# Hunter-Gatherers
# in History, Archaeology and Anthropology

# Hunter-Gatherers
# in History, Archaeology and Anthropology

*edited by* Alan Barnard

Oxford • New York

First published in 2004 by
Berg
Editorial offices:
1st Floor, Angel Court, 81 St Clements Street, Oxford, OX4 1AW, UK
175 Fifth Avenue, New York, NY 10010, USA

Berg is the imprint of Oxford International Publishers Ltd.

**Library of Congress Cataloging-in-Publication data**
Hunter-gatherers in history, archaeology, and anthropology / edited by Alan Barnard.
    p. cm.
"The book has its origins in the Ninth International Conference on Hunting and
Gathering Societies (CHAGS 9 for short), which was held at Heriot-Watt University,
Edinburgh, in September 2003"--P.
    Includes some papers commissioned specifically for this volume.
    Includes bibliographical references and index.
    ISBN 1-85973-820-6 (cloth) -- ISBN 1-85973-825-7 (pbk.)
    1. Hunting and gathering societies. I. Barnard, Alan (Alan J.) II. International
Conference on Hunting and Gathering Societies (9th : 2003 : Heriot-Watt University)

GN388.H866 2004
306.3'64--dc22                                 2004008969

**British Library Cataloguing-in-Publication data**
A catalogue record for this book is available from the British Library.

ISBN 1 85973 820 6 (Cloth)
     1 85973 825 7 (Paper)

Typeset by Avocet Typeset, Chilton, Aylesbury, Bucks
Printed in the United Kingdom by Biddles Ltd, King's Lynn

**www.bergpublishers.com**

# Contents

# List of Figures and Tables

## Figures

## Tables

# Preface

Hunters and gatherers have always been important in social and cultural anthropology and in archaeology. Many of the great figures in these disciplines, such as A.R. Radcliffe-Brown, Julian Steward and Grahame Clark, and even founders of the social sciences more broadly, like Adam Smith, Karl Marx and Emile Durkheim, developed their ideas through the examination of hunters and gatherers. Images of a hunter-gatherer lifestyle as humankind's natural existence, as the earliest stage of social evolution, or as the antithesis of modernity, have had a profound impact (for better or worse) on the development of countless theoretical ideas on society and culture.

This book is the first to examine in depth the idea of the 'hunter-gatherer' through history. It is important to recognize that this is not (to borrow a metaphor from Steward) a unilinear history, but a multilinear or yet more complex one with differences of emphasis, a diversity of problems and opposing points of view. Equally, it is important to recognize diversity in world anthropology. In this book not only North American and British, but also Japanese, French, German and Austrian, Russian and Soviet, and Indian ethnological and archaeological traditions (as well as perspectives in the ancient scholarly traditions of Arabia, India and China) are scrutinized. And not only old debates, but also those of recent decades and of today, are treated in ways that should be enlightening for academics, students and a wider public alike. The result, I believe, is a unique contribution to understanding the many ways in which anthropologists, archaeologists and other scholars have approached and do approach the study of hunting-and-gathering societies.

The book has its origins in the Ninth International Conference on Hunting and Gathering Societies (CHAGS 9 for short), which was held at Heriot-Watt University, Edinburgh, in September 2003. The majority of the papers here were presented in draft form in one of that conference's thirty-nine sessions, 'Hunting and Gathering as a Theme in the History of Anthropology', while some were presented in other sessions and some commissioned specifically for this volume. This series of conferences is itself testimony to the enduring significance of hunter-gatherers, both to science and scholarship and to the enrichment of human understanding which has come through anthropology's engagement with their living representatives.

I would like to express my gratitude to Tim Ingold, my co-convenor in CHAGS 9, and to the organizing committee, especially David Anderson and Nancy Wachowich, who worked so hard to make that conference such a success. Acknowledgement is also due to the sponsors, especially the Wenner-Gren Foundation for Anthropological Research who funded the travel and conference fees of some of those whose papers appear in this volume. I am also grateful to Kostas Retsikas and Peter Schweitzer for their editorial help, especially with the bibliography.

*Alan Barnard*

# –1–

# Hunter-Gatherers in History, Archaeology and Anthropology: Introductory Essay

## *Alan Barnard*

Until 12,000 years ago, all humanity were hunter-gatherers. Only a tiny fraction any longer subsist entirely or primarily by these means. Yet thousands of people today do remember their hunter-gatherer past. Millions live in cultures with a collective memory of their hunter-gatherer ancestors, and millions more probably believe, as Richard Lee and Irven DeVore wrote in their preface to *Man the Hunter* that 'the human condition [is] likely to be more clearly drawn here than among other kinds of societies' (Lee and DeVore 1968a: ix). Lee and DeVore's statement entails a supposition that hunter-gatherers are, in a sense, more 'natural' or even more 'human' than people who live in agrarian or industrialized societies.

In the early twentieth century, scholars had quite different views. For example, Sigmund Freud (1960 [1913]: 1–2) saw hunter-gatherers, Australian Aborigines in particular, as 'the most backward and miserable of savages' who did not build permanent houses, kept only the dog as a domesticated animal, could not make pottery, had no chiefs, nor beliefs in or worship of higher beings. The Social Darwinists W.G. Sumner and A.G. Keller (1927) cited the social organization of Australian Aborigines and African Bushmen or San as examples of what they called 'primitive atomism'. These hunter-gatherers, they said, 'are full of hostility, suspicion, and other anti-social feelings and habits' (1927: 16). Even Richard Lee, in pessimistic tone some two decades after his famous statement, said that he had been wrong: the 'human condition' is about 'poverty, injustice, exploitation, war, suffering'; anthropologists looking at hunter-gatherers, he added, are looking for 'a vision of human life and human possibilities without the pomp and glory, but also without the misery and inequality of state and class society' (Lee 1992: 43).

These examples illustrate the diversity of views and the changing ideas on hunter-gatherers through time. Over the last century the field of hunter-gatherer studies has had a profound influence on anthropological and archaeological

1

thinking throughout the world, and this book offers a series of diverse perspectives in a wide variety of the world's major anthropological traditions.

## Reflections on the Idea of the 'Hunter-Gatherer'

In order to understand contemporary issues, reflections on the history of the idea of the 'hunter-gatherer' are essential. The problem begins in the seventeenth century, and there is no doubt that seventeenth- and eighteenth-century concerns with 'human nature' form a central part of hunter-gatherer studies, even though hunter-gatherer studies emerged as a subdiscipline only around the 1960s. Those early, especially seventeenth-century concerns, have recently been described by one of our contributors (Pluciennik 2002) and debated by others.

Margaret Hodgen (1964) argued that the basic concepts of modern anthropology, including ideas on culture change and social evolution, were developed in the sixteenth and seventeenth centuries. However, early concern with peoples we would now call 'hunter-gatherers' was largely hypothetical. Seventeenth-century writers tended to be interested not with ethnographically attested peoples but rather with an imagined state of nature. In the words of Anthony Pagden, 'The painstaking description, and the recognition of the "otherness" of the "other", which is the declared ambition of the modern ethnologist would have been unthinkable to most of the writers [of the sixteenth and seventeenth centuries]' (Pagden 1982: 6). It was only in the eighteenth century that subsistence and its relation to society became truly meaningful topics of intellectual discussion (cf. Duchet 1971; Berry 1997). Adam Smith began his *Lectures on Jurisprudence* with a consideration of what he called 'the Age of Hunters'. Smith's idea of hunter-gatherer society was of twenty to thirty families per village, with a general assembly of several villages, government without leaders but by consensus of the whole (Smith 1896 [1763]: 14–15, 20). Property existed in only a limited sense: in one of his examples, a man chasing a hare *gradually* acquired the exclusive privilege of killing (1896: 7).[1]

Today, property has returned as a central focus in hunter-gatherer studies. It has been a major interest of James Woodburn in his Hadza ethnography and his comparative studies (e.g. Woodburn 1980; 1982). Indeed, a conference on Woodburn's contribution to the study of property in hunting-and-gathering society was held just a few years ago (in June 2001) at the Max Planck Institute for Social Anthropology in Halle, Germany. From the late 1970s, Woodburn began to talk of two types of economic system: 'immediate return' and 'delayed return'. Economies based on an immediate-return principle reject the accumulation of surplus; people either consume or share. Those based on a delayed-return principle allow for planning ahead. Only *some* hunter-gatherers fit the immediate-return category; those who invest time in keeping bees, raising horses, or making boats or large traps, are, like non-hunter-gatherers, consigned to the residual, delayed-return category. In his paper for the London hunter-gatherers conference of 1986, Woodburn (1988) argued that delayed-return economies are adapted to pastoralism and agriculture, whereas immediate-return ones are not. It is not that people in immediate-return systems have any technical difficulty with food production; what keeps them from doing so are their social organization and value systems, which are based on egalitarianism and sharing. Rousseau said much the same thing in his *Discourse on the Origin of Inequality* (1973 [1755]). Moreover, delayed-return economies depend on the acquisition and maintenance of assets, and the loss of these can result in delayed-return economies becoming immediate-return. There is ethnographic evidence for this in central Africa, for example, where hunter-gatherers have yielded control over both material and ritual aspects of life to their agricultural neighbours (Grinker 1994). Thus, evolution is not a simple, one-way process, and ecological relations are bound up with social relations – both within and beyond the community. That represents a challenge to the viewpoint within hunter-gatherer studies that sees the subdiscipline as essentially evolutionist.

Marshall Sahlins (e.g. 1972: 1–39) represents another modern viewpoint, with his emphasis on the notion of the 'original affluent society'. Also echoing Rousseau, he suggests that if affluence is measured in free time, hunters and gatherers are often more affluent than their agricultural neighbours. Except in times of scarcity, hunter-gatherer populations need spend only a few hours per day in subsistence-related activities, and they survive times of general severity, such as drought, better than neighbouring agricultural peoples. He articulated the theoretical position that really lay beneath the hard data being uncovered in the 1960s: if hunter-gatherers maximize, they maximize their free time, not their wealth. This realization, which became apparent in the Chicago 'Man the Hunter' conference of 1966 (Lee and DeVore 1968c), was to transform hunter-gatherer studies into perhaps the most theoretically challenging branch of anthropology of that time.

Strangely though, it was twelve years before another major hunter-gatherer symposium came to be held. That was the Paris symposium of 1978, first in a series now numbering nine. After Paris came Quebec (in 1980), Bad Homberg, Germany (in 1983), London (in 1986), Darwin, Australia (in 1988), Fairbanks (in 1990), Moscow (in 1993), Osaka (in 1998), and the one on which this volume is based, Edinburgh (in 2002). The tenth is planned for Bhubaneswar, in the state of Orissa, India, in the near future. Since the fifth, Darwin, conference, the series has carried the convenient acronym CHAGS ('conference on hunting-and-gathering societies'). While the first six were dominated by Western models (and to some extent indigenous ones, especially in the case of Darwin), from the seventh (Moscow) broader and more diverse anthropological traditions came to be represented.

From the time of the Paris conference (retrospectively, CHAGS 1), a new generation of fieldworkers began to focus on changes in social structure in emerging nation states; new interests included rapid acculturation, ethnic pluralism, and class relations. Among questions raised: if hunter-gatherers are affluent, do they lose their affluence as they adapt to the modern world? Resolutions to the controversy have begun to appear, following synthetic approaches like that of Nurit Bird-David. In her paper 'The giving environment', Bird-David (1990) emphasizes hunter-gatherers' perceptions of their environments as rich and kind to their inhabitants. She also emphasizes sharing between people, rather than environmental exploitation or the work effort exploitation requires. This is the way hunter-gatherers themselves often see the world: the environment contains the necessities of life in sufficient amounts, provided that one's lifestyle remains based on the principles of mutual aid and communal good will. In another paper, Bird-David (1992b) has gone on to reformulate Sahlins' notion of 'original affluence' to correct some of its inherent flaws. Sahlins, she argues, confused ecological and cultural perspectives. The key distinctions he drew were insightful, but he remained too much a formalist in his emphasis on labour time. What Sahlins failed to realize is that, to hunter-gatherers, what matters most is one's relationship to other people and to the environment.

While these theoretical foundations were being moulded, ethnographic (and to some extent archaeological) studies throughout the world served both to bolster theoretical speculation and to build up pictures of regionally specific forms of hunter-gatherer society. In addition, regionally specific themes emerged: for example, kinship in Australia, band organization in the Subarctic, shamanism in the Arctic and South America, the hunter-gatherer/cultivator divide in South America and Southeast Asia, forager/cultivator relations in central and southern Africa, and so on. Of course regions have much to teach each other: for example, current debates in southern Africa over the acquisition and loss of non-hunting-and-gathering means of subsistence reflect long-standing concerns with that issue in South America (see e.g. Rival 1999).

While diversity in hunter-gatherer ways of life is now commonplace in anthropological discourse, and even in the titles of anthropological monographs (e.g. Kelly 1995; Kent 1996), there remains nevertheless a recognition that hunter-gatherer societies have enough in common to make them a category to go on discussing. Or at the very least, there remains a consensus that such an invented category has produced sufficient insights for CHAGS conferences to continue! Themes such as 'original affluence' have an enduring presence and could not have existed without the notion of hunting-and-gathering society as a specific type. In both 'noble savage' and evolutionist frameworks, the idea of the hunter-gatherer as ultimate alien other has been strong. It has gained and regained prominence at various points in the history of anthropology (especially but not exclusively in evolutionist periods such as the 1870s, 1930s, and 1950s and 1960s). Interestingly, debates of the 1980s (perhaps especially at the 1986 London conference) about the salience of the category have now subsided. Hunter-gatherer studies had long been the last vestige of anthropology's quest for natural man (cf. Barnard 1994). Whereas once anthropologists expected a greater cultural purity (in the sense of the absence of non-hunter-gatherer means of subsistence), it seems now that the acquisition of a few goats or the occasional planting of vegetables need not exclude a people from the category 'hunter-gatherer'. (Barnard 1989). Were this not to be the case, no doubt there would be few peoples left for hunter-gatherer specialists to study.

## Recent Developments

In a paper presented at CHAGS 6 (Fairbanks, 1990), Richard Lee mentioned in passing six key issues in (mainly Western) hunter-gatherer studies since the 1960s: evolutionism, optimal foraging strategies, woman the gatherer, world-view and symbolic analysis, hunter-gatherers in prehistory, and hunter-gatherers in history (Lee 1992: 32–3). I would add a seventh and an eighth: relations with outsiders and indigenous voices. Let me touch on each, both in broad terms and in light of developments since 1990.[2]

Evolutionism was the prevailing anthropological perspective in the nineteenth century, but it rose to prominence again in the 1950s and 1960s, partly as a result of Julian Steward's *Theory of Culture Change* (1955a). Lee's own work with the Ju/'hoansi was inspired by Steward. In the 1980s some, such as Tim Ingold (e.g. 1986: 79–129), looked to the boundary between human 'hunter-gatherers' and animal 'predators-foragers'. Among archaeologists, this boundary took on new meaning as models derived from evolutionary ecology and ultimately from economic theory, came to be applied to human foraging strategies. In the 1990s, new trends in evolutionary theory led to great interest in the search for the origins of language, ritual and symbolic culture. Previous gradualist approaches are being challenged by new models, based loosely on recent hunter-gatherer ethnography. Among these models is that of Chris Knight and his followers (e.g. Knight, Power and Watts 1995) which has overturned the post-Enlightenment concern with families and clans as the basis of society, with a seventeenth and eighteenth-century 'social contract' view. According to this view, all symbolic culture emerged as a result of a social contract among females of a primeval band perhaps 60,000 or 70,000 years ago. Collectively, the theory goes, they denied men sex and forced them to hunt between new and full moon, and then enjoyed an orgy of sex and food from the full to the new moon. Although only a small number of anthropologists accept Knight's theory, nevertheless it has sparked a surprising amount of debate and even interdisciplinary research among anthropologists, archaeologists and linguists over the last decade.

The second key issue involves the study of optimal foraging strategies. These are in fact theoretical models of behaviour, based on the premise that humans (and animals) seek to maximize their chances of finding food with the least effort. The volume *Hunter-Gatherer Foraging Strategies*, edited by Bruce Winterhalder and Eric Alden Smith (1981), led the way in this trend. Their model is based on the idea that both hunter-gatherers and animals exhibit a kind of economic 'rationality' in their subsistence strategies, and that that 'rationality' is a product of evolutionary adaptation. For this very reason, the model has become interesting to those who *cannot* accept it. For example, Ingold (1996) has argued that optimal foraging theory is misplaced because it confuses adaptation with rationality. It proposes abstract models of behaviour as though they were explanations for behaviour. In other words, it goes too far towards biology in seeking explanations for cultural behaviour. That said, interdisciplinary efforts over the last few years have led to renewed interest in relations between the biological and the cultural or social, perhaps epitomized by the volume *Hunter-Gatherers: An Interdisciplinary Perspective* (Panter-Brick, Layton and Rowley-Conwy 2001) to which Winterhalder was a contributor.

Thirdly, 'woman the gatherer' was a catch-phrase of feminist anthropology, within hunter-gatherer studies (or gatherer-hunter studies), even before the Paris conference of 1978. It originated in an article by Sally Slocum (1975) and gained currency in the late 1970s and early 1980s, when women's food-gathering activities, and women's status and political power in hunter-gatherer communities, became popular themes. Today, with the general acceptance of the fact that women produce more than men in so-called 'hunting societies', interest in such themes has waned, although interest in gender relations remains strong.

Fourthly, world-view and symbolic analysis have become, and remain, a very significant area of interest. As Lee himself suggests, this may in part be as an implicit critique of previously dominant interests in ecology and evolution. Within this broad area of interest, however, are two very different sorts of work. On the one hand, there is empirical, ethnographic research on hunter-gatherer worldviews, symbolic culture and ritual. The monographs on Bushman or San religion by Lorna Marshall (1999) and Mathias Guenther (1999) are splendid examples. On the other hand, this interest in symbolic analysis has led to grand theories like Knight's, with their piecing together of ethnographic information from around the world.

Fifthly, hunter-gatherers in prehistory has been a dominant theme since the rise of 'processual archaeology' in the 1960s, and it remains prominent in archaeology wherever the concept of hunter-gatherers is a focal interest (see e.g. Trigger 1989: 289–328). One difficulty is that contemporary foragers, who are largely confined to deserts and jungles and in continual contact with non-foraging peoples, may be quite different from the ancient hunter-gatherers who inhabited the archaeological sites of Europe and temperate North America. Lewis Binford and John Yellen are well-known examples of archaeologists who have succeeded in useful ethnographic analogy. This is because some of their work has included a combination of ethnographic and archaeological fieldwork in the same places, Binford (e.g. 1978) among the Nuniamiut and Yellen (e.g. 1977a) among the Ju/'hoansi or !Kung Bushmen. Related issues are described in this volume, notably in the papers by Shanti Pappu, Paul Lane and Tim Schadla-Hall, and Michael Sheehan.

Sixthly, hunter-gatherers in history poses quite a different question for archaeologists. Let me expound on it with the example of the 'Kalahari Debate' (see also Widlok, this volume). The debate is between those who see Bushmen or San as exponents of a hunting-and-gathering culture and essentially isolated until recent times (the traditionalists), and those who see them as an underclass and part of a larger social system (the revisionists). Although it had been simmering for some time before, the Kalahari Debate proper erupted with the publication of Edwin Wilmsen's *Land Filled with Flies* in 1989. Arguably, the core of the debate consists of a series of articles and comments published in the journal *Current Anthropology* between 1990 and 1995, with a few subsequent articles in other journals. In traditionalist Lee's ethnography (e.g. 1979a) adaptation is seen in a dynamic and theoretical way. Lee takes foraging for granted, as a basic and adaptive way of life, an assumption that is anathema to the hard-line revisionists. He also takes for granted the fact that Ju/'hoan society is a relevant unit of analysis, in spite of the presence of members of other groups (Herero and Tswana) within their territories. The Ju/'hoansi and their cattle-herding neighbours seem to occupy different ecological niches. For revisionists like Wilmsen, the truth is perceived very differently. Traditionalists emphasize cultural continuity and the cultural integrity of Bushman groups. Revisionists de-emphasize these aspects in favour of greater concern with the integration of southern African politico-economic structures taken as a whole. Neither view is necessarily at all close to a Bushman's own view of the world, but the debate has been fundamental to our rethinking the purpose of our theoretical interests in hunter-gatherers.

My last two issues are closely related and follow logically from the interest in 'hunter-gatherers in history'. Relations with outsiders is a complex matter. Some studies have concentrated on relations between hunter-gatherers and their immediate neighbours, such as subsistence herders and horticulturalists (again, see Woodburn 1988). Others have looked beyond to relations with the state and other bureaucratic entities. A notable example here is Sidsel Saugestad's (2001) study of those known in Botswana as Basarwa (another collective term for Bushmen or San) and their predicament as 'inconvenient indigenous' peoples. The latest permutation of this issue is the burgeoning debate on the idea of being 'indigenous' (e.g. Kuper 2003).

Finally, 'indigenous voices' are becoming prominent in hunter-gatherer studies (e.g. Suzman 2000). This is partly a result of the realization in anthropology that writing is a creative process, and one which involves an interaction between writer and reader, and between those studying and those whose cultures are being studied. In recent decades, the latter have come to be included as creators of ethnography too. The interest in indigenous voices is also a result of increasing pressures on indigenous populations throughout the world, and an increasing awareness of their plight. International organizations like Survival International, Cultural Survival and the International Working Group for Indigenous Affairs (IWGIA), as well as national organizations in countries where hunter-gatherers live, have contributed to our awareness of the political role anthropology can play on behalf of the hunter-gatherers and former hunter-gatherers we work with.

I predict that indigenous voices will become yet a more prominent part of hunter-gatherer studies in the very near future, and indeed several of the papers represented in this volume bring together contemporary concerns with indigenous voices and older concerns in the history of anthropological thought. The great thing about hunter-gatherer studies today is that it can and does accommodate both high theory and practical activity, both age-old ideas of Western philosophy and new issues in science and politics alike.

Finally here, it is worth pointing out that, although anthropological ideas in general and ideas within hunter-gatherer studies in particular frequently develop through the efforts of individuals, hunter-gatherer specialists also frequently work as part of larger research programmes and even in fieldwork teams. This was true of Lee's own work, which involved many colleagues in the Harvard Kalahari Research Project (see Lee 1979b), and is the norm among researchers in archaeology as well as in ethnographic traditions such as that of Kyoto University (see Ichikawa, this volume; Sugawara, this volume).

## Plan of the Book

Each of the three parts of this volume represents an interdisciplinary theme within the history of hunter-gatherer studies. The chapters may, of course, be read individually, but taken together they form less a bunch of historical threads and more an interwoven set of histories from different anthropological and archaeological traditions. Throughout the volume there is an element of debate: for example, two papers on Steward, each giving a very different portrayal from the other; complementary perspectives on Siberian hunter-gatherer studies in Russia and the Soviet Union; and two papers on Kalahari Bushman or San, representing different views (if not exactly different 'sides') in and on the debate which has for the last two decades divided anthropologists, archaeologists and historians alike in their perception of the measure of contact between Kalahari hunter-gatherers and non-hunter-gatherer peoples.

*Part I. Early Visions of Hunter-Gatherer Society and Their Influence*
These four chapters trace visions of the hunter-gatherer from the seventeenth to the late twentieth centuries, but the focus in each case is on past ideas and their continuing significance.

Mark Pluciennik traces the history of subsistence-based categories to seventeenth-century northwestern Europe and subsequent developments in the late eighteenth century, when the category 'hunter-gatherers' became widespread in its opposition to herders and farmers. He argues that the use of means of subsistence was related to factors such as theories of agricultural improvement, the growth of agrarian capitalism and the idea of methodological individualism. He also adds comparative examples from indigenous traditions of scholarship in Arabia, India and China.

My own paper looks at the idea of hunting-and-gathering *society*, a concept quite foreign to seventeenth-century thinkers who often equated society with agriculture. It suggests that such a notion only takes on meaning when economics comes to be seen as the basis of society, notably in eighteenth-century Scotland but with some precursors in eighteenth-century France. For some of the Scots, the hunter-gatherer phase was only hypothetical or of passing significance; nevertheless moral philosophers of the Scottish Enlightenment developed an understanding of hunter-gatherer society that is, for the first time in history, comparable to that we recognize today. Their debates, though often grounded as much in speculation as in ethnography, remain enlightening.

L.R. Hiatt argues that, like the Scottish moral philosophers, Edward Westermarck sought the origin of moral ideas in sentiments. Westermarck attributed generic significance to the retributive emotions of resentment and goodwill and related these to the Darwinian principle of natural selection. Over the last century, two views have emerged in evolutionary biology: one maintaining that there is no evidence of morality in nature, and the other that the precursors of morality may be seen even in non-human animals. Against that background, Hiatt discusses the ethical principles of an Australian Aboriginal community and considers the implications for speculation about the origin of morality.

Finally here, Aram Yengoyan examines the nineteenth and early twentieth-century framework of 'difference' that separated hunter-gatherers from other peoples. A key example is Marx's reading of works on Aboriginal Australia: Marx sought an explanation as to how the variable infrastructures there could be accounted for, given the relatively simple and seemingly unrelated infrastructure common to the continent. The first major shift from cultural to non-cultural explanation, Yengoyan argues, comes with Julian Steward, who introduced the distinction between the 'cultural core' and the 'rest of culture' – the latter being that affected by history and diffusion. Further changes in thinking followed, including the 'biologicalization' of small-scale societies, and Yengoyan's paper analyses the implications of these.

*Part II. Local Traditions in Hunter-Gatherer Research*
This set of papers focuses on some of the major local traditions that lie outside the supposed 'mainstream' often defined by French, British or North American studies to the exclusion of others. Each of the traditions discussed here has a special significance for hunter-gatherer studies: German-language, Russian and Soviet, Japanese, and Indian-archaeological. The significance of these traditions is highlighted by the different emphases in the two papers on Russian and Soviet studies; and by the intriguing similarities and differences implicit in the two papers on Japanese approaches – one dealing with central Africa and the other with southern Africa.

Peter Schweitzer aims to counter the common Anglophone assumption that modern hunter-gatherer discourse began with the 'Man the Hunter' conference of 1966. His beginning is with nineteenth-century German-language anti-evolutionism, the consequent emergence of economic anthropology (a compromise between evolutionism and anti-evolutionism), and after that the Vienna School of the early twentieth century. In this essentially diffusionist school of thought, hunter-gatherers came to be seen as representatives of 'primeval culture', thus implicitly signifying a return to evolutionist thinking. Schweitzer offers an analysis of these tendencies and an exploration of their influence on contemporary regional traditions and post-Second World War developments. He also stresses the relation between theoretical paradigms and field data.

Olga Artemova notes that in Russian usage, 'ethnography', 'ethnology' and 'social anthropology' are seen essentially as synonyms. Nevertheless, she argues, hunter-gatherer studies in Russia emerged within two separate traditions: an ethnographic or ethnological tradition developed for the study of hunter-gatherers within the country, and a library-based tradition that focused on foreign literature on the world's hunter-gatherers. Whereas the former tradition held back from generalization, the latter aimed to build a general theory of human prehistory and social evolution. Artemova describes in detail the development of these traditions through pre-Soviet and Soviet times, and notes the arguments concerning the latter tradition, not least that of A.N. Maksimov whose anti-evolutionism was reminiscent of Boas and that of some in the German-language tradition described by Schweitzer and also anticipated Radcliffe-Brown.

Anna Sirina focuses on the other Russian tradition, specifically the Siberian research in which the Russian Imperial Geographical Society had leading role. She investigates the assumptions and methods of this school, its practitioners' interests in culture history, folklore and shamanism, and the isolation of its scholars from theoretical concerns elsewhere in the world. She argues that the Marxist-Leninist focus on the construction of theories of the 'primitive' owed much to Siberianist scholarship; and further, that in the current era of international scientific cooperation the study of regional traditions in Russian ethnography is developing as a new tradition in its own right.

Mitsuo Ichikawa describes the Japanese tradition of central African hunter-gatherer research as occupying a unique position, forming as he says a 'triangle' with the French and American traditions. French studies (perhaps influenced by the 'Encyclopédists' of the eighteenth century) emphasize ethnographic description with particular interests in ethnoscience and ethnomusicology, whereas American ones (influenced by behavioural ecology, itself linked to neo-classical economics) are much more 'scientific', presenting a hypothesis and verifying it with quantitative data. The Japanese tradition has both French and American elements and is characterized by 'ecology in a broad sense', which consists of cultural ecology, historical ecology and political ecology. Ichikawa ends with a discussion of recent trends towards convergence.

Kazuyoshi Sugawara examines the theoretical framework and historical background of Japanese research on the Central San (or Bushmen) of Botswana's Central Kalahari Game Reserve. He notes that early research, from the 1960s, was dominated by an ecological paradigm, and that changes towards a more sedentary existence led to new interests in acculturation and social change. Accompanying these changes, and the growth in numbers of Japanese researchers, has been a shift in focus towards a more detailed concentration on communication and face-to-face interaction. In all these cases, Japanese research has had at its core a concern with the cultural-behavioural basis of egalitarianism – a concern, he argues, that was inspired by the intellectual movement of animal sociology and primatology dominant at Kyoto following the Second World War. Both Ichikawa and Sugawara are products of this school.

Shanti Pappu traces the history of Indian archaeology of hunter-gatherers to the work of R.B. Foote in the late nineteenth century, and contrasts that early approach with that developed as a result of the influence of the 'New Archaeology' of the 1960s. The change was marked by a shift away from the construction of culture-sequences and type-lists towards attempts to study past behaviour. Pappu's focus is different approaches to ethnographic analogy in the interpretation of prehistoric hunter-gatherer behaviour. She situates these approaches in a context of Indian archaeology taken as a whole.

## Part III. Reinterpretations in Archaeology, Anthropology and the History of the Disciplines

Part III explores changes in thinking within social anthropology and archaeology through the second half of the twentieth century. The first two chapters, both mainly on archaeological interpretation, touch on the relations between these two disciplines. The second pair of chapters is devoted to the work of Julian H. Steward, whose *Theory of Culture Change* (1955a) was so influential in the development of modern hunter-gatherer studies in North America. Yet they represent two very different views of Steward and his influence, the first paper emphasizing

his positive influence on American anthropology, and the second suggesting negative associations in the context of indigenous land rights in Canada. The last pair
of chapters takes up explicitly the idea of 'history', both in the context of southern
Africa. The authors represent quite different views though, with Suzman
employing the concepts of San or Bushmen themselves, and Widlok focusing on
the Western discourse of the 'Kalahari Debate'.

Paul Lane and Tim Schadla-Hall examine the long history of interpretation and
reinterpretation of the famous Mesolithic site of Star Carr (seventh century BC) in
northern England. They relate the site to others in the area in order to situate it, in
its different phases, among cycles of seasonal activity and patterns of cultural
change and continuity. They argue that the understanding (and misunderstanding)
of Star Carr reflects changing (and sometimes unchanging) theoretical views over
the more than half a century since it was first excavated. Their general conclusion
is that the case study they examine has the potential to provide more general
insights into the manner in which archaeological knowledge is produced.

Michael Sheehan explores the issue of ethnographic analogy and the 'limited'
applicability of contemporary foraging theory and asks the question: is this a
problem with theory, or with the data available to test theory? His exploration and
his answer involve tracing the historical development of hunter-gatherer studies
and foraging theory, especially the approach known as optimal foraging theory
(which holds that an economic strategy of rational choice governs the activities of
hunters and gatherers). Like many North American archaeologists, he regards his
field as a subdiscipline of anthropology, and he argues for an approach to the modelling of human behaviour which might help bridge the gap between archaeology
and other branches of a larger discipline of anthropology.

In the first of the papers on Steward, Daniel Myers traces modern hunter-gatherer studies to Steward's ecology-based paradigm of multilinear (cultural) evolution. He assesses Steward's contributions to the study of hunters-gatherers
(including his early field studies in the Great Basin of California), his influence on
later practitioners of hunter-gatherer studies, and more broadly his influence of
anthropology in the United States. Myers discusses, in particular, relations
between Steward's work and other paradigms, including the linguistically focused
'New Ethnography' derived from Ward H. Goodenough's work from the 1950s,
and a much more recent 'postmodern' ethnography of the 1980s and 1990s.

Marc Pinkoski and Michael Asch take quite a different view of Steward, in
assessing his negative influence even as an 'expert witness' on hunter-gatherer
lifestyles. Their main concern is with the doctrine of *terra nullius*, the idea that territory supposedly empty of inhabitants who understand the notion of land ownership might legally be claimed by the state or some other entity. Pinkoski and Asch
argue that Steward's ideas of cultural ecology and multilinear evolution support
that doctrine, as indeed did his testimony on Great Basin issues in the 1950s. They

argue further that the impact has been a denial of indigenous rights in Canada too, where the Crown's sovereignty and jurisdiction has been assigned without consideration of the claims of indigenous peoples already living in such territories.

James Suzman takes up a reconsideration of the issues of indigeneity and historicity among Ju/'hoansi in the western Kalahari. He makes use of the Ju/'hoan distinction between 'old times' and 'new times', and argues that such a distinction is useful in our reconceptualization of the history of hunter-gatherer/non-hunter-gatherer association. Perhaps surprisingly, he ends up with a framework explicitly less historicist than that of the 'revisionist' side of the Kalahari Debate (which argues for a greater emphasis on history and a view of hunter-gatherers as subjugated minorities). He then uses his findings to challenge the popular human rights discourse of today that sees 'Indigenous Peoples' as special and different from others. In his view, so-called 'indigenous rights' are indistinguishable from human rights in general, not a separate category privileging one kind of people over another.

In the final chapter, Thomas Widlok also reflects on the Kalahari Debate, but in his case the argument more directly concerns the terms of the debate itself. He suggests that it is not history that is problematic, but an exclusive focus on the contemporary – in the suggestion sometimes made that hunter-gatherer studies ought to be turned into 'contemporary history'. He focuses on time and analogy in the recent history of ideas on hunter-gatherers, and suggests that anthropology needs to preserve its concerns with ethnography and comparison, interests that are quite different from those of history as a discipline, and that have specific implications for taking account of the dimension of time.

## Notes

1. There are different published versions of these lectures. The edition quoted here differs from the version cited in my paper later in this volume.
2. The first six issues discussed here are those identified by Lee, but the discussion is my own. A more detailed account, presented in a lecture in Posadas, Argentina in September 2000, has been published in Spanish in the journal *Avá* (Barnard 2001).

# Part I
# Early Visions of Hunter-Gatherer Society and Their Influence

# 2

# The Meaning of 'Hunter-Gatherers' and Modes of Subsistence: a Comparative Historical Perspective

## *Mark Pluciennik*

Our preference for using anthropological categories such as hunters, pastoralists and farmers can be traced back to mid-eighteenth century northern Europe, when social evolution or 'progress' was first widely expressed and systematized as universal histories, and stadial schemes of human development defined by subsistence categories (Meek 1976, Trigger 1998, Barnard 1999, Rudebeck 2000, Pluciennik 2001). The most recent phase of hunter-gatherer studies dates from the 1960s (Bender and Morris 1988; Bird-David 1994: 583–7; Lee and Daly 1999), and can be linked with broader currents of neo-romanticism and environmentalism. Since then, many have queried its utility or definitional content both ethnographically (e.g. Barnard 1983) and archaeologically (e.g. Bender 1978). Although one can in principle simply define hunter-gatherer societies, the extent to which the term is useful has been widely discussed. There are various issues embedded here: they include recent history and encapsulation – how far are colonialism, demographic, agricultural and territorial expansion, state formation, industrialization, environmental change and modern capitalism responsible for the current nature of these groups? How commonly is foraging as a mode of subsistence a 'secondary', recent or cyclical response? How do contemporary 'hunter-gatherers' combine foraging, wage labour, state benefits and perhaps agriculture, and what maintains their separate identity? How do they relate to nearby groups and institutions, and what historical depth do these relations have?

In short, there is increasing recognition of the variability and historicity of hunter-gatherer societies. This is crucial for both ethnographic and archaeological attempts to describe and explain distinct ways of life in relation to subsistence. One response has been to develop subcategories such as immediate and delayed return or 'simple' and 'complex' hunter-gatherer societies (Woodburn 1980;

Testart 1982; Rowley-Conwy 1983; 2001; Price and Brown 1985; Arnold 1996). Others emphasize that while there may not be universals, useful generalizations can still be made: thus Bird-David suggests that hunter-gatherers are characterized by an attitude that she describes as the giving environment (1990; 1992a), or the importance of public sociality (1994), though this latter is not confined to hunter-gatherer groups. Lee and Daly (1999: 3) propose that modern hunter-gatherers are *typically* characterized by a cluster of traits: 'subsistence is one part of a multi-faceted definition of hunter-gatherers: social organization forms a second major area of convergence, and cosmology and world-view a third'. Sharing is also recognized as a common trait (Kent 1993), even if 'simple' egalitarian nomadic societies are now recognized as only part of the forager spectrum (Lee and Daly 1999: 5–6). Barnard (2002b) has argued that a useful distinction can be made between foraging and accumulation modes of thought (but see Kenrick 2002). Brody (2001: 353; cf. Woodburn 1997) notes that 'the distinction between hunter-gatherers and herders and farmers' is widely incorporated in linguistic categories, and that there are essential differences in worldview.

This question of variation is even more challenging for archaeologists (cf. Zvelebil and Fewster 2001: 152–3). Inevitably dealing with situations with no direct parallels in the present, archaeologists cannot use existing variation as a *template* for the past; and dispute how far it can be used even as a *guide*, whether favouring adaptionist or culturalist formulations of hunter-gatherers. If we cannot easily point to non-tautological characteristics for contemporary and recent forager societies, it is highly unlikely that we can do so for the more distant past. Comparative study offers a starting point for historical awareness and self-reflection on these issues. Conditions are examined pertaining to societal categories and philosophies of history elsewhere, at roughly the same time as social evolution arose in eighteenth-century Europe. The European materials are contrasted with three other 'regions' with distinct religious, philosophical, economic and perhaps other traditions: southern Asia, China and Islamic southwest Asia.

## Cosmologies, Histories and Time

Two broad ways of constructing anthropological difference may be given varying weights in contrasting intellectual, cultural and historical contexts. The process of *abstraction* compares similarities and differences across classes of objects, and is typically how anthropologists have attempted definitions of, say, hunter-gatherers. An alternative is the process of *subtraction*, working from self-understanding outwards: heathens are us without 'proper' religion; savages are us without aspects of civilization or culture. The results of these processes for producing discursive difference can be arranged along axes of real or mythical time or space, or of cultural values. In surviving ancient texts with reference to non-farming peoples or times, the second process appears to dominate. In many Sumerian, Babylonian, Indian, Roman and Judaeo-Christian texts there is an idea of a paradise or Golden Age when people did not have to work for food. This primitivism (Lovejoy and Boas 1965) can be traced to before the end of the third millennium BC. Albright (1965: 425) refers to a Sumerian poem which 'describes the condition at the beginning, when mankind had been created, but had not learned the art of living. Men did not know how to make bread or beer, or clothing of woven stuff, but lived in the reed thicket. Then they were taught how to plant grain, to raise domestic animals, and to build houses of brick, etc.'.

For many (sub)cultures and most periods, such Golden Age myths are a common form of history, in the sense of comparing then to now; a reference to 'sacred time', the *in illo tempore* of Eliade (1991). Such explanations are produced by imagined comparison with present conditions (there was a time before language, cities, farming, or work . . .), and perhaps in answer to questions such as: Why do we have to live like this? Why is there disease, disaster, death? It is thus perfectly possible to point to the existence of 'non-farming' people in the cosmologies of most agricultural societies, without assuming that they necessarily refer to actual hunter-gatherers (contra, e.g. Pandey 1989; Prasad 1989; M. Zvelebil 2002). From India Paddaya (1995: 117) notes a Jain text which describes how people were once ignorant of farming because 'prior to Nabhi's reign there were *Kalpavrikshas* or wish-fulfilling trees which granted people whatever they wished.' Similarly a Sanskrit text of eleventh-century central India records how 'in the [period of the] Kritayuga men were dwelling in groves, hills and forests, and near rivers and lakes, along with gods. The wishing-tree *Kalpavriksha* catered for all kinds of needs. It was subsequently lost, so the people were forced to make use of tree-foods. Later on they reaped the grains of wild rice.' (1995: 117).

Warder (1961: 49) describes Buddhist texts in which early societies were morally perfect, and there was

> no state or kingship, no sex or marriage, no property, no work, no caste, no war, no old age, or disease. The earth itself consisted of a delicious edible substance: at first no one touched it, but after a time it was tasted and found enjoyable, whereupon all took to eating it . . . the edible substance disappeared but was replaced by edible fungi and eventually by edible plants . . . Afterwards it was discovered that food (rice) could be stored. As soon as this was done there was a shortage of wild rice. The land was then divided into private holdings to ensure fair distribution, but as a result of this theft was invented.

Such accounts making an eventual virtue out of necessity are explanatory in a particular way. Although they may draw on empirical observations, these 'myths by subtraction' are a qualitatively different mental operation to those of 'ethnography' and social evolution which rework real and imagined people into a contemporary and/or historical hierarchy. One of the keys is the attitude towards time in general and human history in particular.

Until the eighteenth century in western Europe (A.B. Ferguson 1993) most Eurasian ideas of history emphasized a general decline during contemporary times, or since Creation, albeit with eventual salvation (but see Janko 1997). The Judaeo-Christian version of history and the Fall of Man is paralleled in part by Hindu and Buddhist understandings, in which we are living towards the end of particular periods characterized by darkness and degeneration (P.-E. Dumont 1965). Thus within the vastness of Hindu and Buddhist cyclical reckonings covering billions of years (Layton 1989: 6–7; Paddaya 1995:113), each subcycle typically incorporates not progress but decline. 'Progress' is compressed into instantaneous, between-cycle, rebirth or re-creation. Thus 'on the human plane, [there is] a decrease in the length of life, accompanied by a corruption in morals and a decline in intelligence. This continuous decadence upon all planes – biological, intellectual, ethical, social, and so on – assumes particular emphasis in the Puranic texts' (Eliade 1991: 113). Paddaya (1995: 114) notes that many have felt that these elements of destruction and retrogressive movement found in the Hindu concept of time inhibited development of the notion of purpose in history. However, others have pointed out that these cycles are 'essentially cosmological in character and did not prevent recording of the [historical] past in a form considered socially relevant and necessary to the present and future. Such a cyclic concept emphasized continual change . . . it was maintained that the past can and does teach lessons, usually moral lessons . . .' (Thapar 1984, cited in Paddaya 1995: 114).

There is however a clear contrast with the much shorter 6000–year-long Judaeo-Christian chronology including both creation and human genealogical history, which puts particular constraints on the production and understanding of difference through time. It requires either the foundational creation of difference (e.g. the unique relationship of a chosen people with God, or variable racial endowments), or a fast-moving history to explain differentiation. It was this tension which led to the debates between monogenists and polygenists, and Creationists and evolutionists in nineteenth-century Europe and America (Stocking 1982; Bieder 1986; Patterson 2001: 7–34). In contrast both Hindu and Buddhist attitudes relate to almost infinite time-spans, which are themselves cyclic. Although one can relate this to forms of stasis or fatalism antithetical to 'history', such long cosmic time-spans also allow for intra-cycle histories. They still potentially enable a separation of cosmological and 'human' historical events and ages. Nevertheless Eliade contrasts two ends of a spectrum: at one, typified in southern Asia, people often 'defended themselves' against the vagaries and uncertainties of history 'by periodically abolishing it through repetition of the cosmogony and a periodic regeneration of time' (Eliade 1991: 142), whereas the (Judaeo-) Christian view involved a more linear sense of history and life, with a '"concrete and irreplaceable" time, and involving unique events such as incarnation, crucifixion, and redemption' (1991: 143). This attitude towards time was one of the factors enabling the production and acceptance of a progressive social evolutionary history in Enlightenment Europe, with 'primitive' non-farmers placed at the misty beginnings of human history, at the base of an historicized hierarchy full of *telos* and change.

## South Asian 'Tribals'

The experience and conceptualization of difference is culturally and historically variable (cf. Khare 1990; Toby 1994), although comparison of Asian and European perceptions shows that some significant characteristics are shared, such as the contrast between sedentary and mobile people – perhaps a classic case of difference by subtraction. In mainland Southeast Asia, suggests Reid (1994: 270), the 'riverine kingdoms . . . all saw themselves surrounded by "wild" upland peoples, potentially able to be brought within . . . lowland royal control and settled wet-rice agriculture.' He also notes an indigenous 'dichotomy between civilized/cosmopolitan peoples of the cities and coasts and barbarous/isolated people of the interior or of remote islands'. In south Asia the urban and village plains-dwellers were distinguished from those of the mountain and forest. However there were and are other important axes of difference, such as religion, purity and language. In India terms such as 'forest-dwellers', 'hillmen' and 'tribals' – not coterminous with, but including 'hunter-gatherers' – were and are used. The protected 'Scheduled Tribal Areas' is a category taken over from the colonial British to retain particular control over the most 'backward' and 'primitive' of India's inhabitants. In subsistence terms they were considered to be pastoralists, swidden cultivators and (rarely) foragers, and were thus typically associated with less- or non-agricultural areas (mountains, forests) and with more mobile populations. In 1981, however, foragers in the strict Western sense numbered only about 20,000 (Bird-David 1999: 231). Under colonial conditions and subsequently, many were forced out of the forests and are now landless agricultural labourers or employed in fishing, hunting, mining, quarrying and construction (Savyasaachi 2001: 71). According to the Ministry of Tribal Affairs (2002), tribal communities are characterized by 'primitive traits, geographical isolation, distinctive culture, shyness of contact with outsiders, economic backwardness' (but see K. Singh 1994: 1–15).

In many ways 'tribals' can be seen negatively as the repository of non-Hindu values: they live in the hills rather than plains, or forest rather than villages, and are perceived as free and individualistic in comparison to caste-based and hierarchical Hindu society. They are also described as non-Aryan and as non-Sanskrit users, though some of these 'tribal' attributes are also shared by lower castes (Omvedt 1980: 16). Formerly they could also be characterized as non- Christian,

Hindu, Buddhist, Jain, Sikh or Muslim, though many have converted (Singh 1994: 10–13). 'Tribals' were rarely characterized directly by subsistence regimes in the past, although there are many references to 'forest-dwellers'. Singh (1988: 322, fn. 12), for late medieval/early modern Punjab, notes that some named tribals were pastoral and others settled agriculturalists. Other studies (e.g. Guha 1996; Dash 1998) of this period, emphasize the spectrum of ways of life present in Indian society, and the presence and persistence of 'tribals', despite a continuous and long-lasting process of Hinduization ('Sanskritization') of peoples and culture (Omvedt 1980; Dash 1998), suggesting recruitment from the lower castes socially or spatially marginalized on the edges of village society. What has been seen as particularly intriguing is how, against the Western idea of historical progress, many of these groups have survived among empires and other 'advanced' agricultural, military and trading polities (cf. Layton 2001 for other areas). Fox (1969) argued that these regionally distinctive south Asian hunter-gatherers were performing a kind of caste-like economic specialization, providing forest products in exchange for commodities from the plains. More recent work, tellingly, suggests that many of the tribal agriculturalists also hunt and gather and may possess 'forager-type' social and cultural characteristics. 'Features of their way of life are much like those of [hunter-gatherer] peoples . . . yet they are excluded from consideration because they also practise subsistence activities like shifting agriculture or animal husbandry. The degree of overlap between domesticative and foraging activities is considerable in the forests of South Asia' (Bird-David 1999: 233). Many foragers may have been forced to take up other subsistence practices because of colonial, environmental, demographic or commercial pressures, but other processes have led in the opposite direction. Extremely complex histories may characterize these groups and processes of classification.

Earlier in the last century followers of Gandhi encouraged tribal peoples to take the name Adivasi or 'original people'. This was in part a reaction to prior colonial ascription of statuses. Bayly (1999: 197) notes that, especially in areas with many tribals, 'it was as colonial subjects with anxieties about the preservation of status and economic advantage that Indians came to sharpen boundaries of rank which had in the past been far more fluid and ambiguous.' Savyasaachi (2001) emphasizes how geographic and cultural distance had reinforced European views of history and progress, and schemes of classification. Conversely he argues that for indigenous inhabitants of India 'the nature of social distance between the forest-dwellers and the outsiders was conditioned by the geographical proximity' (2001: 80). There were marked sociocultural differences – the 'ritual hierarchy' of medieval Hinduism was a feature of the 'sedentary agricultural communities' of the plains, cities and towns, but not of the forest-dwelling tribal people (2001: 79–80). However he claims that the spatial inter mixture of these environments and societies meant that within India '[t]here was no notion of the centre and the frontiers, and no notion of the dominant/mainstream versus the marginal/peripheral. These notions developed on account of colonialism' (2001: 80).

This seems an oversimplified reading of the complexities of responses within the heterogenous communities of South Asia. Bayly (1999: 208) notes that while many forest-dwellers 'were disparaged by the British as "gypsies" and criminal predators', they were also considered as 'uncivilized vermin-handlers by the status-conscious village people for whom they trapped snakes, hunted game or collected forest produce'. Colonialism thus also served to heighten pre-existing internal differentiation and hierarchies, such as the increasingly highlighted traditional distinction between the 'clean' and 'unclean'. Colonial stereotypes included the "feckless" hill and forest-dwelling "aboriginals"', but these 'both echoed and enhanced the differentiations which many Indians were now making . . . between the upright man of Brahman or merchant *ahimsa* values and the various aggressive, parasitical or "uncivilized" peoples from whom they were now seeking to distinguish themselves' (Bayly 1999: 124).

Such south Asian values and categories necessarily drew on prior local understandings of difference. Halbfass (1988: 172) argues that Hinduism especially has been isolationist or at least self-contained. The internal complexities of the hierarchy enable non-Hindus or the lowest castes to be seen as deviant, impure, irrelevant and unnecessary as 'the Other' to Hindus. Traditional Hinduism 'has neither recognized the foreign, the other as a possible alternative, nor as a potential source of its own identity'. Hindu categorization may usefully be considered as:

> a sequence of concentric circles, which surround the centre of ritual purity and perfection. Seen from this center, the most distant members of the social structure, the *candalas* [indigenous outcastes including tribals], constitute the transition to the *mlecchas* [foreigners, outsiders]. These in turn form the transition to the animals. The perspective is, of course, that of the Brahmins . . . They see themselves at the center of this system of concentric circles, in which foreigners appear as an extension or continuation of the internal structure of Hindu society. (Halbfass 1988: 180)

The *candalas*, though excluded from rituals and sources of sacred tradition, 'are part of the dharmic system, though in a negative fashion'. *Mlecchas* on the other hand are outside it. For Halbfass,

> Classical Hindu thought has developed . . . a complex, internally differentiated framework of orientation, a kind of immanent universe of thought, in which the contrast of the "indigenous" and the "foreign," of identity and otherness, seems *a priori* superseded, and which is so comprehensive in itself that it is not conducive to any serious involvement with what is different and apart from it – i.e. the 'other' in its otherness. (1988:187)

## China and History

As in India, all strands of Chinese historical thought (Confucian, Taoist and Buddhist) ultimately consider cosmologies and histories to be cyclical (Bodde 1981). Unlike many other European and Asian systems drawing on a personal Creator, these even have no fixed starting point from which to measure events (cf. Black 1989: 40–1). However, there is a widespread Confucian conception 'which sees the days of the ancient sage-kings as a truly golden age, and all human history since that time as a process of steady degeneration' (Bodde 1981: 245). For most Taoists the earliest times were also golden, but (as with some Buddhist writings) because of a lack of government, people were living in a 'state of nature'. Although history is cyclical, the writers are living in the downswing portion. Only a small minority have been associated with a 'progressive' or linear strand in Chinese historical thought. Bodde (1981: 250) gives the early example of Ho Hsiu in the second century AD, who conceptualized history as passing through three ages of Disorder, Approaching Peace and Universal Peace, and suggests that this framework is 'the first in Chinese thought which explicitly recognizes the possibility of positive human progress according to a fixed pattern of historical evolution'. Needham (1965) prefers rather to emphasize the linearity of much Chinese thought about historical time, in contrast to India, including the second century BC *Huai Nan Tzu* with a chapter 'devoted to proving social change and progress since the most ancient times, with many references to material improvement' (1965: 23, fn. 2). Many Chinese thinkers displayed an interest in history, whether dynastic, regional, linguistic or archaeological, with much early work on corpuses of inscriptions, for example. Needham explicitly contrasts Chinese and much later Western European ideas about prehistory (1965: 34–8), and points to the tripartite Stone–Bronze–Iron technological sequence offered by Yuan K'ang in the first century AD. Concepts of social evolution are clearly possible.

One of the most interesting later thinkers is the seventeenth-century Wang Fu-chih (Wang Ch'uan-shan) (1619–92), whose philosophy, suggests Gernet (1982: 499) 'looks like a naturalist and "materialist" one'. For Wang Fu-chih 'the traditional picture of ancient times as a golden age is contrary to what can be rationally deduced about the past; the history of man has been marked by the uninterrupted evolution and constant progress of societies' (1982: 499) He suggested that changes are:

the result of historical forces, which operate according to a definite pattern, irrespective of the intentions of the historical individuals involved ... Not only are such changes inevitable, however, but they belong to a definite pattern of social improvement which has moved China forward from tribalism to feudalism and from feudalism to centralized empire ... there has been a steady subsequent growth in civilization. (Bodde 1981: 251)

Tellingly, Wang Fu-chih's writings, against the mainstream of Chinese philosophical thought, remained largely unpublished for two centuries, but later became important as a precursor for explicitly materialist and progressive thinkers including Chinese Marxists. Bodde adds (1981: 295, n. 22): 'though Wang's theory of historical progress makes him quite exceptional . . . certain similar tendencies are discernible in a few other scholars of his and the next century.' The timing of these exceptionalist Chinese philosophies of history is interesting: they overlapped (as in Europe: Tribe 1978) with the publication of numerous agricultural treatises (Gernet 1982: 442) from the earlier seventeenth-century Late Ming dynasty onwards. According to Gernet (1982: 523), through Jesuit missionaries, '[t]he importance attributed to agriculture in Ch'ing China inspired the thinking of the [French] Physiocrats' who were important in promulgating subsistence-based social evolution. There were other rare later exceptions to mainstream Chinese historical thought, such as Liao P'ing, and the leader of the New Text School of Confucianism, K'ang Yu-wei (Bodde 1981: 252–3; see also Fung 1953: 680–3, 712–13). However, Bodde (1981: 254) argues that these later nineteenth-century Confucianists' unusual stance 'very probably reflects Western influence, in the form of either scientific writings or the theory of evolution or of theological literature about a coming millennium'.

## Ibn Khaldûn and Islamic History

A third brief comparison highlights the contingency of the perceived significance of anthropological categories. Medieval Islamic scholars and those of Judaeo-Christian tradition, had ancient and Classical texts, a personified Creator, and environmental and other experiences in common. They might thus be expected to demonstrate other commonalities regarding the form of cosmologies, time and hence history. But the example of Ibn Khaldûn – one of the few pre-modern Islamic scholars to write extensively about history – suggests that other factors were more influential. His *The Muqaddimah: An Introduction to History*, was written at the end of the fourteenth century. Partly because of common sources, some of his statements prefigure the ideas of European Enlightenment writers (see e.g. Pluciennik 2002: 100). Thus in his 'First prefatory discussion' (In Khaldûn 1967: 89–93) he argues that 'civilization' or 'human social organization' is the result of the need for food, defence and hence cooperation. He also ascribes aspects of difference to the effects of climate: while Montesquieu reasoned that France offered the most perfect conditions, Ibn Khaldûn proposed that 'The Irâq and Syria are directly in the middle and therefore are the most temperate' (1967: 168). Residents of extreme zones – 'black' Africa, Slavic northern Europe – are correspondingly intemperate, ignorant and less refined. Diet and hence subsistence is important in determining character:

he contrasts agriculturalists and pastoralists, and shows an admiration of asceticism or restraint. Thus,

> desert people who lack grain and seasonings are found to be healthier in body and
> better in character than the hill people who have plenty of everything. Their complexions are clearer, their bodies cleaner, their figures more perfect and better, their characters less intemperate, and their minds keener as far as knowledge and perception are
> concerned ... the inhabitants of fertile zones where the products of agriculture and
> animal husbandry as well as seasonings and fruit are plentiful, are, as a rule, described
> as stupid in mind and coarse in body.' (Ibn Khaldûn 1967: 177–9).

A series of binary values is used to contrast people and conditions, such as urban:rural and urban:desert; softness:bravery, corrupt:pure and so on. Distance from corrupting urban civilization is a measure of purity, rather than any ethnographic information: his exemplars are the Mudar tribes of the Arabian Peninsula who 'lived a hard life *in places where there was no agriculture or animal husbandry*. They lived far from the fertile field of Syria and the 'Iraq, far from the sources of seasonings and grains. How pure have they kept their lineages! These are unmixed in every way, and are known to be unsullied.' (Ibn Khaldûn 1967: 266, emphasis added).

Ibn Khaldûn displays much ambivalence towards both 'civilized' and 'savage' people. He sees many praiseworthy qualities in nomadic 'desert life', as well as benefits in sedentary civilization. Although aware of lengthy human histories (including ruined cities), he does not present a framework of social evolution, and nowhere expressly mentions hunter-gatherers or non-farmers as a group. Much of his philosophy is overlain by a short-term cyclical idea of 'history' on familial, dynastic and political/urban levels, typically with three to four generations between those typified by 'desert' qualities and vigour, and subsequent urban luxury, decadence and overthrow. Ibn Khaldûn does not always distinguish between nomadic and sedentary peoples, but rather contrasts rural (including nomads) to urban life. Rosenthal (1967: lxxvii) observes that 'the term *badâwah* was applied to the largely sedentary rural people living at some distance from the great population centers, and Ibn Khaldûn preferably used it in this sense'.

> Ibn Khaldûn's 'Bedouins' were not, as a rule, nomads living in the desert, but dwelt
> chiefly in villages, and practiced agriculture and animal husbandry for a livelihood...
> . Cities in his day permitted, and required, a good deal of agricultural activity. In Ibn
> Khaldûn's thinking, the sociological distinction amounted to no more than a quantitative distinction as to the size and density of human settlements. (1967: lxxvii)

Ibn Khaldûn's ambivalence extends to the term 'savage', sometimes used to mean 'natural' or 'wild' in a valedictory or at least not wholly condemnatory way.

Thus nomadic camel pastoralists are described as 'the most savage human beings that exists. Compared with sedentary people, they are on a level with wild, untamable (animals) and dumb beasts of prey' (Ibn Khaldûn 1967: 252). But elsewhere he offers praise for such qualities. 'Since . . . desert life no doubt is the reason for bravery, savage groups are braver than others' and hence *ceteris paribus*, will 'beat' sedentary tribes. They also display superior 'group feeling' or social solidarity (Ibn Khaldûn 1967: 282–3). Only in a few places are there indications that Ibn Khaldûn had some sense of linear progression. He argues at one point (1967: 252–3) that 'Bedouins are prior to sedentary people. The desert is the basis and reservoir of civilization and cities . . . It has thus become clear that the existence of Bedouins is prior to, and the basis of, the existence of towns and cities.' As a consequence, his Bedouin share aspects of the Noble Savage: 'As compared with those of sedentary people, their [the Bedouin's] evil ways and blameworthy qualities are much less numerous. They are closer to the *first natural state* and more remote from the evil habits that have been impressed upon the souls (of sedentary people) through numerous and ugly, blameworthy customs' (Ibn Khaldûn 1967: 254, emphasis added).

## Discussion and Conclusion

The cultural conditions for producing universal histories, such as social evolution, comprize three interrelated aspects: identifying certain differences, explaining and evaluating difference, and organizing and expressing such differences chronologically.

The early modern European perspective on cultural differences between humans was enhanced by intensified, expanded and increasingly published contact with others in a variety of colonial and mercantile settings. This was especially true of encounters with the 'New World', which offered extra-biblical challenges to existing cosmologies, mythologies, theologies, geographies and histories. The geographical remoteness and enormity of the Americas in particular, coupled with the lack of ancient textual authority, allowed the New World and its inhabitants to become the vessels for all kinds of fantasies and explanations (*cf.* Todorov 1984). The perception of discontinuity enabled and promoted the formation of particularly rigid and bounded categories which were a prerequisite for stadial schemes. These particular conditions of geographical and cultural rupture were not replicated in southern and eastern Asia.

The European choice of subsistence tells us something of the cultural preoccupations of those writing the conjectural histories – often economists and lawyers, and/or landowners and 'improvers'. They were men interested in the material conditions of life, work, colonization and trade. These and other aspects can be linked to the growth and expression of agrarian and mercantile capitalism as practice, culture and ideology both 'at home' and abroad in the colonial context (Pluciennik 2002). Though complex, the category of 'hunters' was Other to the ideal of seventeenth- and eighteenth-century European men – property-owning farmers with enclosed lands. Specific attitudes towards the relative merits, ideal locations and characteristics of culture, cultivation and nature (e.g. Cosgrove 1993; Glacken 1967) also coloured attitudes towards and the connotations of 'hunters'.

Early modern Europeans engaged with difference under specific conditions and in a particular way. Linear tropes for time and history existed and progressive interpretations were favoured by changing conditions. The fact that Ibn Khaldûn and later Islamic scholars, despite many commonalities, did not develop or show interest in subsistence-based social evolution, reinforces the argument that it was the product of a very specific set of circumstances and sense of history. European conjectural historians were using their own and proxy experiences as the marker against which to measure progress and improvement. The sense of a personal journey towards the achievable end of salvation became important as a model of and for secular achievement, collective histories and modern political philosophies. In much of south Asia, though, the comparable understanding was one of karmic debt and reincarnation over many lives; in China the concept of cosmic balance militated against linear histories. Even Wang Fu-chih saw human history in part as an alternation between prosperity and chaos, representing the dominance of *yang* and *yin* respectively (Teng 1968; Liu 2002). For southern Asia, the Hindu commitment

> to the rules of dharma and to transempirical, soteriological goals [i.e. those pertaining to salvation] limits or supersedes the interest in science and technology, and with it the openness for the scientific achievements of foreigners. Furthermore, the traditionalistic tendency to regard all "sciences" (*vidya*) as timeless, all-inclusive configurations of knowledge is incompatible with the ideas of progress and an open-ended empirical accumulation of knowledge. (Halbfass 1988:186)

If the arguments above are correct then the particular societal categories which continue to shape our disciplines are more contingent than is generally accepted. This is not to say that such terms have no 'real' content or anthropological interest or application. Others, however, are also concerned with the distorting effects of the 'capacious and radically underdetermined subsistence categories' typically used by anthropologists and archaeologists (Roscoe 2002: 160). The salience, meaning and even presence of such distinctions – and the uses to which they are put – is historically and culturally variable. It is for particular reasons that we preferentially use subsistence as a primary axis of variability, however much we have recently debated definitional contents and boundaries. This suggests that viewing the range of societies with which we are concerned through differently constituted lenses, whether those of history, or of *other* indigenous sociologies and philosophies, may be an intellectually and perhaps also ethically worthwhile exercise.

## Acknowledgements

My thanks for advice, references and comments from my former colleagues at Lampeter: Gary Bunt, Kathy Fewster, Gavin Flood, Paul Rainbird and Xin Yang Wong.

# –3–

# Hunting-and-Gathering Society: an Eighteenth-Century Scottish Invention

## *Alan Barnard*

'Hunter-gatherer society' was in essence a late eighteenth-century invention, and it came to be realized as meaningful in social theory largely within Scotland. I do not claim that no one before the eighteenth century or beyond Scotland had any idea of hunting and gathering as preceding other means of subsistence. Nor am I suggesting that no one before had conceived of these means of subsistence as characteristic of early human existence. Rather, my argument is that it was only with some of Montesquieu's ideas as developed in eighteenth-century Scotland that a theoretical understanding of hunter-gatherer society comes into being. We know today that the overwhelming part of humanity's existence has been spent in hunting-and-gathering societies. Our intellectual antecedents in the seventeenth and eighteenth centuries did not know this.

There has been some debate in recent times about whether it is better to speak of hunting-and-gathering *society*, or instead hunter-gatherer *sociality* (itself, a seventeenth-century concept, which the eighteenth-century Scots were to call *sociability*). Tim Ingold (1990; 1999), in particular, advocates the notion that hunter-gatherers live 'socially', but not in 'societies', partly because the notion of 'society' as he sees it is embedded in a discourse of social domination. Two requirements need to be met before there can exist a theory of hunter-gatherer society. First, there needs to be a notion of progress with *more than two stages* – in other words, to use the language of the day, not simply savage/civilized, barbarous/polished or brutish/sociable. Rather, we need a notion of at least three or four stages of human social evolution. Secondly, there needs to be a concept of society as based on *economic relations*. The reason for the first requirement (more than two stages) is substantive rather than formal: eighteenth-century thinkers and their immediate predecessors simply could not conceive of a dualist classification which placed only hunter-gatherers in one category and all the rest of humanity in the other. The reason for the second is, at the simplest level, that hunting and gathering are by definition economic activities. Any notion of 'hunting-and-gathering society' must therefore be an economic notion; and any theory about such a society must, at least in part, be an economic theory.

Let me add a final disclaimer. The possibility that sixteenth-century Jesuits may have had ideas on hunter-gatherers that influenced the eighteenth-century Scot William Robertson, for example, would not refute my argument. Nor would the suggestion that hunter-gatherers themselves, or their neighbours, would have had a pre-eighteenth-century notion that they lived in a 'society' that did not practise herding or cultivating.[1] That is, at least in part, because invention as much as discovery is a process of awareness – not necessarily a single event. Take the analogy of another eighteenth-century phenomenon, the 'discovery' of oxygen. Historians of science debate over who truly discovered oxygen: Carl Wilhelm Scheele, Joseph Priestly, Antoine Lavoisier, all in the 1770s, or even seventeenth-century alchemist Zbigniew Szydlo, 170 years before. There is no single point of discovery, because it all depends on the relation between events (in this case experiments) and the understanding of events in the context of systems of knowledge. Most textbooks credit either Scheele or Priestly with the 'discovery' of oxygen, but Scheele and Priestly defined their experimental results in terms of the (erroneous) phlogiston theory. Lavoisier's supporters point out that only he had a reasonably correct theory of oxygen, as an element within air required for combustion (see e.g. Donovan 1996). Accepting the argument of Lavoisier's supporters, I suggest it is much the same with the invention of hunting-and-gathering society. An accepted set of theoretical premises is required before the concept becomes truly meaningful.

## Seventeenth- and Eighteenth-century Precursors

Before the middle of the eighteenth century there was virtually no notion of a kind of society comparable to what we call 'hunting-and-gathering society'. Instead, the concern was with the dichotomy 'natural man' versus either the state or civil society; or with individualism versus sociality; or with the influence of climate on temperament and culture. What scholars sought was an explanation of the innate, natural human existence, whether it was 'original' or simply embedded deep in the human psyche. Compared to the debates on whether humankind was innately good or evil, naturally social or naturally solitary, mode of subsistence was inconsequential.

Even some of the greatest seventeenth-century thinkers seemed not to have made a distinction between hunting and herding, or between gathering and primitive cultivation; and none of them place any significance in the idea of a type of society in which hunting and gathering were the principal subsistence activities. Samuel Pufendorf, famed for asserting an innate 'sociality' (*socialitas*) of humankind, wrote that 'the earliest men sought to fill the empty world and to find more ample living space for themselves *and their cattle* . . .' (1991 [1673]: 116; emphasis added). John Locke (1988 [1690]: 300) too suggests that 'man in the state of nature' possessed sheep and cattle, and that the earliest stages of society might be characterized by the exchange of wool and for other goods.

Or consider the best-known of all passages on the state of nature, from Hobbes's *Leviathan*:

> In such a condition, there is no place for Industry; because the fruit thereof is uncertain: and consequently no Culture of the Earth [cultivation] . . . ; no Knowledge of the face of the Earth; no account of Time; no Arts; no Letters; no Society; and which is worst of all, continuall feare, and danger of violent death; And the life of man, solitary, poore, nasty, brutish, and short (Hobbes 1973 [1651]: 64–5).

Hobbes's concern was with a hypothetical 'Naturall Condition of Mankind' and *not* with the nature of a specific known type of human existence. There is no evidence that Hobbes meant this description to apply to real hunter-gatherers, whose existence in his own time may indeed have been unknown to him. Rather, he simply imputed that before the social contract (when men agreed to band together for their own protection), there would have been no cultivation.

Such visions of hunters and gatherers change in France in the middle of the eighteenth century. In that time and place, we come much closer to a vision of hunting-and-gathering society we would recognize today. Yet still subsistence, and more broadly production, are undervalued in contrast with the way they are treated in later times. The shadow of hunting-and-gathering society may exist in the writings of Francophone intellectuals of the mid-eighteenth century, but it is not a fundamental type even in the writings of the two chief protagonists: Montesquieu and Rousseau. Turgot may have originated the idea of three stages of society in terms of subsistence (hunting, herding and farming) as early as the late 1740s, but it is difficult to assess his influence, particularly given that his essay was not published until long after his death (cf. Meek 1976: 68–76).

In *The Spirit of the Laws*, Montesquieu (1989 [1748]: 290–2) has really very little to say about hunter-gatherers. His main purpose, of course, was to classify societies according to political system (republican, monarchical and despotic) rather than according to subsistence. In general, he lumps hunters and herders together as a single type: 'peoples who do not cultivate the land' (*les peuples qui ne cultivent point les terres*). Yet he does distinguish 'hunting peoples' (*les peuples chasseurs*) from 'pastoral peoples' (*les peuples pasteurs*) in that hunters, such as those of Siberia, could not feed themselves if they were to unite like the Tartar hordes with their livestock. Rather, hunters live in small camps or bands, each of which itself forms a small 'nation'. For reasons that are not entirely clear to me, he sees hunters as living mainly in marshy forests.

In Rousseau's *Discourse on the Origin of Inequality* we see the emergence not only of a hunter-gatherer but, arguably, even a kind of 'original affluent society' (cf. Sahlins 1972: 1–39) – except that for Rousseau there was yet no society. Rousseau describes his natural man as 'satisfying his hunger at the first oak, and slaking his thirst at the first brook . . . and, with that, all his wants supplied' ('. . . *et voilà se besoins satisfaits*') (1973 [1755]: 52). According to Rousseau early people lived scattered in the forests, without society. Because humans are more intelligent and adaptable than animals, each could use his or her ingenuity to extract food from a great variety of resources. Some of Rousseau's points are similar to those of the Scottish intellectuals who followed. Yet there is a crucial difference: Rousseau describes an age *before* society, not a type of society.

Arguably, the first truly to think of 'hunting-and-gathering society' as a clearly-defined stage of evolution was Turgot. His incomplete, posthumous treatise *On Universal History* was sketched out in the late 1740s and early 1750s, and was later edited and first published (in French) in 1808. Yet even here, it is difficult to know whether the 'nations' (*les nations*) of hunters he describes are in fact *societies* in the sense of later Scottish or modern anthropological discourse. Turgot's hunting stage begins after the biblical Flood, when all humanity was but a single forest-dwelling family with no fields to cultivate and presumably no possession over the animals released from the Ark.

> Without provisions, and in the depths of forests, men could devote themselves to nothing but obtaining their subsistence. The fruits which the earth produces in the absence of agriculture are not enough; men had to resort to the hunting of animals, which, being limited in number and incapable in a given region of providing many men with food, have for this very reason accelerated the dispersion of peoples and their rapid diffusion.
>
> Families or small nations widely separated from one another, because each required a very large area to obtain its food: that was the state of hunters. (Turgot 1973 [1808]: 65)

Turgot's ideas undoubtedly anticipate those of Adam Smith and others among the Scots, and indeed French writers such as Condorcet, Quesnay, Helvétius and Goguet (Meek 1976: 91–8). Yet it is with the Scots, and their belief in economics as the driving force of social being and social evolution, that 'hunting-and-gathering society' becomes a significant concept.

## Hunting-and-Gathering Society in the Scottish Enlightenment

The Scottish tradition was certainly built upon a foundation of economic concerns. These related to early eighteenth-century periods of economic as well as social instability in Scotland, and to a time in the middle and late eighteenth century when Scottish farming practices, as well as other economic concerns, were undergoing great change. Several of the key protagonists, such as Lord Kames and Adam Smith, were active in their advocacy of specific reforms in farming practice and commercial practice. There was also a key interest, held collectively among Scottish intellectuals, in progress, or as it would later be called, social evolution. Montesquieu was the figure the Scots most admired. Indeed, a French edition of *The Spirit of the Laws* was published in Edinburgh just two years after it first appeared in Geneva, and several English-language editions were published in the eighteenth century, in Aberdeen, Edinburgh and Berwick-upon-Tweed, as well as in London. However, while Montesquieu, like his nineteenth-century successors, saw progress in terms of a transition from savagery to barbarism to civilization, the Scots tended favour a line more akin to that of Turgot, from hunting to herding to farming, and in some cases (most famously Adam Smith), to commerce.

The first Scot to consider the idea of hunting-and-gathering society was Sir John Dalrymple, in his *Essay Towards a General History of Feudal Property in Great Britain* (1758 [1757]). Like seventeenth-century thinkers Grotius, Pufendorf and Locke, his understanding of the stages of progress is embedded in a theory of property (cf. Meek 1976: 101). However, unlike almost all of his predecessors, including the French, Dalrymple states clearly that he is talking about *a kind of society*. In the second (corrected and enlarged edition), he writes:

> The first state of society is that of hunters and fishers; among such a people the idea of property will be confined to a few, and but a very few moveables; and subjects which are immovable, will be esteemed to be common. In accounts given of many American tribes we read, that one or two of the tribe will wander five or six hundred miles from his usual place of abode, plucking the fruit, destroying the game, and catching the fish throughout the fields and rivers adjoining to all the tribes which he passes, without any idea of such a property in the members of them, as makes him guilty of infringing the rights of others, when he does so (Dalrymple 1758 [1757]: 75).

His second stage is of 'pasturage', when the hunting and fishing life proves inconvenient and dangerous. His third (and arguably, final) is a stage of agriculture, induced through population expansion and insufficient resources.

The second Scot to comment on the problem, a year later in his *Historical Law Tracts*, and subsequently in several other publications, was the famous judge Lord Kames. Yet interestingly here, Kames, like Ingold in our own time, holds back on calling the hunting way of life a 'society'.

> Hunting and fishing, in order for sustenance were the original occupations of man. The shepherd life succeeded; and the next stage was that of agriculture. These progressive changes, in the order now mentioned, may be traced in all nations, so far as we have any remains of their original history. The life of a fisher or hunter is averse to society,

except among the members of single families. The shepherd life promotes larger societies, if that can be called a society, which hath scarce any other than a local connection. But the true spirit of society, which consists in mutual benefits, and in making the industry of individuals profitable to others as well as to themselves, was not known till agriculture was invented. (Kames 1758: 77)

Later Kames was to argue that hunting preceded fishing: 'Water is not our element; and savages probably did not attempt to draw food from the sea or from rivers, till land-animals became scarce' (1788: 88). Typically among Scottish thinkers, he argued that the sense of property is *not* the exclusive preserve of humans, it being found also among beavers, sheep and monkeys. For Kames, the practice of hoarding was inherent in human nature. From this, hunter-gatherers, or more accurately hunter-fishers, developed barter. And from barter, commerce eventually ensued (1788: 116–27). Later too, Kames seems to have come round to the idea of early hunters as having society, for he refers to hunting, fighting and love as 'the sole occupations of men in the original state of society' (1789: 244).

Kames's most vociferous opponent in many matters was his judicial colleague, Lord Monboddo. Whereas Kames regarded Native Americans as a different 'species' from Europeans, Monboddo regarded even orang-utans and chimpanzees as members 'of the human species'. Monboddo's (e.g. 1774) main scholarly interest was in the origin of language, which he argued could not exist until after the invention of society. Rightly or wrongly, he regarded the 'Orang Outang' (including the chimpanzee) as a gregarious and even a societal human being, but one without language. And unusually for his time, this led him to speculate (though attributing the idea to ancient Greek writer Plutarch) that gathering preceded hunting:

Man did not become carnivorous till he became a hunter, and he could not be a hunter till he had invented some kind of arms; and not even immediately after that; for the Orang Outangs, though they use sticks, do not hunt, but live upon the natural fruits of the earth. It is therefore necessity which drove man to this unnatural diet, and luxury has continued it . . . (Monboddo 1774: 225).

Interesting though Monboddo's arguments were, and as important as he was among Edinburgh's literati, his views were not those of mainstream Scottish thinking. Nor did his ideas quite anticipate Darwin's, some nineteenth- and twentieth-century commentators have argued. My own view has long been that his ideas are, in a sense, the inverse of Darwin's: it is not that man is an ape, but that the ape is a pre-linguistic, pre-hunting food-gatherer who lives at the very earliest stage of *human* society (see e.g. Barnard 1995).

With hindsight, the most important of all the Scots (at least on economic progress) was, of course, Adam Smith. He, and those who followed him, wrote of four distinct 'Ages' of human society: those of Hunters, of Shepherds, of Agriculture and of Commerce (or sometimes: hunting, pasturage, farming and commerce). The first published treatment of these was in *Wealth of Nations* (1776), but the earliest and fullest source in his writings comes to us through his *Lectures on Jurisprudence* as recorded by his Glasgow students in the academic year of 1762/3. It has been suggested that he may have given some of this material in Edinburgh lectures on 'Rhetoric and Belles Lettres' as early as 1748, which would probably place him prior to Turgot in the development of 'four-stage theory' (Meek 1976: 110; cf. 1977). At any rate, let me quote from his Glasgow lectures.

If we should suppose 10 or 12 persons of different sexes settled in an uninhabited island, the first method they would fall upon for their sustenance would be to support themselves by the wild fruits and wild animals which the country afforded. Their sole business would be hunting the wild beasts or catching the fishes . . . This is the age of hunters. (Smith 1978 [Dec. 24, 1762]: 14)

In the age of hunters it is impossible for a very great number to live together. As game is their only support they would soon exhaust all that was within their reach. Thirty or forty families would be the most that could live together, that is, about 140 or 150 persons. These might live by the chase in the country about them. They would also nat-urally form themselves into these villages, agreeing to live near together for their mutuall security. (1978 [Feb. 22, 1763]: 213)

In the age of hunters there can be very little government of any sort, but what there is will be of the democraticall kind. A nation of this sort consists of a number of inde-pendent families, no otherwise connected than as they live together in the same town or village and speak the same language. With regard to the judicial power, this in these nations as far as it extends is possessed by the community as one body. (1978 [Feb. 21, 1763]: 201)

'Regular government' emerged after the appropriation of animals as property, and it gave rise to inequalities, with some individuals acquiring more than their neighbours. Property in the age of hunters existed in only a very limited and tran-sient sense. Smith's famous example, later repeated in *Wealth of Nations*, was that of a man chasing a hare over a period of some time who would acquire an exclu-sive privilege to hunt that hare (1978: 17–18). For Smith, a key difference between hunting and herding societies is in their respective attitudes towards theft. Hunters (he cites Amerindians) have almost no notion of property, and theft is of little concern. Herders, in contrast (he cites the Tartars), punish theft by immediate death. Smith concedes that cultivation of the soil may follow directly from a hunting-and-gathering existence (in parts of North America), but his central argument on the origin of property is that it evolved as part of the transition from hunting to herding.

He does attribute both a division of labour and an incipient form of commerce to those peoples living in the age of hunters, for example in suggesting that a good arrow-maker might exchange arrows for venison (1978: 348).

Adam Ferguson (1966 [1767]: 81), an Edinburgh professor (of various subjects), also noted that some 'savage nations' subsist by 'hunting, fishing, or the natural produce of the soil', though their existence, for his argument, was far less important than it was for that of Smith. Ferguson did take more account of contemporary ethnographic descriptions than Smith, but Ferguson's comments on the age of hunters, or as he preferred to see it, 'the rude nations prior to the establishment of property', was still more conjectural than ethnological. He saw their existence as useful for armchair conjectural historians, like himself, in order that such men might better speculate on the origins and prehistory of society. Ferguson noted that those who subsisted by hunting and fishing had only the property they carried with them, and had not yet appropriated food as property. In his words: 'The food of to-morrow is yet wild in the forest, or hid in the lake; it cannot be appropriated before it is caught; and even then, being the purchase of numbers, who fish or hunt in a body, it accrues to the community, and is applied for immediate use, or becomes an accession to the stores of the public' (Ferguson 1966 [1767]: 82). In other words, food not caught is not property, though once acquired it becomes what later thinkers would describe as 'communal property' (as opposed to 'individual property').

The great historian of the age, and long-time Principal of the University of Edinburgh, was William Robertson. Working from several hundred sources in various languages, Robertson outlined the existing ethnography of the Americas in his four-volume *History of America*. Like Rousseau, he gave prominence to the individual over society. He regarded Amerindians as averse to labour, especially for men. He saw those in the more primitive states as essentially nomadic. In opposition to Kames, he believed that fishing preceded hunting, and that 'as the occupations of the former do not call for equal exertions of activity, or talents, with those of the latter, people in that state [fishing] appear to possess neither the same degree of enterprise nor of ingenuity' (Robertson 1809 [1777]: 101). His sequence was: gathering (including small animals), fishing, hunting, agriculture. He added that 'hunting nations' were mainly 'strangers to the idea of property', and that 'The forest or hunting-grounds are deemed to be the property of the tribe, from which it has a title to exclude every rival nation', while 'no individual arrogates a right to any district of these in preference to his fellow citizens' (1809: 115). Interestingly, in light of twentieth-century discoveries, Robertson's hunter-gatherers lived a 'free and vagrant life' (1809: 107) in preference to the drudgery which agriculture entailed. According to one recent historian (Wood 1995: viii), Robertson's emphasis here on subsistence and more generally economic relations, coupled with David Hume's (1987 [1748]) insistence on moral over physical causes, marked a move away from the previous dominance of climate as the prime cause of human diversity.

In any case, John Millar, Smith's friend and colleague at Glasgow, was (a few years before Robertson) the first major thinker to consider the importance of property with respect to sex and gender relations (Millar 1806 [1771]: 14–16). Millar's idea of hunting-and-gathering society was that it entailed great hardship and afforded few pleasures: 'A savage who earns his food by hunting and fishing, or by gathering the spontaneous fruits of the earth, is incapable of attaining any considerable refinement in his pleasures . . . His wants are few, in proportion to the narrowness of his circumstances' (1806: 14–15). Hunters and gatherers had little 'refinement' in courtship, and consequently little sexual passion, because, he argued, passion is derived from the difficulty of obtaining what one seeks. By this reasoning, we may imagine that hunting, rather than sex, was the more passionate pursuit of the male forager. What is significant for Millar is that both gender hierarchy and other aspects of social differentiation emerged along with the development of agriculture and the increase in importance of property.

James Beattie, Professor of Moral Philosophy at Marischal College, Aberdeen, like others, grouped hunting, fishing and food-gathering together, and saw this as the first stage, preceding the stages of herding, of agriculture, and of commerce. However, he was unusual in suggesting that geographical variation should be such an important factor that this scheme might only be applicable in some countries. In others, e.g., those by the sea, he noted that fishing may dominate and that commerce from the sea may exist without the introduction of either herding or agriculture (1817 [1793]: 96–7). Agriculture, Beattie claimed, depended on combining several skills, such as woodwork or metallurgy (to make ploughs), which implies that arts such as these began in a food-gathering state (1817: 93–4).

Some conjectural historians, such as Gilbert Stuart (1797 [1791]), make no mention of hunter-gatherers because their chief concerns lie with later stages of society, while others ignore subsistence in favour of other topics of the time such as the history of language and its relation to communication and intellectual development. For example, James Dunbar, Professor of Moral Philosophy at King's College, Aberdeen, writes very much in the spirit of the four-stage theorists yet makes no explicit mention either of the age of hunters or of any other of the three stages of production. Instead, he conjectures that 'Man may have subsisted, in some sort, like other animals, in a separate and individual state' (1781 [1780]: 2). His second stage was one of a linguistic proficiency which conflicts with the equality, freedom and independence of the earlier stage; and his third and final, a stage developing from 'slow and imperceptible transitions' to 'the protection and discipline of civil government' (1781: 2–3). Dunbar couples this Rousseauian argument with, among others, a Montesquieuian essay 'Of the relation of Man to the surrounding elements' that influence language, art and intellect (1781: 321–47).

David Doig, a Stirling schoolmaster who coupled antiquarianism with religious conservatism, added a new twist: an emphasis on degeneration (degeneration was implicit in Dunbar and Monboddo, but to a lesser degree). Like Dunbar, Doig shunned hunting, herding, cultivating and commerce in favour of savagery, barbarism and civilization. In his *Two Letters on the Savage State Addressed to the Late Lord Kaims* (*sic*) (1792) he argues that progress is not inherent in human nature and that chronological sequences reveal degeneration as well as progress. According to Doig's account, while contact of peoples of lower stages with civilization may sometimes yield advancement, this is the exception rather than the rule. Moreover, he questions the truth of ancient Greek and Roman sources which hint that wandering, fruit-and-herb-gathering savages populated the earth before the dawn of civilization. He suggests, against Ancient writers and their eighteenth-century admirers, that such views stand 'contrary to our natural ideas of the divine beneficence' (1792: 9). God would not create savages without also creating some in a state of civilization. Given this, as well as his assumption that, when disasters came, some with superior knowledge would survive to pass the knowledge on, he argues that 'the empire of the Savage State could neither have been universal, nor of long duration' (1792: 23). The argument in Doig's treatise is complex and difficult to follow, if not convoluted and obtuse. Nevertheless, it should stand as a reminder that opinion in eighteenth-century Scotland on these issues, and other issues, was divided – so much the better for debating in the clubs and societies which proliferated in Edinburgh and elsewhere.

Finally, consider the Revd John Adams of Ayre, little known today but widely read in his time. He was essentially a compiler of the ideas of others. Adams borrows heavily from many writers (often without citation), both those named in the title of his book (Kames, Monboddo, Dunbar and Montesquieu) and others as well (such as Robertson, Ferguson and Smith). Following Montesquieu he saw man as a 'social creature', but argues too that society was first established in order for 'self defence' (1789: 6–7). His comments on climate are interesting in light of the fact that living hunter-gatherers, then as now, tend to occupy the least fertile parts of the world: 'In fruitful countries, and benign climates, men may live in the natural state; but in rude climates, and barren countries, they cannot subsist at all without society and arts' (1789: 8). He repeats this claim several times, arguing always from first principles rather than from example. However, he does argue from implicit example (though he mentions no specific societies), that:

> With respect to hunting it may be observed, that as it becomes less and less necessary in the progress from cold to hot countries, the appetite for it keeps pace with that progress. It is vigorous in very cold countries, where men depend on hunting for food. It is less vigorous in temperate countries, where they are partly fed with natural fruits; and there is scarce any vestige of it in hot countries, where vegetables are the food of men, and where meat is an article of luxury. (Adams 1789: 11)

Adams also does say explicitly that 'it is probable' that hunting preceded 'planting, sowing, or any kind of culture of the ground', as well as the taming and breeding of flocks and herds (1789: 11). For Adams, agriculture generally precedes pastoralism. He cites (erroneously, of course) a lack of agriculture in North America as the reason why the Indians there have not developed 'the pastoral life'; though he suggests that the Laplanders, and to a lesser extent the Tartars, are forced into 'the shepherd-state' because of their harsh environments (1789: 12). Following a brief general discussion of 'the shepherd-state', Adams makes the point that hunting societies require more land, and therefore have smaller populations, than other kinds of society. Where he disagrees with most of his contemporaries is in his assertion that a sense of property pre-dates the transitions from hunting and indeed is prevalent both in human nature and in the nature of some animals, including beavers and sheep (1789: 15–18).

The idea of a hunting-and-gathering society, or in the language of the eighteenth century, a society of hunters, is an economic idea. The basis of four-stage theory was economic. However, it is true that not all envisaged the progress of humankind in economic terms, all the time. Hume, Ferguson and Robertson pointed to the existence of the stages but de-emphasized subsistence or production as a prime cause of progress or social 'improvement'. Hume seemingly had little interest in the matter; Ferguson saw the transitions from savagery to barbarism to civilization as dependent at least as much on intellectual outlook and political domination as on subsistence; and Robertson consistently regarded the search for simple causes, such as means of subsistence, as inadequate in light of the complexity of human existence (Spadafora 1990: 271–2).

Yet the economics of four-stage theory taken as a whole was not merely about subsistence. It was equally, for many in Scotland in the late eighteenth century, about society and about property. As political theorist Christopher Berry has put it, four-stage theory was: 'a tool to identify certain coherences in social institutions. As such it did not explain these institutions. Nowhere do the Scots say that the mode of subsistence causes the form that social institutions take. Rather it was a device that highlighted the central role that property played since it was how property was organized that gave coherence' (Berry 1997: 114).

## Conclusion

I have been looking at the notion of hunting-and-gathering society through examples of early modern Western discourse. This may seem ethnocentric, and in a sense it is. But it is with good reason: anthropology as an academic discipline is in theoretical continuity with eighteenth-century Scottish moral philosophy, through Smith's disciple Dugald Stewart at Edinburgh, and to his students James Cowles Prichard and Thomas Hodgkin, the founders of organizational anthropology in

Great Britain in the early nineteenth century (see e.g. Augstein 1999). Also, Marx read Smith; Lewis Henry Morgan read Kames; and Evans-Pritchard and Radcliffe-Brown, who saw the Scottish Enlightenment as their inspiration, read and applauded the works of the Scottish conjectural historians despite their disagreements with them about methodology (see e.g. Barnard 1992a).

Ingold's problem on hunter-gatherer society versus sociality owes its problematic nature to the conception of society formulated in the Scottish Enlightenment and handed down in social theory to the present day. This was a conception of society based on material as well as social concerns, and indeed one in which economic concerns began to overtake the more simply political ones of the seventeenth century (cf. Barnard 1999: 375–7). The theoretical positions of our contemporaries Sahlins, Lee, Testart or Woodburn would not seem that out of place in an Edinburgh tavern of the 1770s. The same could be said of discussions of empirical interests in the transition from hunting and gathering to herding and cultivation. Examples in my own ethnographic region would include writings by Kalahari ethnographers such as Tanaka, Sugawara, Osaki and Ikeya in the Japanese tradition; or the quite different writings of 'revisionist' archaeologists such as Denbow and Wilmsen, who argue that hunter-gatherers in the Kalahari only exist as part of a larger political economy of domination by agro-pastoralist peoples.

In that regard, perhaps it is worth some reflection that the current Kalahari 'revisionist' debate began with an article by a historian on seventeenth-century subsistence strategies (i.e. Marks 1972). Later revisionists (e.g. Wilmsen 1989a) have criticized modern hunter-gatherer studies for their overemphasis on the pristine nature of hunting-and-gathering society; yet they have failed to consider the possibility that the world-view of seventeenth-century Europeans might have influenced what they 'saw' in their descriptions of the Cape. The fact is that Europeans before the Scottish Enlightenment had very little idea of a 'hunting-and-gathering society'.

To return once again to the question of society versus sociality, it is worth reflecting that this is, quite possibly, both a linguistic and a deeply cultural problem. It may be differently determined, for example, in Japanese, where 'society' and the 'social' are equated (the word *shakai*) and 'sociality' is definable simply as the essential nature of society (*shakaisei*).[2] If, however, we concede that the sociality of hunters and gatherers is pre-society, then equally it is meaningful to think of it as post-society as well, in that it is today maintained in opposition to the larger state-based societies of domination.[3] The fact that hunter-gatherer specialists around the world meet periodically for an 'International Conference on *Hunting and Gathering Societies*' (not merely '. . . on Hunter-Gatherers') is testimony to the endurance, rightly or wrongly, of this Scottish idea.

# Notes

1.  For example, there is a widespread notion in 'traditional' Africa of hunter-gatherers as the original peoples in lands they now share with pastoralists and cultivators. Indeed this notion sometimes features in the symbolism and rituals of non-hunter-gatherers (see e.g. Woodburn 2001: 3–5).
2.  This example was suggested by Kazuyoshi Sugawara (Kyoto University) in discussion of related issues in another paper of mine.
3.  I am grateful to Yasushi Uchiyamada (University of Tsukuba) for discussion of this point.

# –4–

# Edward Westermarck
# and the Origin of Moral Ideas

## L.R. Hiatt

Man: A species of ape who believes in the gods and who imitates *them without ceasing to be an animal.*

From the World War I prison memoirs of André Lorulot, French pacifist

Despite his formal classification as a sociologist, Westermarck's two major works (*The History of Human Marriage*, 1891; *The Origin and Development of the Moral Ideas*, 1906) are in the best traditions of evolutionary anthropology. As an empiricist, he based his speculations about origins and early human history on massive digests of ethnographic evidence, and was sceptical of notions such as 'group marriage' which he regarded as fanciful and counter-intuitive. As a theorist, he was guided by Darwin's principles of natural and sexual selection. The first edition of *The History of Human Marriage* contained an introductory note by Alfred Wallace.

Paradoxically, the early beneficiaries of Westermarck's empiricism and scepticism (most notably Malinowski) became the founders of an anthropology that eschewed conjectures about the origins of culture and promoted instead a comparative sociology of contemporary small-scale indigenous populations. Darwinian theory was left to zoologists and marginalized survivors from the nineteenth century such as physical anthropologists. With the rise of postmodernism in the late twentieth century, what had been initially a strategic disciplinary indifference to human evolution became a covert taboo as anthropology sought to distance itself from any inference that tribal peoples exemplify primordial stages of social development.

Meanwhile a resurgence of interest among biologists in the problem of altruism gave rise to what is now known as kin-selection theory. Initially directed to non-human species, the implications for human evolution were too attractive to be ignored, with the result that cohorts of sociobiologists and evolutionary psychologists have come to occupy the territory where Westermarck once reigned supreme. Given the indifference not to say hostility of anthropologists, it is perhaps inevitable that a trademark of the new order is a bias away from ethnography towards what is often commonplace and intuitive data from the highly evolved culture of its own practitioners (cf. Ingold 2000b).

The present paper represents a first step towards a basically Australianist project in which Westermarck's work on the natural history of marriage and morals is taken as a convenient starting point for evaluating the contribution made to these subjects by evolutionary biology during the twentieth century. I confine myself at this stage to speculations on the origins of morality, since to begin there highlights a difference between human and non-human species that in the case of reproduction is perhaps less critical. In other words, while continuities in the sphere of reproductive strategies enable central features to be encompassed by evolutionary biology, moral accretions seem peculiarly human. The issue is whether these can also be encompassed by evolutionary biology and, if so, how.

I make no pretence at exhaustiveness, either on the biological or the anthropological side. I merely look at some of the views advanced by leading thinkers in evolutionary biology, then ask myself whether the anthropological material I know best has any bearing on them.

## Morality and emotion

Although Westermarck sets himself apart from philosophical inquiry, his outlook has evident affinities with the empiricist Scottish tradition exemplified by Hutcheson, Hume and Smith.[1] Like them, he traces moral ideas to feeling; and his stated priority, as theirs, is to analyse rather than prescribe. Behaviour is neither inherently good nor bad but is deemed to be so depending upon whether it is conventionally approved or disapproved. Moral judgments may, and do, differ from one culture to another, and even between subdivisions of the same culture. There is no legitimate sense in which science can discover what all human beings ought or ought not to do. The object of ethical science (if the expression is to be used at all) can only be to study and account for moral consciousness as a fact.

Westermarck locates the beginnings of morality in the 'retributive emotions', using 'retributive' inclusively to designate positive as well as negative reciprocity. Evolution will tend to favour individuals who react angrily, aggressively or resentfully towards those who would injure them. It will also tend to favour those who display affection and goodwill towards those who would aid them: 'As natural selection accounts for the origin of resentment, so it also accounts for the origin of retributive kindly emotion; . . . by resentment evils are averted, by retributive kindliness benefits are secured' (1906: 94–5). In a general sense we can say that individuals approve of behaviour that supports them and disapprove of behaviour that threatens them. In its earliest stages morality is a consensus reached by individuals about hurtful and beneficial behaviours. Hurtful behaviours are the subject of general disapproval, beneficial behaviours the subject of general approval. The former are said to be bad, the latter to be good.

Westermarck's argument contains a difficulty he left unresolved. If morals are conventions, to locate them in individual advantage and disadvantage begs the question of their origin. While it is to A's advantage not to be hurt by B, it is not self-evidently to B's advantage to refrain from hurting A. Sensing this difficulty, Westermarck invokes a principle of 'sympathetic identification with the other' (you know what it's like to feel pain, so you refrain from inflicting it on a fellow human). How such a propensity evolved is left unexplained. If natural selection operates at the level of the individual, do the restraints imposed by sympathy and morality generate benefits in excess of those available through the unfettered pursuit of individual self-interest?

The problem remains as one of the central issues in human sociobiology. In the wake of Darwin's thoughts on the matter in *The Descent of Man*, two distinct traditions have emerged. One maintains that morality is absent from nature and that its emergence cannot be explained in terms of the principle of natural selection. Its occurrence as a cultural artefact in humans is therefore biologically enigmatic.The other finds precursors of human morality in non-human species, especially higher primates, and sees no difficulty in accounting for them along orthodox selectionist lines as evolving forms of mutual aid. The first tradition is exemplified by Thomas Huxley and George Williams, writing nearly a hundred years apart towards the ends of the nineteenth and twentieth centuries respectively. Their adversaries, Peter Kropotkin and Franz de Waal, exemplify the second.

## Nature: Bad Through and Through

In 1888 Thomas Huxley published an essay entitled 'The Struggle for Existence' in which he suggested that, although in a strict sense civil society is as much a part of nature as anything else, it is convenient and appropriate to regard it as distinct from all other forms of social life. The reason is that it possesses a unique characteristic or objective called morality, lacking not only in non-human species but in human savages as well. In consequence, 'the course shaped by the ethical man – the member of society or citizen – necessarily runs counter to that which the non-ethical man – the primitive savage, or man as a mere member of the animal kingdom – tends to adopt' (1888: 165). The savage, like any other animal, inhabits an amoral world in which the struggle for existence is fought to the bitter end. For countless generations of human history the weak and stupid have gone to the wall, while the strong and shrewd have survived. In circumstances that must remain obscure, members of certain populations began to exercise self-restraint and to pursue their interests only to the extent that they did not interfere with the interests of others. Morality was born, war gave way to peace, and ethical man sought the common weal as much as his own.

In 1893 Huxley was invited to give the Romanes Lecture, which he entitled 'Evolution and Ethics'. This added little to its antecedent, except an even greater emphasis on the opposition between nature and morality. The object of the ethical process is survival not of the fittest but of the virtuous. In place of competitive individualism, it advocates benevolence and cooperation. Huxley deplored the laissez-faire market philosophy of the day and exhorted his audience to 'understand, once for all, that the ethical progress of society depends not on imitating the cosmic process, still less in running away from it, but in combating it' (1894: 81).

G.C. Williams is one of the founders of modern sociobiology. In the 1960s he spearheaded the attack on Wynne-Edwards's group-selection theory, thereby clearing the way for gene-centred sociobiology in the 1970s (Williams 1966). In 1989 he endorsed Huxley's position on morality in an essay entitled 'A Sociobiological Expansion of 'Evolution and Ethics''. With the benefit of a further century of biological understanding, Williams maintained that Huxley's judgment on nature was too soft. As well as the bloodstained beak and claw, we now have proof that the forests and seas are rife with cuckoldry, rape, incest, infanticide and cannibalism, not to speak of manipulation, desertion and wasteful predation. To make matters worse, those rare examples of morally attractive behaviour like altruism and mutuality turn out to be manifestations of genetic selfishness. We have all the more reason, therefore, to refuse any longer to be instruments of the evolutionary process. The time has come to rebel against the tyranny of the replicators.

## Nature: Some Good There

In 1890 Peter Kropotkin published a reply to Huxley entitled 'Mutual Aid among Animals'. On the basis of his reading and of his own observations of wildlife in Siberia, he argued that mutual aid in animal species was as important in evolution as competition and struggle. Darwin, it is true, had dwelt upon competition between individuals of the same species; but he had also acknowledged the importance of cooperation. Communities with the greatest number of mutually sympathetic members would flourish best and rear the greatest number of offspring. Huxley, in common with numerous lesser exponents of Darwinism, stressed the selfish aspects of social life in animal species to the virtual exclusion of altruism.

Huxley's representation of primitive communities as agglomerations of unruly, brawling savages was, Kropotkin argued, manifestly untrue. No better proof of human social instincts could be imagined than the section organization of Aboriginal Australia, where countless communities lacking any form of government nevertheless conformed to complex systems regulating marriage eligibility.

To describe such people as creatures devoid of ethical principles could be pardoned only on the grounds of lamentable ignorance. Altruism and hospitality abounded, and within the tribe a principle of 'each for all' reigned supreme. The same sociability and spirit of solidarity characterized primitive communities everywhere.

A century later Kropotkin's argument was taken up and developed by the eminent primatologist Franz de Waal in his book *Good Natured: The Origins of Right and Wrong in Humans and Animals* (1996). In de Waal's view, the orthodox sociobiological approach to morality is a curious convergence of religious, psychoanalytic and evolutionary thinking which pits morality against nature and in doing so puts it beyond a naturalistic explanation. But if the antithetical forces reside in nature itself, the mystery evaporates. It is not a case of morality versus nature but of certain tendencies in social life in contrast or opposition to others. Field biology of the twentieth century has amply confirmed and extended Kropotkin's anecdotal material on cooperation and altruism. Fuelled by empathy and an impulse to help, they form building blocks of morality to be found in animals and human infants alike. As the Scottish philosophers of the eighteenth century maintained, the moral sentiments come first, moral principles later.

The question remains, what natural forces assemble the blocks into the shape of an ethical structure? Two complementary developments in classical sociobiology provide obvious starting points: W.D. Hamilton's thesis (1964) on the selective advantage of altruism within groups where kinship coefficients are high, and Robert Trivers's demonstration (1971) of the selective advantage of reciprocal altruism even when kinship coefficients are low. In anthropological terms, the first will generate a willingness to look after the interests of close kin even if doing so entails a degree of individual self-sacrifice; the second will generate pragmatic arrangements whose success depends on trust and honesty. Empirical verification is provided by the study of hunting-and-gathering societies, which suggests that kin altruism and balanced reciprocity have been central features of human social life from the outset. So far, so good. The problem is that if these tendencies are the product of natural selection, moral approval of generosity and honesty would seem to be redundant and moral disapproval of selfishness and cheating unnecessary. Why indoctrinate children with values that come naturally?

The best inference is that morality developed as an adjunct to pre-existing cooperative tendencies, reinforcing them in a chronic struggle against their natural enemies. How to take such an hypothesis beyond mere speculation is not easy to say. For what it is worth I set out below the lineaments of morality and propriety as they occurred in an Aboriginal hunting-and-gathering community with which I have been associated for forty-five years. I tentatively suggest that the description has some generality, at least within the Australian continent. I am also inclined to believe that it presents the essential features of a system that has persisted for a very long time. The ancestors of contemporary Aborigines arrived some 50,000 years ago and for the last 10,000 years were isolated by sea from the rest of the world. It is likely that whatever core values they share with peoples elsewhere represent not independent innovations but a common biological and cultural inheritance of great antiquity.

## A Hunter-Gatherer Case Study

The moral lexicon described in this section forms part of an Aboriginal language called Gidjingarli or Burarra, spoken by people of the Blyth River in Arnhem Land. The data are drawn mainly from two sources: *Burarra-Gunnartpa Dictionary* (Glasgow 1994) and *People of the Rivermouth: the Joborr Texts of Frank Gurrmanamana* (Gurrmanamana, Hiatt and McKenzie 2002). The former publication is by Katherine Glasgow, who worked at Maningrida in Arnhem Land for many years on behalf of the Summer Institute of Linguistics. The latter is a CD-Rom made by Kim McKenzie on the basis of texts I recorded in the Gidjingarli language in 1960. In places I have used my own acquaintance with Gidjingarli to amplify Glasgow's translations; and I have drawn on my own observations and knowledge of the culture to contextualize the specific topics under discussion.

### 'Good' and 'Bad'
The standard Gidjingarli terms for expressing approval and disapproval are *molamola* and *werra* respectively. They are normally translated as 'good' and 'bad'. As with their English equivalents, both adjectives can be used to make nonethical as well as ethical valuations: depending on context, *molamola* may be an expression of moral approval (e.g. 'he is a good man') or it may mean good at something (skilful), good-looking, in good spirits, in good health; similarly, *werra* may be an expression of moral disapproval ('he is a bad man', 'he's no good') or it may mean defective, of poor quality, in poor health.

### Altruism
When qualifying in a moral sense, *molamola* indicates a disposition to look after others, particularly by sharing goods and possessions. Conversely, *werra* indicates a disposition to harm others, or at least not to act kindly towards them. Although such evaluations are expressed objectively, their articulation may often have a subjective underpinning derived from the speaker's experiences, expectations, and prejudices.

The Gidjingarli assume that benevolence is a property of *borrmunga*, glossed as 'kin' or 'countrymen'. *Gurrurta*, conceptually linked with *borrmunga*, is translated as 'neighbourliness, loving concern as for a relative or friend, kinship love that fulfills responsibilities'. *Gurrurta-gurrurta* is 'reciprocal kinship love'. The word *guburrmaymba* connotes kinship terminology as an ideology of amity and mutual aid. Beyond its limits are people referred to generically as *werranga* (from *werra*, 'bad'). They are 'others' or 'aliens', potentially malevolent and therefore to be treated with caution.

Altruism is thus a central value of Gidjingarli morality. In practice a good person is one who cares for others, where 'others' means 'us', 'one of us', or specifically 'me'. The verb 'to be married to' is *marrpa*, which also means 'to look after'. The verb *worija* means 'to have sympathy, compassion, worry, or concern'. A man who responds ungrudgingly to requests is said to have a soft heart (*mun-molma mun-nyarlkuch nula*), as compared with a selfish fellow whose 'mouth is hard and dry' (*ngana an-derta an-gorla*, i.e. he refuses) or who must be deaf (*an-bongarrowa*, which also means 'stupid' or 'incorrigible').

## Equity

Altruism lies within and permeates a broader field designated as *joborr*, which English-speakers gloss as 'custom-law'. The cognate term *rom* signifies the metaphysical foundation of *joborr*: the realm and deeds of the ancestral spirits responsible for introducing shape and structure to the cosmos. First and foremost among the consequences of their actions was an equitable distribution of land among patrilineal descent groups. Hardly less important were marriage rules inhibiting the monopolization of women by aggressive and powerful males. *Joborr* provides a foundation for the rights of all men and women (*joborr rrenyja*, 'stand on the law'). Political rights and influence are widely distributed among adults, and in public life there are no formal hierarchies of power and control. *Wana negiya*, 'make oneself big', is an expression of disparagement. Behaviour in accordance with *joborr* is said to be *jechinuwa* ('straight').

## Contracts

Some of the most important aspirations of Gidjingarli men and women, particularly in the domains of marriage and trade, are realized through contractual agreements or partnerships sanctified by tradition. The act of bestowing a girl in marriage consists of a formal declaration of intention, which is made by the bestowers and communicated to the chosen man (*jibirriny-urrjanga nula*, 'they promise her to him'). If he accepts, he must make gifts to the bestowers while waiting for his bride to reach marriageable age. Promises require trust (*yagurrma, bama balcha*, 'believe, trust'); unfulfilled promises give rise to bitter feelings (*nguna-gaypurda*, 'I have been cheated'). Trading partnerships (*gerra abirri-wuchichiya abirri-workiya*, 'they give each other goods') operate on a similar basis of trust and may result in similar disappointments. The kin relationship between wife-givers and wife-receivers, and between trading partners, is often not a close one; and, though stated in kinship terms, may not in a strict genealogical sense be traceable.

Breaches of marriage contracts are at the heart of the most serious conflicts in Gidjingarli society. The injured party is typically a man who, having honoured his part of a bargain, is faced with a promised bride who refuses to marry him. The situation becomes worse if she shows interest in other men, and worse still if she elopes with one of them. The scene is set for argument (*ngarndarrk*), accusation (*jabarrk,* 'harangue, shouted monologue of blame'), fighting (*mari*), and violence (*rra,* 'to spear'; *bu,* 'to hit, kill'). Threats (*ngu-derta ngi-rrapa,* 'I'm a hard man, I'll spear you'), insults (*ny-merdaberper,* 'you are a coward'), and obscenities (*murdila nggu,* 'you cunt') are exchanged. If fighting breaks out (*gu-mari ngana wu,* 'the fire of trouble is lit'), close kinsmen come to each other's aid (*gung-gachichiya,* 'help one another') and neutral parties try to quell the flames by conventional methods of fight control (*an-goma a-rrimarrmiya,* 'they grip [the antagonists] around their bodies'; *jobujoba,* 'restrain'). If serious injury or death nonetheless occurs, revenge and feuding are set in train (*mari bu,* 'attack arising from [previous] trouble', *guna-wangarra,* 'vengeance on behalf of a dead man's spirit'). But if angry words (*gun-bachirra*) give way to calm and reason (*yabulu*), compensation (*jawalaka*) may be offered and injured parties may agree to forgive and forget (*baywarra ni,* 'to be forgiving', *mari bamapa,* 'to forget the trouble').

When marriage takes place, morality requires sexual fidelity (*galginy miliba,* 'eye stay-close-to') and condemns adultery (*mobula borrkpa,* 'mock behind the back'). Promiscuous men and women are poorly regarded (*jalmuna,* 'damp'). Nevertheless flirtations and affairs (*mararrach*) are commonplace and give rise to jealousy (*mey*) and trouble (*mari*).

Trade goods are transmitted over long distances along chains of traditional partnerships and include commodities of practical value as well as religious objects. The dominant ethic of trade is to pass things along and to resist a temptation to keep too much for oneself (*gopa*). A man who hoards (*jordaja ga*) or shows off his wealth (*gorlk bulawa*) runs a risk of being ensorcelled by an aggrieved partner (*mu-galk a-rra*).

## Etiquette

Many customs designated collectively as *joborr* are prescriptions for tact, consideration, and good form. Wherever possible people's feelings should be protected, their fears and anxieties alleviated, and their rights and privileges respected. The recently published Joborr Texts of Frank Gurrmanamana can be read as an introduction to manners and protocols at various phases in the Gidjingarli life cycle. Here are some examples.

> A woman tells her husband she is pregnant. He replies: 'Ah, so. Very good. Shortly I shall give you fish. I shall spear something and give it to you. We mustn't both go. You shouldn't come with me. Soon I'll spear something. The baby mustn't get hot, he must be kept cool.' (Gurrmanamana et al. 2002: 5)

After the baby is born, the mother's mother says to her daughter: 'Rear him properly. Your husband has given me food and I have eaten it. You have lived together and he has watched you for me. I am satisfied.'(Gurrmanamana et al. 2002: 12)

The son has speared a big fish. His father says to his wife: 'Take some and eat. When he was small, only I ate what he speared, but he's a big boy now so I can give you some. Eat it.' The wife replies: 'Not yet, you haven't eaten.' The father says: 'No, but you eat. You're his mother.' (Gurrmanamana et al. 2002: 27)

The boy's father decides it is time for him to be circumcized. He formally approaches the lad's maternal great-uncle for approval. F: 'Regarding your grand-nephew, I have listened for your agreement'. MMB: 'It's fine, we can't stand in your way'. F: 'I would rather not speak to my wife about it. I'm afraid of upsetting her.' Later the grandmother speaks to the boy's mother. MM: 'I'm here to speak about your son's initiation'. M: 'I don't object'. (Gurrmanamana et al. 2002: 34–5)

A man expresses gratitude to the father of his future bride: 'Your daughter is mine. Your wife and her brother have given her to me. She is my wife. I shall keep her always.' When she becomes a young woman, her mother speaks to her: 'Go and sleep together. Do not cry. He will give you food so that I may eat. No-one else is my son-in-law, he is the one. I have given you to him and that is the end of it.' The daughter replies: 'I am agreeable, mother. I want him, your son-in-law. He will give you food from his own hands, and you will be full. When you are hungry, he will be there calling to you.' (Gurrmanamana et al. 2002: 81–3)

A man speaks to his elder brother: YB: 'Our [trading partner] 'brother' has sent metal spearheads, grinding stones, red ochre, and a sacred icon. Look at it. That's the lot.' EB: 'Our 'brother' in the east has been generous. Except that I thought he might have given you some milkwood spearshafts.' YB: 'Here is the sacred icon'. EB: 'A sacred icon, good!' YB: 'We will keep it here with us. The metal spearheads, grinding stones, and red ochre we will send on to our 'father' and 'brothers' in the west. As for the icon, our 'brother' in the east will come and tell us he will hold a ceremony. Afterwards we will give the icon to our 'father' and 'brothers' in the west.' (Gurrmanamana et al. 2002: 152–3)

A man dies. His sister's son takes charge of funeral arrangements. He says: 'Women and men should assemble here. There should be no fighting. Let us ritually cleanse ourselves by brushing with leaves. Otherwise trouble will descend on my brother and me.' (p. 164) Later he speaks to the widow: 'You must not be afraid. My brother and I might have speared or beaten you when your husband died, but we have no quarrel with you.' She replies: 'You have no cause to be displeased with me, because your uncle was dear to me. I cared for him while he was alive, and now I shall care for his remains.' (Gurrmanamana et al. 2002: 167)

## Capital Punishment

Gidjingarli ethics clearly serves sociality, amity and mutual advantage. If antisocial behaviour nevertheless reaches intolerable levels, the community may have no option but to resort to corporate violence against offenders. An elder addresses a meeting about two lawbreakers:

> *Elder*: All of you here, I shall speak to you. Perhaps you will agree with what I say.
> *Citizen 1*: Yes, speak to us. After you've spoken we'll see whether we agree with you.
> *Elder*: Those two men are of a fierce and ruthless nature. They have speared both men and women. They have killed again and again. So let us spear them without delay. For they are fierce and ruthless men.
> *Citizen 1*: It is only a matter of time before someone from somewhere else tries to spear them.
> *Elder*: Yes. Those of you here should discuss it, then spear them so that we can all live in peace.
> *Citizen 1 (to Citizen 2)*: Why don't you and I try out something on them? Later, if there's trouble, the rest of you can protect us.
> *Citizen 3:* Yes. We don't want murderers. Spear them and be done with it.
> The two volunteers search for the law-breakers.
> *Citizen 1*: There's the camp where they usually sleep.
> (*The sun is going down. The law-breakers are having their evening meal by a fire.*)
> *Citizen 1:* You spear one and I'll spear the other. If things go wrong, we'll join forces against them.
> (*They attack.*)
> *Lawbreaker 1*: Help, brother! Who is throwing spears at us?
> *Citizen 1*: Give up, murderers!
> (*The law-breakers die. The two volunteers return to the camp and speak to their countrymen. At first they pretend things have gone badly.*)
> *Citizen 1:* We bungled it!
> *Citizen 3*: Tell us the worst.
> *Citizen 1*: Don't worry, we annihilated them!
> *Citizen 3*: The deed is done. Your throwing-arms were good. It is over, and now we can sleep, go into the bush to defecate, urinate, and move around in safety. For we lived in fear of them, those two men.
> *Citizen 1*: Later, if there is trouble from their relatives, you should all be ready to help us.

(Gurrmanamana et al. 2002: 154–8)

## Discussion

The degree to which Gidjingarli moral ideas typify indigenous Australian ethics remains to be determined.[2] If an examination of Aboriginal lexicons were to reveal a widespread distribution of moral expressions in the Gidjingarli sense, a further task would be to establish how they are deployed in practice. My impression is that the Gidjingarli apply the term 'good' not so much to primary caretakers like mother, father and other close kin but to individuals beyond the family circle from whom generosity and care are less likely to be taken for granted. An extended def-inition of a 'good person', then, might include 'someone who behaves towards others like a close relative'. A 'bad person' is 'someone who behaves towards others like a non-relative'; and, of course, it is in precisely such a pejorative sense that an aggrieved individual uses the adjective to censure a relative. On this basis we might surmise that at an elementary level moral language represents an attempt to extend or generalize the succour inherent in genetic closeness and to diminish the hostility inherent in genetic distance.[3]

This tendency, which may be a characteristic of moral systems everywhere, is complemented in the Australian case by a remarkable generalization of kinship terminology itself. As Kropotkin's friend A.R. Brown argued, Aborigines were able to develop a wide-ranging and complex social order by using family kinship as a conceptual microcosm for the world at large. Through the operation of a small number of simple principles, identified by Radcliffe-Brown with labels such as 'the equivalence of brothers', terms designating primary relationships of blood and marriage were extended outwards along ramifying genealogical networks to everyone whom an individual was likely to encounter in his or her lifetime. Since kinship was equated with goodwill, the extension of terms and their associated sentiments beyond the narrow confines of closely related families created a wider polity for the purpose of establishing reciprocal arrangements such as trade and marriage. Succour and trust thus evolved as twin pillars of an expanding, albeit fragile, ideology of benevolence and mutuality.[4]

Against this background we can now return to methodological individualism and the problem of explaining how sentiment is converted into conventions, or self-interest into moral values. The most popular solution, even among gene-centred sociobiologists, is to postulate some form of 'group selection' on the assumption that early human communities were internecine and that moral indoc-trination conferred selective advantages by reducing internal conflict and fostering solidarity.[5] Darwin himself, with the help of his antiquarian friend Lord Avebury, launched this idea in the *The Descent of Man* by stressing how important loyalty, discipline, and obedience must have been in 'the never-ceasing wars of savages' (1871: 162–3).

Whatever the evidence from antiquity, it is not hard to find examples among the savage nation-states of the twenty-first century. The Australian Aboriginal case, while not exempt from such considerations, nevertheless reminds us that compas-sion and trust can be deployed not only to improve the war effort within the kinship unit but to transform external enemies into friends. The policy of expanding amity, symbolized by the dove, may be something of an evolutionary novelty; but, when the hawks hover, it is comforting to remember that its roots in the human heritage run very deep.

## Notes

1. Francis Hutcheson, *A Short Introduction to Moral Philosophy*, 1747; David Hume, *An Enquiry Concerning the Principles of Morals*, 1751; Adam Smith, *The Theory of Moral Sentiments*, 1759.
2. I am currently pursuing this objective through an examination of available lexicons. Excellent modern dictionaries, such as the Arrernte dictionary by John Henderson and Veronica Dobson (1994) and the Warlpiri Lexicography Group's unpublished computerized dictionary, facilitate the task by including numerous utterances in which terms with moral connotations occur. Another invaluable source is the published work on Pintupi emotions by F. Myers (1979,1986,1988).
3. Gurrmanamana once said to me that the term *gurrurta* ('kinship love'; see under subsection 'Altruism' above) means 'good friend' and can be applied to 'Chinaman', 'Japanese', 'anyone', not just close relatives.
4. For a more detailed account of Radcliffe-Brown's treatment of the relationship between kin classification and political organization, as well as his connection with Kropotkin, see Hiatt (1996: ch. 5). See also Singer (1981) for an extended argument on the transcendence of nepotistic tendencies by universalistic ethics.
5. See especially Richard Alexander's book *The Biology of Moral Systems* (1987).

# –5–

# Anthropological History and the Study of Hunters and Gatherers: Cultural and Non-cultural

## *Aram A. Yengoyan*

The emergence of the category 'hunters and gatherers' has had a long history within anthropological theory and in part changes in the study of foraging societies reflect theoretical changes in anthropology. This paper deals with three aspects of these shifts which have had a critical bearing on current developments. The first part is a general survey of the category 'hunters and gatherers' and it will direct attention to certain pivotal shifts in writings since the publication of *Man the Hunter* (Lee and DeVore 1968c). The second section attempts to evaluate the impact of Julian Steward's work as a threshold transitory point in which cultural factors became marginalized in the study of small-scale foraging societies. And the last section turns the case back to Marx's writing on small-scale societies with special reference to his reading of the works on the Australian Aboriginal.

### The Category of Hunter and Gatherer

In the early works on such societies, the term 'hunters and gatherers' seldom appears but after the publication of *Man the Hunter* the use of the category is widespread. It is not possible to fully inventory all the works before and after 1968, but a number of issues can be set forth. In most cases after 1968, the differences and complexities of different societies are virtually lost and even denied within the categorical rubric which is used. Forde (1934) places the Semang, Bushmen and Paiute along with the Nootka and Kwakiutl under the category of food gatherers. Yet, within this category the differences in social structure, economy and political complexity are so vast as to render the category effectively void of any heuristic utility. Coon's (1948) anthology to a certain extent avoids this problem by not using food gatherers. Thus Coon devises three levels (simple family bands; the band contains several families; and the rise of specialists and multiple institutions) which in many ways are more specific. But again the problem emerges in having to merge the Kurnai of southeast Australia with the Trobrianders in his third level. Foraging is combined with agriculture and animal husbandry, thus the problem takes another form.

Service (1962; 1978 [1958]) dealt with the problem by avoiding the label 'hunters and gatherers', thus utilizing a framework based on political complexity such as bands, tribes and chiefdoms. As expected, most foraging societies were placed under bands and the Nootka, which are hardly foragers, were listed as a chiefdom. To a certain extent, Service moved away from the problem of hunters and gatherers but created others such as having to label the Kalinga as a chiefdom which they are not.

A few writers like Birdsell used hunting and collecting populations as early as 1958, the shift to hunters and gatherers accelerates after 1968. Although there has been a plethora of work in the past thirty years, a few examples might be noted since the research under the rubric hunters and gatherers now includes archaeology, ecological anthropology, social and behavioural approaches, population ecology, systems analysis, evolutionary biologists, optimization models, neo-Darwinian theories of cultural transmission, Marxist and structural Marxist approaches, and the list continues. Foremost in these new approaches are works by Bettinger (1991), Kelly (1995), and a volume edited by Panter-Brick, Layton and Rowley-Conwy (2001). Each of these works covers a broad range of theoretical and empirical developments all of which focus on foraging, hunting and gathering.

At the same time, one also notes a number of developments from previous work on foragers. The convergence of these approaches is not isolated and they should also be interpreted within the pioneering work of Julian Steward which will be discussed later. The lasting impact of the category 'hunters and gatherers' is that, after *Man the Hunter*, the use of the category homogenized cultural and social structural differences among local societies which were the initial foundations of the study of non-literate peoples. Cultural differences might have been magnified by fieldworkers up to the 1940s and 1950s, but the homogenization of particular societies under 'hunters and gatherers' created an almost total collapsing of differences. Thus the Eskimo, the Nootka and the Kwakiutl are now forged into one category. Differences between such societies are truly broad and they are also vast in terms of the cultural core.

The obliteration of cultural differences also reflects other long-term changes. Nearly all early descriptions of foraging societies dealt with cultural features which are difficult to compare. Thus, each cluster of authorship and description – be it Gusinde in Tierra del Fuego; Schapera among the Bushmen; Boas on the Northwest Coast; Kroeber and his students in native California; Spencer and Gillen, Strehlow, Stanner and others among the Australian Aboriginal; etc. – all stressed culture and cultural features as the centrality of their efforts. But in the past three decades or so, culture alone is no longer seen as a viable means of analysis for these small-scale societies. As noted above, this change results in part from the use of 'hunters and gathers' as a category, which allows the stressing of similarities from region to region; whereas, in fact, such similarities are seldom found within and throughout local cultures or among their cultural features.

In this shifting perspective of analytical concepts, culture, associated with the ideas of a people, may be viewed as occupying one end of a continuum that moves on to society, and hence to an opposite end, the population, with its basis in the dominance of biology. The initial progress from culture, which was highly local and variable, to society, which was less local and less variable, allowed for regularities to be found among hunter gatherer societies in a way that had comparative implications, but now along social parametres. Thus Service (1971) could find parallels by using a model of social organization based on bands, tribes and chiefdoms. Although Service saw the problem within evolutionary perspectives, the synchronic focus does indicate parallels within each form of structural complexity and one can accept this without evoking an evolutionary framework. The final move along the continuum from society to population, however, is critical, for the current shift to population means that now hunters and gatherers may be compared and contrasted with non-human primate societies. The idea of a population has its roots in genetic and evolutionary theories of how a biological unit reproduces itself. From Mendel, Galton and Fisher, the population could be demarcated by certain markers which the analyst could define and whose transmission across generations could be understood. Thus populations, such as fruit flies, are an isolate through which evolutionary principles are operative as a means of explaining the characteristics of the population and the kinds of changes which are predictable.

For many anthropologists and evolutionary ecologists, small foraging populations can be understood within a biological paradigm through which biological and evolutionary models are utilized. Thus, foragers are only one step above other populations; they might be somewhat more complex, but one can possibly detect how evolutionary forces work on small populations. Furthermore, the biological paradigm is also the basis of a set of critical models such as optimization, maximization and time/resource management which will provide insights and comparisons with non-human primate societies. This departure from earlier anthropological efforts has recast actors in foraging societies as bereft of any local and particular cultural foundations. It goes without saying that culture is no longer an issue, it is now non-existent. Thus, the combination of the category 'hunters and gatherers' and the move towards population analysis as it is reflected in small-scale societies has not only impacted on the subject matter of hunters and gatherers, it has also created a new discourse in which evolutionary and economic models have reduced human actors to disemboweled humans who no longer have cultural anchors.

## Julian Steward and the Question of Culture

Earlier, it was noted that the change from culture to society to population was in part due to the work of Julian Steward (1955a). It should be made clear that the directions in terms of population analysis is not found in Steward's work. The impact of Steward's approach takes another form which is necessary to explicate for understanding the kinds of changes that have taken place in hunting and gathering studies and also to explain why the idea of culture was marginalized by Steward.

In his concern for drawing cross-cultural regularities either among hunting and gathering people or in the development of early civilizations, Steward set forth a contrast between the cultural core and the 'rest of culture'. Based on his fieldwork on the Great Basin Shoshone, Steward developed three levels of sociocultural complexity for hunters and gatherers: the family level of sociocultural integration, which characterized the Shoshone; the patrilineal band which was found among most foraging peoples; and the composite hunting band found among northern Algonkians, Canadian Athabaskans and the Andamanese. The cultural core as a heuristic device was a set of features which were closely linked to subsistence activities and economic arrangements which sustained the social unit. This would include technology and its extractive efficiency, economic organization and forms of exchange, and social groupings which had a role on how society is sustained. Yet, Steward (1955a: 37) notes in passing that political and religious patterns would be part of the core if they could be empirically determined to have an effect on technology and economy.

The 'rest of culture' (which is my term, not Steward's) would include myth, ritual, cosmology, religion and even political factors which might not impact on the cultural core but which exist in every society. Thus, the cultural core is adaptive and is the source of cross-cultural regularities while the 'rest of culture' is a result of history and diffusion and might not be adaptive. It is local and regional, and it is the cultural framework of each society; thus cross-cultural regularities would not be expected within this domain. This division within society has a bearing on the Marxist contrast between the infrastructure and the superstructure, though it is not clear if Steward ever read Marx. It was only later that the neo-functionalists in the 1960s and 1970s made the 'rest of culture' also adaptive but that is another matter.

For Steward's purposes, the contrast between the cultural core and the 'rest of culture' was probably the only means of establishing cross-cultural regularities but it was done only through making culture an epiphenomenon which had little or no bearing on the core, and also, relegating culture to the periphery. The impact of the cultural core/rest of culture contrast has been drastic on any understanding of hunters and gatherers. Not only did it marginalize the idea of culture, it also partly moved the investigation to population analysis, which was hardly what Steward would have envisioned. Thus while at an earlier time the study of small-scale for-aging societies was central to anthropological theory, it is now an appendage of biological and economic modelling.

## Marx and the Australian Aboriginal

Marx's reading on non-literate cultures comes primarily from his copious notes on Morgan and other writers previous to Morgan. As Krader (1972) notes, Marx's reading of Morgan along with Phear, Maine and Lubbock starts in the winter and spring of 1880-1 and the only evidence we have are his notes, since Marx died in 1883. Yet, his analysis also covers various other writers of the time such as Grey on Australia; McLennan; and some notes from Tylor, Bachofen and Bastian. But the majority of his thoughts on the 'primitive' come from Morgan's *Ancient Society* as well as *Systems of Consanguinity and Affinity of the Human Family*.

From this broad reading, which is given in outlines that are far from completion, Morgan was his chief proponent and Maine in many ways was the opposition. Yet, Marx was also sceptical of the scientific doctrines which were the intellectual foundations of Morgan's approach as they were in Darwin and Lubbock. Marx saw the problem as one of history and historical developments which a scientific approach would have to minimize.

Yet, from Morgan and what else he read, Marx developed a certain under-standing of the issues which he had to account for. Morgan's *Ancient Society* relies heavily on the descriptions by the Revd Lorimer Fison on the Kamilaroi of south-east Australia but other sources are also cited. Marx (Krader, 1972: 109, 125–6, 139–46) refers to the Punaluan groupings and structure which embrace the Aboriginal systems of classes and rules of exogamy. By noting that the Punaluan family structure is older and prior to the emergence of the gentes, Marx accepts Morgan's conclusion that the class system must have preceded the gentes. However, Marx's analysis attempts to go beyond Morgan by ascertaining what are the internal contradictions in Kamilaroi social structure that can be traced to the rudimentary emergence of the idea of property. The gentes structure, which Marx notes must overthrow the preceding Punaluan class structure, is a result of prop-erty and property arrangements that foster and fortify the emergence of a gentes structure, which in turn is the basis of the idea of government. If Morgan interprets the Kamilaroi as a natural historian with the aim of identifying particular devel-opments that can be linked to an evolutionary process, Marx is asking another set of questions. Here, Marx's concern is the determination of what factors limit or curtail these developments and to what extent internal contradictions are resolved by the domination of one institution over another. Thus, Marx's reading focuses more on the preconditions which must be found among Australian Aboriginal societies which create true forms of property.

But, Marx's curiosity about the Australian Aboriginal is not limited to the issue of property arrangements and social groups. His notes also indicate that he was puzzled by the infinite number and range of different totemic categories and groupings which are found not only among the Kamilaroi but also in other indigenous societies. Thus, the Kamilaroi have totemic terms and rules of exogamy for namesake totems such as iguana, kangaroo, opossum, emu, bandicoot and blacksnake just to name a few. Not only is the listing of totemic names infinite and highly variable in one society, they also differ markedly from one local group to another. In some cases, totemic namesakes are connected to exogamous groups, but in other cases totems exist without any connections to groups. In some cases, certain totems are linked to gender differences, in others they also exist as personal nomenclature.

Marx's notes on religion and cosmology are limited to what he had to work with, but again he is concerned with the highly variant quality of these belief systems. If the Punaluan structure were predictable and the possible conflicts with a system of gentes could be partly explained, nothing could be predicted from the foundational basis of economic arrangements and social organization to the realm of totemism and religion in general. In a more general way, Marx is left to ponder an imponderable problem. Throughout his notes, he points to an issue that is still with us as anthropologists; namely, in a continent of three million square miles one finds a very broad common pattern of hunting and gathering technology and local organization, which is fundamentally uniform from coast to coast. Yet, cultural features like some aspects of social organization and more so in totemism, religion and cosmology, are intricately variable from one local society to another.

Thus, to place this in more contemporary terms, there is a marked and critical dysfunctionality between the infrastructure and the superstructure. Not only is the superstructure unpredictable in any single case, its variance exists throughout the continent. As Marx would have predicted, one would expect to find some kind of convergence from the base to the superstructure; but none exists. It is as if there are two or more layers of cultural thought and social activity which do not converge on one another. Myths are highly local and variable from one society to another. In some cases ritual and myth are interconnected, but in others they are not. And the content of the superstructure (religion and cosmology) operates along lines which cannot be predicted from the base and in some cases cannot be explicated from what we know about general theories of religion and cosmology.

For Marx, the 'primitive' as a mode of production cannot be comprehended as a totalized social formation in which all levels of society can be understood within the whole. Differences within any particular society must be interpreted as institutional levels which do not mirror one another. It has always been a vexing problem and one which Marx comprehended. Since Marx's reading, many generations of anthropologists have attempted to overcome this problem, more recently through structural Marxist approaches. An older generation of anthropologists, such as Goldenweiser and Radin, saw the problem as one of involution and play, which were highly unpredictable within any one society. Here the issue is one of cultural creativity that exists primarily in activities and thought, which are not determined by the infrastructure. Goldenweiser thought that involution as a creative activity was a primary characteristic of 'primitive' people though he also claimed that it existed in classical music such as the changes in Bach's fugues.

In many ways, we benefit from the hindsight provided by more empirical evidence and different ways of analysing these problems, but there is no final closure. Marx's preliminary reading of fragmentary accounts probably whetted his interest in what was a moot issue within his total contributions, but it is still a perplexing concern for many a generation of anthropologists.

## The Culture Issue

If the study of hunters and gatherers has turned away from cultural accounts let alone cultural explanations, anthropologists still do fieldwork in the quotidian life and nuances of small-scale communities. Culture might no longer be glamorous nor does it carry the weight of cutting-edge recognition which academia and its practitioners are always seeking.

Barnard (1983; 2000) has also questioned this trend by dealing with subjects such as the hunter-gatherer mode of thought. From his work with the Central !Kung and also cases from other areas, Barnard (2000) notes that there is a resilient quality among hunters and gatherers even though economic and political changes within the state apparatus have either ended or muted the material basis of foraging. However, certain qualities of social life still exist. Thus sharing is valued over accumulation and sharing throughout broad non-discrete kinship units is the source of sociality. Furthermore, politics is by consensus, decision-making is a group matter, knowledge is ideally collective, and personal self-interest is curtailed socially or through force.

These features are also found among the Pitjantjatjara of the western desert in Australia. Generalized reciprocity is the common rule and rights extend to all by age and gender. Ideally this form of cultural expression is still dominant but given the encroaching commodification of social life, an increasing number of tensions pit one generation against another. A few examples will suffice. Commodities that have no commercial value and are intended for the hearth group (those who cook and eat together) do not cause social disruption. Thus a kangaroo or wallaby is divided among the hearth group and others along certain principles. Those individuals who are either non-productive or the least productive (the aged, nursing mothers, pregnant women, young children) are usually given the best portions of the carcass. Individuals who are productive receive minimal portions and the individuals who killed the kangaroo are barely provided for. There is a very strict code which governs these allocations.

The breakdown and questioning of this ethos occurs when European-derived commodities have entered the local scene. A good example is a truck, which might be purchased individually or, more likely, by a few individuals who pool their resources. Trucks, new and used, are very expensive and petrol costs are exorbitant. Social tensions occur when the wider kin-based network feels that they should have access to the vehicle and this pits them against those who purchased the vehicle. Reciprocity might cease or it might be fought over, with charges of selfishness directed at the owners. At times these conflicts can become violent and bad blood might ensue.

Another example not involving commodities should be noted. Like most Aboriginal societies, the Pitjantjatjara are heavily gerontocratic. Older males are the guardians who make sure that ritual and ceremonial activities are carried out in ways that are traditionally connected with myths and the unfolding of the ancient Dreamtime. But the generational differences have been enhanced by men in their thirties and early forties who speak English and are thus utilized by the Anglo-Australian white bureaucracy to deal with the Pitjantjatjara on a broad range of issues. The emergence of this new class of 'Black Bourgeoisie' has now taken control of community relations with the external world (Yengoyan, 1998). The conflicts for control between generations have become a difficult problem and one which has caused severe strains in aboriginal communities. And since the Pitjantjatjara are virtually monolingual, the problems are even more enhanced.

Apart from these cultural features which have parallels with what Barnard (2000) has discussed, the cultural logic in the realm of language, myth and religion is still viable. Myth is the critical link which combines the most ancient past to the present and that is done through language and physical markers which emblemize how the past is propelled into the present. But, the matter is also more linguistically technical and has its roots in various forms of tense and aspect that are highly abstract in Pitjantjatjara. To summarize this, one must note a fundamental difference between the past tense and the imperfect tense. The past tense is only used for events which are secular and non-continuous. Events which have occurred once and will not re-occur. But myth, which is the basis of all religion, is always conveyed through the imperfect. Myths are sacred and the use of the imperfect means that events in the ancient past are conveyed into the present and the future. There is no closure or finality, thus in Eaglehawk myths, Eaglehawk was falling off of a branch, but never fell off. The continuity of the event or action has no finality.

Comparatively, these kinds of connections between myth, language and locality are also found in hunting and gathering societies such as the Chipewyan and Sarce, but also among the Tewa of New Mexico who are not hunters and gatherers. There are also other interesting parallels between many of the Pueblo cultures in the American southwest and the Australian Aboriginals.

Barnard's account of modes of thought has an important and critical bearing on my analysis of Aboriginals. Where I would differ from Barnard is his utilization of the concept of ideology to describe what he sets forth in a lucid style. What he calls ideology, I would call culture. To summarize what could be a lengthy issue, I understand culture as a set of conscious and unconscious givens or ontological axioms which normally are part of prior texts which actors bring to bear to understand events. Normally, these prior texts or ontological axioms are not questioned by participants though it can occur. Culture in this sense is a form of stability and also a product of shared thought. By contrast, ideologies are also shared but they are consciously developed through reasoned and rational action. It is the ideological domain that emerges through group or class interests as a means of either providing unity to a body politic under rapidly changing situations and/or controlling individuals and social groups within the body politic.

Yet, ideologies are not created in a vacuum. They must be connected to prior texts which are found in the cultural logic. To make ideologies meaningful and even acceptable to actors, they must possess the prior texts to understand, accept or reject what ideologies embrace and transmit. Thus, I agree with Barnard in his development of the idea of sharing among hunters and gatherers. But I would interpret it as a cultural given which is not only basic to the social life of foragers but it also provides emotional sustenance and resiliency when different social formations and capitalistic structures, such as the free market, are encountered.

## Conclusions

The fundamental issue is the conflict in how economy is projected against culture. Culture and its conservative quality is an attribute of inertia to change. Social institutions and political structures might change through economic transformations and/or revolutions, but the source of change is seldom if ever realized in culture.

Culture(s) are not only transmitted inherently through its own logic and prior texts, they also exist within broader social and cultural contexts which are not of their making. Local differences among hunters and gatherers are not only internally generated based on traditions, they are normally magnified in terms of the oppositions which exist between adjacent societies. Propinquity creates and enhances differences which in most cases are historically derived. It goes without saying that culture is local and it is the source of differences regardless of how former foragers encounter other traditions which only enhance their own primordial sentiments.

## Acknowledgements

I would like to thank Bruce Winterhalder and Shannon Tushingham for their assistance in regards to the development of the hunter-gatherer category.

# Part II
# Local Traditions
# in Hunter-Gatherer Research

# No Escape From Being Theoretically Important: Hunter-Gatherers in German-Language Debates of the Late Nineteenth and Early Twentieth Centuries

## *Peter P. Schweitzer*

Until recently, the genealogy of debates about the structural properties of hunter-gatherer societies was supposed to be rather shallow. Due to the Anglophone bias of much contemporary anthropology, the 1966 conference 'Man the Hunter' has often been viewed as the starting point of the modern hunter-gatherer discourse. More historically oriented overviews, on the other hand, traced the beginnings to the works of A.R. Radcliffe-Brown and Julian Steward. Thus, it is a positive development that the history of hunter-gatherer studies has received more attention lately. Alan Barnard has been most active in restoring the extended genealogy of hunter-gatherer discourses, either by putting the subject into the wider realm of European social thought (Barnard 1999) or by pointing out that the notion of 'hunting-and-gathering society' is an eighteenth-century Scottish 'invention' (this volume). Similarly, Mark Pluciennik has recently identified seventeenth and eighteenth-century Europe as the birthplace of a sustained discourse about hunter-gatherers (Pluciennik 2001; 2002; this volume).

My intention here is not to deal with the origins of a Western hunter-gatherer discourse – which, if you really want, can be traced back to the ancient Greeks (see e.g. Vajda 1968) – but to present an intervening and now forgotten chapter in the history of hunter-gatherer studies. I am referring here to a number of German-language texts written by ethnologists and geographers between the 1880s and the 1930s. This corpus of texts does not constitute a single debate but, instead, represents several interrelated scholarly discussions in which hunting-and-gathering societies figure – directly or indirectly – as main points of theoretical reference. On the one hand, my goal is simply to counter the above-mentioned English-language bias when discussing the history of hunter-gatherer studies. On the other hand, I want to use those German-language contributions as a foil to investigate the relationship between theory building and ethnographic field studies.

A major incentive to present this material here is the fact that there is hardly anything published (either in English or in German) about this particular episode in the history of hunter-gatherer studies. A notable exception is a detailed article by Jasper Köcke published in 1979 (Köcke 1979). Although Köcke does not approach the material with hunter-gatherer studies in mind (instead he is concerned with early contributions to economic anthropology), many of the authors he discussed will be prominent in my review too. Other than that, there have been a few anthropologists who looked at the works of several nineteenth-century German economists to make more general points (see e.g. Dumont 1977; Kahn 1990). Alas, neither the anthropological side of the debates nor the hunter-gatherer aspect have been addressed adequately.

Now a few clarifications. I use the awkward expression 'German-language anthropology' consciously since the debates to be discussed were not limited to Germany but included Austrian anthropologists as active participants (but hardly anybody from Switzerland). The label German is reserved for contexts which were explicitly restricted to Germany. I use the word 'anthropology' – despite the fact that is it a misnomer in the German-language context – for English-language convenience. The more appropriate term would be 'ethnology', which I will use rather selectively. In the remainder of the article I will proceed by first portraying the scholars and their thoughts about hunting-and-gathering societies in more or less chronological order. As I believe that anthropological (and other) ideas are best understood within the intellectual and social framework of their times, I will provide a limited amount of background information to that effect. Finally, I will attempt to generalize about the central concerns of the debates in question, thereby trying to approach several key questions about the place of theoretical reasoning in hunter-gatherer studies.

## Hunter-Gatherers and German-Language Anthropology

German-language anthropology during the final decades of the nineteenth century was largely characterized by opposition to British and American treatises of social and cultural evolution. Even Adolf Bastian (1826–1905) – who laid the institutional foundations for modern German anthropology and later became the evolutionist scapegoat for his diffusionist critics – could hardly be called an evolutionist, either in terms of biology or of sociology. At the same time, at the turn from the nineteenth to the twentieth century the academic community witnessed the spectacle of the intellectual battle between anthropologists fighting academic humanism and equipped with natural science methods and ethnologists trying re-historicize the discipline (see Zimmerman 2001).

In addition to rallying for history, ethnologists opposed to evolutionism also included geography into their arsenal. As a matter of fact, the *spiritus rector* of German diffusionism was Friedrich Ratzel (1844–1904), a geographer by education and profession. Although Ratzel made no significant contributions to hunter-gatherer studies, his work influenced most of the people to be discussed below. The notion of hunters and gatherers did not appear in Ratzel's famous *History of Mankind* (1896 [1894]), since he arranged the 'natural races' according to geographic location and not according to subsistence activities. Instead, 'peasant farmers' were Ratzel's main objects of ethnological and political curiosity (W.D. Smith 1991: 147). Nevertheless, Ratzel had great influence on early twentieth-century anthropological discourses, including those addressing hunter-gatherers. For example, Marcel Mauss's (1979 [1904–05]) famous essay on 'Seasonal Variations of the Eskimo' is – among other things – also a refutation of Ratzel's ideas about the correlation between geographical space and social forms.

My starting point, however, is a short article which appeared in 1891 and, in its title, already posed the rhetorical question 'Were the people of primeval times between the stages of hunting and agriculture nomadic pastoralists?' (Hahn 1891). The author, the cultural geographer and zoologist Eduard Hahn (1856–1928), attempted nothing less than challenging the so-called three-stage theory (i.e., a historical trajectory from hunters to pastoralists to agriculturalists) which had been firmly entrenched in Western social thought for centuries (see Vajda 1968: 55–58). Hahn further developed his views about the origins of different modes of subsistence in a multitude of subsequent publications (e.g. Hahn 1914). His primary interest, however, was not in studying the development of hunting and gathering but in a fine-grained typology of forms of agriculture. He distinguished 'hoe cultivation' (*Hackbau*) from 'plough cultivation' (*Pflugbau*) and considered *Hackbau* to have arisen first and independently in several different locations. Hahn considered a gendered division of labour to be the basis of economic life and was among the first to emphasize the role of women – through gathering and food-storing activities – in foraging economies. It was the female activity of gathering which Hahn considered to have laid the basis for hoe cultivation. Despite his emphasis on female subsistence contributions, he considered men to have been the founders of political and legal institutions, as well as of plough agriculture, which to him was not just a technological innovation but rested on specific religious beliefs and rituals.

The next important contribution was also made by an outsider, the art historian and Sinologist Ernst Grosse (1862–1927). When he published *The Forms of the Family and the Forms of the Economy* in 1896, he was little known among anthropologists: his only previous book-length publication was a critique of Herbert Spencer's 'synthetic philosophy' (Grosse 1890). Grosse's main motivation to write *The Forms of the Family* was to counter Morgan's model of unilineal social evolution. At the same time, he adopted an economistic approach; that is, he considered the economy to be the most influential factor in the cultural whole. In the end, he concluded that 'every culture has the kind of family organization which best corresponds to its economic conditions and needs' (Grosse 1896: 245). Along the way, Grosse introduced a distinction of so-called 'economic forms' which became influential in subsequent German-language treatises of the topic: he distinguished lower hunters, higher hunters, pastoralists, lower agriculturalists and higher agriculturalists. Grosse did not understand this list of modes of subsistence as a historic or evolutionary sequence (although he admitted that the first and the last of the five forms represented most likely the oldest and the youngest respectively). For our purposes, it is primarily the distinction between lower and higher hunters which demands attention. Although Grosse was to my knowledge the first to introduce a dual division into the study of hunting-and-gathering societies (which reappeared throughout the twentieth century in various forms: e.g., immediate return/delayed return, simple/complex), he spends very little time on explaining or justifying that distinction.

For Grosse, the difference between lower and higher hunters seems to be primarily a quantitative one, that is higher hunters have much higher yields due to more advanced technologies and a richer environment. His list of lower hunters includes Bushmen and Pygmy societies in Africa; the Wedda on Sri Lanka; tribes on the Andaman Islands, in Sumatra and the Philippines; as well as all groups of Australian Aborigines. In the Americas, his list ranges from Tierra del Fuego to the homelands of the Inuit. Still, North America is also where most of his higher hunters are to be found (along the coastal areas from California to Alaska, around the Great Lakes region). In addition, he names northeast Asia – and the Itel'men in particular – as the home of higher hunters. Grosse's subsequent scholarly work had little to do with hunters and gatherers (instead, he authored an influential work on the origins of art [Grosse 1898]), but he exerted a major influence on the prime figures of the so-called Vienna School of anthropology.

Led by Father Wilhelm Schmidt (1868–1954), a German priest of the missionary order S.V.D. (*Societas Verbi Divini*), and seconded by his fellow clergyman Wilhelm Koppers (1886–1961), the Vienna School of Anthropology built its own brand of diffusionism (and fierce anti-evolutionism) on the works of Ratzel, Grosse, Graebner, Ankermann, and others. The concept of *Kulturkreis* ('culture-circle') formed the cornerstone for their grandiose schemes of universal history; their approach is thus often referred to as *Kulturkreislehre*. Neither Wilhelm Schmidt nor Koppers paid any particular attention to the notion of 'hunter-gatherers', although Koppers was among the first to propose an 'ethnological study of the economy' (Koppers 1915–16). Their key term of relevance here was *Urkultur* ('primeval culture'), which was characterized by lower hunters, primeval monotheism and monogamy (see W. Schmidt 1973 [1939] for an English-language exposition of Schmidt and Koppers's views). This primeval culture circle could be reconstructed through its modern remnants, 'lower hunters', which had been pushed into marginal areas. W. Schmidt and Koppers believed, contrary to Hahn, that pastoralism developed directly out of hunting and considered reindeer herding its oldest form. Parallel to pastoralism developed 'higher hunting' and horticulture, which constituted the three 'primary culture circles'. Further historical development ('secondary culture circles') was achieved through migrations which led to a blending of primary culture circles.

Among the fellow clergymen of W. Schmidt and Koppers, two stand out through their contributions to early fieldwork among hunter-gatherers. Father Martin Gusinde (1886–1969) is primarily renown for his fieldwork in Tierra del Fuego (although he also worked with hunter-gatherers in Africa and elsewhere). His three-volume monograph about the 'Indians of Tierra del Fuego' (Gusinde 1931–39) continues to be a major work of reference (Borrero 1994). The same can be said about the work of his colleague Father Paul Schebesta (1887–1967) who, stimulated by W. Schmidt and his theories, concentrated on fieldwork among Pygmies in Africa and among Southeast Asian Negritos (Schebesta 1952–57). The latter work, conducted in 1924/25 and 1938, constitutes one of the first systematic studies of hunter-gatherer societies driven by general questions about the earliest past of humanity (Lukas 1998: 111).

There were, of course, also German and Austrian anthropologists interested in hunter-gatherer studies not associated with the Schmidt/Koppers school. For example, Fritz Krause (1881–1963), who later became a notorious supporter of the Nazi regime, pursued some kind of 'proto-structuralism', according to which cultures are to be viewed as structured, living entities whose different parts are inextricably intertwined and interrelated. The economic sphere was part of that whole and Krause devoted one of his most popular works, *Das Wirtschaftsleben der Völker* (Krause 1924), to its study. He adopted Grosse's distinction between 'lower' and 'higher hunters' and subscribed to Hahn's position that a direct transition from hunting and gathering to pastoralism was impossible. More problematic was Krause's distinction between 'collective' and 'productive' economies: hunting-and-gathering was classified as 'collective' and characterized as being based on 'passive attitudes' (while 'productive' economies were 'active').

Max Schmidt (1874–1950) had originally been educated as a lawyer but extensive fieldwork in central Brazil and other parts of South America led him to a museum career in ethnology. His topical interests were centred around legal anthropology and economic anthropology. M. Schmidt has a reasonable claim to be one of the founders of the latter, primarily through the publication of his *Grundriß der ethnologischen Volkswirtschaftslehre* (*Outline of an Ethnological Economic Theory*; M. Schmidt 1920–21). His hallmark was a strictly empirical approach, which was equally opposed to evolutionism and culture-circle theory

(Gingrich, forthcoming). Max Schmidt clearly distinguished between two aspects of the economy, the material (which included technology) and the social aspect. Although he provided one of the most detailed descriptions of the material aspects of hunting and gathering at the time (e.g. M. Schmidt 1924), he did not contribute significantly to our understanding of the social aspects of hunting-and-gathering economies. One could argue that he contributed to the long-standing neglect of South American hunter-gatherers in anthropological debates (see e.g. Rival 1999), by analysing his Brazilian data primarily through the lens of producing economies. Max Schmidt had little lasting influence on German-language anthropology and emigrated in 1929 to Brazil and later to Paraguay (Baldus 1951: 302).

Julius Lips (1895–1950) was the successor of Graebner in Cologne but, unlike most of his contemporary colleagues, engaged in leftist politics. Being a member of the Social Democratic Party, he lost his job in 1933 and emigrated via Paris to the United States in 1934 (Fischer 1990: 181–2). His most important contribution to hunter-gatherer studies is his coinage of the term *Erntevölker* ('harvest peoples'), by which he referred to a transitional stage between the gathering of wild plants and the harvest of domesticated plants (Lips 1928). Lips used the Ojibwa wild rice harvest among the Ojibwa as his major example for *Erntevölker*. This transitional form of subsistence triggered particular residence patterns (as the harvest locations were also places of residence), as well as storage practices and a particular care of the wild-growing plants to be harvested (e.g., making sure that nobody would disturb the plants).

Heinrich Cunow (1862–1936) was a social-democratic politician, a scholarly autodidact, and one of the few Marxist anthropologists between the First and Second World Wars. His 'General Economic History' (Cunow 1926) is a material-istic and empirically oriented account which tries to avoid the schematism of nine-teenth century evolutionism. He used the term 'gathering and hunting' economy; to my knowledge, he was one of the first to express the importance of gathering terminologically. Given his Marxist frame of reference, Cunow did not pay too much attention to particular forms of subsistence, such as gathering, hunting or fishing. Instead, he demanded that 'economic history needs to be social history' (Cunow 1926: 22). The early 1930s were the hey-days of the culture-historical approach in German-language anthropology. When German and Austrian anthro-pology re-emerged from the nightmare called Third Reich, the theoretical land-scape had changed significantly. Despite the fact that the most prominent members of the Vienna School returned from exile shortly after the war, the theoretical con-struct was crumbling (and officially renounced by the mid-1950s). Nazis and non-Nazis alike seemed to hide behind a kind of empiricist anthropology which tried to stay away from grand theory.

In the field of hunter-gatherer studies, there was one major publication in the years and decades immediately following the Second World War. Rüdiger Schott's

*The Beginnings of Private Enterprise and of the Planned Economy* (Schott 1956) was a comparative treatment of food distribution among African and South American (Tierra del Fuego) hunter-gatherers. Based not on fieldwork but on careful literature studies, Schott provided some interesting insights into the social and legal aspects of sharing and redistribution. In the final analysis, however, his main point was a negative one: modes of food distribution and of economic organization varied considerably among hunter-gatherers (between the extreme marks of private enterprize and planned economy). Thus, theoretical generalizations were better avoided. This scepticism was understandable in reaction to the Vienna School but seems of little relevance today.

## Conclusions

Let me briefly summarize a few general features of the discussions about hunters and gatherers in German-language anthropology before the Second Word War. German-language anthropology started to get interested in hunter-gatherers as a result of discovering 'economic anthropology' as a legitimate and meaningful sub-field of the emerging discipline (anthropology). This is not particularly surprising but should serve as an instructive reminder that our cherished category of 'hunter-gatherers' cannot be conceptualized without attaching significance to modes of subsistence.

It is often assumed that heightened theoretical interest in hunter-gatherers is causally tied to evolutionist approaches. The evidence presented above clearly suggests otherwise. The anti-evolutionists Grosse, Koppers and W. Schmidt did not attach less theoretical significance to hunter-gatherer societies than the evolutionist Cunow. While it can be argued that the *Kulturkreislehre* was actually a kind of clandestine evolutionism, I believe that this argument misses the point. Instead, scholars who view hunter-gatherers as representatives of 'primitive society' – no matter whether 'primitivity' is reconstructed through evolutionary stages or through historical sequences – are prone to reserve a privileged slot for hunter-gatherers in their theoretical speculations. It is this association between contemporary hunter-gatherers and humanity's past which makes for 'savages of scientific value' (Rosaldo 1982).

German-language anthropology produced a number of interesting theoretical contributions to hunter-gatherer studies between 1890 and the 1930s (e.g., by highlighting the importance of female subsistence activities, distinguishing between simple and complex hunter-gatherers, or by introducing the notion of 'harvest peoples'). Still, none of these contributions seem to be particularly earth-shaking today, since they have long since entered the anthropological canon through other avenues. This means that early German-language contributions to hunter-gatherer studies are primarily relevant from a historicist perspective and not terribly important from a presentist or theoretical point of view. This situation was partly caused by the fact that German-language anthropology (not only in the field of hunter-gatherer studies) had little impact on global anthropology after the Second World War. On the one hand, this was a political reaction to Germany's and Austria's embrace of Nazi ideologies. On the other hand, it had also to do with the 'retreat from theory', typical for post-war German-language anthropology.

The *Kulturkreislehre*, in particular, provides an interesting case study for the relationship between theory and ethnographic data collection. An elaborate (albeit fanciful) theoretical construct (designed primarily by W. Schmidt and Koppers) triggered a series of long-term fieldwork among so-called 'lower hunters' (conducted primarily by Gusinde and Schebesta). It certainly can be argued that without the grandiose speculations of W. Schmidt and Koppers about 'primeval culture' Gusinde's work among the Selk'nam and Schebesta's work in Africa and Southeast Asia would not have been undertaken, at least not with the same intensity. We are confronted with an obvious case of theory driving data collection. If we look at the results of this brand of 'Catholic anthropology' from today's perspective, W. Schmidt's culture circles appear as little more than a bygone aberration, which can be diagnosed as part of the puberty of our discipline. Some of the ethnographic monographs triggered by W. Schmidt's theories, however, remain relevant and useful up to the present day (especially if one skips the passages where the data were interpreted according to the 'culture historical method'). In short, these studies are of little and dubious theoretical value but, if critically assessed, can still yield some relevant ethnographic material.

The title of this paper, 'No Escape from Being Theoretically Important', was initially coined in reference to hunters and gatherers. In other words, throughout the history of anthropology, hunter-gatherers have always been of prime theoretical importance for scholars of various persuasions. The period presented above – the transition from evolutionism to diffusionism – was no exception in that respect. But 'No Escape . . .' refers as well to anthropologists as to hunter-gatherers. As the preceding examples have demonstrated, anthropology cannot create useful data without theoretical input. At the same time, theories often seem to be little less than short-lived triggers of ethnographic reports. Thus, one is tempted to exclaim 'anthropology is theory or it is nothing – as long as we do not forget that the half-life period of theories is generally much shorter than of the data they produce.

## Acknowledgements

I want to thank the participants of the CHAGS 9 session 'Traditions of Hunter-Gatherer Research' for their critical comments, as well as Andre Gingrich (Vienna) for his comments on an earlier draft of this paper.

# −7−

# Hunter-Gatherer Studies in Russia and the Soviet Union

## *O. Yu. Artemova*

In Russia the terms 'ethnography', 'ethnology' and 'cultural (or social) anthropology' have always been perceived as synonyms. Descriptive and comparative theoretical studies were conducted within the boundaries of the same discipline. From the beginning of the nineteenth century until quite recently this discipline was called 'ethnography'. The word 'anthropology' was applied only to studies of the physical constitution and biological evolution of humans.

Some two decades ago several leading Russian ethnographers came to the view that the word 'ethnology' sounded more imposing than the word 'ethnography'. Soon afterwards the institute to which I belong, as well as a number of departments in the main state universities and the major journal in our field were renamed. For example, the journal called *The Ethnographic Review* became *The Ethnological Review*. With *perestroika*, many who in the Soviet period studied and taught so-called scientific communism, historical materialism, fundamental Marxism-Leninism, the political economy of socialism, the history of Soviet Communist Party and so on, found themselves out of work or, at best, in a position of no prestige at all. But they were not accustomed to such a position. Somehow they had to change their professions, at least nominally. And so they found a niche which seemed to be empty: social (cultural) anthropology. They were numerous and quite influential, still having very strong connections with powerful structures at the 'top' of society. A flood of publications came, which in the guise of social (cultural) anthropology contained strange and incomprehensible things. New university departments were created, and new acts (called State Educational Standards) prescribing how to teach social anthropology were issued.

At first the ethnologists, engaged in fundamental studies, kept away from this crude process. Then some grasped the nonsense of what was happening. As one erudite woman announced at a public meeting: 'It is the birth of a new science and the delivery is painful.' The ethnologists began to assure their self-proclaimed colleagues, at their magnificent conference gatherings, that social anthropology had existed in the country for more than 150 years, though it was known by a different name, and that its subject had nothing in common with the 'newborn science'. Of course, this made no sense. It seemed that the only way to correct the situation was to organize new educational structures, where under the name of social or cultural anthropology professional ethnologists would teach students, and where the subject would correspond with the term. Now there are several such departments in state universities, some of which coexist with the departments of ethnology. So the same scholars do research work in ethnology at the research institutions and teach social or cultural anthropology at the universities. Sometimes they also teach ethnology at another university or in an ethnology department of the same university; and many people around them feel themselves quite lost.

It is worth mentioning that the terms 'social anthropology' and 'cultural anthropology' are badly suited to the Russian language. The word 'anthropology' is strongly associated with bones and craniums. Adjectives in combination with this word sound rather awkward. In particular, the word 'cultural' sounds odd – *kul'-turnyy*, in Russian. The connotation is of a knowledgeable person with good manners and good education. I remember when in the late 1990s a certain woman, a member of the editorial board of *The Ethnological Review*, asked my advice. She was editing a paper for publication, and in it 'cultural anthropologists' had been mentioned. She thought that, maybe, it would be better to put the word 'cultural' in quotes, otherwise the readers could think that there were, somewhere, 'uncultural', that is uncultured, anthropologists! I will therefore hereafter use the words 'ethnology' and 'ethnologists' as better corresponding to Russian past and modern situations.

## The Heritage of pre-Soviet Russian Studies

In 1989, in Paris, a conference was convened on the problems of the development of Soviet studies on the so-called traditional (meaning preliterate or stateless) societies. Virtually all the participants from other countries (apart of one, James Woodburn), as well as Russian scholars who were at that time already emigrants, spoke about the backwardness of Soviet ethnological thought. And one of our former colleagues even declared that in our times only Soviet ethnologists are interested 'in an origin of the phenomena', and that no 'properly progressive' anthropologists anywhere in the world nowadays study 'an origin'. I do not know whether this is actually a bad sign, but according to the strong tradition of ethnological education in Russian universities, there is no science at all without aspiring to understand the origin of the various phenomena of social life. In Russia, ethnology is science not simply scholarship. That tradition, in fact, comes from pre-revolutionary times. Also, until quite recent times, hunter-gatherer studies were not distinguished as a separate sphere of ethnology. They were included within the scope of studies on stateless societies, and these, in turn, were conducted first as a means of creating a general theory of the evolution of human social life. Such studies were called the *history of primeval or primitive societies*, in accordance with the principals of nineteenth-century unilinear evolutionism.

Nevertheless, Soviet ethnology retained a viable heritage from pre-revolutionary ethnological studies. There were many highly educated scholars who easily read foreign languages, maintained regular contacts with foreign colleagues, worked abroad for long periods (predominantly in European countries), and kept abreast of the progress of ethnological thought as well as of various theoretical discussions in other countries. Indeed, it was predominantly the wish keep in step with the main lines of the development of Western ethnology that made Russian ethnologists study data on the Aborigines of Australia, the American Indians, African, South Asian, Oceanian and other 'exotic' peoples, using exclusively literary sources. Apart from, perhaps, the epoch of circumnavigations, Russian scholars never had any opportunities to collect their own data among those peoples. But precisely the data on the Australian, African, American and Oceanian natives served as the grounds for a rapprochement of Russian studies with Western thought, because the latter developed predominantly on the basis of these data, and no interaction or theoretical polemics with colleagues abroad were possible without the analyses of the ethnological material which they both knew. So in the period preceding the Revolution of 1917, there was no barrier between Russian ethnology and Western social or cultural anthropology.

## The Work of A.N. Maksimov

The majority of Russian ethnologists enthusiastically accepted the concepts of British and American evolutionism. On the other hand, as in the West, in Russia, at the end of the nineteenth and the beginning of the twentieth centuries, quite sceptical attitudes to evolutionistic speculations had developed. These attitudes were most obvious in the works of A.N. Maksimov. It was precisely due to his efforts that on the eve of the Revolution the avant-garde approaches to the investigation of stateless societies had been expressed in Russian ethnological publications. There was also another very important point: a stable tradition of serious, objective and unbiased, fair, critical analysis of the work of domestic and foreign scholars did exist. Indeed, every issue of the pre-revolutionary *Etnograficheskoe obozrenie (Ethnographic Review)* had a section, comprising half (or even more) of the journal's contents, containing between thirteen and twenty critical reviews of new books. The reviewers who engaged in this labourious and thankless task were all respected researchers, such as D.K. Zelenin, V.F. Miller, N.F. Sumtsov, V.N.

Kharuzina and N.N. Kharuzin. And there was no timidity about criticizing scholars of authority (as in the Soviet period), and no special reverence toward Western authors (which became typical in post-Soviet times). Thus, Maksimov, while quite a young person, wrote numerous particularly critical articles on the works of such writers as Tylor, Lubbock, Grosse, Morgan, McLennan, Lips, Westermarck and others.

In 1898, at the age of 26, this author published a work in which he examined contemporary methods of ethnological studies on marriage and kinship systems in stateless societies. He could not approve any of them. But the main argument of this publication (as well as many of his other writings) was directed against various general schemes of step-by-step evolution in social life (kin and marriage relations, especially) – schemes which were easily created, and no less easily destroyed, even by not-very-strict criticism. The major defect of all such schemes, he believed, was the concept of the uniformity of social evolution throughout the world, a concept he recognized as obviously false. So he postulated a kind of rough-and-ready methodological principle, according to which ethnological studies of stateless societies were to be conducted on the grounds of a general assumption that human societies proceeded in diverse ways, until some other viewpoint could be definitively shown as more reliable. Reasoning from this point, he regarded it as unacceptable to detect a sort of archetype of prehistoric peoples in the Australian Aborigines, for instance (or in the African Pygmies), or to consider modern hunters and gatherers to be 'more primitive' than shifting horticulturists, or to allot various stateless societies to supposed 'steps' of social evolution (Maksimov 1898).

Later on Maksimov wrote works refuting particular evolutionistic hypotheses quite popular among his colleagues. In these works he used, among others, data on hunters and gatherers, and especially often, on the Australian Aborigines. He frequently arrived at conclusions that were only indirectly linked to the primary goals of his studies, conclusions that had autonomous value and that sometimes were completely unexpected. Some of these critical works turned into vast analytical surveys of the data, collected as thoroughly as circumstances in his time allowed. Thus, while proving the groundlessness of Morgan's group-marriage concept, he undertook two monographic studies on Australian Aboriginal kinship terminologies and systems of sections and subsections (Maksimov 1912; 1909). In the first he investigated thirty-two kinship terminologies, using all the data he could find in Russian libraries. And at that time it was possible to find quite a lot, the most famous books or periodicals as well as very rare ones.[1] In his work on sections and subsections (of course, he called them 'marriage classes') Maksimov not only argued that these divisions could not be regarded as 'survivals' of group marriage, but also tried to show that in traditional contexts they did not regulate marriages at all, that they appeared and spread among the Aborigines relatively late,[2] and that, ultimately, they had not been 'genetically' linked to phratries or moieties (1909). To prove the last idea he analysed all the indigenous names of the sections, subsections and the phratries he could obtain. He did similar work to show that totemism should not be perceived as one of the earliest and universal stages of the evolution of religion, and to reject the idea that matrilineal descent always and everywhere had preceded patrilineal decent. Methodologically, and sometimes even in verbal expression, many of his works anticipated Radcliffe-Brown's writings of the 1930s and 1940s (e.g. Radcliffe-Brown 1952: 32–48 ['Patrilineal and matrilineal succession', 1935]; 1952: 49–89 ['The study of kinship systems', 1941]).

For all his scepticism, Maksimov, in accordance with domestic traditions, had done work aimed at finding out 'the origin' of certain phenomena which had attracted the special attention of scholars. His approach to such tasks is also reminiscent of Radcliffe-Brown's (1941) method of searching for 'the sociological origin' (as opposed to 'historical origin') of phenomena. Maksimov was convinced that the scholar, in order to understand the functional sense and the sociological roots of this or that human usage, had not to limit his research basis to the data on the most simple (most 'primitive' or even 'backward' as they used to say at the time) societies but had to collect the data from societies of various types, even those that were called 'civilized'. Thus, while doing a study on avoidance relations and trying to discover 'the sociological origin' of the phenomenon (he used the word-combination 'psychological origin'), he included data on many 'tribal' groups of Australian Aborigines and Siberian hunter-gatherers into the wide survey of the source material, which embraced more than one hundred other peoples (Maksimov 1908).

## Ethnology in the Early Soviet Era

Maksimov had but few followers: maybe only one (S.A. Tokarev), at best two (Tokarev and A.M. Zolotarev), though both did work in the post-revolutionary period. After the Revolution the task of elabouration of the new 'Marxist' ethnological methods had been announced by 'the ideologists' of the country. Paradoxically, this task was realized especially industriously in the field of 'primeval history', which meant, in fact, studies on stateless societies. The subject had provoked special interest among the founders of Marxism-Leninism. Owing to the fact that Marx and Engels had been greatly influenced by Morgan and other nineteenth-century writers, Soviet 'ethnological Marxism' formed a kind of symbiosis with classic unilineal evolutionism. In accordance with the latter, all the societies 'in the early stages of social evolution' were perceived as quite uniform, having a definite set of universal sociological and cultural features. The interest in the genesis of various social institutions and cultural phenomena noticeably overshadowed the interest in the mechanisms of their functioning or their predestination in the contexts of particular cultures. Concurrently, the isolation of Soviet ethnology from Western studies was growing, as a consequence of the exaggerated striving for its own separate way.

However, at that time, the late 1920s, Marxism in Soviet ethnology existed as an assortment of general concepts rather than as an overarching paradigm, ready-made for all cases (the latter sort of paradigm only emerged later). Therefore, in the publications of that period one may find considerable plurality of concepts and a diversity of personal approaches. Besides this, the scholars who had made their reputations before the Revolution, still continued to work in those years, and some of them did not turn to Marxism at all. Maksimov, for instance, proceeded as if Marx and Engels had never existed. In some branches of knowledge, in biology and psychology, particularly, this period (the second half of the 1920s to the very beginning of 1930s) is regarded as 'the Soviet golden age'. It was very short but very fruitful. I do not know whether one could speak of 'the Soviet golden age' in ethnology or not, but the appearance of works which made a contribution not only to domestic but also to world ethnological literature seems to be obvious. Among these were the innovative article 'Primitive Monotheism of Terra del Fuego Islanders' (1929), by P.F. Preobrazhenskiy, and one of Tokarev's early publications, 'On the Kin Systems of the Australian Aborigines' (1929), which was a yet more complete survey of the data on kinship terminologies than Maksimov's.

Two years later young Zolotarev (he was 23) published his first monograph 'The Origin of Exogamy' (1931). The main hypothesis of this work is, perhaps, of no interest nowadays, but its value consists in a number of conclusions and assumptions regarding the social life of hunters and gatherers as a whole and the Australian Aborigines in particular. He made an attempt to show the mechanism of section and subsection formation without resorting to the idea of superposition of matrilineal descent on patrilineal descent – as many authors did before and after him. Zolotarev suggested that sections and subsections (marriage classes) were derivatives of the 'classificatory' kinship nomenclatures. It seems to me that later on A.P. Elkin and still later H.W. Scheffler went a similar way (see e.g. Keen 1988: 98–9). Zolotarev also tried to prove that the systems of two moieties (in those Aboriginal groups which lacked sections and subsections) represented the reduction of section and subsection systems – as the result of the simplification of social structure, which was necessary for the development of 'intertribal' interaction. Such reasoning seems to be not out of date even now. It is worth mentioning that Zolotarev's work was based on a huge number of literary sources. Sometimes he would pull out of nowhere editions unknown to anybody in our country and quite difficult to access.[3]

To illustrate how far the plurality of opinions stretched during that period, the paper, 'The Problems of Pre-Clan Society' by S.P. Tolstov, the would-be 'chief' of Soviet ethnology, might be mentioned.[4] Tolstov argued that by the time of European colonization Australian Aboriginal society had been torn by antagonisms similar to class war: the old men had barely held their positions, power and privileges, constantly resorting to 'murderous religious terror' against younger men and women. But the old order was doomed to fall. Such was the logic of socio-economic development, determined by the universal laws of the historical materialism (Tolstov 1931). (According to the dogma, which was implanted in our literature several years later, Australian Aborigines like all other hunter-gatherer peoples the *had* to be completely egalitarian, and they were described as such until the beginning of 1980s.)

To return to serious investigations, it should be noted that at the end of 1920s a new direction of research merged psychology and ethnology: 'historical-evolutionary study of the phenomenon of personality', initiated by L.S. Vygotsky and his followers, A.R. Luriya and A.N. Leont'ev. They were interested in the development of human personality in various cultural contexts. They conducted cross-cultural research, using literary data and field material obtained in a number of expeditions to the remote regions of the country, performed at the beginning of 1930s. On the basis of this work something similar to the American 'Culture and Personality' school could have arisen (though, of course, the methodological background would not be Freudian). Yet this was not fated to happen.

The end of the 1920s and the beginning of the 1930s were, as is well known, years of a tragic turning point in the internal policy of the Soviet government. A general extreme toughening of the regime influenced the development of Soviet science (including hunter-gatherer studies, which seemed to be so far from the current problems of Soviet life) in the saddest way. In a few years Marxism ceased to be the methodology of research and became a set of dogmas. Any deviation from these threatened the scholars not only with the loss of opportunities to write and publish their works but also with real mortal danger.

Morgan's main concepts concerning the early evolution of human society, which had been worked out in 1860s and 1870s and had been repeated (for the most part) by Engels in *The Origin of Family, Private Property and State* (1972[1884]), were canonized. In addition, the same happened to various fragmentary statements of the 'founders of Marxism-Leninism' from other works, as well as from their private letters and even rough copies of the letters, and even remarks in books. As a result the following scheme of social relations and spiritual life on the stage of 'classical primeval society' was shaped: the matrilineal exogamous clan as the main 'socio-economic unit', group marriage (or, at least, the numerous survivals of group marriage in marriage and kinship systems), and complete social equality. At that, the concept of social equality and 'primitive communism' in an odd way got along together with the concept of matriarchy – the dominance of women. Then, totemism had to be regarded as the universal form of religion in this stage of evolution. Finally, classical primeval society, according to the 'true Marxist approach', lacked human personality: the people's characters and behaviour were quite the same, without any individual peculiarities. The individual's willpower was completely constrained by social norms, which were extremely strict and numerous.[5] The 'stage of classical primeval society' was associated with the European population of the Upper Paleolithic or the Mesolithic, and the latter, with the existent hunter-gatherer societies in the modern world. These, in turn, *had* to conform to the above-described scheme and if the facts showed the opposite, then, 'so much the worse for the facts', as well as for those who relied on such facts.

Thus, it turned out that theoretical thought was thrown back to the second half of the nineteenth century. Really serious cross-cultural work on hunters and gatherers and stateless societies as a whole was, after that, almost completely excluded because the modern data on these societies did not correspond with the dominant scheme nor did the conclusions, made in a number of careful investigations of the previous period. The advantages of this period were very soon forgotten, and in the 1960s and 1970s Soviet ethnologists time and again stood up anew for the ideas which had been published by their compatriots dozens of years earlier. It is notable, that this 'harsh break' happened precisely at the period when ethnology in Western countries was advancing.

## Field Versus Library Studies

Precisely at that period many Soviet authors, now belonging to new generations, abandoned the tradition of careful analysis of the facts obtained from foreign literature. Even studying at least three European languages was no longer obligatory. Many scholars came to manage with only one foreign language (very often German), or none. The so-called 'criticism of bourgeois concepts' changed the in-depth analysis of the new directions of Western ethnological studies. Similarly, in the 'internal scientific life', pure analytical criticism gave place to ideologically motivated charges. Now it was not a shame to rely on insufficient data or to distort the data, but it was frightful to be accused of 'anti-Marxism' or bourgeois delusions such as 'relativism', 'diffusionism' and so forth. All this, besides many other disadvantages, led to a sharp demarcation between the so-called armchair 'theoretical' studies and field research among those Siberian and northern peoples of the Soviet Union, who retained a hunter-gatherer mode of subsistence or, more broadly, 'the main features of traditional pre-literary culture'. This demarcation had existed previously but not in such a harsh form as emerged in the Stalinist period.

Field studies in the Russian North and Siberia almost always developed according to the saying: 'bad lack often brings good fortune'. The early (pre-revolutionary) researchers, such as V. Bogoraz, V. Iochel'son, L. Shternberg and many others, were mainly not professional ethnologists; they were 'professional revolutionists', whom the government exiled to the most remote and severe regions of the Empire. There, they collected invaluable data on the indigenous peoples who inhabited the places of their exile. Later, on return to urban centres, these exiles began to read through the ethnological literature in order to adjust their material to the theoretical concepts. Morgan and some other evolutionist writers impressed them most of all. This (as well as 'the revolutionary past') helped some of them (Bogoraz and Shternberg, for instance) to occupy positions of influence in the first decade of the Soviet period (predominantly in Leningrad). They taught widely in the universities and other institutions for higher education and the obligatory requirements demanded of all would-be scholars included prolonged stationary fieldwork among the native peoples and study of the native languages. Some of their students left Leningrad for Siberia and worked for several years as school-teachers in remote settlements among the indigenous people. Many did long-term field studies (for example, G.M. Vasilevich among the Evenki, I.S. Vdovin among Chukchi; E.A. Kreynovich among the Nivkki and the Yukagir, and S.N. Stebnitskiy among the Koryak). These young scholars later published detailed works, devoted mainly to the languages and the folklore of the investigated peoples. Social structure, kinship nomenclatures, kinship relations, economic systems interested them much less, although some fieldwork on these topics had been done at the end of the 1920s and the beginning of the 1930s.

After 'the break' some of the most conscientious 'library scholars', previously interested in African, American or Australian ethnology, turned to fieldwork in Siberia. Also, many of the newcomers devoted themselves exclusively to collecting and publishing field data. So, a lot of the new and very good quality materials on traditional cultures, including hunter-gatherer cultures (for example, that of the Khanty and the Mansy in Western Siberia, or the Ulchi, the Orochy, the Evens of the Far East of the Soviet Union), were obtained from the 1930s to the beginning of the 1950s. But the subjects of the field studies were limited in a certain way.

To continue the analogy between Soviet psychology and Soviet ethnology: when studies on 'personality and culture' became impossible the students and the followers of Vygotsky (he died in 1934) went deep into specific psychobiological problems. As the psychologists like to say now, the science then turned to be the 'psychology of ear, nose and throat'. By the same pattern, field ethnology became the 'ethnography of food, dwellings and dress'. Now these subjects are sometimes jokingly called the 'standard ethnographic triad'. Those scholars who were still engaged in theoretical work on social evolution, made a lot of fun of such a theme of a master's or even a doctoral thesis as: 'The traditional food of the Evenky' or the 'The traditional dwellings of the Buriat'. In other words, the predominantly descriptive work on the so-called material culture became especially in demand. Apart from this, the great number of descriptions of various festivals, rites and rituals, accompanied (at least in the case of hunters and gatherers) by the search for the 'survivals of totemism', were published.

Those few authors, who, nevertheless, dared to study certain aspects of traditional social organization of Siberian peoples, preferred not to go into structural or functional details of the social units and kin ties. Of course, the traditional social organization of Siberian peoples had been soundly destroyed by the time of the 1930s and 1940s. But the same tendency – to avoid discussion (at least at any extent thorough) of the composition and functions of various native groupings – was also typical of works that aimed to reconstruct the previous situation and relied on the evidence of early writers (travellers, missionaries, administrative officials) or on archival documents. The best example was the famous huge volume *Tribal and Clan Composition of the Siberian Peoples in the 17th Century* by B.O. Dolgikh. It was published in 1960, but contained the results of his titanic work done in the preceding decades. The material on an incalculable number of indigenous groupings (certainly, much more diverse than clans or tribes) in this volume amounted to little more than information about their native names, geographical distribution and ethnic attribution. It looks like the author not only rejected any structural and functional analysis, but also tried to exclude any data that could collide with Morgan's and Engels's definitions of 'clan' (Engels called it the 'gens'; in Russian we say *rod*) and 'tribe' – definitions loyally repeated by the author in the surprisingly brief preface to the volume. The work is wonderful, but it is extremely difficult to understand and to use now. Perhaps one of the few subjects which was not dangerous to discuss analytically – to speculate on, to propose diverse hypotheses, to polemicize with opponents – was the so-called ethnogenesis: the origin and early history of various ethnic groups. In Soviet times (though not today) it was a politically and ideologically 'neutral zone' – at least, as regards the hunters and gatherers of Siberia. So a lot of such work had been done.

## Discussion and Conclusion

The events and processes in Soviet 'ethnological life' did not happen on their own. The harsh break and all that followed had been done 'by the hands' of certain scholars or those who pretended to be scholars because the rulers of the country understood nothing or almost nothing in ethnology, hunter-gatherer studies especially. Unfortunately, modern Russian scholars are not inclined to examine the positions and deeds of their predecessors, although such an examination could be quite edifying. Indeed, we are not yet convinced that such a thing could not happen again. Perhaps hunter-gatherer studies are now out of danger but other spheres of human intellectual endeavour might be at risk.

As far as I know, only one writer has tried to analyse the problem seriously, using the verbatim shorthand records of the ethnological meetings and conferences of the 1920s and 1930s and looking through the literature of these years: T.D. Solovey (1998; 2001). She came to the conclusion that the *main* 'work' had been performed by members of the Communist Party, who could not find a place in the so-called *apparat* (machinery of State and upper structures of the Party) but were eager to rule, to dictate to others what to do and how to do it. They searched for the appropriate niches. Some of those people pretended to control humanitarian knowledge as a whole; some were ready to content themselves with ethnology, the more so as it was responsible for the important task of uncovering the origin of human society and the state. As a rule badly educated, the newcomers were convinced that this was hardly rocket science, especially since the 'founders' (classics) had already taken care of quite a lot of things. They organized a number of magnificent gatherings, during which were discussed such problems as: what is ethnology and what is ethnography? what should this discipline study and what should it not? and even, did the country need ethnology at all? Having clashed with professional ethnologists, who had reputation and knowledge, they did their best to get rid of them. Any means were used, including political denunciation of their 'colleagues'.

Perhaps this should make clear why I have spoken in a roundabout way at the beginning of this paper. The analogy is obvious. Of course, our modern situation seems not to be dangerous; rather, it seems to be ridiculous and annoying. But, maybe, Maksimov at the end of the 1920s (when he did not want to waste time on the meetings of the self-proclaimed 'new ethnologists' as well as to waste energy on the discussions about the subject of ethnology) could not imagine that ten years later he would not be able to say to students what he thought about the functions of matrilineal descent in the societies of Australian Aborigines; that 15 years later he would prefer not to leave his flat and that his fate would be one of the happiest – for he died in his own bed.

So, the newcomers had done the *main* 'work' but the *last* 'work' had been performed by the scholars who were ready to conform and to 'write from dictation' – because of their fear of persecution, or because of aspirations to make their career or simply because of the wish to preserve their current position. But even at that time the people had the opportunity to make their choices. Those scholars who were not arrested and killed at the very beginning of the process (as happened to Professor P.F. Preobrazhenskiy) displayed themselves differently.

Maksimov was discharged from Moscow University in 1930 on the grounds of 'harmful views'. Until his death (1941) he published nothing and worked as a bibliographer in the Lenin Library. He composed a huge systematic catalogue of ethnological books and articles, predominantly devoted to traditional societies: approximately 80,000 index cards with annotations. Zolotarev and Tolstov continued to write and publish books and papers. The content of their new works was quite contrary to the content of their previous works. But then their fates parted. Both of them went to the front in 1941 as volunteers. Tolstov returned and became a prosperous person. Zolotarev was taken prisoner by the Germans, and managed to escape and reach the location of the Soviet army, but later he (along with millions of other Soviet soldiers who had been imprisoned by the Germans) was arrested by the Soviet security service. He perished in 1943 in one of the Soviet strict-security camps. Just before the War Zolotarev published two papers, in which he tried, rather carefully, to argue against some points of Morgan's (and Engels's) official scheme.

Tokarev, like Maksimov, was discharged from Moscow University in 1930. He worked in other institutions, did a lot of fieldwork (though not among hunters and gathers), published a historiographical study and never discussed any 'sharp' questions. After the War he ws invited to work in the Institute of Ethnography and in Moscow University, where he later became the head of the Department of Ethnography. He was one of the most respected and beloved Soviet scholars: 'the ethnologist number one', as everybody called him. His erudition was incredible; he was extremely honest while expounding the data and published a lot of quite adequate data from foreign books, including those on hunters and gatherers. And it was his students who from the 1960s to the 1980s began to try to get rid of Morgan's and Engels's scheme. These scholars were exclusively library researchers and they used the Australian Aboriginal data especially often. But that is another story.

## Acknowledgements

I am grateful to Drs A. Barnard, P. Gray and N.N. Sadomskaya who helped me to correct my English style.

## Notes

1. For example, *Journal and Proceedings of the Royal Geographical Society of New South Wales* or *North Queensland Ethnography Bulletin*. By comparison, now our central libraries receive almost nothing from the foreign anthropological literature on hunter-gatherer societies.
2. Later, at least some of these conclusions were confirmed by the field studies (see e.g. Keen 1988: 97–100).
3. Such as *Report of the Australian and New Zealand Association for the Advancement of Science* (Vol.16.Wellington, 1923; Vol.17, Adelaide,1924; Vol.18, Perth,1926; Vol.19, Hobart,1928; Vol.20, Brisbane, 1930). This also shows the state of our libraries at the time.
4. Tolstov was later director of the Institute of Ethnography and head of the Ethnography Department in Moscow University. He was very influential and despotic.
5. Indeed, this dogma had been proclaimed later, after the Second World War.

# 8

# Soviet Traditions in the Study of Siberian Hunter-Gatherer Society

## *Anna A. Sirina*

I commenced my studies in the 1980s when ethnography was still wearing the mantle of Sovietism. I remember at the time disliking the dry scientific text, devoid of life that, in keeping with established canons, did not allow authors to show their positions or attitudes to the phenomena, events or facts they described. Such a style has not always been characteristic of ethnographic writings. Rather, it was a reflection of a society where demonstration of individuality was not encouraged. As early as the 1920s, works were published where ethnographic text was presented in a different manner. I had a desire to understand for myself the reasons for the difference between these two periods; so I started to take an interest in the history of ethnographic studies.

For most of our Western counterparts the Soviet period seems to be a time of ideological dogmas reflected in the recognized impossibility of getting into the Siberian field, with the corresponding stereotype, namely that ethnographic data collected by Soviet scholars had been chosen to match a certain theory, hence they were biased. Also because northern indigenous peoples' culture and subsistence economy had been changed under the long-term influence of the Russian/Soviet State, there was a view that they were not 'real' hunter-gatherers anymore. So, these data have 'dropped out' of the factual base of world anthropology thereby impoverishing the science itself. Today, Siberian ethnographic data are increasingly used for analysing the key subject matters of international anthropological studies – social structure, ethnic identity, property, religion, consequences of contacts with a dominating society, and experience in resolving legal problems such as those of the Australian Aborigines (Vakhtin and Sirina 2003).

From the outset I should note that the term 'hunter-gatherers' had rarely been used in Russian ethnography. Before the revolution these peoples were called *inorodtsy* ('peoples of different/other clans') that were classified into the cate-

gories of vagrant, nomadic and settled.[1] This classification was made on the basis
of the subject's mode of life, which depended on the mode of production or subsistence economy. In Soviet times the term 'indigenous numerically small peoples
of the North' came into use. Such classification was based on the following criteria: geography, small numbers, low level of socio-economic development, specific attributes of existence and mode of life. Basically, the level of socio-economic
development was the basis of this classification. The specific features of a particular culture were not taken into account and were regarded as 'survivals' of the
'primitive' society. The definition implicitly had an idea of backwardness of these
peoples. Hence the goal of the Soviet State was to help them in overcoming their
backwardness. During the Soviet period reindeer herding was greatly expanded
among people who were previously hunter-gatherers, and education programmes
were implemented.

More and more frequently the people became labelled 'indigenous' or 'aboriginal'. There is a special register of such peoples, which has grown from twenty-six
to thirty over the last seventy years. They belong to various language families, and
have specific cultural characteristics. Many of them are involved in reindeer
herding to various degrees (Tishkov 1994). The new definition stresses the specific
cultural characteristics, including traditional way of life and subsistence economy,
which was necessary for the laws to be implemented.

After publication of Tokarev's monograph (Tokarev 1966), studies of the history
of Russian/Soviet ethnography were suspended. In post-Soviet Russia intensified
interest in the history of ethnography has been caused by the institutional crisis in
the humanities, and by renunciation of Marxist-Leninist ideology and theory
(Solovey 1998; 2001). A search for new methodologies and theoretical approaches
has commenced. Attention to both Western theories and the heritage accumulated
from Soviet times has become more acute.

To quite a considerable degree, the traditions and theoretical approaches of
Russian ethnography have been formed on the basis of studies of 'hunter-gatherer'
societies. The territory of Siberia, together with the peoples populating it, had
become a component part of the Russian State earlier than the others, during the
sixteenth and seventeenth centuries. However, the history of Siberian ethno-
graphic/anthropological studies has only nowadays started to attract the serious
attention of researchers both in Russia and abroad. One may say that a new tradition is being formed in the study of Siberian hunter-gatherer (Krupnik 1998;
Schweitzer 2000a; 2000b; Slezkine 1994; Vakhtin and Sirina 2003).

## Theories and approaches

Ethnographic studies in Russia were primarily empirical in character. Russian
ethnography has always been characterized by the secondary nature of theoretical

approaches. Theories, for instance evolutionism, arrived from the West. There were at least two reasons for that situation. The first reason was internal, being based on the logic of the development of the discipline. For a long time Russian ethnography had developed within in the framework of geography, in close connection with the natural sciences, which is probably the cause of the special interest in evolutionism. The second reason was external, connected with the penetration in Russia of Marxist ideas (and, more broadly, liberalism) which was characterized by an unrestrained apologetic of progress, and which also was closely connected with evolutionism (Solovey 1998: 32–3).

Russian philosophy was not the basis for ethnographic studies since it was itself formed relatively late in comparison with Western philosophy. Philosophy, which developed within the framework of Orthodoxy, was characterized by its anthropocentrism and extreme sociologism. During the Soviet period Russian philosophy was the captive of political and ideological dogmas of the elite. However it would be a mistake to assume the absence of any other theories and trends of thought in Russia during that time. A.N. Maksimov, had an understanding of recent theories of foreign ethnography, and was a severe critic of evolutionism in the first years of the twentieth century (Artemova 1997). Moscow University professor P.F. Preobrazhenskiy, on the other hand, tried to combine evolutionism with diffusionism (Ivanova 1999); and the Irkutsk University professor G.S. Vinogradov followed A. Bergson and N.O. Losskiy in his attempts to understand culture as a living entity (intuition theory) (Sirina 1993). Some other scholars, especially in the field of linguistic studies (such as P. Bogatyrev and V. Propp) developed their own approaches which differed from evolutionism.

Marxist-Leninist theory attempted to create new approaches. Marxism-Leninism became the major methodological approach in studies during the Soviet period, together with historical materialism with its theory of socio-economic formations, progressive development, and the decisive influence of the mode of production in the historical process. Soviet ethnography, in its Marxist garb, followed the research line of evolutionism, with its quaint combination of idealism and materialism. Marxism gave special attention to the problems studied by evolutionism, namely the origin of social structural forms, and the origin and history of religion. Nevertheless, within the framework of official Marxism there were different streams and approaches. I would stress that dividing the history of Russian ethnography into pre-Soviet, Soviet and post-Soviet periods would be quite artificial. I would rather point out the continuity between these periods and the permeable boundaries between them. Soviet ethnography inherited some traditions from pre-revolutionary times, as well as acquiring new features during the Soviet era. Society was changing, and this reflected on scientific research.

The history of Soviet (including Siberian) ethnography has usually been divided into four main periods. Of course, the division is quite relative. The first lasted from 1917 till the end of 1920, and was characterized by a variety of theoretical approaches, the great rise of the scientific perspective, as well as studies of local lore, history and economy. Should this period be evaluated as 'Soviet' or as an organic continuation of the pre-Soviet? The second period (1930s to 1940s) was marked by the predominance of vulgar Marxism and dogmatism. The accusation of anti-Marxism was very dangerous for the career, safety and even the life of a researcher. In the early 1930s Soviet ethnography went through a crisis. There was heated discussion about the subject matter of ethnographic studies. Suggestions were made that it should be completely abandoned as a bourgeois science. Olderogge, an outstanding Soviet specialist in African languages and cultures, wrote this ironical verse ('V. Aptekar's letter to the Ethnography'[2]) as a reaction to the Meeting of the Ethnographers from Moscow and Leningrad (1929):

> Are you still alive, grandmammy Ethnography?
> In my opinion, you do not exist at all.
> Just yesterday, with a public epitaph,
> I sent you to the other world.
>
> (Osnitskaya,1993: 371)

Ultimately, instead of a geographical discipline ethnography was recognized as a historical science that should first of all serve as the history of 'primitive' society. Hunter-gatherer societies were viewed as remnants of 'the archaic world'. In this connection ethnographical empirical data from Siberia in the Soviet times served as the basis for studying the problems of 'primitive' society's history: social arrangements, specificity of kinship relations, tribal composition, correlation between fratria, clan and community, and the evolution of family development; the role of implements of production in the 'primitive' economy; and of specific archaic beliefs. The Moscow Institute of Ethnography even used to have a special theoretical section for the history of 'primitive' society. The scholars who worked in this section, as a rule, had never been in the field either in Africa, Australia (which was understandable), or even in the Russian North.[3] They used ethnographic data extracted mainly from foreign sources, because ethnographic data from Australia and Oceania were regarded as 'classical' for reconstruction of the history of 'primitive' society. In so doing, scholars implemented the cross-cultural or comparative method of analysis. The heyday of those studies was connected with the third, and partly the fourth, periods of Soviet ethnography.

Using archeological and ethnographic data, as well as foreign literature, during the 1960s some Soviet scholars started to revize some statements of Marxist theory of the history of 'primitive' society. For instance, conclusions had been made about the ancient character of the family, about community (*obshchina*) as a main socio-economic unit of 'primitive' society, and about the unequal status of people in such communities. Vasilevich, using her rich field materials, collected among Siberian taiga-forest hunters, arrived at conclusions about the specific character of their social organization. They did not live by tribes, and their main socio-economic nomadic unit consisted of extended families, being represented by members of different clans. Matriarchy was not considered anymore as a universal stage of human history. Attention was paid to the complex and complicated process of adaptation to natural conditions, which led to different types of social organization and subsistence (Reshetov 1972). The concept of 'group marriage' was criticized as well. Thus, the ethnographers in the second part of the twentieth century, understanding the crisis in theory of 'primitive' society, tried to use different approaches, which were close to neo-evolutionism, cultural ecology and functionalism.

Some Siberian ethnographers, although they were not encouraged to do so, tried to make theoretical speculations based on their own field ethnographical data. These attempts were officially thwarted, as they sometimes led to new theoretical approaches which were far from the official dogmatic approach. Thus, the scientific researcher from the Leningrad branch of the Institute of Ethnography of the Academy of Sciences of the USSR, Andrey A. Popov, wrote an article about traditional beliefs of the Dolgan people (Popov 1958). [4] Popov's materials contradicted the official Soviet concept of the origin of religion. He considered using the term 'supernatural' with regard to the 'primitive' worldview as a mistake. He did not consider the 'primitive' worldview as religious and idealistic, and so suggested a psychoanalytic approach for considering archaic beliefs from the point of view of the psychology of the perception.[5] To some extent his theoretical position was close to Durkheim and Lévy-Bruhl. Popov had been heavily criticized for the 'implementation of subjective psychology-analytic method' instead of the 'objective' Marxist method of analysis (Shakhnovich 1958: 76). Soon after this studies of archaic beliefs and perception of the world were suspended for years. Scholars restricted themselves to the description of particular phenomenon and did not analyse them from new methodological positions (Gracheva 1993).

The third period in the history of Soviet ethnography (late 1940s to the early 1960s) was characterized by an expansion in the collection of field data. New theories of economic/cultural types and historic/ethnographic regions had been developed. At the same time the study of ethnogenesis and ethnic history were priorities on the agenda (Vainshtein and Kryukov 1988: 114–24). The historical approach to research did not emerge from nowhere. Even before the Revolution scientists had demonstrated heightened interest in the simultaneous study of ethnography, archaeology and physical anthropology as well as archived data. The interdisciplinary nature of this research, together with the historical approach, became predominant in Soviet Siberian studies. That led to the dominance of the theme of ethnogenesis and the ethnic history of different ethnicities. Another approach – a geographical one – used to be traditional for Russian ethnography. In Soviet times this was based in many respects on the works of the proponents of the theory of cultural circles and diffusionism. Levin and Cheboksarov (1955) created the theory of economic-and-cultural types and of historical-and-ethnographic regions based on the dependence of economy and culture on geographical conditions. In particular, Siberian materials became the basis for developing the theory of economic-and-cultural types. Predecessors of Levin's and Cheboksarov's theory were papers by N.N. Koz'min, P.F. Preobrazhenskiy and B.F. Adler.

In the framework of the historical approach outlined here, the theory that ethnic groups and ethnicities should be the major object for ethnographic studies was elabourated by Yu.V. Bromley (Bromley 1983) and the Institute of Ethnography (Moscow Section) and became predominant in Soviet ethnography in the 1960s to the 1980s (fourth period). Ethnicity was viewed as a historically established category possessing certain characteristics. The first attempts to develop the theory of ethnicity were made in the 1920s by N.M. Mogilyanskiy and S.M. Shirokogorov who, in particular, had been using Siberian materials in their work (Mogilyanskiy 1916; Shirokogorov 1922). Neither the culture nor the society but the people, or ethnic group, became the key object of ethnographic studies. The gradual narrowing of research objectives in domestic ethnology began, together with reducing it to the study of types of ethnic communities and of the ethnic specificities of sociocultural phenomena. The concept of ethnic self-consciousness was created in the framework of the ethnicity theory. It was assumed that self-consciousness, arising on the different ethnic criteria, is quite independent and self-sufficient.

At the end of the Soviet period L.N. Gumilev developed a theory of environmental determinism, the theory of 'passionarity' which means the fluctuating oscillation between periods of dynamic activity and periods of stagnation of ethnic group. He emphasized the biological nature of ethnicity. (Gumilev 1989) Followers of his theory of passionarity are especially proactive in St Petersburg. In Soviet times, studies of language and of folklore were continued, and are especially pertinent to communities of hunters-gatherers. At this point, not only scientific but also practical objectives were set for the academics, namely to create the writing and literature in the languages of those peoples.

## Topics

Within the framework of the historical approach, an important dimension was the study of ethnogenesis and ethnic history – the origin of the peoples, sometimes from the most ancient times, using archaeological, anthropological, linguistic and archived data (Tokarev 1949; Levin 1958). Special interest in the problem of ethnogenesis could be explained not only by Marxism's historical tradition, but also by the specifics of the Siberian field, where on one and the same territory scholars could find archaeological artefacts from different historical periods. The question of ethnogenesis is natural for Siberian (including hunter-gatherer) studies also because of the existence of ancient written Chinese texts. Essentially, archaeology, ethnography and physical anthropology became differentiated from one another approximately in the middle of the twentieth century. The main role in ethnogenesis studies was played by ethnographic sources, namely historical legends, the clan composition and the elements of material and spiritual culture. The themes mentioned above were developed independently as well.

Studies of so-called 'traditional' culture had a major role. They were of importance in view of fundamental changes in family life and domestic patterns of the peoples of the USSR, especially in Siberia, in view of the rapid disappearance of the old way of life. Traditional economy, material and spiritual culture were studied. This effort resulted in the composition of historical-and-ethnographic atlases (Levin and Potapov 1961) as well as summarizing papers about practically all peoples of the North, in the form of historical-and-ethnographic monographs (1950s to 1970s) (Alekseenko 1967; Vasilevich 1969; Menovshchikov 1959; Smolyak 1966; Lar'kin 1958; Kreynovich 1973; Lyapunova 1975). Usually, the time-frame covered was the period of the late nineteenth to the early twentieth centuries. These monographs were organized in line with a general and common pattern: ethnogenesis and ethnic history, social organization, economy, material and spiritual culture. Summarizing the results of studies in the form of a monographic description helped subsequently in developing individual problems of the ethnography of those peoples.

One of the best examples of hunter-gatherer studies in the second part of twentieth century was Yurii B. Simchenko's monograph entitled 'The culture of deer hunters of Northern Eurasia. Ethnographical reconstruction' (Simchenko 1976). There he analysed a great deal of archeological, ethnographic, physical anthropological and linguistic materials, including his own field data, and reconstructed the genesis and culture of the first inhabitants of this polar region before the spread of domestic reindeer-herding. The book is full of new ideas and hypotheses. His conclusion about interconnection between the people of the Ural language family and eastern-Siberian Yukagir cultural elements became the core of the current concept of mutual kinship of some peoples of the Russian North. He reconstructed the subsistence cycle of tundra hunters using the concepts of ecology.

During this period the collections of articles on uniform themes (ethnogenesis and ethnic history, family rituals, social structure, problems of social consciousness, shamanism, etc.) were published. Of paramount importance in studies of Soviet researches were the religious beliefs of the peoples of the north, especially of Siberian shamanism and its specific features. Theoretical papers had been written using the Marxist approach, where religion was considered as a way of struggle for existence, as a fantastic reflection in the human mind of the elements of the objective world. Taylor's animism theory, while moderated, laid the basis for studying the world-view of hunters, gatherers and fishermen.

Scholars were interested in the question of the origin and of the phenomenon of Siberian shamanism, the correlation between shamanism and different 'primitive' beliefs and rituals. There are brilliant papers and monographs in this field written by Soviet scholars (Vdovin 1976; 1981; Gracheva 1984; Smolyak 1991). Shamanism was regarded as quite a late phenomenon in Siberia, which existed primarily in the southern part of Asia. Studying Siberian hunter-gatherer societies, researchers came to the conclusion that different beliefs and practices, such as the hunter's magic rituals, elements of totemism, the cult of fire, and the cult of deceased ancestors had ceased before the spread of shamanism. Assuming the universal character of the human mode of thinking, some scholars did not deny the role of pathological elements in spiritual creations. Another dimension of research dealt with folklore and language studies. It was in Soviet times that dictionaries were compiled and huge amounts of folkloric materials recorded. Since 1970, many research workers dealing with language and the folklore studies have been representing hunter-gatherers by themselves.

## Organizations and Institutions

In the Soviet period, popular theory was of a convergence of all nations and nationalities within one united state; and the notion of elimination of ethnic features of a culture was a popular view. Ethnographers studied those things that sooner or later (it was the official point of view) inevitably had to die. Hence they were lacking in prospects. In the Soviet Union ethnographers studying hunter-gatherer societies were very scarce, numbering not more than two or three dozen. In Soviet times, a monopolism of approaches and monopolism of researchers shaped out in ethnography. In the 1960 and 1970s the researchers worked essentially alone in dealing with the ethnography and archeology of hunter-gatherers and of fishermen. That situation did not contribute to the development of scientific contacts and of scientific exchange. The situation has now changed with the internationalization of Siberian studies.

Research has been carried out in the Siberia Studies Department at the Moscow Institute of Ethnography and at its Leningrad branch, which has been operating independently since 1992. The Moscow section was called the Department for Studying Socialist Construction amongst the Peoples of Siberia and the Extreme North, while in Leningrad the main focus was on museum-management studies and studies of socialist construction of so-called 'traditional culture'. Later on, ethnographers studied the impact of process of socialist construction, and the formation of current cultural traditions. A special department at the Council of Ministers of the RSFSR on the problems of development of the North supervised a sector at the Moscow Institute of Ethnography. Following expeditions, researchers wrote field reports where they provided the materials that were not presented in scientific articles describing the real situation and the status of the peoples of the North. Having received the necessary information, the Government took concrete steps.

The study of hunter-gatherer societies was conducted also in Siberia within universities, museums and academic institutes. There were different approaches in the different centres dating back to the pre-revolutionary or early Soviet periods. Tomsk, one of the oldest Siberian cities, had a tradition of linguistic and ethnographic studies; in Irkutsk and some other Siberian cities the study of archaeology and anthropology was combined with ethnographic themes and the main focus of attention was the problems of ethnogenesis and material culture. Researchers in Novosibirsk studied both archaeology and contemporary problems of the numerically small peoples of the North, including their integrity in the modern Soviet society. Besides this invisible but important circles of non-formal scholarly social intercourse also existed.

## Methods and Ethics

Continuity between pre-revolutionary and Soviet ethnography lay in the tradition of long-term fieldwork among the people being studied. This tradition comes from Russian Orthodox missionaries, some of whom used to collect ethnographic materials and studied languages (I. Veniaminov 1984; 1993; Anderson and Orekhova 2002). People convicted of political crimes in the late nineteenth and early twentieth centuries, who became the ethnographers in their Siberian exile, were the other source of the tradition. The practical need to create language models, together with these traditions of pre-revolutionary Russian ethnography, also forced researchers to spend not less than two years 'in the field'. The most vivid example of that would be A.A. Popov who in 1936 to 1938 worked in the tundra among the *Nganasans*. During that time he walked over 8,000 kilometres with them, learned the *Nganasan* language and also knew the *Yakut* language. He amassed a museum collection of 500 items and 800 photos, made drawings of working industries, recorded the folklore and used it all as the basis for the unique papers that he wrote (Popov 1966; 1984). Most Soviet ethnographers working during the first post-revolutionary years combined research activities with work at Soviet bodies or at boarding schools. It was an impulse of romanticism in ethnographic studies that was influenced by the spirit of the official period of 'great construction sites' as well as the romanticism of the first phase in the development of Soviet society.

In the post-war years, the methodology of long-term participatory observation (residence) gave way to comprehensive intensive expeditions where each member worked according to a certain programme. Later on, short-term group or individual trips were introduced. The generation of Siberia researchers of the 1950s to the 1970s spent from between six or eight weeks and six months working in the field for up to thirty years or more. Pursuing their studies every year over many years enabled them to observe the dynamics of the phenomenon concerned.

Evgeniya A. Alekseenko, who has been studying the *Ket* people (Western-Siberian hunters) since the early 1950s, shared with me her experience in the methods of her fieldwork.

> There was this man, Egor Sutlin, whom we met during our fieldwork. He used to hunt with his son for musk-rat on the river. He was about 50. He was a man, with whom later on I worked on shamanism. One obtained the experience of fieldwork not only from literature, but directly from field experience.
>
> I asked him from the very beginning not about his notions of spirits, for instance, but about more ordinary things: I asked him how did he make the wooden frame for the shaman's drum. He started to tell me all the details of this process. And later he said: actually, the size of the wooden frame depends on the drum, whether it (the drum) is the first, second or third one. From the Anuchin's articles[6] I knew there were several drums, perhaps up to seven. The seventh drum was only for the big shaman. But Egor told me that all the drums were regarded as one and the same drum. Once every three year the status of the shaman was changed/arisen and the shaman did the ritual of animation of the new drum. The new drum had been made larger, but it was still perceived as the first drum that had grown.
>
> All the drum's design, all the pendants, all the cross-beams on the drums were added in a special system, in a special order, manner, number. . .The topography of the drum, all the materials depended on the status of the shaman. I felt it. I was struck by it. When I felt it, it was the moment of the truth. I said to him: Egor, would you please stop for a while. I came out on the front steps. I wanted to stand on my head. Later on I didn't ask strange questions, I did know what should I asked. Further I checked the information among the other informants, in different places. When it was confirmed, it was splendid. In some sense it was self-education, as among the shamans.[7]

In contrast to this method of Alekseenko's, with the shortening of the usual fieldwork period the methods of observation were reduced, and various forms of questioning including massive use of questionnaires increased. All that could not but effect the formation of research outcomes.

Soviet Siberian ethnography was characterized by its social missionarism, servicing the practical interests of the State. The new power needed to know its population numbers, for instance, in order to perform social changes. As long as the peoples of the North were considered backward in Soviet times the objective was to restructure their life and family patterns, to introduce new forms of economic activities, to give them access to Russian and, more broadly, to European culture. This effort engaged the practical participation of ethnographers who collabourated with the Committee of the North (from 1924 to 1935), who worked at the Institute of Languages of the Peoples of the North, who created written languages for many peoples of the North and who taught at national schools.

There are no officially implemented ethical rules for studying hunter-gatherer societies. Nevertheless, the tradition of Russian humanism in research, particularly in Siberia, still exists. It had been connected, however, with the idealization and romanticization of those peoples, their social structure, traditions of sharing and others features of their life. I will give just two vivid examples. Well-known Russian ethnographer Lev Ya. Shternberg used to work with the hunters and fishers of the Russian Far East at the end of the nineteenth to the beginning of the twentieth centuries. Later he became the tutor of the new generation of Soviet ethnographers in Leningrad. His students, who worked in the same places, remembered:

> Lev Yakovlevich did not stop at relating to the *Negidal* people as equal to equal, he also told them, as it is turned out, that all the peoples are equal, and the time will come when nobody will exploit them. He also tried to awake their national self-consciousness, or, as they say, 'asked them to take care of their old law.[8]

Vladimir K. Arsen'ev was a well-known explorer, writer, traveller and ethnographer of the Russian Far East of the first quarter of the twentieth century. He considered the *Udege* people, the Ussuri deep forest hunters, with whom he spent many months in the taiga, as his best friends. Having experienced the horrible years of the Civil War, and the early stage of the Soviet regime, he wrote in one of his letters:

> ... if I were alone, I would have gone to the far mountains, far from the city, with its crowds, trickery, lies, envy, and malice, which have now soaked into us, like water saturating a sponge in the sea. Three or four families of aborigines would go with me. We would have been gone to such jungles, where nobody except us could penetrate, and nobody would ever find us. (Luganskii 1997: 323)

Scholars not only studied the peoples, but also tried to help them to get health assistance and education. They also encouraged and helped them in studying their own culture and language, and a new generation of the indigenous linguists and ethnographers was created.

## Conclusions

The Soviet tradition of studying hunter-gatherer societies was in many ways built on the pre-revolutionary approach. In Soviet times, the secondary nature of theoretical approaches in ethnography persisted although the theory of ethnicity was elaborated and the historical approach to research was developing. The evolution of ethnography took place within the framework of history rather than philosophy as in the West. Marxism-Leninism in ethnography mostly consisted of vulgar Marxism containing some elements of evolutionism. Many researchers studying

Siberia only paid verbal tribute to it; they were pure empiricists, preferring not to theorize but to collect concrete ethnographic data.

Taking an empirical look at the whole period of development of Siberian research in Soviet times, one cannot but be amazed by the vast areas studied and by the tremendous amount of materials collected. The Soviet period, in comparison with the pre-revolutionary period, was beyond any doubt a step forward in accumulating ethnographic data, and not infrequently without any pressure from Marxist or any other theoretical directives. The basis for Siberian studies was laid down by Russian ethnography including the tremendous contribution of Soviet ethnography. An urgent objective currently is to bring theoretical and interpretive analysis to this material and to integrate it with world hunter-gatherer debates.

## Acknowledgements

The paper was prepared with the aid of research grant from the Jubilee Fund of the Sweden Bank in the framework of the project 'Post-Soviet Political and Socio-economic Transformation among the Indigenous Peoples of Northern Russia: Current Administrative Policies, Legal Rights, and Applied Strategies'.

I would like to express gratitude to Professor Alan Barnard and Professor Tim Ingold for enabling me to attend the conference. The Russian Fund for Fundamental Researches sponsored my travel expenses. My special thanks to Dr Deborah Bird Rose (ANU) and Dr Patrick John Sullivan (AIATSIS) for their attentive and productive editorial work.

## Notes

1. The population of Russia in pre-Revolutionary times was divided into estates (*soslovie*) in accordance with the professional association of certain groups of people. There were no strict boundaries between them, it was possible to cross from one estate to another. After the October revolution all the estates were abolished and every member of the population officially became citizens with the equal rights.
2. V. Aptekar had a leading role in that meeting.
3. The exception is Vladimir R. Kabo's trip to Sakhalin island and his studying of the social structure of the Nivkh people (Kabo 1981).
4. *Dolgan* people are hunters for wild deer and white fox and they also conduct reindeer-herding. They live in Siberia, in the tundra north of the Krasnoyarsk region and in the north-west of Sakha (Yakutiya) Republic.
5. Although the name of the method retained Freud's concepts, it had nothing else in common with it.
6. V.I. Anuchin was an ethnographer who in the years 1920 to 1930 worked with

the peoples of the southern part of Western Siberia. He published some interesting papers.
7. Author's personal archive, 2002.
8. State Archive of St. Petersburg branch of the Russian Academy of Sciences,
   282/1/110:79.

# 9

# The Japanese Tradition in Central African Hunter-Gatherer Studies, with Comparative Observations on the French and American Traditions

## *Mitsuo Ichikawa*

### Early Research on the 'Pygmies'

The central African hunter-gatherers (generally called 'Pygmies') live mostly in rainforest zones of the Congo Basin, in such countries as the Democratic Republic of Congo (DRC, formerly Zaire), Congo-Brazzaville and Cameroon. They also inhabit forest margins and montane forests, but are not found in savannahs or wood-land. When some years ago I investigated the distribution of Efe Pygmies in the north-eastern part of the Congo Basin, the Efe were found only in forest patches, even in the areas with a mosaic vegetation of forests and grassland. Given their low body height and other physical characters adaptive to forest life, coupled with their life highly dependent on forests, the Pygmies may well be called 'Forest People'.

The people generically referred to as the 'Pygmies' in the Western world have different local names. They are called 'Baka' in south-eastern Cameroon, 'Aka' in Central African Republic and the northern part of Congo-Brazzaville, 'Mbuti' and 'Efe' in the north-eastern part of the DRC, and 'Sua' in western Uganda. These groups with different local names use different languages. The Baka in the west use the Ubangian language of the Adamawa Eastern group; the Aka, Mbuti and Sua speak different languages of a Bantu group; and the Efe are Sudanic speakers. Based on these differences, some have argued that these groups should be called only by their local names instead of bundling them all together under the name 'Pygmies'. But in this paper, I use 'Pygmies' in some cases as the generic term to refer to all these groups, because there are many non-linguistic cultural elements held in common. I believe that these similarities are of greater importance than the differences among the languages they speak.

Despite the fact that some of them live as far as 2,000 km apart in the Congo Basin, they not only share a similar forest environment, but other cultural similarities as well: the hunter-gatherer way of life, rituals in which the spirits of the forest play an important role, dances and songs performed at such rituals, and a close but somewhat dependent relationship with neighbouring agricultural peoples. Musical performances, in particular, show their distinctive identity. When I arranged for a group of Pygmies to listen to a chorus sung by another group of a distant region, the listeners immediately recognized the singers as their fellow people.

In the ancient dynasties of Egypt, it was already known that people with very low height lived in forest areas in the upper reaches of the Nile. It was Georg Schweinfurth (1873), a German explorer and natural historian, who introduced them to the modern world. When Schweinfurth was exploring in the southern part of Sudan, he encountered a group of low-height people, called 'Bakke-Bakke' by the Monbutto (nowadays known as the Mangbetu). He found that they called themselves 'Akka', that they had close ties with the Monbutto village where they obtained farm products, and that they came from the forests in the south where many more of their people lived. Taking the body measurements of some of these people, Schweinfurth concluded that they were in fact the 'Pygmies', the mysterious people he had been looking for. Being a natural historian in the era of imperialism, Schweinfurth tried to take an Akka man back to Germany. This man subsequently travelled through northern Africa with Schweinfurth for a year and a half, but in the end, he died of illness in Berber Land in northern Africa.

Georg Schweinfurth's 'rediscovery' of the Pygmies in the upper reaches of the Nile marked the start of anthropological investigations into the Pygmies' life. Father Paul Schebesta, an Austrian, conducted an extensive survey of the Pygmies in the Ituri Forest in the north-eastern part of the Congo Basin in the 1920s. He found different Pygmy groups called the Efe, Basua (now called the Mbuti) and Aka, and also conducted surveys on the physical characters, languages, social organization and religion of these respective groups. Schebesta's research, having been influenced by the Viennese School of ethnology, placed particularly strong emphasis on religion and languages. The results of his work were put together in his voluminous monograph (Schebesta 1938–50), published 20 to 30 years later.

Schebesta did not stay long at a Pygmy's forest camp, but instead stayed in a nearby agriculturalists' village and invited them there to obtain information, which was still common research practice in those days. This method was subjected to mounting criticism, particularly after the practice of participant observation gained wider acceptance in anthropological research. Especially in the case of the Pygmies, the old-fashioned methods of investigation contained a fatal flaw. The Pygmies' attitude varied according to whether or not the interview was made in a village. Colin Turnbull, a British anthropologist, indicated the problems inherent in the research by Schebesta, and launched a new investigation in the 1950s.

Turnbull rejected Schebesta's views concerning social organization and ritual systems among the Mbuti, and pointed out that these were not essentially Mbuti characteristics, but had been borrowed by them from neighbouring agricultural peoples. The Mbuti, argued Turnbull when describing their social organization and ritual system, were really trying to pay compliments to the agricultural people when they were interviewed in a village. Back in the forest, without agricultural people present, they returned to their original way of life. In the forest, Turnbull argued, the Mbuti were not subject to the clan system that was derived from the agricultural people, but frequently changed the groups to which they belonged, through a process of 'fission and fusion'. Moreover they put performances of dancing and singing, considered to be a form of talking to the forest, at the core of their religious life, in total disregard of formalized rituals. Turnbull underscored these points about the Mbuti in *Forest People* (1961) and *Wayward Servants* (1965).

However, Turnbull, who so vividly described the human aspects of the Mbuti and who gave unstinting praise to their life in the forest, hardly showed concern with the forest itself. He emphasized that the Mbuti can obtain everything they need to support their livelihood from the forest, but offered little explanation as to the nature of the things they needed and how they obtained them from the forest. The same can be said about Schebesta. Their books were mainly devoted to descriptions of the languages, religion and social life of the Pygmies, and made little mention of their everyday material life. In particular, the ecological relationships of the Pygmies with the forest environment were virtually ignored.

## Research by Japanese: The Ituri Forest Survey

Japanese research on the Pygmies started in the early 1970s. Shortly after the end of the civil war in Congo, known as the Simba rebellion, Junichiro Itani and Reizo Harako from Kyoto University embarked on their research on the Mbuti Pygmies. Itani was already internationally known as a primatologist for his studies of Japanese monkeys (*Macaca fuscata*) and chimpanzees. Harako studied anthropology at Tokyo University after working as a surgeon and ship's doctor, and joined Kyoto University in 1970. Both of them had studied natural science, and both belonged to the anthropology laboratory of the university's Faculty of Science. Their backgrounds thus largely influenced the initial phase of Japanese research on the Pygmies. From the start, our interest focused on ecology; in other words, the relationship between people and the forest. Today, environmental problems are in the spotlight, and much more attention is being paid to the traditional and sustainable ways of forest resource use. Back then, however, when we began our work, few anthropologists other than us cared about the ecological aspects of research on the Mbuti Pygmies.

After a preliminary survey conducted with Itani, Harako selected a village in the central part of Ituri as his study site, located in the border zone between the net hunters and the archers. Harako conducted comparative studies on the net hunters and archers for a year. Just before Harako retuned to Japan in 1973, Tadashi Tanno arrived from Kyoto to take over, and he then moved the research site to another village, deeper in the Ituri Forest, to continue with more detailed work on the net hunters. The papers written in English by Harako (1976) and Tanno (1976) were actually the first detailed reports describing the subsistence activities of the Mbuti, particularly their hunting methods, the animals hunted and their hunting efficiency. These reports were received with high acclaim, particularly among the anthropological community of the United States, where there was a growing interest in hunter-gatherer subsistence activities. After Tanno, I took over the research activities in the Ituri Forest (Ichikawa 1978).

The objective of our research was to find clues concerning the evolution of human society by studying the life of existing hunter-gatherers who depend heavily on nature. The behaviour patterns and societies of early human beings have not been left behind in the form of fossils. In order to understand them, we need to gain some clues from the life of existing hunter-gatherers as well as from the contemporary primates proximate to humankind. As a result, the initial phase of research on the Pygmies focused on such matters as subsistence activities, dietary life, food sharing and social organization of hunter-gatherers who had adapted to the rainforest environment, and the research results were examined for their implications for our understanding of human evolution.

Investigating present-day hunter-gatherer societies in this way, with the purpose of reconstructing the evolutionary history of humankind, sometimes becomes a target of criticism in that the approach allegedly distorts the image of contemporary hunter-gatherers. Certainly, hunter-gatherers of the present day are not 'survivors from the Stone Age' or anything of that kind, but are indeed our contemporaries and as such are susceptible to the modern world in varied ways. When the existing way of hunter-gatherer life is studied in the context of human evolution, researchers simply use various fragments of modern hunter-gatherer cultures as clues to the way of life of early humankind. They have no intention of attempting an exhaustive depiction of the present-day life of hunter-gatherers. Various elements of the present hunting-and-gathering life are intentionally severed by the anthropologist from their cultural and social context (decontextualization) and then used to reconstruct the path of human evolution. As long as researchers pursue this method of study while fully conscious of what they are doing, we can safely argue that criticism that it distorts the real image of the hunter-gatherer society is wide of the mark.

At the same time, however, we intended our research to be significant in itself, and not just work aimed at reconstructing the early history of humankind. As ecological anthropologists, we explicitly aimed at the detailed description and analysis of such matters as the correlation between the natural environment and subsistence activities, material culture, the exchange economy, dietary life and the utilization of plants. The descriptions by Harako of children's play (1980) and religious life (1984), the ethnobotanical research by Tanno (1981), and the study of food avoidance by Ichikawa (1987) were all done out of the desire to understand the life and culture of the Mbuti, and not particularly for the reconstruction of human evolution.

## Expansion of Research Areas and Research Interests

In 1978, Hideaki Terashima (1983) embarked on a survey on the Efe Pygmies who live in the north of the Ituri Forest, and Masato Sawada joined the Efe project in 1985. The scope of the research came to cover such topics as the relationships with agricultural peoples (Terashima 1986) and contemporary social changes (Ichikawa 1991), in addition to subsistence activities, ethnobotany and social organization. Sawada (1990) in particular became deeply involved in studies of the Efe's performances of dancing and singing and their religious backgrounds. Pygmy songs are polyphonic, with multiple rhythms and melodies proceeding simultaneously with very few accompanying lyrics. It is a music that can be described as an 'orchestra of human voices'. All of us were deeply moved by their performances of polyphony. But it was a different matter whether we should make polyphony a subject of our research. For one thing, we were somewhat at a loss about how to conduct research into such things as songs and dances. For another, our belonging to the Faculty of Science became something of an implicit barrier. Yet, younger-generation researchers like Tsuru (2001) and Bundo (2001) are already developing new types of research into the Pygmy musical performances. For analysing how the Pygmies participate in the performances and reach the climax, they use methods that they have devized themselves, while partially adopting the methodology of behavioural observation used in primatology.

Such Japanese research activities may be characterized by a kind of fearlessness. To put it another way, we were trying to enjoy anthropology as a young and 'soft' science. Partly because of the short history of anthropology in Japan, Japanese research is often given to following and confirming, through fieldwork, the hypotheses and theories advanced by Western researchers. In the midst of a prevailing fashion such as this, we wanted to try something new on the basis of first-hand data that we had gathered in the field, braving the comments of our authoritarian peers that our research could hardly be called 'professional anthropologist's work'. It was as though we had been drawn by the attractiveness of research that has something in common with a handicraft item made at a small factory in downtown Osaka, or a product devized for a 'niche market' of goods that no one else may think of.

From the latter half of the 1980s, we extended our research into areas other than the Ituri Forest. In 1987, Tanno studied the Aka Pygmies in areas along the Ubangi River in the western part of the Congo Basin. Tanno's research was later taken over by Kiyoshi Takeuchi (1994; 1995) and Koichi Kitanishi (1995; 1998), who developed the detailed quantitative studies on the Aka Pygmies' subsistence activities, diet, food sharing and food restrictions, in the Région de Likouala of Congo-Brazzaville. Around the same time as Tanno began his research in the mid-1980s, Hiroaki Sato (1992) started the research on the sedentarized Baka Pygmies in northern Congo. But we were forced to suspend research activities in both countries with the deterioration of political conditions around the mid-1990s. As an alternative, we began research on the Baka Pygmies in the forest zone in Cameroon, on the western tip of the Congo Basin. This has been carried forward to the research now being undertaken by a younger generation.

As described briefly above, studies on the Pygmies by Japanese researchers began with the Mbuti in the Ituri Forest and have now been extended to cover other groups such as the Efe, Aka and Baka. It means that all the major Pygmy groups in Africa have been studied by Japanese researchers during the last thirty years, involving more than twenty researchers and graduate students. The scope of research has also been expanded significantly during this period, embracing research on a diversity of topics such as ritual performances studied by Tsuru (1998; 2001) and Bundo (2001), interactive behaviour including conversation and non-verbal communication investigated by Daiji Kimura (2001) and socialization process studied by Nobutaka Kamei (2002). Most of the research was based on detailed behavioural observations and quantitative data, adopting research approaches different from the methods used by conventional Western anthropologists. If we add to the above some other ongoing studies on infant care (Hirasawa 2002), and research into the relationship with a nature conservation project (see Ichikawa 2002), our activities cover a broad array of subjects. More than ten researchers, including some graduate students, have already participated in the Baka research project that began several years ago in Cameroon.

## Research by French Scholars

As France established colonies in Africa's rainforest region where the Pygmy people live, it has a long history of research on the Pygmies, and has accumulated a vast amount of research data and documents. French research on the Pygmies displays three noticeable characteristics: a unique method of ethnomusicological research, a naturalistic interest in the forest fauna and flora, and precise linguistic description. On the strength of these research activities and because of the historical background, France has produced many internationally distinguished researchers on the Pygmies. In particular, the research project on the Aka Pygmies in Central African Republic, launched by Arom Simha, Jacqueline Thomas, Serge Bahuchet and others in the early 1970s, can be counted as one of the most remarkable ethnographic studies of the twentieth century, for the far-reaching scope of the research, its high quality and the depth and breadth of its impact.

The research on polyphony of the Aka Pygmies by Arom (1991) and the publication of the music via compact discs (1987) and other musical media helped Pygmy music to become famous throughout the world. Being a classical horn player, Arom became entranced by the Aka music when he visited the Central African Republic in the latter half of the 1960s to teach a military band there. By employing his specialist knowledge of music, and by making use of rich sound archives, Arom showed that Aka music consists of a very deep polyphony of multiple rhythms and melodies that draw on all kinds of human voices, handclaps, drums, clappers and occasionally such household utensils as pans and machetes. Also, using the 'playback method' in which Aka players, while listening to the base melody (called 'the mother of the song'), add new parts to it sequentially, Arom shed light on the actual composition of the Aka polyphony. His work takes an approach different from that of British-style social anthropology, which primarily tries to link such performances to their ritual and social meanings. Arom's method of research clearly demonstrates the tradition of French ethnography, a tradition that places emphasis on the detailed description of cultural phenomena based on their inherent characteristics. Arom Simha's research was followed by Susanne Fürniss, Emannuelle Olivier (1999) and others who undertook comparative research of the Aka with other hunter-gatherer and agricultural groups. In addition to musicological analysis based on the playback method, these researchers are also beginning to pay attention to musical syncretism and the social and historical backgrounds that have stimulated the syncretism.

French ethnology is renowned for its theoretical constructs, as represented by the work of Lévi-Strauss. But French ethnology also has a long tradition of 'description' dating from the days of the Encyclopédistes. The traits of this tradition of 'encyclopedic description' can be discerned in French research on the Aka Pygmies. A remarkable example of this is the Aka ethnography by Serge Bahuchet (1985), which describes in detail the material and technical relationships between the Aka and the forest, a subject ignored by Turnbull. Researchers studying the Aka, or the Baka living nearby, carry Bahuchet's ethnography to the field and check what they see or hear against his book, or find points of difference between what they observe and what Bahuchet wrote. Bahuchet's Aka ethnography has itself become a kind of encyclopedia, reference to which is frequently made by researchers in these areas. A museum boy who frequented museums since his mid-teen years, Bahuchet combined his strong interest in natural history, obtained during those days, with the linguistics he learned from Jacqueline Thomas, particularly ethnolinguistics, and used this knowledge to conduct highly detailed descriptive research. He is not alone in this. Elizabeth Motte's research into plant medicine of the Aka (1980) and Edmond Dounias' ecological study of wild yam utilization (2001) also exhibit strong interests in natural history and ethnolinguistics.

French research on the Pygmies is notable for detailed and exhaustive descriptions, centring especially on folk categories. The summarization of these research activities is embodied in the *Encyclopédie des Pygmées Aka* (1981 onwards), which was compiled over a period of twenty years and is still being published. French researchers have also made available a wealth of information on the Aka Pygmy culture via the medium of CD, an enterprize appropriate to the multimedia era (Arom et al. 1998). Taken together, their research on the Pygmies fittingly reflects the cultural tradition of a country that produced intellectuals such as the Encyclopédistes. Alain Epelboin has been recording video images of the same Aka individuals over a quarter century since the late 1980s. His method of using video camcorder can be termed a new initiative in ethnographical research.

Japanese and French researchers share a strong interest in natural history and ethnography, but they have clear differences of approach as well. French researchers have combined their interest in natural history with the methodology of linguistic description, but their research still steadfastly adheres to investigation of the 'culture' of humankind. By contrast, Japanese researchers are drawn more to 'evolution', in which animals and humans are viewed in continuity (but not 'identical'). For this reason, Japanese research is oriented more than French research toward natural science.

## Research by North American Scholars

An interesting similarity exists between Japanese and American scholarship on African hunter-gatherers. In both countries, anthropological work on African hunter-gatherers has undergone a three-stage shift, from generation to generation, in the topics that have interested teachers and their students. The first generation is represented by Kinji Imanishi and Sherwood Washburn (Imanishi visited Washburn in California on the return journey from his first visit to Africa in 1958); the second generation by Junichiro Itani and Irvin DeVore who were trained by the first generation; and the third generation is represented on the Japanese side by Tanno, Ichikawa, Terashima and others taught by Itani, and on the American side by Robert Bailey and other students of DeVore. The first-generation researchers embarked on the studies of human evolution. The second-generation researchers focused on the ecology and society of non-human primate species, seeking for a clue to understanding the history of human evolution. The third-generation researchers approached the questions of human evolution on the basis of their research on modern hunter-gatherers. The third-generation researchers took up the leading role in the research on hunter-gatherers in central Africa, and then gradually extended their research activities into areas outside human evolution.

However, while Japanese research gradually moved closer to cultural anthropology, American research on the Pygmies, beginning in 1978 among the Efe in Ituri, has continued to focus on physical anthropology, using the methods of natural science, with only Grinker (1994) and a few others being the exception. Robert Bailey (1989), the leading figure in American research on the Efe, has written that their major topics of interest have been demography, nutrition, growth and the correlations among these factors. As such, the social and cultural aspects of life have attracted their attention only in relation to the above-mentioned topics. In addition to ecological studies by Bailey and others, a separate team of anthropologists carried out work on child development and infant care. In Central African Republic, Barry Hewlett (1991) conducted research on children of the Aka Pygmies and infant care. There are also ethnoarchaeological studies on the Efe in the Ituri Forest (Laden 1992). In most of these studies, the Americans adopted the methods used in primatology and animal ecology, such as focal individual sampling and spot observation, for the quantitative analysis of the behaviour patterns of the hunter-gatherers. Particularly noteworthy has been the attempt to evaluate the reproductive fitness of individuals' behaviour from a cost-benefit viewpoint. These research methods have been developed in evolutionary ecology or sociobiology targeted at animals (Winterhalder and Smith 1981; Bailey 1986). As is widely known, the cost-benefit discussion in evolutionary ecology is based on *homo economicus*, or 'rational' individuals in pursuit of self interest, the key idea underlying neo-classical economics (see also Barnard 2002a).

Pygmy studies by American researchers are similar to those by Japanese researchers in their concern with human evolution and the use of primatological research methods. But they are mainly oriented toward physical anthropology and rely more on natural scientific methods developed in animal ecology, such as evolutionary ecology and sociobiology. In other words, they are studying the behaviour of humankind using methods identical to those used for animals. This is where the American research stands in contrast to studies by Japanese researchers, whose studies also sprang from an interest in 'evolution', or the reconstitution of the continuity from animals to humankind. In the case of the Japanese, Pygmy studies gradually shifted towards topics relating to the inherent culture of mankind.

What brought the American research into the spotlight was perhaps the hypothesis advanced by them to the effect that 'it is impossible to sustain the hunter-gatherer life in rainforests', rather than their empirical research based on evolutionary ecology. The controversial discourse by Bailey and others (1989) argued that rainforests do not offer a stable year-round supply of energy-rich food, and went on to suggest that humankind did not inhabit rainforests before agriculture was introduced. They have also argued that no group of people that truly live entirely by hunting and gathering is found in rainforests, anywhere around the globe. Some French and Japanese researchers (Bahuchet, Mckey and de Garine 1991; Sato 2001) have deployed counter-arguments against the Americans. While the issue still remains inconclusive, recent archaeological research (Mercader et al. 2000) has discovered traces of human habitation dating back several thousand years in the forest-like environment of the Ituri region.

## Three Types of Ecology

Japanese research activities have taken a holistic approach, first focusing on the ecology and behaviour of hunter-gatherers and then considering correlations with other cultural and social aspects. They do not, however, subscribe to ecological determinism or sociobiological reductionism. In a nutshell, Japanese research can be described as research of 'ecology in a broad sense'. In what follows, I will explain some of the recent development this 'ecology in a broad sense' as a combination of the three types of ecology, namely cultural ecology, historical ecology and political ecology. By using these three types of ecology, what have we established and what are we trying to establish about the relationship between the nature of the central African forests and people who live in them?

The first question is how and to what extent the hunter-gatherers in central Africa depend on forests. By staying with them for a few days at a forest camp, we can understand how many aspects of their life are so closely connected with forests, from material aspects such as food and housing to rituals and other non-material aspects. Certainly, these forest people have a surprisingly rich store of knowledge about the animals and plants in the forests. But our knowledge about their rich forest culture is still very limited. Thus, the first question has to do with cultural ecology, that is, to describe their unique forest culture in detail and shed light on the relationship between their culture and the forest environment. As part of this interest, we have been involved with the 'Aflora' project (see http://130.54.103.36/aflora.nsf) since the latter half of the 1980s. This aimed at building a database of their knowledge about plants, an endeavour to document the intellectual legacy these people have accumulated through careful observation over centuries.

The second question involves historical ecology, studies on the history of interactions between humankind and the forest environment. Most of the forests we see now are the products of interactions between humankind and nature over a very long period of time. The forest people do not merely depend on the forest products; they contribute at the same time, by living in forests and utilizing resources found there, to sustaining the ecological system of forests in a variety of ways, such as improving light conditions within forests, spreading plant seeds, and concentrating soil nutrient elements by making piles of domestic waste (Ichikawa

1996; 2001). We therefore interpret the ecological system of an area as the system of interdependence between humans and nature with a long history of interactions between them. This way of thinking may open up the ground for a new approach to the conservation of nature. The conventional scheme of nature conservation is to build a sanctuary for shutting out human activities, as exemplified by the 'paradise of wildlife' scheme. If we can prove that the human impact on the forest environment has positive aspects, it will become feasible to establish protected zones that can accommodate some human activities.

The system of coexistence of humankind and forests no longer exists in complete isolation from the outside world. At present, in varying degrees, that system comes into contact with a broader world of a state or international economic and political systems. The third question, therefore, is pertinent to political ecology, or efforts to elucidate the relations between the microscopic aspects of the life of the forest people and the broader world, in particular the relations with macro-level political and economic systems. Since political and economic crises currently confront central African countries, these relations host a variety of problems. I have elsewhere (Ichikawa 1991) described a suggestive example of how the Mbuti Pygmies were maintaining a stable barter economy at a time when the former Zaire was mired in trouble, its national economy devastated by rampant inflation. The forest people are not just a group of vulnerable people buffeted by the raging waves of globalization, by forces such as the market economy, destruction of the environment and nature conservation movements. From now on, it will be necessary to understand how the forest peoples are coping with these forces and to identify the ways in which they can maintain their autonomy.

By means of the three types of ecology, we intend to place the way of life of the forest people in three kinds of context, in the natural environment, historical and political contexts. Only after we have undertaken research along these lines can we begin to comprehend the hunter-gatherers of central Africa in their entirety.

## Convergence of Interest – Integration of Rainforest Problems and Hunter-Gatherer Research

In respect of research on the hunter-gatherers in central Africa, the Japanese tradition occupies a unique position, forming a 'triangle' with the French and American traditions. Japanese researchers have followed the approach of 'ecology in a broad sense', conducting their research by adopting ecological methods to study the various aspects of the life and culture of the forest people. French researchers, for their part, have excelled in the ethnographic description of the forest people and to this end have employed to good effect their command of ethnomusicology, ethnolinguistics and natural history. American researchers have mainly pursued the natural scientific approach of presenting a hypothesis and then verifying it through research, relying on recent ecological theory such as sociobiology. However, research interests are beginning to converge in recent years, mainly as a result of the destruction of the rainforest, which is the forest people's living environment, and the conservation movement against such destruction.

The destruction of the rainforests has become one of the major global environmental problems of our times. In central Africa, deforestation has been accelerating at a tremendous rate since the early 1990s (Ichikawa 2002). At the same time, forest conservation programmes have also been introduced. Against this background, there is an urgent need to maintain the life and culture of the forest people, particularly the hunter-gatherers, who are caught in the crossfire between forest exploitation on the one hand, and attempts to protect the natural environment on the other. It has now been widely accepted that the forest conservation plans cannot succeed without taking into account the people living in the forest. Many ongoing conservation programmes begin to show an understanding of the cultural or social dimension of nature conservation, and try to recognize the importance of the life and culture of people who have long coexisted with the forests, emphasizing the need to get the forest people actively involved in conservation programmes. In these circumstances, researchers studying the hunter-gatherer people in central Africa are actively committed to research related to environmental problems.

The APFT (Avenir des Peuples en Forêts Tropicales) project, an EU program launched in 1995, emphasized the need to support coexistence between the forests and the people living in them. The project set up one of its research bases in Cameroon, central Africa, and its activities there are being led by Pygmy studies specialists such as Daou Joiris and Serge Bahuchet (1994). Meanwhile American anthropologists with experience of Pygmy research, such as David Wilkie (Wilkie and Carpenter 1999), known for the bushmeat research, and Bryan Curran (Curran and Tshombe 2001), who was also involved in a rainforest conservation project in Cameroon, are taking part in forest conservation programmes in central Africa being promoted by the Wildlife Conservation Society (USA). A similar situation is found in Japan. In the Eastern Province of Cameroon, young Japanese researchers are engaged in research that integrates forest conservation with anthropological studies of Baka society (Ichikawa 2002). Moreover in countries such as the United Kingdom, as is illustrated by the works of Justin Kenrick (2001; 2002) and Jerome Lewis (2001), many scholars are taking up research on themes that relate directly or indirectly to social and cultural aspects of forest conservation. In this way, Pygmy studies are bringing together research interests in the environmental problems of the tropical rainforests, and are exhibiting a hitherto unparalleled degree of research activity among dozens of anthropologists from various parts of the world.

# 10

# The Modern History of Japanese Studies on the San Hunter-Gatherers

## *Kazuyoshi Sugawara*

In Japan the discipline of anthropology originated more than 100 years ago: the first volume of the Japanese journal of physical anthropology was published in 1886.[1] However, it was almost half a century later, in 1934, that the formal society of cultural anthropology (the Japanese Society of Ethnology) was founded (Yamashita 1998). Soon after the the Second World War, the University of Tokyo became the prominent centre for Japanese cultural anthropology. In particular, Hitoshi Watanabe's (1968) study on the Ainu, former foragers in Hokkaido, was the most pioneering work of the new discipline that has been called 'ecological anthropology'. The studies based on intensive fieldwork among extant hunter-gatherers were initiated by the research focusing on the San in Botswana, Southern Africa. Succeeding researches, mainly organized by the scholars of Kyoto University, have continued for more than thirty-five years to the present. In this chapter I will review many articles arising from these enduring researches. This academic history will also mirror the modern history the San hunter-gatherers themselves have gone through.[2]

The most conspicuous characteristic of Japanese studies in anthropology in Africa is that they were pioneered by researchers from a primatological back-ground. Among others, Jun'ichiro Itani paved the way with ecological studies of hunter-gatherers, pastoralists and slash-and-burn cultivators in eastern and central Africa. Greatly influenced by this academic tradition, most studies on the San have been characterized by the following features, even though some of them cannot be lumped under the headline of 'ecological': (a) a positivistic method-ology based on direct observation of behaviour (including speech acts), (b) an interest in the relationship between people and their natural environment, and (c) the pursuit of a synthetic theory of the evolution of human society. On this point, the studies reviewed below may show a contrast with current trends in cultural anthropology that adopt a sceptical stance towards the evolutionary approach to human culture.

## Studies of Traditional Life of the G/wi and G//ana

The Japanese studies of the San were initiated by Jiro Tanaka. His host groups are the G/wi and G//ana, closely related dialect groups of the Khoe-speaking Bushmen peoples (Barnard 1992c). I will use an abbreviated notation, G/wi-G//ana, to refer to both dialect groups. Approximately 1,000 G/wi -//Gana were making a living by hunting and gathering in the Central Kalahari Game Reserve (CKGR) which was demarcated in 1961. Among them, the population living in the Xade Area, in the mid-western part of the CKGR, has been the focus of attention from Western and Japanese anthropologists. The modern history of the Xade area began in 1958 with the first anthropological survey by G.B. Silberbauer, who contributed to the establishment of the CKGR. The borehole at !Koi!kom drilled under his supervision became the centre of the settlement in the fifteen years that followed (Silberbauer 1981). Soon after Silberbauer left, Tanaka started his own research in December 1966.

### *Subsistence Ecology and Social Organization*

After his initial research for sixteen months from 1966 to 1968, Tanaka published a preliminary report (Tanaka 1969), and a book which was the first to introduce the San's self-sufficient hunting-and-gathering economy to Japanese readers (Tanaka 1971). He identified the lack of permanent bodies of water as the most striking feature of the habitat in the Central Kalahari. He also found that there was a division of labour by sex in their subsistence activity: hunting was monopolized by men and gathering was carried out mainly by women. Tanaka also showed that the G/wi-G//ana relied on a diet built around eleven major foods among about eighty species of edible plants. Meat was of secondary importance, making up only 20 per cent of the diet. By observing the allocation of time in daily activities by each member of a 'camp' (defined below), he found that the women used to go out to gather for between one and five hours almost every day, while the men used to go out to hunt between three to five days a week, for between five and twelve hours. Thus, he estimated the daily average work time per person to be 4 hours 39 minutes. Based on these results, Tanaka emphasized that the gathering and hunting economy was not at all precarious but was sustained by quite a stable and varied food resource base.

Another important contribution of Tanaka's book to the study of hunter-gatherers in general is that it showed the fluidity of their social organization. He found the residential group was composed of between one and twenty families (on average ten families including forty people) usually connected by bilaterally traced kinship or affinal relationships. As the main food plants changed during the year, people had to move from place to place in accordance with the distribution of these plants. Though some related families tended to form a relatively enduring cluster throughout the process of group fission and fusion, any clear-cut boundary between sociological entities or bands with exclusive membership was hard to recognize. In order to emphasize this point, Tanaka applied rather a neutral term, 'camp', to the residential group of the G/wi-G//ana.

## Comparative Perspectives

From 1971 to 1972 Tanaka carried out his second field study, as a participant in the so-called 'Harvard University Team', organized by R. B. Lee and I. DeVore. Integrating the results from this research with the findings mentioned above, he compared the subsistence ecology of the G/wi-G//ana with that of the Ju/'hoan (formerly called !Kung) in the Dobe Area, in the north-western part of Botswana (Tanaka 1976). Analysing the quality and nutrient composition of eleven main species of plant food, he concluded that the G/wi-G//ana subsistence was primarily based on the two species of *Cucumis* and *Coccinia* tubers, and secondarily on the seasonal concentration of two species of *Bauhinia* beans. He also pointed out that the Ju/'hoan could utilize the nutritious *mongongo* nuts (*Ricinodendron rautanenii*) as a primary food (Lee 1979a), while the G/wi-G//ana, lacking this species, showed a more varied pattern of diet than the Ju/'hoan. He argued that poorer dietary conditions and the lack of permanent water in the Central Kalahari resulted in migration over a much larger area, and that it took approximately twice as long to obtain food as in the Dobe area.

The comparative perspective was extended to other hunter-gatherers living in a contrasting environment. The habitat, material culture, mode of subsistence and structure of social units among the G/wi-G//ana were compared with those of the Mbuti Pygmies inhabiting the Ituri rainforest in former Zaire (Tanaka 1978). In relation to material culture, the most conspicuous difference was that the Mbuti used almost exclusively plant materials, but the G/wi-G//ana used about 50 per cent animal products. Focusing on the hunting methods, Tanaka contrasted the bow-and-arrow hunting of the San, usually carried out by a single man, with the net hunting of the Mbuti, which required close cooperation among male and female participants. Finally, Tanaka examined the correlation between the differences in hunting methods and the difference in the formation of social units: fluid open grouping among the G/wi-G//ana, and solid patrilineal groups among the Mbuti.

Most of the issues discussed above were integrated into Tanaka's principal monograph (Tanaka 1980). The most prominent contribution of this volume was that it presented concrete data on the processes of camp fission and fusion. Based on the analysis of these data, he attempted to compare the group structure of the

San with that of social carnivores and chimpanzees. Although this method of comparison is rather speculative, it explicitly incorporates the academic tradition in primatology. As another important consequence of regarding fluid grouping as the basis of G/wi-G//ana social organization, Tanaka rejected the concept of territoriality in discussing the spatial arrangements among residential groups. Several clusters of families formed in turn larger clusters, the core area of each of which were segregated from each other. But, due to the great fluctuation in ecological conditions, no cluster could be tied permanently to a fixed segment of land. Thus, periodic concentration in a particular site with abundant food, as well as constant interaction between camps, rendered the concept of territoriality meaningless.

## Egalitarian Society Undergoing Change

The primary interest that motivated Tanaka's studies was to clarify the way of life of humans who are thoroughly dependent on the 'blessing of nature'. Thus, while recognizing that 'the ancestors of the modern hunter-gatherers must certainly have undergone some social change themselves during the last 10,000 years', Tanaka confidently stated that 'there is no doubt that the ethnographic facts relating to the present-day hunter-gatherers hold many important keys for us as we try to reconstruct man's past history' (Tanaka 1980: 138).

In the last two decades the ecological/evolutionary paradigm that had characterized many articles of the San, including those by Tanaka, has been subjected to serious criticism by so-called 'revisionists' (Wilmsen 1983; Wilmsen and Denbow 1990). Tanaka and Sugawara (1996: 3) admitted that 'the previous studies of the ecological anthropology of the San ha[d] been biased to some degree, in that they ha[d] concentrated on the homeostatic mechanism of adaptation within a closed system, while having paid relatively little attention to either historic changes or their persistent contact with the outside.' Even before the start of the revisionism debate, Tanaka's interests had been moving towards ongoing socio-economic changes. Faced with the drastic changes which have affected the culture and society of the G/wi-G//ana of the Xade area since 1979 owing to the Remote Area Development Programme (RADP) of the Botswana Government, Tanaka has organized a number of research teams since 1982 in order to study these changes. He also published several articles that described the process of transformation (Tanaka 1987; 1991). The people formed a large community with a population of over 600 persons settled around the borehole at !Koi!kom. They became dependent on aid distributed by the government. A particularly crucial period was that of the provision of infrastructure in 1984, including a primary school, a medical clinic and a shop. The concentration of the population had resulted in various kinds of social conflicts, which were often exacerbated by alcohol.

*Changes in Hunting Method and Their Influence on 'Egalitarianism'*
The most important of the San's traditional hunting methods was the hunting of big antelopes with bows and poisoned arrows. After these species had been driven away from around the settlement, one-day hunting trips on foot became difficult (Tanaka 1987). Focusing on 'equestrian hunting' (hunting on horseback), Masakazu Osaki (1984) investigated its methods, activities and productivity, and its effects on social relationships in 1982–83. During the five months of his investigation, Osaki recorded ninety-one large animals killed by hunting, eighty-seven of which were killed with horse. The meat thus obtained was estimated at 22,800 kg, of which 88 per cent was obtained by group expeditions. Osaki found that the amount of meat per capita in 1982–83 was very similar to Tanaka's (1980) estimate of its amount obtained with bows and arrows in a camp of fifty people.

Kazunobu Ikeya paid special attention to the fact that hunting with dogs was actively carried out during the period of his investigation in 1987–8. Comparing the differences in the pattern of distribution of the meat produced using dogs and horses, Ikeya pointed out that most of the meat obtained by the latter method tended to go to the owner of the horse used in the hunting expedition. Interpreting these results that were originally published in a Japanese article in 1989, Osaki discussed the problem of to what extent the egalitarian system which had governed the traditional San social life had been influenced by sedentarism (Osaki 1990). He pointed out that the unequal sharing of the meat obtained from equestrian hunting had brought about a 'one-way flow of distribution', which had not existed in traditional San society. By contrast, the meat from hunting with dogs was distributed equally among the participants, who also shared it with non-participants within the same camp. Thus, Osaki regarded the sudden spread of hunting with dogs among sedentary groups as the manifestation of a persistent orientation towards egalitarianism that was deeply rooted in the psychology of the people.

However, in the English version of his original article, Ikeya (1994) criticized Osaki's interpretation. He emphasized two points as factors promoting hunting with dogs: (a) the rapid growth of the dog population after settlement; and (b) the increased demand for the hides of small-sized animals, which were used as materials for making handicrafts for sale. Ikeya (1994: 132) concluded that Osaki was 'mistaken in his interpretation' which stressed only the sociopsychological factors. Thus, Ikeya warned against the tendency of researchers to regard the concept of 'egalitarianism' as self-evident for the characterization of hunting-gathering society.

*Behavioural Analysis of the Gathering Activity*
Kaoru Imamura, a female anthropologist, investigated the gathering activity of women in 1990–1, about ten years after the commencement of sedentarism (Imamura 1996). Even in this period gathering was frequently carried out, espe-

cially because of the necessity of collecting firewood. Comparing her results with those of Tanaka (1980), Imamura pointed out that while the women used to gather within the range of five kilometres around the camp in their previous nomadic life, the distance to the gathering place had doubled to about ten kilometres. Accordingly the burden for one gathering trip had become greater and the time for gathering had increased from between one and five hours to between one and thirteen hours. Imamura identified sixteen species of plant food which were not included in Tanaka's (1980) list of eighty species of edible plants. Thus it was ascertained that the G/wi-G//ana utilized nearly 100 species of plants as food.

Imamura also analysed the group formation and time allocation in gathering activities. For collecting firewood, individual gathering alone was more common, while for collecting food or grass, gathering in groups was more common. In a given period, group gathering was more efficient than individual gathering, but the longer the time spent in group gathering, the lower was the efficiency. While enumerating the advantages of group gathering such as avoiding danger and collecting reliable information, Imamura emphasized the importance of societal function of secondary activities such as conversation, singing songs and passing around tobacco. She concluded that 'the gathering activities [we]re social as well as determined by ecological factors and confirming their cultural identity' (Imamura 1996: 61).

## New Ways Making a Livelihood

According to Tanaka (1980), some G//ana people raised several dozen goats in the Xade area in 1967. Later on, in 1982, Osaki carried out a census all the livestock raised in the settlement and counted 543 goats, of which 406 (76 per cent) were kept by only four (6 perc ent) out of seventy-one households, while forty-seven households (66 per cent) had no goats (Osaki 1990). Based on the observations between 1987 and 1989, Ikeya (1993) analysed the technical and socio-economic aspects of goat raising. According to his census, the number of goats had increased strikingly, to about 2,700. This rapid population growth was mainly due to the promotion of goat raising by the government, as well as their purchase using cash obtained from laubor in road construction and the selling of folk crafts. I have also drawn attention to the fact that a complex network of keep-and-entrusting relationships for goats has spread through the community (Sugawara 1991).

Ikeya (1996b) carried out an intensive investigation of farming in the rainy season of 1993. Following studies were also conducted in 1994 and 1995. In this period, watermelons (*tsama* melon), cowpeas, and maize were cultivated in various combinations in forty fields around the camps. Comparing the locations of the field with those recorded by Osaki in 1982–3, Ikeya found that the distance from the central area of the settlement had increased to an average of ten kilometres. Ikeya concluded that the system of joint-cultivation described by Osaki had broken down and there was a shift to cultivation of fields by individual households. Tanaka (1991) pointed out that even in the 1970s the San occasionally sold furs at shops in Ghanzi, 170 km north-west of Xade, and bought various items with the cash they obtained. However, he also pointed out that by the 1980s the construction of buildings, road, the laying of water piping and the establishment of the handicraft trade provided the people with a lasting source of cash income. Ikeya (1996a) focused on road construction labour and the sale of handicraft. The data from his own observations in 1987–8, together with official documents since 1983, showed that very few people worked continually in road construction throughout the four years 1983–7. Ikeya also pointed out that it was difficult for the G/wi-G//ana men to adapt their production quickly to the changing market trends in handicrafts.

In 1987, I analysed the 'catalogue of belongings' in each of fifteen households in three adjacent G/wi camps (Sugawara 1991). The social distance between partners involved in barter and purchase was not significantly different from that in gift-giving. This result negates the general assumption that barter and purchase represented a more depersonalized relationship than gift-giving. It was concluded that a wide-ranging gift-giving network was prevalent, while the G/wi seemed to be oriented towards the profit-seeking principle of expecting an immediate return, even from their close kin.

## Studies of Face-to-Face Interaction and Communication

Along with the ecological paradigm focusing on subsistence, Japanese studies of the G/wi-G//ana have made a distinctive contribution to the development of the description and analysis of social interaction and communication.

### Face-to-Face Interaction as a Basis of Society

The approach to face-to-face interactions among the G/wi began with my own work on interpersonal proxemic behaviour and physical contact (Sugawara 1984). Using primatology as a basis, I applied quantitative sampling methods to the collection of data on the spatial proximity among the residents of several G/wi camps. They were in far more frequent proximity with members of the same sex than with the opposite sex. In the same generation, proximity and physical contact were avoided between siblings or siblings-in-law of the opposite sex. Paying special attention to grooming behaviour (i.e., the removal of lice), I showed that this behaviour had not only hygienic but also social functions: it was usually performed by females for juveniles or other females, while males never groomed females. The primary function of the grooming of juveniles was maternal care or reassurance, while between females, it functioned as a social transaction.

During the research period of 1984–5, I analysed patterns of visiting in the sedentary community (Sugawara 1988). The most important point proposed by this study was that the camp could be characterized as a multilayered micro-terri-tory occupied by the residents. Greeting interaction deserved special attention, as specific way in which the intruder into a micro-territory established focused inter-action with its occupants. The essential features of greeting represented two main themes that were contradictory to each other: the openness of a camp and the def-inite distinction made between residents and non-residents. The residents were not able to prevent the visitor from entering their own micro-territory, but instead enjoyed the right to begin mutual interaction by initiating greeting. It was con-cluded that the latent message conveyed by this programme was that of the 'situa-tional dominance' of the residents.

Koji Kitamura, a member of the same research team as myself in 1984–5, also made a unique contribution to the study of face-to-face interaction among the G//ana. Kitamura (1991) abstracted four distinctive characteristics of cultural con-ventions in social interaction from seemingly trivial everyday behaviour: (a) hesi-tating to act towards others, (b) ignoring proposals for interaction by other party, (c) frequent overlapping of utterances, and (d) suspending one's own proposal for interaction as something provisional. The essential point was that when people intended to draw others into immediate interaction, they regarded as extremely important the spontaneous actions of the other party in response.

## Analysis of Everyday Conversation
In 1987 I began the analysis of everyday conversation among the G/wi, and con-tinued this study in successive periods of research in 1989 and 1992. Part of the results was combined with my previous research on proxemics and greetings (Sugawara 1990). I pointed out that a particular form of bodily co-presence could be interpreted and treated as a symptomatic sign of a particular type of social rela-tionship. I used the term 'body idiom' to refer to the process through which human beings not only express something by means of bodily behaviour but also fix this expression in a verbal idiom. In particular, I argued that not only the G/wi, but we ourselves have a general tendency to attain a more accurate interpretation of reality depending on the 'evidence of the body'. These arguments and another findings were integrated into a Japanese book (Sugawara 1993).

In the ensuing article, I criticized the principle-centred theory of conversation and emphasized the proposition that G/wi conversational organization should be examined within the context of the social relationships between participants (Sugawara 1996). I compared the organization of interaction using two contrasting examples: seemingly polite dialogue and frank argument. The former was charac-terized by 'formalization', which was defined as a systematic differentiation of speaker and hearer into complementary roles, while the latter was characterized as 'immediate-reflexive responsiveness'. By applying these concepts to actual social relationships, I reconsidered the model of joking/avoidance relationships.

In an article that aimed at reconsidering egalitarianism in the perspective of communication theory, I paid special attention to prolonged simultaneous discourse, or overlaps, which was one of the most remarkable characteristics of G/wi conversation (Sugawara 1998a). I classified these overlaps into the following three types according to the context in which it occurred: (a) cooperative, (b) antagonistic, and (c) parallel. Cooperative overlaps were closely connected with the intimate behaviour such as speaking in unison and repeating or completing the other speaker's sentence. In such cases, the main reason for overlaps was to 'entrain' into the other speaker's activity. In contrast to this, long 'parallel overlaps' could be understood in terms of 'egocentric relevance' that not only allowed the speaker to search his memory, but also made it easy for the participants to avert their attention from the focus of ongoing interaction. I argued that such a 'sense of interaction' formed the basis of San's unique sociality that enabled the people to disperse without any explicit sign of antipathy.

In a further article, I attempted to clarify the logic of negotiation (Sugawara 2002a). I analysed the whole process of a negotiation transaction between two men recorded in 1992 into several sets of intelligible proposition components. These sets were quite consistently ordered and alternated with other phases of exchanging more explicit 'illocutionary acts' of requirement and refusal. This analysis demonstrated that the G/wi negotiators speak to each other using consistent line of logic. Finally, paying attention to the interactive features that served to transform the serious negotiation into a joking game, I examined what were the conditions under which this kind of meta-communication was successfully attained. These arguments and a number of another findings from the G/wi conversation analysis were compiled in two voluminous Japanese books (Sugawara 1998b,c).

## Ethnographic Studies of Habitual Thought and Practice

Another line of studies has developed side by side with the studies on socio-economic changes and face-to-face interactions. Although this line covered rather heterogeneous domains of social life, it is characterized by ethnographic interest in the G/wi-G//ana's mental world that is interwoven both with ecology and embodied experience.

### Cognition and Practice towards Animals
Tanaka's (1996) important contribution was to link the G/wi-G//ana subsistence ecology with the ideological and cognitive aspects of the natural environment. This work, integrating his data and insights on the G/wi-G//ana view of animals accumulated through his continuing research, established a basis on which ethno-zoological, folk-taxonomic and folklore studies could be developed. Here, he clarified

the very practical classification of animals into the categories of 'eat-things' (i.e., animals to be eaten), 'bite-things' (i.e., harmful animals) and 'useless things'. Furthermore, by presenting representative folk tales and myths, he outlined the symbolic world of the G/wi-G//ana which was closely connected with their minutely detailed knowledge of animal habits.

Ken'ichi Nonaka (1996) pioneered the new area of study of 'ethno-ento-mology'. Eighteen kinds of insects and three kinds of honey were recognized as food according to the G/wi-G//ana classification. Nonaka also pointed out that other insects were also essential to the quality of the G/wi-G//ana diet, even though they were scarce in quantity. Furthermore, he described other interesting use of insects for medicine, beauty, decoration and children's play, which is supported by strikingly minute knowledge with more than 130 vernacular names. This wide range of usage is based on the characteristics of insects which differ from those of mammals and plants, such as chemical and physical qualities and the external skeleton.

I investigated three fields in which the G/wi-G//ana think and act with animals: (a) interpretations on peculiar features of game animals, (b) ethno-ornithology, and (c) food taboo or avoidance (Sugawara 2001). The hunters interpreted peculiar behaviour or appearance of animals in terms of some influential process that acts beyond mechanical causality. A number of folk-tales explained the origin of salient habits and morphology of specific bird species. Privileged enjoyment of some kinds of meat by elder people was the principal factor that organized the food taboo. Based on these analyses, I proposed a theoretical model of cognitive space that schematized the G/wi-G//ana's knowledge, belief, and practice towards animals. I also argued that the beliefs organizing the food taboo or avoidance were based on embodied experience, which was different from deictic identification, and no more amenable to indirect cognition.

## *The Extramarital Sexual Relationship (Zaaku)*

Tanaka (1989) first pointed out that persistent extramarital relationships called *zaaku* are quite prevalent among the G/wi-G//ana society. Scrutinizing many cases of marriage, divorce, remarriage, and *zaaku* relationships, he argued that the sig-nificance of *zaaku* relationship lay in the uniting of two or more married families through a sexual relationship.

Following this article, I reconstructed a number of episodes of *zaaku* relation-ships from the analysis of topics in everyday conversation (Sugawara 1991). I shed light on the unique cultural value attached to this relationship, as well as the ambivalent attitude of people toward it. In the emotional life of the G/wi-G//ana, *zaaku* relationships were regarded positively. One of the factors supporting this feeling was an economic mutualism, which was most distinctly embodied by the 'ideal type' of *zaaku*, that is, mate-swapping. On the other hand, there was a negative side to the *zaaku* relationship. It sometimes provoked conflicts in which not only the concerned parties but also their kin (or even their past 'lovers') were involved. It was believed that a man, as well as his children, might suffer from a disease caused by intercourse with a woman other than his wife.

Integrating further topics in the life-history narratives of senior G/wi men into the analysis, I attempted to solve the question of 'what does it mean to possess another person?' in egalitarian societies (Sugawara, in press). Based on the theory of 'pair-gestalt inhibition' in primatology, I regarded the triadic relation among the possessor, the possessed and the rival as the prototypical form of possession. Contrasting the conflict derived from triadic relation with the reciprocal mutualism in 'quadruple relation' in which two couples were involved, I emphasized that the sexually-emotionally-engaged relationships with another were always vulnerable to trespass. I argued that the essence of G/wi's social attitude was characterized by their persistent effort to undergo this contradiction that was intrinsic to the possession of another person, and concluded that this 'dialectic of emotional life' was negotiated and renewed over the course of continuing face-to-face interaction.

## Ritual Practice

In his principal monograph, Tanaka (1980) examined the ideological and aesthetic aspects of the G/wi-G//ana social life, especially the function of dancing, the most important of which was the 'gemsbok dance', in exorcising evil spirits and re-establishing peace within the community. He also described another important repertoire of dance; i.e., the 'eland dance' which was performed only by women to celebrate the menarche. While enumerating several magical practices, Tanaka (1980: 114) pointed out that '[r]eligious ceremonies among the San [we]re surprisingly rare'. This statement seems to reflect Tanaka's basic ecological framework that puts less emphasis on the people's 'beliefs about supernatural power' than on their 'basically realistic and rational' lifestyle (1980: 110).

The whole range of G/wi-G//ana ritual practice had not been systematically investigated, until Imamura (2001) conducted intensive research in 1994–5. She pointed out that the G/wi-G//ana practised certain rites every time one passed critical phases in their life or when something unfortunate happened. Because all these rites were a kind of curing, various kinds and parts of plant or substance from the human body (i.e., urine, sweat, fingernails, etc.) were used as medicine. Imamura identified more than fifty species of plant that were used for medicine. Although some of the rites were supposed to have been imported from the Bakgalagadi agropastoralists, the G/wi-G//ana rites were characterized by the attribution of strong efficacy to the bodily substance rather than to the medical plants. Imamura also proposed a unique view on *zaaku* relationships. The rite of 'mixing urine' was usually held for removing the 'dirt' that arose from a *zaaku* relationship. Imamura argued that all those involved in *zaaku*, including their young children, were connected with one another through the medium of 'water' exchanged by intercourse, suckling or close contact. If any of them had bad feeling, this same 'water' would be changed into 'dirt' that caused the illness. The rite of mixing the substance from all the participants' bodies not only revealed the problem underlying the relationship but also reified the agreement, which in turn changed the same substance into strong medicine. Imamura developed this demonstration into an inspiring interpretation of the G/wi-G//ana view of life and vital power.

## Towards the Future

Under the influence of primatology, Japanese studies of ecological anthropology have been characterized by an orientation towards a synthetic theory of the evolution of human society. Concerning the studies of hunter-gatherers, this orientation was most distinctively expressed in a number of attempts to elucidate the ecological, sociological and behavioural grounds for 'egalitarianism'. In this regard, Itani's (1988) article entitled 'The origin of human equality' was seminal.

Itani claimed that the most important task for anthropology was to understand the phylogenetic grounds of human equality in the context of the social evolution of non-human primates. Although 'egalitarianism' was a term usually used for characterizing hunter-gatherers' social and economic systems, Itani pointed out that many traditional societies of African slash-and-burn cultivators and pastoralists also exhibited 'fear of civil inequality'. He carried out a grand survey of the evolutionary process, from 'equipotency' in the elementary societies of nocturnal prosimians, through the 'a priori inequality' prevailing in most social units of anthropoids, to 'conditional equality' emerging from various kinds of social interaction (for example, play, greeting and food-sharing) in the societies of great apes. Thus, Itani tried to demonstrate that the egalitarianism most typically found in extant hunting-gathering societies was deeply rooted in the legacy from prehominid and proto-hominid ancestors.

Previously in this chapter, referring to the criticism by Ikeya of Osaki's interpretation, I have noted the tendency of researchers to regard the notion of 'egalitarianism' as self-evident. Radical re-examination and reorganization of this notion is required in order to establish a new theory concerning the evolution of hunting-gathering society. However, I have to admit that this prospect might be too idyllic in the light of the recent situation the G/wi-G//ana are undergoing. In 1986, the cabinet of the Botswana government decided to relocate the people living in the CKGR to new places, outside the reserve. Eleven years later, in May 1997, the first wave of people began to migrate from Xade to the new settlement Kx'oensakene, or New Xade. In the course of four months until September 1997, all the residents of Xade successively left their home. The outline of this process, as well as the responses of the people to the government policy, was described by

Ikeya (2001). Even after the enforcement of this 'relocation programme', the Japanese research on the G/wi-G//ana people in which several graduate students have participated is still under way. These researchers in younger generation are challenging the new issues that are relevant to the concentrated life in New Xade. For example, Junko Maruyama (2002) analysed the distribution of the dwellings, and revealed the differentiation into central and peripheral components. Comparing the exchange networks in which these two components were involved, she elucidated the socio-economic factors that prompted the orientation towards the peripheral residence.

In order to understand fully the present difficulties the G/wi-G//ana people are going through in face of the overwhelming power of the state, it is indispensable to re-examine the historical context of relationship between the hunter-gatherers and the agropastoralists in the Central Kalahari. From 1993 Osaki began to reconstruct the history of the Central Kalahari, by collecting the narratives of senior G//ana men, as well as official documentation dating both from before and after the British colonial administration. As the clues to estimate the chronology, Osaki (1998) paid attention to several specific events such as the swarms of locusts in 1924–5 and 1934–5, and the epidemic of smallpox in 1950–1. He assumed that very early in the twentieth century the Tswana had begun to visit the G/wi-G//ana's land, and had introduced chiefdomship and a tribute system, as well as agriculture and livestock. In a recent article (Sugawara 2002b), I have described various aspects of the G/wi-G//ana interactions with the outside, using three different kinds of material: narratives of life history (including the incidents after which the newborn babies had been named), everyday conversations and discourses drawn from informal interviews, which corresponded to three chronological stages: before sedentarism, during the settlement life at Xade and after the relocation. I characterized the G/wi-G//ana strategy to cope with the power from the outside as 'optimistic realism' that is apt to result in 'opportunistic subordination'.

Three years before the enforcement of the relocation programme, in a Japanese book entitled *The last hunter-gatherers*, Tanaka (1994) warned against the arrogance of civilized societies that only advocated the conservation of nature, without regarding the long history of symbiotic relationship between human beings and nature. He was also seriously concerned about the many problems caused by sedentarism, which threatened the people's ability to sustain a life of peace. Tanaka claimed that anthropologists have a responsibility to the people to be committed to the solution of these problems. It is an epistemological, as well as practical task left to not only the researchers of the San but to all anthropologists struggling with the 'modern' system, to know how to solve these problems. Tanaka and Sugawara (1996: 6) wrote: '[W]e do not believe that the persistent effort to understand more thoroughly the uniqueness of the San must lead to the alienation of them into Others. We hope that we ourselves will be changed by this understanding.'

## Notes

1. Although the main part of this chapter is a shortened version of another article (Sugawara 1998d), several new arguments are added.
2. For the convenience of non-Japanese readers, I will focus my attention only on the English articles with the exception of a few important books in Japanese.

# –11–

# Down Ancient Trails: Hunter-Gatherers in Indian Archaeology

## *Shanti Pappu*

Place him on the earth before he dies, He must stay close to where his four walls grew – And where his copper coin and silver thread and arrowhead lie hidden, He must remember when his home was new.

Bhil song from Khare, The Singing Bow

South Asian archaeologists invariably work within an atmosphere influenced by a diversity of socio-economic and cultural forces, the outcome of the coexistence of varied religious, caste and tribal groups. Within this context, the image of the 'hunter-gatherer' is one created, not only by anthropological writings, but also by a personal awareness of such groups existing on the fringes of, or within towns and villages, as nomads passing through cities, or as groups increasingly assuming a more forceful role in Indian polity. The 'hunter-gatherer' as portrayed in myths and legends, epics, folk songs (as in the Bhil song quoted above), historical records and ancient literature dating back to the third century AD, has infused a time depth rarely met with elsewhere. It is this seeming continuity, which has deeply influenced the structure of Indian ethnoarchaeological studies.

The use of ethnographic analogies drawn from studies of modern hunter-gatherers may be traced to the work of R.B. Foote and other scholars in the late nineteenth century (Pappu 1991–2). Foote established the science of prehistoric archaeology in the subcontinent, and was perhaps the first to use analogies drawn from hunter-gatherers to reconstruct Palaeolithic lifeways. The importance of his work lies in the fact that in addition to discovering and documenting sites, he made a conscious attempt to integrate diverse kinds of evidence to arrive at a comprehensive picture of prehistoric lifeways in this region. Despite the constraints of working within the profit-oriented Geological Survey, largely in the field, devoid of the 'luxury of a library' (Foote 1881: 326), and distant from the European academic mainstream, his interpretation of the physical and cultural landscapes of this region, gave a new dimension to nineteenth-century archaeological thought. It is here that his field experiences 'exposed to risks from violent storms and from wild beasts in jungly regions' (Foote 1881: 326) compounded by the influence of Darwin and Huxley comes into play. In particular 'palaeolithians' were thought to have been struggling in the 'school of necessity' subject to tropical seasonality, diseases and predators. At the same time they were of comparable intelligence with European hominids and not merely dominated by climatic alterations (Foote 1868). His observations of local tribal and caste groups led him to visualize images of 'palaeolithians' foraging in catamarans across the coast, from where tools were lost within mud banks. He was also the first to use analogies drawn from natural and cultural forces to interpret artefact distribution and settlement patterns (Pappu 1991–2). Images of prehistoric hunting technology were created using observations drawn from the tribal use of bamboo implements, thorn arrowheads and boomerangs. Subsequently, the impact of the 'New Archaeology' led to changes in conceptual approaches among some Indian scholars (Paddayya 1990, 1995). In prehistoric archaeology, this marked a shift away from the construction of culture-sequences and type-lists towards attempts to study past behaviour. Among other approaches adopted, analogies drawn from modern hunter-gatherers and actualistic studies influenced the way in which prehistoric settlement and subsistence patterns were interpreted. This paper examines different approaches used by archaeologists in interpreting prehistoric behaviour through analogies drawn from modern hunter-gatherers. It situates these approaches within the context of Indian archaeology as a whole, and attempts to examine how results of these studies have influenced interpretations of Indian prehistory.

## Hunter-Gatherers in Modern Indian Archaeology

The first few decades of the twentieth century, witnessed a shift in emphasis in Indian prehistory towards constructing grand sequences linking cultural phases and Pleistocene environmental changes. Emphasis was thus laid on stratigraphy, geomorphology and tool technology, and anthropological studies did not form an important part of research aims (Paddayya 1995). It was the impact of the New Archaeology that spurred Indian prehistorians towards investigating modern hunter-gatherers once again. The importance of ethnography was first emphasized by Malik (1968), although impetus was achieved through the writings of H.D. Sankalia, V.N. Misra, K. Paddayya and M. Nagar, and with the establishment of a chair in ethnoarchaeology at the Deccan College, Pune in 1972 (Misra 1989a; Paddayya 1979). Subsequently, most research has been carried out by students of the Deccan College. The post was first held by Malti Nagar, who carried out pioneering work in the field for more than two decades (Nagar 1967, 1969, 1977, 1978, 1982, 1983, 1985; Nagar and Misra 1989, 1990). For many years, she was the sole woman ethnoarchaeologist in India, and worked under taxing conditions; both in the field and in a largely traditional, male-dominated social and academic world. Subsequently, numerous scholars worked on hunter-gatherer communities in various parts of the subcontinent, and it soon became incumbent on any student of prehistory to include a chapter on hunter-gatherers inhabiting their study regions (Allchin 1985, 1994; Boivin and Fuller 2002; Fuller and Boivin 2002; Mohanty and Misra 2002; Sinopoli 1991). Despite claims of following a processualist approach, little consistency exists in the use of analogies, leading to a wide range of interpretations of what ethnoarchaeological research constitutes. No clear definition of 'hunter-gatherers' is present (Bender and Morris 1988; Bettinger 1991), although this term is generally assumed to refer to a particular mode of life characterized by hunting, gathering and fishing. Principle approaches towards the archaeological study of hunter-gatherers are presented below.

## *The Question of Continuity: Hunter-Gatherers and Traditional Ways of Life*

The apparent continuity of traditional ways of life in India, has largely conditioned a firm belief in the efficacy of ethnographic analogies in reconstructing the prehistoric past. Owing to the paucity of organic remains at most Palaeolithic and Mesolithic sites; it is widely believed that modern hunter-gatherers are the key to gaining an understanding of prehistoric subsistence and settlement strategies. This general opinion is seen in Murty's (1981: 57) observation that '. . . broad similarities in subsistence strategies in the hunter-gatherer ecosystems from Stone Age times to the ethnographic present can be predicted on the basis of ethnographic analogy, in combination with archaeological reasoning and environmental reality'. He however cautions that construction of Stone Age realities with the help of living traditions may not always be valid for the prehistoric period, but that historical documents offer scope to examine the dynamics of hunter-gatherer cultures.

This continuity is often examined in terms of biological continuity. Thus, hunter-gatherers of the Gangetic plains are thought to be 'almost certainly descended from the pioneering Mesolithic colonizers of these plains' (Nagar and Misra 1989: 86), and that despite degeneration and change, they provide clues to Mesolithic lifeways. The Van Vagris and other tribes are traced to earlier Mesolithic communities of Rajasthan (Misra 1990: 91). Cooper (1997: 96) states that the Kuruk fisherfolk of the Chitrakot Falls region may be descendants of early Mesolithic settlers, although no direct line can be traced owing to migration and fluid social structures. She believes that ethnoarchaeological studies of the Kuruks may reveal fundamental 'truths' about the best ways to exploit resources of the area 'which are true at all times and with all peoples in this place, even though the two sets of communities, prehistoric and modern may not have any direct lineage' (Cooper 1997). Murty (1981: 57) notes that the traditional economic behaviour and dietary habits of tribes like the Chenchus, Yanadis, Yerukulas and Boyas of the south-east coast of India, can in fact be seen as ontogenic survivals from the Stone Age past.

Continuity is also interpreted in terms of environmental and cultural factors (Allchin 1994: 1; Misra 1989b). Nagar (1967: 236) argues that culture is a historical process and although modified, some older practices survive, preserved in the lifestyles of various tribes. Despite this, she concludes that it is difficult to draw comparisons between Chalcolithic Ahar and modern Bhils, there being few common factors between the two. Among the tribes of Rajasthan, Misra (1990: 91) believes that harsh ecological conditions imposed severe restrictions on economic growth and contributed towards the continuation of traditional adaptive strategies of hunting and gathering. Subsequent degeneration of the environment forced certain groups into agriculture or craft-traditions and into a symbiotic relationship with local communities, while others took to crime.

## *Encapsulation and Change*
The 'encapsulation' and acculturation of modern foragers, in terms of their interaction with farmers, pastoralists and urban societies has long been recognized in Indian archaeology. This recognition coexists with studies highlighting continuity of lifeways, and in such cases, attempts are made to filter selective information thought relevant for the study of prehistoric lifeways. Allchin (1985: 25) aptly warns that while communities appear to retain their identity, changes have occurred and their lifestyles need not reflect the past merely because of the survival of certain traditions. In this context of continuous change, Murty (1985a: 192–193) believes that analogical reasoning may be used only if there is evidence in the archaeological record to demonstrate a continuity from past to present. Chakrabarti (1994) presents a holistic picture of the tribal landscape in the Chhotanagpur region, with interactions between hunter-gatherers, shifting cultivators and plough agriculturalists. In the case of the Van Vagris and other tribes of Rajasthan, Misra (1990) traces their adaptation through time within different ecozones. With depletion of game, some tribes took to agriculture, while others continued as hunter-gatherers but entered into symbiotic relationships with local communities. Nagar and Misra (1989) use historical documents to trace changing subsistence and settlement patterns among tribes in the north Indian Gangetic plains, considering population demography and variability in settlement and subsistence patterns through time, as well as the symbiotic relationship between hunter-gatherers and other groups.

Murty (1985a; 1994) utilizes inscriptions, medieval literature and colonial accounts, archaeology and folk culture for a period ranging from the fourth century AD to the nineteenth century, in order to trace dialectics between forest peoples, cultural systems and the state, and to 'explain the dynamics of hunter-gatherer cultures' of the Eastern Ghats. Cultural trajectories of hunter-gatherers are traced in a changing physical and social environment in which the state is seen to act as an intermediary. This research stresses a continuum from medieval to modern times in hunter-gatherer lifeways and displays how forest cultures were integral to the functioning and maintenance of organization of the state. An ethnohistorical study of the Andaman islanders is also presented by Cooper (1994).

Studies such as that of Hooja (1988; 1994), trace interactions between Bhils and non-Bhils from post-700 AD in Rajasthan, and dwell on recent transformations within their society. Drawing on archaeological data, she notes that early farmers of Chalcolithic Ahar (c.2500–1500 BC) and Gilund were in close interaction with hunter-gatherers of Mesolithic Bagor (Phase I, and Phase II, c.2700–2000 BC). Hooja believes that even without raising the issue of whether Bhils or non-Bhils are descendants of prehistoric communities, ethnoarchaeology can provide case studies of 'contact, conflict and co-existence between two distinct cultures in historical and modern times' (Hooja 1994: 139). Data from the Mesolithic sites of Langhnaj, Pushkar, Ganeshwar, Bhimbetka, Lekahaia and Adamgarh also point to this early interaction. Jacobsen (1985) points out that hunters and farmers have coexisted for almost five millennia, and draws on evidence from Mesolithic and Chalcolithic sites in the Raisen-Sehore complex rock shelters, where stone chipping technology and tool kits coexist with late Chalcolithic or Early Iron Age material and historical goods.

Evidence of the exchange of items between Mesolithic and settled Neo/Chalcolithic communities, is discussed by Misra (1989b), who believes that with the emergence of village-based economies in Mesolithic habitats, hunting-gathering populations came into closer interaction with the former, and possibly became marginally enclaved. Guha (1994) and Possehl and Kennedy (1979), stress the role of hunter-gatherers in Harappan socio-economy. The latter argue that the location of Lothal (Harappan) in relation to Langhnaj and other North Gujarat Mesolithic sites indicates that the hunter-gatherers of the North Gujarat Plain were supplying raw materials to the city of Lothal. Khanna (1988) uses archaeological and ethnographic data to postulate a model for the site of Bagor. A pastoral hunter-gatherer economy is proposed for Phase I (after c.2635 BC), outside the periphery of settled agriculturalists and with a multi-resource exploitation system. In Phase II, he argues for contact with neighbouring Chalcolithic populations (2765–2110 BC).

This situation prevails in Peninsular India as well, where hunter-gatherers were integrated into the wider community as specialized castes, involved in either visible or invisible trade with local communities or as dispossessed victims of expansion by kings/cultivators (Morris 1982), or pushed into refuge zones (Gardner 1982; Morris 1982). This 'acculturation' is documented in South India as far back as the first or second centuries AD in Sangam texts and in the Mackenzie

Manuscripts (see Morris 1982; Raman 1959: 5); and is inferred from trade in forest products with Rome (Morris 1982). From medieval times onwards, hunter-gatherers were employed by kings in the army (e.g. Vellans) or incorporated into the social structure (*kiratas, pulindas, nishadas,* etc.). During most of the nineteenth century, they were driven into forest refuges (Morris 1982: 19). A study of the Irulas reveals that as per old legends in the *Colapurvapattayam,* (sixteenth to eighteenth centuries AD during the reign of the Cola king Kullotunga), the Irula chief Kovan ruled over Coimbatore (Kovanputtur, Koyamutturu or the 'New Town of Koyan') and that the tribe disbanded following the death of Kovan (K. Zvelebil 1988: 52–3).

## *Ethnographic Documentation*
These approaches may be seen in the form of studies where individual artefacts or aspects of the material culture of tribes are described with a view towards interpreting the archaeological record of a particular site/region. Two approaches may be detected here.

The first approach provides detailed descriptions of hunter-gatherers, focusing primarily on settlement and subsistence systems, highlighting aspects of material culture that anthropological studies often ignore. These studies are conducted in regions rich in prehistoric archaeology, and are directed towards interpreting the archaeological record of the region under study. In most cases modern groups are regarded as offshoots of original prehistoric communities. Archaeological data may be minimal in these studies although references to other works abound. These studies supply a wealth of information on fast-vanishing lifeways, and provide a base which may be utilized by prehistorians. This approach is seen in the work of M. Nagar (1982; 1985) on the Gonds and other tribes of Central India, by M. Nagar and V.N. Misra on the Kanjars (1990) and Pardhis (Misra and Nagar 1993) and tribes of the Gangetic plains (1989, 1994), by V.N. Misra on the Van Vagris (1990) and T. Kaping (1998) on the Southern Nagas. Ethnographic studies are also noted in combination with intensive archaeological surveys and studies of lithic assemblages, in the work of S.C. Nanda (1983) on the Parjas and other Orissan tribes, P. Mohanty (1989) on the Juangs of Orissa, J.S. Jayraj on the Yanadis (1983), T. Kaping (1998) on the Southern Nagas, and P.C. Pant and V. Jayaswal (1991) on the Kodas of the Kharagpur hills near Paisra.

The second approach deals with studies of individual aspects of material culture from which parallels may be traced in the archaeological record. Here, Nagar's (1977) study of tribes in the vicinity of the Bhimbetka group of rock shelters, and her analogies drawn from Gond memorial stones and iron implements to study Iron Age burials and copper hoard cultures are significant. Analogies drawn from modern tribals were used to identify a possible shrine (a rectangular stone platform with a triangular stone with circles) at Baghor II (Upper Palaeolithic), which aids in tracing a long continuity of mother-goddess worship (Kenoyer, Clark, Pal, and Sharma 1983). Ansari's (2000) study of modern Kols and Musahars focuses on construction and use of different types of storage bins/pits, which is compared with evidence from Mesolithic Chopani Mando.

Tool functions are often interpreted on the basis of ethnographic analogies. This is seen in analogies drawn by Murty (1981) and Raju (1988) to interpret stone tool functions along the south east coast of India. This is particularly evident in studies of Upper Palaeolithic and Mesolithic tool types, including backed blade elements, microlithic blades, arrowheads and crescentic backed pieces. Parallels are also drawn from bored-stones used by the Yanadis, Voda Balijes and others as net sinkers in fishing and which are also found at Upper Palaeolithic sites in this region (Murty 1981). Grinding stones at Upper Palaeolithic sites are thought to have been used for processing wild food such as rice (*Oriza nivara*), found even today in the Eastern Ghats. Analogies have also been drawn from the study of specific plant species (Kajale et al. 1991) to explain probable uses of wood remains of *Cassia* cf. *fistula* found at Betamcherla (Upper Palaeolithic and Mesolithic). Murty (1981) also draws on modern analogies of the use of resins/gums (gums of several species of Acacia, lacquer from the nests of tree ants and milky juice of *Excoecaria agallocha*) in interpreting hafting of Upper Palaeolithic tools. Ethnobotanical studies were also conducted by Nagar (1985) in Central India, in which she highlights species utilized, as well as the fact that most collection is done by women and children.

## General Ecological Models

Models drawn from human ecology as well as from studies of modern and Pleistocene geographical and environmental changes represent a movement away from particularistic studies. In a comprehensive paper Misra (1989b) draws together archaeological and ecological data and proposes a broad picture of settlement and subsistence patterns spanning the Palaeolithic and Mesolithic. Varied ecological niches in ecosystems were occupied from the Upper Palaeolithic onwards, as seen in the presence of archaeological sites in regions occupied by modern tribals. He believes that this concurrence in site location indicates that present-day resources must have been used by Terminal Pleistocene populations, possibly on a much larger scale (Misra 1989b: 24). Similar reasoning is used to push back the exploitation of aquatic resources of water bodies in the Eastern Ghats, to the Terminal Pleistocene, based on analogies drawn from the Yanadis (Murty 1981, 1985a). Murty (1985a; 1985b) argues that the tremendous tribal knowledge of plant species results from ecological adaptation and exploitation over a long period, and thus justifies the use of analogies drawn from recent tribal subsistence patterns along the south-east coast to predict past subsistence strategies.

Murty (1981) was perhaps among the first to integrate ecological, archaeological and ethnographic data to categorize sites based on their physiographic location and microenvironment, sedimentary context, assemblage composition, and their relationship with modern tribal settlements, in order to propose models of changing prehistoric subsistence and settlement patterns. He also uses general ecological models and those based on Maruyama's deviation-amplifying to study causes and antiquity of the Kunchapuri Yerukula subsistence strategies based principally on hunting aquatic birds (Murty 1978–9) He argues that temporary periods of environmental instability, during the Pleistocene, must have led to a reliance on a narrow spectrum diet. Assuming that the strategy proved advantageous, following climatic amelioration, it would have been favoured by cultural selection and become an established economic tradition. He suggests that in the late Pleistocene and Holocene, wild cattle were plausibly tamed on a limited scale as an aid (acting as a concealing shield) in bird hunting, even as is done today, and that the tradition of maintaining small herds of cattle/pigs possibly dates back to their symbiotic association with Neolithic stocks.

This approach may also be noted in Paddayya's model of Acheulian land-use patterns in the Hunsgi valley (Paddayya 1982). He considers environmental factors, seasonality, types of water sources, archaeological site sizes, distribution and density of artefacts, and ethnographic data drawn from the !Kung and Chenchus among others. He postulates a model of dry season coalescence of groups around scarce water bodies such as springs, and wet season dispersal when resources were diverse. Ecological approaches form an integral part of research, which includes middle range models and actualistic studies, discussed below.

## Middle Range Research and Actualistic Studies
Such studies often invoke theoretical approaches of the New Archaeology (Binford 1982; 1983; Schiffer 1987), but differ in their application and methodology. They generally involve the following aspects: (a) a description of one/more tribes inhabiting the study region, focusing on their subsistence and settlement strategies, (b) a description of the archaeological record stressing on site location, function, artefact density, (c) (optional): studies of site formation processes (both cultural and natural), and (d) proposal of hypotheses of past mobility and settlement patterns based on comparison with modern data. These studies draw largely on the residential versus logistic mobility models proposed by L.R. Binford (1982; 1983). The use of such analogies may or may not include the establishment and subsequent testing of hypotheses (Wylie 1985).

D.R. Raju (1988) considers archaeological and ethnographic evidence in the Gunjana valley to reconstruct Upper Palaeolithic lifeways. In addition to drawing analogies between the location of modern and prehistoric sites, and site sizes, he also draws on similarities between Yanadi activity areas and the patterning in artefact clusters at Upper Palaeolithic sites, which possibly represent similar activity areas. He notes that, 'while it is hazardous to correlate the Yanadi lifeways with Terminal Pleistocene hunter-gatherers, it does demonstrate the resource potential of the region and its carrying capacity to support considerable hunter-gatherer populations' (Raju 1988: 93). Owing to the absence of any significant environmental change from the Terminal Pleistocene in the Gunjana valley, he uses ethnographic evidence to predict the range of resources which may have been used by Upper Palaeolithic populations and puts forward estimates of palaeodemography.

Similar approaches were used by Selvakumar (1996), whose aim was to understand how modern Paliyans adapt to their environment and how this may be used to study Mesolithic cultures of the Gundar basin, Tamil Nadu. He identifies three types of archaeological sites created by the Paliyans, namely base camps, temporary camping sites, off-sites and rock-painting sites, and discusses choices in settlement location and activities at individual settlements. Drawing on ethnographic and archaeological data, and using Binford's model of logistic versus residential systems, he puts forward a model of dry season migration in the post-monsoon period to the hilly areas of the Upper Gundar basin, and wet season migration to the western part, as influenced by game movement. He identifies three types of Mesolithic settlements, namely base camps, temporary camps and specific activity areas. He also draws on general ethnographic studies in estimating band size and palaeodemography.

In terms of actualistic studies, specific mention may be made of Cooper's work on the Kuruks in the Chitrakot Falls basin, Madhya Pradesh (Cooper 1997), and in the Andaman islands (Cooper 1990; 1992; 1994). In the Chitrakot Falls, her approach is based on a combination of intensive archaeological survey, documentation of modern Kuruk fishermen's settlement and subsistence patterns, and on modern and past ecology. The distribution of Mesolithic sites in this region may be understood by a study of modern Kuruk settlement and by ecological factors. The waterfall formed the focus of the subsistence cycle, with hunting-gathering and fishing being carried out in the dry season along the river. During the monsoon, with the dispersal of game, humans exploited streams where traps/weirs were used to catch fish/crustacea, hunting was minimal and gathering was conducted along numerous small water courses. She also notes that most Mesolithic sites occur on physiographic boundaries between the plains and the rivers, providing access to two different kinds of resources. She proposes that the Chitrakot Falls and environs provided predictable sources of sustenance year round in the Mesolithic, as it does today.

Cooper's study of the Onge encampments in the Andaman islands is the first study in India that attempts to document various stages of abandonment of middens and other sites, and record observable items. Functional attributes of these sites are examined in the light of their possible reoccupation. Cooper believes that this, together with a consideration of the variable patterns of discard and conditions of preservation, might explain the presence of cultural items most commonly found on archaeological midden sites in the Andamans, although she admits that processes determining the internal structure of these mounds would be difficult to determine. Her studies include patterns of refuse disposal and variability in ways in which refuse is disposed of; taking into consideration questions of abandonment and reoccupation. She also notes, as others have done, that transient camps disappear rapidly under the action of animals/vegetation. At the site of Chauldhari, archaeological data, chronology, changing composition of midden species, methods of extraction/procurement and the lithic assemblage are considered. She concludes that the numerical predominance of a particular species or artefact at a site is not always an accurate measure of the major dietary items that were consumed, or tools commonly used. Evidence from the Hava Beel cave (AD 410 ± 110, ANU-5340, from a 4.4 m trench) is important as it marks the complete absence of any faunal remains and artefacts save lumps of resin (*Canarium eyphyllum*), used by modern Andaman tribes for making torches. She suggests that the cave was used as a temporary shelter while maintenance and procurement activities were carried out 100 m away in a shell midden (Cooper 1990).

Deshpande-Mukherjee's (2000) study of midden formation describes contemporary shellfish gathering along the Konkan coast by the Son Koli fishermen, taking into consideration techniques of collection, division of labour, seasonality, processing and discard strategies, as well as modern lime manufacture and other factors influencing midden formation. This study of midden formation, along with that of Cooper, constitute new lines along which actualistic studies are being conducted in India.

Special mention may also be made of Rao's (1994) work on the Gonds in the Kuntala region, Andhra Pradesh and the Vasavas of Akkalkuwa, Maharashtra. Her aim was to understand past settlement and subsistence patterns by reviewing modern practices. In addition, she also considers ecological factors and acculturation, as well as a detailed study of lithic assemblage variability. Her study follows a rigorous methodology in the construction and testing of hypotheses. She identifies short-term sites, transient loci and long-term camps, and suggests that the perennial pool at Kuntala was the nucleus around which populations wandered with wet-season dispersal and dry-season aggregation patterns. She is also one of the few scholars who contrasts this evidence with that drawn from a study of the Vasasvas in a region where water is not the main criteria for mobility. Here modern and prehistoric settlements are located on high grounds (permanent camps) close to the river Narmada facilitating exploitation of the river and interior forested regions (transitory loci).

Actualistic studies were also conducted to investigate Upper Palaeolithic and Mesolithic settlements in the Son valley (Mishra and Clark 1983). Here temporary shelters constructed by farmers to guard over fields, and by pastoral nomads were studied, and important observations were made on the distribution of stone manu-ports, commonly found at prehistoric sites. Based on studies of the Baigas, Clark and Sharma (1983), conclude that models of settlement types and mobility patterns applicable in Africa were not very relevant in India. They put forward a hypothesis for Holocene communities in India, which includes a model of frequent movement over short distances, splitting for short periods during the monsoon and early fall when resources were abundant, and aggregation for socio-religious causes.

Pappu's (2001) research formed a part of a broader aim of investigating behavioural variability during the Middle to Late Pleistocene in the Kortallayar basin, South India. Fieldwork and literature surveys revealed great variability in modern South Indian hunter-gatherer settlement and subsistence strategies resulting from ecological, cultural and historical processes, from which alternate expectations on long-term land-use patterns could be suggested. These expectations were considered after taking into account the influence which the rate and scales of geomorphic processes had on site visibility, location, assemblage composition and long-term settlement patterns. Models were proposed on seasonal movement between the river and the hills, although it was acknowledged that ethnographic analogies could be used only in a very general way as regards the Lower and Middle Palaeolithic archaeological record.

Site formation studies have in recent years led to the development of productive information on the Indian prehistoric record, although in most cases, these have focused largely on natural processes (Petraglia 1995). Taphonomic studies of bone dispersal were conducted in Tamil Nadu (Badam and Sathe 1995) focusing on natural rather than human elements. Research also includes Paddayya's study of the dispersal of modern water buffalo carcasses (Paddayya 1987), studies of animal remains in vacant plots and abandoned workers camps (Faculty and Students 1989), methods of meat processing by the Dabba Yerukulas and Boyas, and implications for Late Mesolithic hearths, bearing charred bones (Murty 1981).

In recent years such studies have focused increasingly on palaeodemography and palaeopathology (Kennedy 2000; Possehl and Kennedy 1979; Tavares 1997; Walimbe and Tavares 1992) wherein analogies drawn from modern human populations are increasingly utilized.

## Discussion

Ethnoarchaeological studies in Indian prehistory include a wide range of approaches in the use of analogies drawn from modern hunter-gatherers. Conceptual approaches do not appear to reflect developments through time, and are not only dependent on the theoretical orientation of authors, but also on the nature of the archaeological database available, and the state of the tribal group under study. The greatest contribution of modern Indian ethnoarchaeological research lies in the documentation of aspects of material culture, often ignored by social anthropologists. Thus issues such as settlement patterns, site-types, -structure and activity areas, refuse disposal methods, midden formation, abandonment and reoccupation, material culture, and methods of resource exploitation are discussed, providing details not available in anthropological literature. This is of immense importance when one considers that traditional ways of life are rapidly vanishing in modern India. Beginnings have been made in ethnobotanical studies, taphonomy and bioanthropology. A growing realization of the importance of adopting ecological approaches is also closely associated with ethnoarchaeological research in India. Above all, such studies have guided Indian prehistorians away from construction of type-lists and culture sequences towards thinking about understanding past behaviour.

Despite these advances, much remains to be done in the archaeological study of modern hunter-gatherers. While the influence of processualist schools of thought has led to greater methodological rigour, hypothesis testing remains confined to the works of a few scholars. With a few exceptions, most scholars focus on a single tribe generally occupying the region that is being surveyed for archaeological sites. Such analogies often constitute chapters within doctoral dissertations, or take the form of research papers; there being a marked absence of ethnoarchaeological monographs on hunter-gatherers. Thus, variability between tribes arising from ecological, cultural or historical processes is either ignored or largely simplified. Owing to the paucity of organic material at archaeological sites, complex statistical modelling of subsistence patterns using modern analogies is non-existent. Most analogies of hunter-gatherers stop with the study of prehistoric sites, and few scholars (Guha 1994; Murty 1994; Hooja 1988; 1994; Misra 1989b; Khanna 1988) take into consideration the important role played by hunter-gatherers in later periods. Analogies drawn are selective, and comprise those elements thought to be most relevant for reconstructing prehistoric lifeways, with few studies focusing on trajectories of change within tribal groups. Questions of time and change are ignored, little attention is paid to the question of palimpsests and rates and scales of archaeological and ethnographic time, and often a single tribe may be used to provide analogies ranging from the Palaeolithic to the Mesolithic.

To a large extent, ethnographic studies have not influenced mainstream prehistoric research. In the case of the Lower and Middle Palaeolithic, behavioural models have little to do with ethnographic data; with site location, palaeoenvironmental changes and lithic technology playing greater roles in interpreting behaviour. Attempts to model past behaviour based on modern foragers are rarely integrated with other sources of information or serve to provide broad generalizations, with models of transhumance as related to seasonal water availability being most commonly used (Paddayya 1982, Pappu 2001). Apart from highlighting continuity in the exploitation of ecological zones and use of similar resources from the Lower Palaeolithic onwards, ethnographic studies have not produced any models of past behaviour, which are unique to the Indian palaeoecological context (but see Clark and Sharma 1983). This is not the case as regards the Upper Palaeolithic and Mesolithic with a richer canvas of chronometric dates, structures, organic remains, burials and art. Ethnographic studies have not only contributed towards identification of aspects of material culture, but have also led to the proposal of plausible hypotheses, which in some cases have been tested against the archaeological record.

In general, models used tend to draw on that proposed by L.R. Binford (1982). Thus site types and settlement patterns are often approached with the aim of identification of categories, and few studies attempt to consider patterns of reuse/multiple occupation or questions of long or short-term abandonment (but see Cooper 1992; Murty 1981; Paddayya 1987; Pappu 2001). This has led to a rather static rendering of all archaeological data, which must be seen to fit within one or more site categories, or settlement types. This assumes importance when considering sites of a different nature, in particular those of the Ganga valley Mesolithic complex (Sharma et al. 1980), which appear to reflect a more sedentary nature of occupation among hunter-gatherer groups.

Analogical reasoning in India has yet to develop greater rigour and theoretical sophistication in order to explore new avenues of investigating hunter-gatherers. There is a need to develop an awareness of contemporary anthropological thought and to move beyond studies of subsistence and settlement, towards issues related to gender studies and the individual. Ethnoarchaeologists must also attempt to involve contemporary hunter-gatherers in studies related to prehistoric archaeology in regions exploited by them. This should form a part of a wider aim of educating the Indian public on the antiquity and complexity of this mode of life, and the wealth of knowledge, which may be derived from such groups. This would contribute towards creating a positive attitude towards addressing problems in the lives of contemporary Indian hunter-gatherers.

# Part III
# Reinterpretations in Archaeology, Anthropology and the History of the Disciplines

# –12–

# The Many Ages of Star Carr:
# Do 'Cites' Make the 'Site'?

## *P.J. Lane and R.T. Schadla-Hall*

By and large the chances are good of finding other Star Carrs. (Clark 1972a: 9)

Archaeologists usually base their interpretations on particular sets of data – pots, flints, bones, seeds, sites – or on observations based on those data: interpretations are, in a sense, the pendant consequences of the chosen data. Widely accepted interpretations then become the conventional framework for further discussion and research, and the conventional interpretation becomes traditional. (Clarke 1976: 449)

The Early Mesolithic hunter-gatherer site of Star Carr, in the Vale of Pickering, North Yorkshire, ranks with Stonehenge as one of the best known archaeological sites in Britain. Like such places as Olduvai Gorge, Teotihuacan and Great Zimbabwe, the site also occupies an important intellectual space within global archaeological discourse. Well-known to interested members of the public and amateur archaeology groups in Britain, Star Carr is currently receiving wider exposure through the Internet. Physical evidence from the site and certain inter-pretations of this material have also been used recently by various 'green' and 'new age' groups for their own agendas. Here, we examine the changing fortunes of Star Carr within archaeology and its post-excavation history, and discuss some of the reasons for the site's continuing significance. Following from this, we aim to show how this specific case study can provide more general insights concerning how archaeological knowledge is produced and reproduced.[1]

A central question is whether the development of archaeological models of hunter-gatherer settlement systems and land use have been in line with those gen-erated by anthropologists. On paper, given that since the initial investigations of the site anthropological understanding of hunter-gatherer communities has advanced enormously, one would expect to find evidence for a steady convergence of under-standing and analytical approaches. In particular, when viewed in cross-cultural perspective, it is now clear that hunter-gatherer societies exhibit considerable variation in terms of their settlement systems, hunting strategies, subsistence logistics, patterns of mobility, use of space, butchery practices and responses to fluctuations in the seasonal availability of resources (e.g. Ingold, Riches and Woodburn 1988; Kelly 1995). No single interpretative model of hunter-gatherer behaviour, therefore, is likely to fit all archaeological manifestations of this mode of subsistence. As we discuss below, new models of hunter-gatherer behaviour have certainly informed more recent interpretations of the evidence from Star Carr, as have other changes in archaeological theory and analytical techniques. Of these, methodological advances in faunal analysis and detecting seasonal signatures from archaeological remains, as well as improved awareness of site formation processes and preservation biases have been particularly significant.

Yet, despite such easily identifiable trends, the two quotations that open this chapter continue to have resonance within British, and arguably European, Mesolithic studies. Specifically, as Grahame Clark held, there is still a very strong belief within archaeology that Star Carr is representative of a typical Early Mesolithic lowland settlement or activity base, albeit an exceptionally well-preserved example. Consequently, it is still widely believed that in time other 'Star Carrs' will be found. The fact that fifty years on from the original excavation no comparable example *has* come to light, still seems to be attributed by most archaeologists to either insufficient or incompetent fieldwork, and sometimes both. That such views are so deeply entrenched within archaeological consciousness seems extraordinary considering the extensive literature on the site, much of which concerns reinterpretations and restudies of material recovered during the initial excavations. Moreover, both the site and its broader setting within the Vale of Pickering have also been the focus of renewed fieldwork campaigns over the last twenty-five years (e.g. Cloutman 1988; Mellars and Dark 1998; Schadla-Hall 1987, 1989). While aspects of the work have yet to be fully published (Lane and Schadla-Hall in preparation), the main results have been discussed at numerous conferences and seminars and are also summarized in the Mellars and Dark report on Star Carr. Although some more recent studies make reference to this material, it is apparent that, in much the same way as David Clarke observed for archaeology in general (1976), conventional concepts continue to drive interpretation of the site and its contents. In this case the pertinent concept is that of the archaeological 'site', which in virtually all studies so far published has been regarded as the primary analytical unit from which subsequent archaeological interpretation should proceed. Below, we attempt to explain why this has been the case and in our concluding remarks offer an alternative interpretative lens through which the data from Star Carr and other Early Mesolithic sites in the vicinity might be viewed.

## Star Carr

The archaeological site of Star Carr is situated at the western end of a former lake known erroneously in much of the archaeological literature as 'Lake Pickering', and more correctly as 'palaeo-Lake Flixton' (Moore 1951). Lake Flixton formed during the terminal stages of the last glaciation roughly between 13,000–11,500 BP, as a consequence of earlier glacial modification of the local landscape and drainage, and the release of melt-waters by retreating glaciers (Catt 1987). Over the ensuing millennia, the lake was gradually infilled as part of a natural hydroseral progression leading ultimately to the formation of extensive peat and other organic deposits, which now seal the former Mesolithic land-surface (Cloutman and Smith 1988; Mellars and Dark 1998). Almost half a century of palaeoenvironmental studies indicates that during the early postglacial period, *c*.10,600–9,000 BP, Lake Flixton was over four miles in extent and up to a mile-and-a-half wide in places, replenished by spring-fed streams running off the Yorkshire Wolds and the North York Moors. At least three prominent islands existed down the centre of the lake, separated from the shorelines by stretches of deep open water. The shoreline topography was highly varied. In places it shelved steeply into deep water, while at the far eastern end of the lake it appears to have comprised a patchwork of narrow channels and islets. Elsewhere, the gradient was far more gentle with shallow embayments that allowed the formation of fringing reed beds. Archaeological surveys and excavations conducted in the Vale of Pickering since the 1940s have revealed extensive traces of human activity attributable to the early Post-Glacial era, including the now world-famous site of Star Carr, first excavated by Grahame Clark (1954).

Since its initial excavation, this 'site' has occupied a key position in studies of the Early Mesolithic of Britain and more generally northern Europe. However, over the years Star Carr has also acquired an international reputation which far outweighs its regional significance (Table 12.1). Numerous introductory textbooks refer to the site, and the methods and interpretations of the original excavator, Clark, have been widely cited as exemplars of the potentials of wetland archaeology, environmental and scientific archaeology, the use of ethnographic analogy, the characteristics of archaeological inference, and as setting standards for excavation, analysis and speedy publication. The site has also been acknowledged as a source of inspiration for similar field studies in other parts of the world, including North America (Kirk 1974) and New Zealand (Shawcross 1972). At a more popular level, the evidence from Star Carr has been widely used as a model for Mesolithic society in museum displays throughout the UK, as well as in a range of encyclopaedias (e.g. Sherratt 1980), archaeological dictionaries and histories (e.g. Bray and Trump 1970) and general guides to British, European and world prehistory (e.g. Clark 1975; Champion, Gamble, Shennan and Whittle 1984; Longworth, Ashton and Rigby 1986).

**Table 12.1** The academic impact of Clark's excavation and interpretation of Star Carr

| Topic/Theme | Selected Reference |
| --- | --- |
| *British Mesolithic* | 'Britain's best-known Mesolithic site, Star Carr, was examined by Professor J.G.D. Clark between 1949 and 1951' (Darvill 1987: 26). |
| *NW European Mesolithic* | 'Star Carr could well be seen as one of the earliest examples of a fully-fledged, classically "Mesolithic" settlement so far documented in northern Europe' (Mellars 1998: 240). |
| *Wetland Archaeology* | 'Clark's major excavations at Star Carr . . . mark the beginning of modern wetland archaeology in western Europe' (Coles and Coles 1989: 58). |
| *Site Catchment Analysis* | 'Clark has suggested . . . that the dwellers on the Mesolithic site at Star Carr . . . were exploiting . . . a wide range of habitats and resources . . . within one or two hour's walk' (Ashton 1985: 21). |
| *Environmental Archaeology/ Ecological Approaches* | 'Prior to the excavations in the early 1950s at Star Carr interest had largely centred around the study of flint artefacts . . . but with the publication of this excavation the importance of organic materials . . . were to be thrust into the foreground' (Longworth, Ashton and Rigby 1986: 19). |
| *Settlement Mobility and Seasonality* | 'The seasonal cycle involved "fission and fusion" of the band similar to that observed in modern hunter gatherers' (Roberts 1989: 83). |
| *Archaeological Inference and Ethnographic Analogy* | 'The assumptions and information on which a chain of argument is constructed are presented to the reader . . . to show the relationship between food waste . . . and the Mesolithic community' (Shawcross 1972: 591). |
| *Excavation & Publication Standards* | 'An example of what would seem to be the proper measure of care in recording, consistent with the importance of flint-reject material, is the work . . . at the Mesolithic site of Star Carr' (Hester, Heizer and Graham 1975: 121). |
| *Quality of Preservation* | 'Star Carr . . . provides such a vivid insight into Maglemosian life that it is as if . . . a TV camera has filmed the past . . . the remains so well preserved that it was possible to reconstruct life and the environment . . . unusually fully' (Laing and Laing 1980: 68). |
| *Contribution to development of new approaches* | 'Clark's ecological researches were important catalysts for the theoretical ferment that burst on American archaeology in the 1960s. Clark's Star Carr monograph and his writings on ecological archaeology were essential reading to anyone interested in the canons of the new archaeology' (Fagan 1999: 70). |

Star Carr has also been the subject of a series of restudies, which have involved reconsideration of the original interpretations, re-examination of some of the faunal and artefactual material recovered and, most recently, renewed archaeological and environmental investigations of the site and its setting (see below). In addition, it is one of the archaeological sites most frequently cited by scholars in other cognate disciplines (e.g. Simmons 1969; Roberts 1989). A rapid Internet search conducted in August 2002 using just one search engine, produced over 100 'hits'. The bulk of these related to either university course work and bibliographies from institutions around the globe or 'general popular archaeology' entries in a variety of languages. However, they also point to a growing interest in the site by environmental activists and 'new agers', as also illustrated by Julian Copes's use of the site in his book *The Modern Antiquarian* (1998), where he comments on its 'brilliant shiny name of possibilities' (1998: 270), while at the same time misspelling it.

## On the 'discovery' of Star Carr

In the first few decades of the twentieth century virtually nothing was known about the Mesolithic archaeology of the Vale of Pickering, in marked contrast to its reputation as place where Neolithic polished stone and flint axes were commonly recovered. In Elgee's review of the archaeology of NE Yorkshire, no isolated finds spots in the Vale let alone sites of Maglemosian date are mentioned. Instead, his review gave the impression that the North York Moors, the Durham coastline and the wetlands of Holderness had been the centres of Mesolithic activity (Elgee 1930, 26–31). Even this had been challenged by Sheppard, who insisted that the finds of Maglemose barbed points from Holderness were forgeries (Sheppard 1923). This situation changed during the 1940s, when a local archaeologist, John W. Moore, began conducting fieldwork at the eastern end of the Vale. By examining sections of freshly cleaned drainage ditches, Moore located a number of sites containing pieces of worked flint, bone and other material dating from the Early Mesolithic, *c*.10,600–8,600 BP. He labelled these Sites 1 to 10 (Moore 1950).

Moore drew his discoveries to the attention of Harry Godwin, Director of the Sub-Department of Quaternary Research at Cambridge University. In 1948, Godwin and A.P. Clapham, visited Moore's excavations at the Flixton sites, and obtained a pollen core from the vicinity. Following advice from Godwin, Moore sent a sample of the flints to Clark (Clark 1954: xviii). Clark later wrote of his excitement on receiving the 'parcel of flints' Moore had sent to him, which he initially assigned to the Maglemosian:

> The possibility was there of recovering this industry in early Post-glacial deposits. The vital clue would be animal bone. Mr Moore responded by systematically exploring

ditches on the northern margin of the alluvium. Sure enough, he was able to lead me on my first visit to a site where decayed bone and antler were visible in a dike profile at the same level as the flints. This site was Star Carr. (Clark 1972a: 4)

Clark subsequently directed excavations at the Star Carr site over three seasons, each of approximately three weeks long, between 1949 and 1951. At Star Carr, Clark found what he took to represent the remains of a residential base camp for a small band of mobile hunter-gatherers, who had occupied the site during the winter and spring months (Clark 1954). During the same period, Moore continued to work at Flixton, and some of his preliminary results were included in the final Star Carr report (Moore 1954). The speed with which Clark put together a thorough and comprehensive report contributed to an immediate interest, as did Alan Sorrell's reconstruction of the site first published in the *Illustrated London News* (Sorrell 1951), and subsequently reproduced in popular books (e.g. Jessop 1967). This created a powerful visual image of hunter-gatherers at Star Carr, reinforcing Clark's preferred interpretation of the evidence, and subsequently formed the basis for museum exhibitions about the Mesolithic throughout the UK. Even more fundamental for ensuring the site's subsequent popularity was that Clark's report was in English. Far richer, in terms of the range and quantity of organic and faunal remains, and more meticulously recorded sites had been excavated decades earlier on the continent (e.g. Ulkestrup, Denmark) but, either left unpublished for decades or published in a European language, the evidence from these has tended to be overlooked by all but a few specialists with knowledge of the requisite languages.

Following Clark's excavations at Star Carr, the site rapidly came to be considered as a 'type-site' for the Maglemosian in Northern England, not least because it was the only site of its kind to have been investigated in Britain. Another reason for the rise in prominence of the Star Carr site was the quality of preservation of faunal remains and organic artefacts never before encountered in the UK on Early Mesolithic sites, which gave further significance to Star Carr and the research potential of waterlogged sites in general.

The integration of data from specialist analyses of the faunal assemblage (Fraser and King 1954), and the pollen remains and peat deposits (Walker and Godwin 1954), was an additional key contributory factor. In particular, by providing information about the site's environmental setting, possible seasons of occupation and the diet of its occupants, these studies illustrated more than any other comparable work at the time the great potential of scientific analyses within archaeology. As a consequence, the Star Carr approach to 'economic prehistory' (Clark 1952a, 1953, 1973) came to be regarded as a model for others to follow and was widely cited in archaeological textbooks.

Yet another contributory factor to the rise in prominence of Star Carr within Mesolithic studies, and more generally British archaeology, was the discovery and investigation during the 1960s of Early Mesolithic sites on the Pennines in West Yorkshire, interpreted as representing the summer counterparts of Star Carr (Radley and Mellars 1964). The view that Star Carr was a fairly typical, if exceptionally well preserved, example of an Early Mesolithic winter and spring-time base camp became further entrenched in the mid 1970s, following the publication of a reappraisal of the evidence from Star Carr and the sites in the Pennines by Clark (1972b). Clark's model was further extended following Jacobi's interpretation of Early Mesolithic flint scatters on the North York Moors at sites such as Pointed Stone 2 and 3, as representing the remains of short-term summer hunting camps (1978).

Aside from these factors, Clark's work at Star Carr was integral to the consolidation of his reputation as a specialist on Mesolithic Europe. In 1929 and again 1933–4, as a postgraduate, he had undertaken major study tours of northern Europe, during which he had had the chance to visit important Early Mesolithic waterlogged sites. During these visits he also came to know the Danish archaeologist Therkel Mathiassen, whose familiarity with the various Canadian Arctic cultures helped draw Clark's attention to the potential value of ethnographic analogy (Fagan 2001: 72). The outcome of these study tours was the publication of the first major synthesis of the Mesolithic (Clark 1936). Curiously, many of the themes with which Clark was later to become most associated with, and especially his concern with the reconstruction of prehistoric economies and the use and production of artefacts from organic materials, are largely absent from this text. Nevertheless, Clark was clearly aware of the potential of waterlogged sites, as evident from his enthusiastic involvement in the work of the Fenland Research Committee over the following decade, that included excavations at Peacock's Farm. However, both here and on his earlier 1937–8 excavations at Farnham with Rankine, Clark's efforts to find suitably rich and well-preserved deposits were unsuccessful (see Fagan 2001). In view of this, his stated enthusiasm at receiving news of the discovery by Moore of waterlogged Early Mesolithic sites in the Vale of Pickering becomes far more significant. Simply put, even before Star Carr was excavated Clark had determined that this type of site held the key to 'understanding' the British Mesolithic, and in hindsight it seems very unlikely that his subsequent interpretations of the evidence were not conditioned by this perception.

One final contributing factor to the speed with which the results of Clark's excavations entered into common archaeological discourse, must have been Clark's own position within academia. Specifically, in 1934 he was appointed honorary editor of (what became in 1935) *The Proceedings of the Prehistoric Society*. In 1935, when he was appointed assistant lecturer at Cambridge he had almost thirty papers in print. In 1952 he was appointed Disney Professor of Archaeology at Cambridge. He had already developed a strong interest in the economic basis of prehistoric society, and was working on the text of a major synthesis of the evidence from Europe (Clark 1952a) at the time he began work at Star Carr. Many of his interpretations of the site are clearly informed by this broader research, while at the same time he used the emerging evidence from Star Carr in sections discussing the use of organic materials such as birch bark and antler during prehistory (e.g. Clark 1952a: 134, 208–9, 222). In addition, after the Second World War many of his former students, several of whom had worked on the Star Carr excavations, began to establish their own archaeological careers around the world (Coles 1999, 210–4), which also did much to embed Star Carr in global archaeological literature.

## Star Carr Reappraised

Clark's original interpretation of Star Carr was that it represented the remains of an exceptionally well-preserved winter base camp, utilized by a small band of mobile foragers (1954). He developed this position further in his 1972 reappraisal of the 'site' providing supporting evidence for the possible summer locations of these bands. This was further strengthened by Noe-Nygaard's identification of healed lesions on deer and elk bones (1975), indicating at least two separate encounters between hunters and their prey. This was taken as further proof of 'winter yarding' around Star Carr by these species. Numerous shorter syntheses by Clark of the research at Star Carr, as well as cross-referencing to the site and its contents in his own more general works of synthesis on world prehistory (e.g. 1975 and subsequent editions), prehistoric Europe (e.g. 1952a,) and hunter-gatherer archaeology (e.g. Clark 1967), helped disseminate information about the site and reinforce his particular interpretation. This was reproduced in turn by others to illustrate a variety of points about archaeological techniques, interpretative methods and the preservational biases of the archaeological record (see Table 12.1).

Also, during the first two decades from the commencement of archaeological work at Star Carr, all of the publications relate to the analysis and synthesis of primary data (Table 12.2). The only challenge to any of the data and interpretations presented in the main site report during this period was Degerbøl's (1961) confirmation of the presence of domesticated dog, originally identified as wolf (Fraser and King 1954). This had no immediate impact on broader interpretations of the site or Clark's models of settlement mobility and seasonality. Instead, what attracted attention was that for a while this was the earliest known example of animal domestication from Europe. Once again, this was taken up by other archaeologists in the way in which the site was portrayed, and added to the growing number of 'jewels' in Star Carr's metaphorical crown.

From the mid 1970s, however, a series of alternative interpretations of the function of Star Carr, its season of occupation and place within a larger settlement

**Table 12.2** Major research themes with reference to Star Carr: analysis of publications by decade, 1949–2003

| Theme | 1949– 1959 | 1960– 1969 | 1970– 1979 | 1980– 1989 | 1990– 1999 | 2000– | Total |
|---|---|---|---|---|---|---|---|
| Report/Interpretative Overview | 5 | | | | 1 | | 6 |
| Artefact Studies | 5 | | | 6 | 3 | 1 | 15 |
| Palaeoenvironment | 5 | | | 3 | 6 | | 14 |
| Faunal Remains | 4 | | | 1 | 1 | | 6 |
| Related Sites – field reports | 2 | 2 | 1 | 5 | 1 | | 11 |
| Subsistence/Economic Basis | 2 | | 1 | 1 | 1 | | 5 |
| Seasonality | 4 | | 1 | 6 | 5 | | 16 |
| Dating | 2 | | | | 3 | 1 | 6 |
| Domestication | 1 | 1 | | | | | 2 |
| Ritual | 1 | | | | | | 1 |
| Settlement Mobility | 1 | | 3 | 1 | 2 | 1 | 8 |
| Taphonomic Processes | | | 2 | 2 | | | 4 |
| Reassessment | | | 4 | 3 | 1 | | 8 |
| Interpretative Reasoning | | | | 4 | 1 | | 5 |
| Human Impacts & Environmental Management | | | | | 4 | | 4 |

system began to emerge. Jacobi's suggestion that Star Carr was a winter to early summer hunting and processing site, was the only one arising from the results of new fieldwork. Perhaps significantly, like Star Carr, these sites were not discovered as a result of targeted fieldwork carried out by a professional archaeologist, but instead were found by a pair of dedicated 'amateur' field workers, J.V. and A. Taylor. This lack of concern among professional archaeologists with conducting new fieldwork so as to augment the data set assembled by Clark from the Vale continued well into the 1970s. Even then, the new phase of excavations at Seamer Carr was only prompted as a result of an external threat to the archaeology, and the consequent need to mount a rescue excavation. It would seem therefore that, as with so many other aspects of Star Carr's post-excavation history, the success of Clark's model at this time acted as much to constrain archaeological enquiry as it did to enhance understanding of the past.

The most significant reappraisals during the third to early fourth decade of Star Carr's post-excavation history, however, were all *literature-based* studies heavily influenced by changing models of hunter-gatherer behaviour and economic organization, as well as newly emerging analytical techniques and concern with site-formation and taphonomic processes. Between 1978 and 1982, four separate reinterpretations of Star Carr were published. These ranged from a suggestion that the site had been a butchering station and possible kill-site (Caulfield 1978); a specialized locality for summertime processing of antler and animal skins (Pitts

1979); a hunting and butchering station used episodically throughout the year (Andresen, Byrd, Elson, McGuire, Mendoza, Staski, and White 1981); and a base camp occupied repeatedly and during more than one season (Price 1982). The merits of these different models have been discussed elsewhere (e.g. Legge and Rowley-Conwy 1988; Mellars and Dark 1998; Dincauze 2000: 489–93), and need not be repeated here. More significant, perhaps, is that these studies acknowledged that hunter-gatherer communities make variable use of the landscape and as a result the archaeological traces of their activity are likely to include a range of special-purpose sites in addition to the remains of settlements and base camps (cf. Binford 1980, 1982). There is also evidence for a growing concern during these decades with the depositional context of the site and potential biases introduced by a variety of natural processes and human activities (e.g. Noe-Nygaard 1977, 1988; Wheeler 1978; Coles and Orme 1983).

For the next two decades, the focus of debates about Star Carr consequently turned to reconsideration of the physical evidence from the site regarding the season or seasons of occupation and the range of activities conducted at the 'site'. Until the most recent phase of environmental research (Mellars and Dark 1998), as in the original site report, evidence from faunal remains has dominated discussions concerning the seasons of occupation and/or activity at Star Carr (e.g. Klein, Alwarden and Wolf 1983; Legge and Rowley-Conwy 1988; Clutton-Brock and Noe-Nygaard 1990; Day 1996; Carter 1997, 1998; Schulting and Richards 2002; Dark 2003). In several cases, these have taken advantage of the development of new techniques for detecting seasonal and dietary signatures. By far the most influential of these studies has been that by Legge and Rowley-Conwy (1988), whose comprehensive reanalysis of the entire faunal assemblage from Clark's excavations reversed some of the original assessments of body part and species representations, thereby providing an alternative perspective on the contribution of different species to the diet, hunting practices, and season of site use. Moreover, in their analyses of the faunal assemblage from Star Carr, Legge and Rowley-Conwy drew heavily on Binford's work on butchery practices and bone discard patterns among the Nunamiut Eskimo (1978), so as to generate a more behavioural understanding of the structure of the deposits.

Over the same period, parallel restudies of the lithics from the site, with emphasis on the evidence from use-wear analysis, were being conducted by J. Dumont (e.g. 1989). The results of these provided a wider understanding of the possible range of activities being performed either at Star Carr, or at least elsewhere in the landscape by Star Carr's occupants. More recently, the various bone and antler artefacts have been the subject of restudy (e.g Smith 1989; Bonsall and Smith 1990) from a typological perspective. As with the more extensive work on faunal remains from the site, the results of these disparate studies have all added information about the function and seasons of occupation of the Star Carr site. Moreover, it is these two issues which continue to dominate discussions of the site and its context, even in the light of new excavations and environmental research (Mellars and Dark 1998). This is well illustrated by the changing fortune of the Star Carr dog. Initially, the presence of dog bones at the site was regarded as significant simply in terms of the history of animal domestication (Degerbøl 1961). Subsequently, following the discovery of more dog bones at one of the Seamer Carr sites, and the application of recently developed techniques of isotope analysis (Clutton-Brock and Noe-Nygaard 1990), these bones were drawn into the debate on seasons of occupation and mobility, and like Star Carr as a whole continue to generate contrasting interpretations (Day 1996; Schulting and Richards 2002; Dark 2003).

## Changing Archaeological Approaches to Hunter-Gatherers

At the time of Clark's excavations at Star Carr, anthropological models of hunter-gatherer societies remained heavily influenced by nineteenth-century evolutionary thinking. While the crude categorization of past and present societies into unilineal stages of savagery, barbarism and civilization was no longer dominant, modern hunter-gatherer societies were still widely regarded as living representatives of a way of life that other, 'more progressive' societies had left behind. Importantly, especially as a result of Radcliffe-Brown's research among Australian Aboriginal societies, and the more general theoretical formulations advanced by Julian Steward, anthropologists had begun to focus their attention on the principles of social organization among hunter-gatherers rather than purely on their technological and economic characteristics. By the 1950s, the dominant model of hunter-gatherer society was that of the patrilineal band. Typically, these were characterized as consisting of local, exogamous and politically autonomous groups of between fifty to a hundred individuals, each with their own distinct communally owned territory, to which members claimed rights of access through the principles of patrilineal descent and patrilocal residence. It was this model which became virtually synonymous with hunter-gatherer society, especially following Service's reformulation of Steward's typology (see Kelly 1995: 11–12).

Although Clark was probably aware of these models, in his original report he makes no explicit reference to current or earlier anthropological theory, making only fairly restricted use of ethnographic analogies to flesh out certain of his interpretations, often citing some of his own syntheses of the relevant ethnographic literature (for analyses of this aspect of Clark's interpretation see e.g. Wylie 1985: 74–7). Instead, Clark relied much more heavily on other comparable archaeological data, especially that from north-west European sites, no doubt in part influenced by having completed his work on the economic basis of prehistoric Europe (1952a) immediately after concluding his excavations at Star Carr (see also Fagan 1999: 69). Clark's 1972 reassessment similarly show signs of having been influenced by recent developments in archaeology and anthropology, notably the notion of 'site catchment analysis' as being proposed by Vita-Finzi and Higgs (1970), and the general definition of hunter-gatherers as 'living in small groups' and 'moving around a lot' as proposed by Lee and DeVore in their introduction to the *Man the Hunter* volume (1968b: 11). Clark, nevertheless, made no explicit reference to any of these broader studies in his paper.

By the late 1970s, both site-catchment analysis and more importantly in this context, the 'Original Affluent Society' model of hunter-gatherers that had emerged from the *Man the Hunter* volume and Sahlins' *Stone Age Economics* (1972), were starting to be critiqued. In archaeology, perhaps the most influential development was Binford's distinction between 'foragers' and 'collectors' (1980), although Woodburn's somewhat similar distinction between 'immediate return' and 'delayed return' procurement systems (1980), has also had an impact as has, at least in some quarters, the extensive literature on optimal foraging theory. Essentially, Binford saw all hunter-gathering societies as occupying points along a continuum. At one extreme Binford placed those societies characterized by high annual residential mobility and low logistical mobility which he termed 'foragers'. At the other extreme, were those societies characterized by low annual residential mobility and high logistical mobility, described as 'collectors'. From this categorization, Binford, and subsequently other archaeologists, generated a series of archaeological indicators that he believed could be used to differentiate between the two extreme forms.

Most archaeologists now accept that it is likely that different hunter-gatherer societies probably fall somewhere between these two extremes, such that their subsistence-settlement systems exhibit elements of both a 'foraging' and 'collection' mode of resource procurement. No single interpretative model of hunter-gather behaviour, therefore, is likely to fit all archaeological manifestations of this mode of subsistence. By the late 1970s, archaeologists generally were also beginning to address various problems perceived to derive from different types of biases that can affect the composition of the data base available to them (e.g. Clarke 1973; Schiffer 1976). As a consequence, it is now conventionally understood that at least four major categories of bias need to be taken into consideration. Namely, preservational biases created by differential deposition, survival and recovery of material; geographical/locational biases created by the differential pattern of fieldwork and effects of post-depositional processes; interpretational biases arising from initial preconceptions about the relationship between the archaeological record and past human behaviour; and paradigmatic biases regarding the nature of society in the past (see Rowley-Conwy 1986 for a discussion of the impact of these ideas on understandings of the European Mesolithic).

As discussed above, these general trends are clearly reflected in the literature-based and object-based reassessments of Star Carr published during the last few

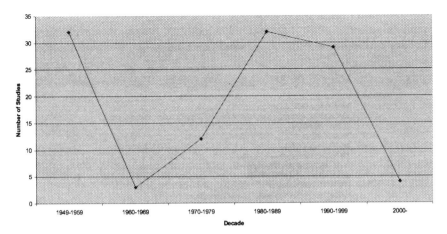

**Figure 12.1** Changing intensity of research activity concerning Star Carr and its environs, 1949–2003

decades. As shown in Figure 12.1, the cycle of academic activity relating to the site has followed a fairly standard trend of discovery, initial acceptance (marked by a dip in activity), reassessment and debate taking into account new theoretical perspectives and the opportunities provided by the development of new techniques of analysis, followed by renewed field activity aimed at augmenting the available database and addressing some of the issues raised during the reassessment phase. This is also confirmed in Figure 12.2, which indicates that like most other archaeological research, considerable energy has been directed repeatedly at the analysis of the artefacts and faunal remains from the site; at establishing a secure chronological framework for these; and reconstructing the site's economy and environmental context. The growing number of alternative interpretations of the site has also served to draw attention to the possible range of different 'site types' that might be encountered within any particular Early Mesolithic landscape, and especially that around Star Carr. The long history of debate and reassessment has also generated new research questions, particularly concerning the possible human impacts on the local environment during the Mesolithic, which are only now being addressed.

However, it is also possible to discern a number of lacunae and issues that have been virtually neglected since Clark's original excavations. Thus, as is evident from Figure 12.2, there has been no attempt to consider the site as a place of ritual significance, despite the widespread publicity that has been given to the antler frontlets recovered by Clark and his proposal that these were used in some kind of shamanistic practice. The numerous beads found at Star Carr during Clark's excavations have also been almost entirely overlooked. Also, to the best of our knowledge, there have been no published attempts to considered the site and its contents

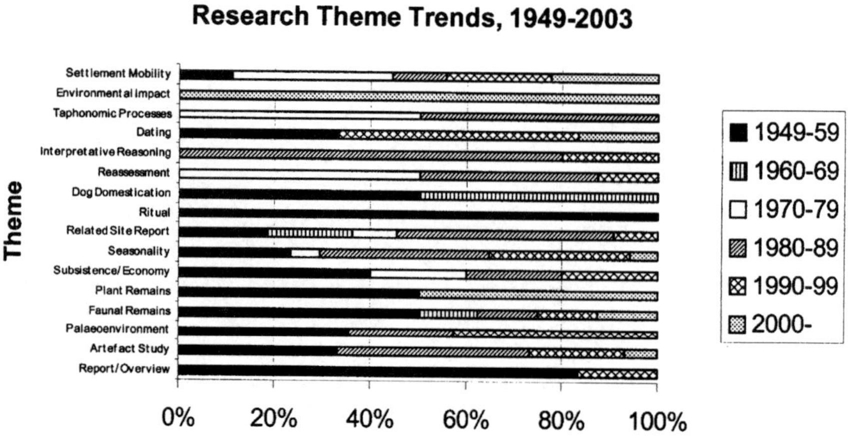

## Research Theme Trends, 1949-2003

**Figure 12.2** Trends in research on Star Carr and its environs, by decade, 1949–2003

either from a gendered perspective or in terms of a more general symbolic reading – both themes being now commonplace in other branches of archaeology. Equally, none of the previous interpretations of Star Carr and its broader context has sought to offer anything other than a cultural geography based entirely around issues of subsistence and seasonality. Questions such as how this landscape may have been perceived and given meaning by its Mesolithic inhabitants, and the extent to which their categories of space and place resemble or diverge from those used in archaeological analysis, remain to be asked despite the fact that these issues are now of central concern to anthropologists of hunter-gatherer societies (e.g. Ingold 2000a: 40–60).

Instead, the key questions archaeologists seem to want to ask about Star Carr remain 'What time of year was it occupied?', 'What activities were carried out there?', and 'What was the site's role within a broader settlement system?'. Important though these are, it seems remarkable that the debate about Star Carr has hardly moved on during the last fifty years. Moreover, the reasons for this almost certainly lie in the process of academic citation. Of course, it is well known that the history of an archaeological 'site' does not cease either at the time of its original abandonment or at the moment of its 'discovery' and archaeological investigation. Instead, both the contents of the abandoned 'site' and the interpretations of them continually undergo various transformations. However, not all sites have the same post-excavation history, or are as equally well documented. Only a few sites generate the number of restudies and reappraisals as has been the fate of Star Carr, but when they do, like Star Carr, these fresh contributions to the archaeological literature help to reinforce widespread belief within the discipline of the site's significance. In other words, certain archaeological sites that are perceived (for whatever reason) to be 'important', 'representative' or 'exceptional' tend to have this status reinforced through the process of academic citation. In this way, the intrinsic properties of the 'site' cease to be the sole criteria of importance to such an extent that occasionally the 'cite' becomes more relevant than the 'site' itself.

## Conclusion

Having looked at the different uses of the site as portrayed in the literature, we want to conclude by emphasizing that most of the time archaeologists have failed to consider the nature of Clark's 'site' itself. Even after half a century, no one can fault the expedition with which the report was published, or the quality of the excavations or the report itself. It remains a key site in global terms for considering early Post-Glacial hunter-gatherers for all of these reasons. It is cemented in the literature, as indeed are many of the conclusions which Clark originally propounded. And yet, the site opens up – or should have opened up – a more vigorous debate about the nature of 'site' itself. Our subsequent work in the Vale, some of which is foreshadowed by Mellars and Dark, clearly indicates that Clark excavated no more than 10 per cent of the area of known deposits. His original interpretation of the site as a tightly drawn area is clearly contradicted by the exposure of a substantial timber platform to the east of his trenches (Mellars, Schadla-Hall and Lane 1998). Recent field walking across the area of the Star Carr site has demonstrated a total area of dry-land flint scatter in excess of 4000 square metres and a lake edge zone of over 2000 square metres. This suggests the likelihood that even in terms of the narrow concepts of the 'site' of Star Carr, conclusions about the nature of its occupation and utilization have been generated from a very small sample. This may go some way to explaining the discrepancies between different categories of evidence regarding the season of occupation and the range of activities possibly performed at Star Carr. The function of the site is further confused by the lack of reconsideration of the nature of early Mesolithic society in broader, regional terms.

The recent programme of high-resolution radiocarbon dating, coupled with equally high-resolution palaeoenvironmental studies has also demonstrated that the area of Star Carr was utilized repeatedly over a number of centuries, and at least three peaks in activity can be discerned (Mellars and Dark 1998). Given such evidence for long-term repeated use of this area of the lake-shore, it is seems highly likely that the locality was used for a quite divergent range of activities at different times. This may also account for why it has been possible to interpret the small part of the site at Star Carr excavated by Clark as a seasonal camp, a processing centre, a hunting station and a ritual site, and also why it has been seen as both typical and atypical, and occupied for both long (if interrupted) periods and shorter intervals. At various times in its occupation history, the area that is now embedded in the literature as 'the site of Star Carr', may have fulfilled all of these roles either consecutively or successively, and perhaps other roles as yet unimagined by archaeologists. Reconstructions of the periodicity of site use is further complicated by the existence of a 'radiocarbon plateau' around the time of the main phases of site occupation (Day and Mellars 1994).

More radically, the work of the Vale of Pickering Research Trust elsewhere in the Vale, coupled with the results of the large-scale area excavations at Seamer Carr, has placed Star Carr in a wider landscape setting and context. The archaeological place known as 'Star Carr' is clearly located at the exit from an extensive lake, around which a further nine 'sites' (so far) have been located. All of these 'sites' certainly fall within the wider date bracket for Star Carr itself. They are also all situated on the lake margins. They have similar flint assemblages to Star Carr, and at least two of them have similar densities (based on the samples thus far recovered). However, none appears to have comparable faunal assemblages either in terms of diversity or quantity, and only an additional three fragmentary barbed points and one worked antler have been recovered from elsewhere in the Vale. No traces of beads have been found. Thus, contrary to Clark's hopes it is unlikely that other 'Star Carrs' will be discovered – at least in the eastern Vale. Whatever Star Carr was, compared with the other traces around the Vale it was a quite 'different' place within the Early Mesolithic landscape of palaeolake Flixton. Indeed the palaeolake (which effectively disappears by the seventh millennium BP) may be critical to the existence of Star Carr and the other related archaeological sites, and hence should be regarded as the *real* 'site'.

Additional pollen and related studies since Clark's day are beginning to provide a picture of manipulation of the environment. For instance, there is evidence for regular burning around Star Carr and other areas (Mellars and Dark 1998; Cummins et al. forthcoming), although there is little evidence to suggest widespread deforestation. It is now clear, also, that a series of powerful springs maintained the lake and that these acted as foci for human activity. The islands in the centre of the lake were also being utilized for settlement and the processing of resources. Between these places of intensive activity are numerous, more ephemeral traces that include small flint caches and localized scatters of flint and animal bones, all of which presumably represent activity as well – and in some cases different types of flint occur at different patches. Conceivably, all of this evidence could be integrated within a general model of 'forager' or 'collector' behaviour of the type now popular within hunter-gatherer archaeology. Indeed, this is precisely how some recent analysts have approached this body of data (e.g. Smith 1992; Rowley-Conwy 1995; Mellars and Dark 1998). However, further away from the margins of the lake there is a relative dearth of activity – at least in terms of flint scatters – all of which suggest that it was the lake itself, which served as 'the site', not particular localities. Thus Star Carr, the Seamer 'sites' and all of the others now known to exist around the lake margins were merely components of this.

In this paper we have attempted to demonstrate the continuing dominance of one relatively small excavation in terms of overall perception of the hunter-gatherer past, and to show how even the data from these excavations are likely to be incomplete. Perhaps as a direct consequence of this, the site has lent itself to multiple and often contradictory interpretations by at least two generations of archaeologists, each borrowing successively from a changing backdrop of anthropological theory and observation. One crucial and mistaken aspect of most of these has been the failure to appreciate the true significance of the evidence that was in the original report (and has since been confirmed by more recent work), of the many ages of Star Carr and its multiple occupation histories. We have also shown how the results of the original excavation came to assume such overwhelming importance in the discipline, and how this continues to be maintained. Through our own research, we may well have placed Star Carr in a wider context, and can begin to demonstrate the complexity of the system of hunter-gatherers in one area; but Star Carr and its much published image remains almost as popular as ever. Mobility and seasonality still dominate the agenda, as does the idea of 'site' on a small scale. In many respects then, despite opening up a wide range of new avenues of enquiry within British archaeology, and setting standards for recording and publication, Clark's work at Star Carr, albeit unintentionally, by its very popularity also stifled wider thinking about the nature of human societies in early Post-Glacial Europe. If anything still seems certain at this stage in the research, it is simply that these early Post-Glacial hunter-gatherers did not share our perceptions of landscape or settlement, and that if archaeologists wish to come closer to understanding these they will need to change the spatial scale of their analyses away from that of the 'site' narrowly defined, to one that is far more encompassing and holistic in conception.

## Note

1. Space does not permit comprehensive listing of all relevant citations compiled for this paper. For further details, see Lane and Schadla-Hall (in preparation).

# –13–

# Ethnographic Models, Archaeological Data and the Applicability of Modern Foraging Theory

## *Michael S. Sheehan*

For an archaeologist trying to 'reflesh' the figurative 'bones' of the archaeological record, ethnographic data can be very seductive indeed. One of the most important challenges confronting archaeology over the past five decades has been developing a consensus regarding the appropriate use of ethnographic data in archaeological interpretation. The development and application of contemporary foraging theory in archaeology brings that challenge into sharp focus.

Hunter-gatherer studies have long been a theme of archaeological inquiry. Archaeology has looked to the ethnographic record for guidance in the interpretation of food residues. This is particularly important with regard to establishing the broader implications of resource procurement as they relate to behavioural patterning in mobility, settlement and subsistence. In recent years, optimal foraging theory has been useful in elucidating these behavioural patterns. Optimal foraging theory encompasses a set of mathematical formulations that describe the theoretical relation between populations of consumers and the resources they exploit. More specifically, it 'provides a cluster of simple models, partially derived from neo-Darwinian postulates, which produce operational hypotheses about foraging behaviours expected in different environmental circumstances' (Winterhalder 1981: 13). It has been widely utilized to good effect in a variety of studies, but it is not without detractors. Optimal foraging theory has considerable explanatory potential for archaeologists. However, as with any body of theory, it should be used with an awareness of its limitations. The position taken here is that the fundamental limitation of optimal foraging theory as an analytical method in the archaeology of hunter-gatherers has less to do the inherent qualities of the theory, than it does with the archaeological data the theory is used to interpret. Optimal foraging theory requires, in many cases, detailed environmental information that is readily available to the ethnographer and not to the archaeologist. This disparity in data detail is a recurring theme in the development and application of foraging theory in archaeology (Thomas 1986).

In the discussion that follows various applications of ethnographic data, especially as it relates to foraging behaviour, to archaeological analysis will be examined. Of particular interest are conventional ethnographic analogy, cultural ecology and middle range theory. The primary objective of this examination is to highlight the impact of the disjunction of data detail noted above, and to summarize efforts to minimize or negate that impact. The models comprising optimal foraging theory will also be reviewed with the intent of showing why many of them are difficult to apply to archaeological data sets. An effort will also be made to show how archaeologists might employ intensive sampling strategies that would allow broader use of these models.

## Ethnographic Data and Foraging Theory

The roots of contemporary foraging theory lie in attempts to link observable behaviour with the material correlates of that behaviour (direct analogy) and culminates with sophisticated approaches to linking 'inferred' behaviour with observable material correlates of that inferred behaviour. As early as 1948, calls were being made to look beyond archaeological data to the development of more powerful interpretative frameworks (Taylor 1948). Ethnographic data have played an important, and changing, role in this process.

Some of the earliest efforts to reconstruct prehistoric foraging patterns employed a very simple, and ultimately misleading, form of ethnographic analogy. In its classic form, ethnographic analogy incorporated an element of behavioural uniformitarianism. Behaviours observed in the ethnographic present were assumed to operate in the archaeological past, and therefore represented a valid tool for interpreting and understanding prehistoric human behaviour. As its use became more common, this kind of 'direct' analogy between behaviour in the present and behaviour in the past became very controversial.

By the mid-twentieth century, mounting concern over the appropriate use of ethnographic data in archaeology caused many to rethink these interpretive frameworks. One of the first venues for the comprehensive treatment of this issue was the now famous 'Man the Hunter' conference held at the University of Chicago in April 1966. At that meeting a number of seminal approaches to the use of ethnographic data in archaeological interpretation were offered, and each represented a move away from traditional, direct, forms of ethnographic analogy. In a discussion of foraging behaviour among Pleistocene hunter-gatherers in East Africa, Isaac (1968: 254) offers three suggestions for the appropriate use of ethnographic data in archaeological interpretation, especially as it relates to foraging. First, he argues that comparative study, of the type represented by ethnographic analogy, 'helps establish terms of reference for an archaeological inquiry'. A second area where ethnographic analogy can be profitably employed is to provide 'inspiration for the interpretation of archaeological evidence, the significance of which might otherwise be obscure.' The critical question here of course is: at what point does an 'inspiration' become a 'blueprint'? The boundary can be difficult to discern, and treacherous to navigate. Finally, Isaac indicates that 'The application of archaeological methods to ethnographic material can test the validity and limitations of archaeological inferences.'

Assuming a position that is, in some ways, diametrically opposed to the one offered by Isaac, Binford argues that the only appropriate use of ethnographic data is as a basis for forming postulates regarding the behavioural context of ethnographically and archaeologically observed phenomena (1968: 268–73). This represents an elabouration of comments he published the year before indicating that it is methodologically unsound to use ethnographic analogy for the interpretation of archaeological data (1967: 1–12). Some of Binford's comments find support in Freeman's position, when he observes that the extensive reliance on ethnographic data in archaeological interpretation has actually impaired the development of explanatory frameworks based primarily on archaeological data (1968: 262). Not surprisingly, Freeman goes on to recommend that the use of 'analogical reasoning from modern behaviour be kept to a minimum' (1968: 265).

Early in the history of modern archaeology, the use of 'direct' ethnographic analogy played an important role in reconstructing hunter-gatherer foraging behaviour. Nowhere is this more evident than in early attempts to understand settlement and subsistence patterns in the North American Great Plains. In the ethnographic present, the horse represented a critical bridge between human populations and their principal faunal resource, bison. Therefore it was argued, prehistoric settlement of the Plains would have been impossible prior to the introduction of the horse because that bridge between consumer and resource was lacking (Sterns 1918; Wissler 1914). In other words, indigenous Plains populations needed the horse to ensure adequate food supplies, in the form of bison, in the present; therefore they needed the horse in the past for the same reason. Needless to say, many scholars were shocked when archaeological sites, predating the horse and complete with bison bone, began popping up all over the Great Plains. Although this is but one example, it illustrates very clearly the pitfalls of using direct ethnographic analogy in archaeological interpretation.

The lure of ethnographic data stems from the level of observational detail obtainable in an ethnographic context. That level of detail is so much greater than that which can be obtained in an archaeological context, that the temptation to draw direct conclusions based on these data is extremely difficult to resist. Unfortunately, succumbing to the temptation produces results that exhibit little in the way of validity. A valid analogy requires congruence in material culture and behavioural context. Historically, archaeological use of ethnographic data involved congruence at the material culture level only.

In contrast to conventional ethnographic analogy, cultural ecology represents a more rigorous means of integrating ethnographic data into archaeological analysis, especially with regard to foraging behaviour. Cultural ecology is 'a way of obtaining a total picture of how human populations adapt to and transform their environments' (Fagan 1997: 417). The concept of cultural ecology was spawned from inspired fieldwork conducted by Julian Steward in the Great Basin of North America over a ten-year period spanning the late 1920s and early 1930s. In Steward's seminal study of the Great Basin Shoshone, Ute and Paiute, he intended to analyse the functional relationships among the different parts of these cultures to one another and to the local environment (Steward 1938). In so doing, he hoped to shed important light on the patterns and processes of culture change. Steward argued strenuously that culture change, especially among hunter-gatherers, could be understood in terms of adaptations to specific environments and that human ecology represented the pivotal bridge between culture and the natural environment. Not surprisingly subsistence strategy and regional resource structure figured prominently in his ideas.

As a method of analysis, human ecology involved the synthesis of information pertaining to the natural environment, the cultural devices used to exploit the natural environment, and the adaptations in human behaviour and institutions that result from the interplay between the natural and cultural environments (Steward 1938: 2). Effective application of this approach required very detailed information regarding flora and fauna, topography, climate, and distribution of water sources (Steward 1938: 10). The critical observation to be made here is that Steward could acquire this information as he conducted his ethnographic fieldwork. Steward continued to develop his ideas relating to the interaction between human populations and the environments they occupied. An important consequence of this development was a reformulation and redefinition of human ecology. The focus shifted away from the 'human community' as a strictly biological construct, to the 'human community' as a cultural construct. Hence the change in nomenclature from human ecology to cultural ecology. In explaining this shift in orientation, Steward argued that culture 'rather than genetic potential for adaptation, . . . explains the nature of human societies' (1955a: 32). He described the theoretical distinction this way: 'Cultural ecology differs from human and social ecology in seeking to explain the origin of particular cultural features and patterns which characterize different areas rather than to derive general principles applicable to any cultural-environmental situation.' (Steward 1955a: 36).

As an analytical method, cultural ecology involved three distinct, but related, procedures. The first involved analysis of the interrelationship between exploitative or productive technology and the environment. The second focused on the behaviour patterns employed in the exploitation of a particular environment by means of a particular technology. The third, and final, procedure emphasized assessment of the extent to which behaviours entailed in exploiting the environment affected other aspects of a cultural system (Steward 1955a: 40–1). The method of cultural ecology placed considerable emphasis on the 'culture core', or those features of a culture most closely linked to subsistence-related activities (Steward 1955a: 37). Given the nature of the archaeological record, especially that produced by hunter-gatherers, it is not surprising that a host of archaeologists welcomed this new analytical method with open arms. Although cultural ecology should not be regarded as ancestral to subsequent foraging theory, it is one of the earliest, carefully constructed, bodies of such theory. Judicious application of its analytical protocols allowed archaeologists to make rigorous inferences about past human behaviour that had a firm basis in carefully constructed theory. The impact of cultural ecology on archaeology in North America cannot be underestimated. Fagan has argued that 'Steward's new cultural ecological approach was, perhaps, the most important theoretical development in North American archaeology in a century' (1995: 51).

Notwithstanding the theoretical value of the concept of cultural ecology, actually applying it using archaeological data was problematical. Once again, archaeologists attempted to employ approaches developed using ethnographic data to interpretation of the archaeological record. In so doing, they confronted a recurring problem: the detailed data, like that Steward relied upon to ultimately formulate the concept of cultural ecology, are difficult if not impossible to obtain archaeologically. For example, Steward was able to 'observe' the distribution of plant and animal resources. Such direct observations are not within the realm of possibility for the archaeologist. Notwithstanding its overall utility and influence in archaeology, the application of cultural ecology to illuminating the archaeological record is hampered by the disparity in data detail between ethnography and archaeology.

In an effort to effectively utilize ethnographic data in a productive manner Binford (2001) and others (e.g. Yellen 1977a, 1977b; Gould 1978, 1980) have explored ethnoarchaeological approaches to archaeological analysis. These efforts were spurred to a significant degree by frustration with conventional usage of ethnographic data in archaeology. Ethnoarchaeology is the study of living societies, by archaeologists, to aid in understanding and interpreting the archaeological record. As it has been applied to hunting and gathering societies, ethnoarchaeology has focused heavily on settlement and subsistence strategy (Binford 1978, 1980; Gould 1981; Yellen 1976, 1977a, 1982). Ethnoarchaeology is one of the most important approaches used to operationalize middle range theory. Much of the work that led to the formulation of middle range theory, stemmed from the observation that a linkage must be made between the archaeological record, which is static and contemporary, and the behaviours in the past that produced the materials comprising the archaeological record (Binford 1977). The absence of such a linkage is one of the main reasons archaeologists began using ethnographic data as aids to interpretation. Middle range theory, therefore, is intended to bridge this gap. A variety of methodologies have been developed to apply middle range theory to archaeological analyses. Ethnoarchaeology represents one of the most successful avenues of middle range research.

In a consideration of the development of hunter-gatherer foraging theory, ethnoarchaeology plays an important role. By conducting ethnographic fieldwork from an archaeological perspective, stronger linkages between material culture and the behaviour producing it can be obtained (Bartram, Kroll and Bunn 1991; O'Connell, Hawkes and Jones 1991). Employing this kind of approach leads to important insights into the decisions that comprise foraging behaviour. Accurate models of hunter-gatherer foraging strategy require thorough understanding of the factors that influence the execution of hunting and gathering activities. In studying prehistoric hunter-gatherers, archaeologists do not have direct access to that decision-making process. The results of ethnoarchaeological investigations provide reasonable, and rigorous, proxies that can be used effectively for modelling foraging behaviour in the past (Binford 2001).

## Optimal Foraging Theory

Optimal foraging theory represents a set of approaches to modelling hunter-gatherer subsistence strategy that has found a receptive audience in contemporary anthropology. Interestingly however, its use in archaeology is fairly limited (Fagan 1995). Given the potential of optimal foraging theory, this seems to be at odds with the widespread need in the archaeological community for approaches that combine predictive value with tangible linkages between the natural and cultural environment. Thomas (1986: 255–6) addresses this incongruity very succinctly when he points out: 'Shifting empirical referent from ethnographic to archaeological data means that neither behaviour nor environment is observed directly . . . Before optimal foraging theory, or any other general theory, can be brought to bear on archaeological data, it is necessary to infer past behaviour from the archaeological record, and also to infer past environmental states from the palaeoenvironmental record . . .'

The roots of optimal foraging theory lie in the fertile soil of evolutionary ecology, which is defined as the 'application of natural selection theory to the study of adaptation and biological design in an ecological setting' (Winterhalder and Smith 1992: 5). The central, and perhaps most controversial, assumption of optimal foraging theory is that human decisions are made such that the net rate of energy capture is maximized (Winterhalder and Smith 1981). Binford (1982) has argued that optimal foraging theory incorporates an inappropriate application of Western microeconomic theory because of its emphasis on 'rational' decision-making. While it is important to remain cognizant of how concepts of 'rationality' can vary from one culture to the next and the implications of that variance, as Bettinger's cogent summary of Weber (1948) points out: 'the fact that rationality was culturally conditioned did not obviate the utility of analyses grounded in concepts of objective rationality' (Bettinger 1991: 106).

The versatility of optimal foraging theory is reflected in the range of studies in which it has been employed (Winterhalder and Smith 2000). Analyses of hunter-gatherers occupying the South American rainforest (Kaplan and Hill 1992), central Australia (O'Connell and Hawkes 1981; 1984), Arctic regions (E.A. Smith 1991) and numerous regions in between, have all relied heavily on the insights provided by optimal foraging theory. In an interesting application, some scholars have also employed optimal foraging theory to illustrate the ways in which hunter-gatherers pattern their subsistence activities to minimize risk (Yellen 1986; Winterhalder 1986, 1990).

## Archaeological Application: Models that Work, Models that Don't

The various models comprising optimal foraging theory fall into several broad categories, focusing on diet, foraging space, foraging time and group size. It would seem that optimal foraging theory has found a wider audience in cultural anthropology and ethnoarchaeology than in archaeology per se. An ample illustration of this is provided by several compilations of anthropological studies employing optimal foraging theory. In Winterhalder and Smith (1981), of the six chapters dealing with applications of optimal foraging theory only two involve archaeological data (Keene 1981; Yesner 1981). In a more recent publication (Smith and Winterhalder 1992), of nine chapters representing tests of optimal foraging approaches to a variety of topics, only one seeks to address problems associated with prehistoric populations (Foley 1992). In light of these observations and for reasons that will be explored in more detail later, it is quite telling that the most common optimal foraging model used among archaeologists is the one focusing on diet breadth (Bettinger 1991: 84; Hegmon 2003).

In a comparison of challenges facing scholars trying to apply middle range theory and optimal foraging theory, Bettinger (1991: 109) points out that the latter can be difficult to operationalize (although no less so than the former). Thomas (1986: 253) poses the question: 'Is it realistic to "test" optimal foraging models against archaeological data?' The answer to that question, in my opinion, is 'yes'. Whatever difficulties exist in the application of optimal foraging theory to archaeological problems, they may have more to do with the data used to test the theory than with the theory itself. Each of the models that make up optimal foraging theory exhibit strengths and weaknesses with regard to their utility in archaeological analyses. An exploration of these attributes is not only worthwhile, but essential, if we are to expand our ability to employ this body of theory in the study of archaeological materials. Such an assessment will allow the identification of sources of data that are frequently overlooked or viewed as unattainable. Only by specifying what our data needs are, will we develop the methodology for meeting those needs.

The component of optimal foraging theory most frequently employed in archaeology is the diet breadth model. Optimal diet, as measured by the diet breadth model, is assessed by examining the addition of low-ranked food resources to the dietary spectrum. The currency used to 'rank' a resource can be caloric returns, pursuit time, search time or prey package size, among others (Bayham 1979; Sheehan 2002; Winterhalder 1981, 1988). An evaluation of optimal diet that employs caloric returns, pursuit time or search time will require detailed information about the spatial structure and content of local and regional resources. If on the other hand prey package size is used as a currency, data pertaining to the physical characteristics of the prey species and evidence that those species actually comprised part of the diet represent the main data requirements. It is clear why the diet breadth model should be popular among archaeologists. Although detailed environmental data, often in the form of a complex vegetative mosaic are readily available to the ethnographer, and desirable for the archaeologist, it is not a prerequisite for the use of the model. It can be tested using data that are commonly retrieved from archaeological deposits: faunal remains, and to a lesser extent floral remains.

The other models comprising optimal foraging theory, those pertaining to foraging space, foraging time, and group size, exhibit much weaker representation in archaeological research. This is directly related to the nature of the data required to test them. The patch use model, often used to evaluate optimal foraging space, requires detailed information about a number of variables that is difficult to obtain using conventional archaeological methods. These variables include, but are not limited to: the proportion of a particular patch in the environment; the usable energetic yield per patch of a particular type of patch, and the time spent travelling between patches of all types (Bettinger 1991: 89). Clearly, extensive information about the local environment is required before any of these variables can be quantified. Consider the task before the archaeologist trying to employ the patch use model. Conventional recovery and analytical methods, usually employing pollen data, simply do not supply the fine-grained picture of palaeoenvironments that will permit the reconstruction of resource patches. Put more simply, how can the archaeologist be assured of the distance separating patches, and thus the travel time needed to move from one to the next, when you have no way of knowing the specifics of patch location or size?

The problem of adequate, and accurate, palaeoenvironmental reconstruction is not unique to the patch use model. It compromises archaeological applications of optimal foraging time and group size as well. Typically, testing these models is set against a backdrop of very detailed, fine-grained, environmental information. In contemporary archaeology most analyses that incorporate palaeoenvironmental data emphasize fossil pollen. While the use of pollen data is an extremely useful and powerful proxy, it will not yield the kind of fine-grained environmental detail required for testing most optimal foraging models. Because pollen is a reproductive structure that relies on some external form of transport, usually wind, to be dispersed, resolution at the regional scale is usually the best that pollen studies have to offer.

The underlying assumptions of optimal foraging theory represent important limiting factors in its application, especially in an archaeological context. However, there is a more basic challenge that must be overcome by archaeologists wishing to employ this evolving theoretical tool. As should be clear, accurate reconstruction of the environmental canvas upon which foraging decisions are made may be the most significant methodological issue confronting archaeologists attempting to work with the full range of optimal foraging theory. The ethnographer can gather this information as part of their fieldwork, and know with certainty that there is a temporal connection between the culture under examination and the contemporary environment. Given the fact that climate can change very dramatically over long periods of time, an archaeologist studying an extinct culture cannot assume that the specifics of the contemporary environment are congruent with the specifics of the prehistoric environment. Because of the potential disjunction between the two, some of the models comprising optimal foraging theory are more effective in archaeological analyses than others.

It is important to be cognizant of the fact that the kind of data that will make detailed, fine-grained, palaeoenvironmental reconstruction possible, is not out of reach. By developing new approaches to data collection and integration, very detailed images of palaeoenvironments and the consequent resource structure should be attainable. As noted earlier, fossil pollen represents an excellent, and oft used proxy for inferring palaeoenvironments. Plant opal phytoliths are another source of palaeoenvironmental information whose importance in the archaeological community is growing steadily (Rovner 1971, 1983, 1988; Pearsall 1985; Piperno 1988). If properly executed and integrated, studies of fossil pollen and phytoliths, might yield the detailed palaeoenvironmental reconstructions required to make better use of the potential offered by optimal foraging theory.

Pollen spectra provide strong indicators of regional climatic and environmental conditions. Phytoliths, by contrast, are strong indicators of local conditions. Phytoliths are minute silica structures formed in plants as part of the maturation process: 'Soluble silica is absorbed with water by the roots and is deposited in and around cells of the plants. These distinct and identifiable plant remains are then deposited in the soil during the decaying process' (Lewis 1982: 353). Perhaps the most important feature of phytoliths, as it relates to palaeoenvironmental reconstruction, is that they are not subject to extensive natural transport (Rovner 1988). The phytoliths from a decaying plant tend to stay within a several metre radius of where it grew. Consequently, phytolith analysis can provide strong evidence for local vegetative cover.

Large scale, intensive, sampling strategies designed to maximize the recovery of phytoliths may well open the door to the kind of fine-grained palaeoenvironmental reconstructions needed to facilitate broader application of optimal foraging theory. Careful study of modern plant communities, and the phytolith assemblages they produce, provide a benchmark for the interpretation of archaeological phytolith assemblages. Since phytoliths inform about local vegetation, implementing such a data recovery protocol would provide the basis for reconstructing resource patches. Once that is accomplished the analytical potential of optimal foraging theory in archaeology can be more fully realized. By combining phytolith and pollen data, the archaeologist can derive insight into the local environment and the regional environmental context to which it belongs. Understanding both levels, and the systemic relationship between them, will provide a solid foundation for creating what might be termed 'palaeo-vegetative' mosaics that can serve as the basis for more creative, intensive, and ultimately more successful, applications of a broader range of optimal foraging theory.

## Conclusion

In the historical development of foraging theory and its applications in the archaeology of hunter-gatherers, early efforts focused on the detailed insights into floral and faunal resource distributions and their exploitation by human populations that could be gleaned from the ethnographic record. However, using ethnographic data to 'interpret' the archaeological record provides problematic results. When ethnographic data are used to develop a 'framework' for interpreting the archaeological record the results are much more promising.

Contemporary foraging theory, particularly optimal foraging theory, provides this kind of framework. Especially if it is combined with the intensive, systematic, collection of palaeoenvironmental data that will permit the full potential of the body of theory to be realized. Notwithstanding the various limitations faced by archaeologists trying to apply contemporary foraging theory in their research, some of these efforts, particularly those employing optimal foraging theory, have opened 'many productive avenues of thought' (Kelly 1995: 110). The critical issue relating to resource exploitation by hunter-gatherers is not the presence or absence of a particular resource in a particular environment, but rather, the distribution of that resource. The archaeological data can enlighten us as to the former, but they are virtually silent on the latter. If the effectiveness of contemporary foraging theory is to be 'maximized', greater effort must be made to open windows on past resource distribution. Perhaps it is time to return to old-fashioned regional studies that employ new approaches to data collection, especially as it pertains to environmental proxies, that will provide the requisite resolution of the palaeoenvironmental picture.

Using innovative data recovery and analytical strategies the door can be opened to the application of a wide range of contemporary foraging theory. This application will significantly enhance our ability to understand and model human behaviour. It will also enhance the feedback relationship that exists between archaeology and the other subdisciplines of anthropology.

# Subtle Shifts and Radical Transformations in Hunter-Gatherer Research in American Anthropology: Julian Steward's Contributions and Achievements

## *L. Daniel Myers*

Hunter-gatherer research may seem to some insignificant or, worse yet, inconsequential to the goals of twenty-first century anthropology. Some scholars might attribute this to a 'specialization in orientation' that has tended to dominate anthropology during the last thirty plus years. They believe that as a subject matter, hunter-gatherer studies are outdated in the midst of globalization, area studies and postmodern specialities. Hunter-gatherer, as a meaningful research category, has been challenged by members from the anthropological community and even hunter-gatherer specialists (Barnard 1983: 193).

There is no debate, however, that as a focus of anthropological enquiry, hunter-gatherer research has had a tumultuous role in the shaping of anthropology as a discipline. Some of anthropology's earliest and most famed practitioners (e.g., Frazer, Morgan, Tyler, Powell, Boas, Durkheim, Mauss, Radcliffe-Brown, Malinowski, Kroeber, Lowie, Radin, etc) employed hunter-gatherer populations as a common ground for theoretical endeavours.[1] Metaphorically, hunter-gatherers are the heart and soul of anthropology, and serve as the foundation for some of anthropology's most cherished beliefs and assumptions. They act as 'shared exemplars' for the discipline, illustrating and illuminating the basic theoretical problems and practical solutions in anthropology. As such, hunter-gatherers are 'models for imitation', and in application create, maintain and perpetuate the discipline of anthropology. These simple societies are 'archetypes' that define what anthropology *is* and has been throughout its historical development. Hunter-gatherer research has provided anthropology with some of its most significant and vigorous debates (L.D. Myers 1987; 1988).

In America, the Shoshonean or Numic-speaking populations (i.e. Southern

Paiute, Western Shoshone and Northern Paiute) are the classic hunter-gatherers, and were so closely intertwined with Julian Hayes Steward as to be inseparable. As the founder of modern hunter-gatherer study (Lee and DeVore 1968a: 5), Steward's (1936; 1938) early research among the Numic peoples was the key to his over-all research efforts (1955a). Revised and revisited throughout his lifetime, Steward's (1970) Numic research served to elabourate one of the most popular and renowned American anthropological paradigms of the twentieth century: cultural ecology. For fifty years, many Great Basin practitioners have viewed the Numic from essentially the same perspective, following Steward's classification of the Numic as gastric orientated (1938: 46), typologically unique, and representing a distinctive and nonrecurrent line of development in a scheme of multi-inear evolution (1955a: 120).

This essay examines Steward's contributions to the ethnographic history of the American Great Basin region and the influence that he had on succeeding generations of Great Basin practitioners. It will be shown that the Numic are shared exemplars, employed to delineate both 'subtle shifts' and 'radical transformations' of thought in several major theoretical orientations developed by Great Basin practitioners over the last fifty years. As such, the Numic hunter-gatherer groups have served as a standard by which to assess the approach, relevancy and effectiveness of theoretical orientations within anthropology. They are used for approval or denial of different theoretical persuasions, specific orientation problems and debates over aims, goals and issues, for instance. Recent re-examinations of Steward's research have been used to show a more positive and, in some ways, radically different view of Numic culture and life ways than Steward presented. This essay addresses these new orientations from a context of current anthropological thought.

## Anthropology of the Great Basin Region

While no comprehensive account of the history of anthropological research within the Great Basin has been published, cursory examinations have been (e.g. Baumhoff 1958; Clemmer and Myers 1999; d'Azevedo 1986b; Fowler 1980, 1986; Fowler and Fowler 1971; Malouf 1966; Shimkin 1964). Most of these practitioners agree that Steward's contributions to Great Basin ethnology, ethnography, and archaeology made him a major force in the study of hunters and gatherers, ecological anthropology and cultural evolution in American anthropology.

## Steward's antecedents

During the latter half of the nineteenth and early part of the twentieth century, the Great Basin region contributed to the development of two theoretical approaches.

The beginning of ethnographic studies within the Great Basin region start in 1869 with John Wesley Powell's exploration of the Grand Canyon. His research efforts continued into the first years of the twentieth century and were funded by federal monies. Powell categorized the various Numic groups (e.g., Southern Paiute, Western Shoshone and Northern Paiute) as the first stage of savagery in the then popular unilinear theory of human evolution. Classed as 'savages', the Numic were seen to have a modicum of cultural features and childish modes of thought (Fowler and Fowler 1971: 21).

The second theoretical approach coincides with the beginning of modern anthropology that began with Franz Boas at Columbia University in 1896. Two of Boas's famed students, Alfred Kroeber and Robert Lowie, played a vital role in Steward's career and shaping of American Anthropology. In 1901, Kroeber founded the University of California's Anthropology Department, at Berkeley. Robert Lowie was appointed Visiting Professor at Berkeley in 1917 and returned as a full-time professor in 1921. In the early 1930s, anthropology at Berkeley was dominated by the 'Culture Elements Distribution Surveys' research programme; a programme to quantify cultural 'traits' or 'elements' of aboriginal populations of the West (Fowler 1986: 25–6). The surveys were an integral part of Berkeley's curriculum of 'salvage' ethnography, and resulted in the 'ethnographic reconnaissance' and ultimate 'ethnographic reconstruction' of over 250 major groups. The surveys were a popular but non-analytical method for collecting ethnographic data that had quantitative properties susceptible to statistical manipulation. The surveys, and justification for them, failed miserably to produce the desired effects of ethnographic reporting on both theoretical and methodological grounds. In both theory and method, common concepts and percepts were taken for granted and exposed a number of underlying assumptions and assertions held by the data collectors (e.g. super-organic culture, work, passive environments, homogeneity, etc.) (Murphy 1970; Myers 1987).[2] Steward conducted these surveys in the mid1930s and published them in two volumes, *Nevada Shoshoni* (1941) and *Northern and Gosiute Shoshoni* (1943), under the University of California Anthropological Records.

Within this university context and with assistance of Kroeber and Lowie, Steward's anthropological experience started in the late 1920s with research among the Owens Valley (Northern) Paiute and was published in 1933. Like Kroeber (1925) and Lowie (1909) before him, Steward took a possibilistic approach that argued that 'the environment was . . . not . . . causative but merely limiting or selective' (Geertz 1963: 2). As such, '. . . only the absence of traits . . . could be predicted from characteristics of the environment' (Vayda and Rappaport 1968: 479). Harris (1968: 662) suggests: 'Steward's position corresponded essentially to that of a rather large number of anthropologists who regarded the natural environment as a vaguely limiting or enabling factor of culture history.'

## Steward's Contributions to Hunter-Gatherer Research

In his career, Steward's (1936, 1938, 1955a) published three major contributions to the ethnography of the Great Basin and the study of hunter-gatherers. In 1970, Steward revised and updated his original position concerning the aboriginal populations of the Great Basin.

Functional in perspective and behavioural by design, Steward's (1936: 331–50) essay 'The Economic and Social Basis of Primitive Bands' constitutes the first systematic 'scientific' study of hunters and gatherers in American anthropology. Relying on an explicit scientific outlook, Steward postulated three types of organization (i.e. patrilineal, composite and matrilineal) under the notion of 'primitive band'. (1936: 332–3) Only two of the three types, patrilineal and composite, were examined and discussed; the third type, matrilineal, was considered by Steward to be hypothetical and undifferentiated. Steward uses the notion of 'economy' to suggest that such factors as ecology, population density, territory, social activity, etc. influenced and maintained the politically autonomous, land-owning, patrilineal bands (e.g. Bushmen, Central African Negritos, Semang, Philippine Negritos, Australia).

The normally larger composite or bilateral bands (e.g. Northern Alqonkians, Canadian Athabaskans, Andamanese) without 'band exogamy, patrilocal residences, or land inheritance by patrilineal relatives' (1936: 338), were the result of special factors contributing to band size, structure, and environmentally sensitive cultural features (e.g. kinship, marriage, economy, residence, inheritance). Of the two, the politically autonomous, land-owning, patrilineal bands were the most significant, both in frequency and typological constancy. The significance of Steward's thesis was its problem-oriented, comparative approach to a systematic and scientific study of 'primitive bands' among the hunter-gatherers populations of the world. This essay was a cornerstone for Steward's theory of cultural evolution, and a measure of the potential of cultural ecology as a systematic method of enquiry.

Two years later, Steward (1938) published the seminal 'Basin-Plateau Aboriginal Socio-Political Groups.' In this monograph, Steward hypothesized that the nuclear or biological (bilateral) family was 'the most stable socio-political group' of hunter-gatherers in the interior Great Basin region (i.e. Western Shoshone, Southern Paiute and Northern Paiute) (Steward 1938: 2–3). A simple sexual division of labour made the family the main self-sustaining economic, political and social unit for most of the year.

> Most of the Basin-Plateau people lived at a bare subsistence level. Their culture was meager in content and simple in structure. Pursuits concerned with the problems of daily existence dominated their activities to an extraordinary degree and limited and conditioned their institutions. (Steward 1938: 1–2)

Confirmed by local and regional histories, Steward (1938: 3–10) claims:

> It is important to an understanding of the entire Shoshonean culture that it was stamped
> with a remarkable practicality. So far as its basic orientation is definable, it was
> 'gastric.' Starvation was so common that all activities had to be organized toward the
> food quest, which was carried on mostly by independent families. (1938: 46)

Through ethnographic reconnaissance, Steward conducted detailed surveys of
twenty-five major groups in thirty-five named localities among the Numic
(Steward 1938: ix-xi). He (1938: 50–230) received most of the basic data from the
'Culture Element Distribution' lists collected in 1935 and intervening research
before and after this date. As a guide, the lists were used to order and control a
wealth of data springing from each of the major groups interviewed. Taking on
such a monumental feat, Steward described and synthesized data into a detailed
synopsis of not only the individual elements, but also relationships and complex
interactions between elements or groups of elements that 'produced the different
kinds of Shoshonean sociopolitical groups' (Steward 1938: 230–58). The type of
sociopolitical groups were 'conditioned to a definable extent by human ecology'
(Steward 1938: 256). Focusing on subsistence patterns, Steward accounted the
various environmental (e.g., topography, precipitation, temperature, plant, animal,
population density) and social (e.g., kinship, marriage, village, chief, sweat house,
festival, property, warfare) factors to determine the latitude of conditions responsible for the types and kinds of sociopolitical units. In this way, Steward analyses
the 'sociopolitical unit' among the Numic (Steward 1938: 256–8).

In the closing pages of the 1938 monograph, Steward (1938: 258–62) provides
an addendum to his 1936 essay to address and reassess certain points in his theory
of 'primitive bands.' After a summary of the patrilineal and composite bands,
Steward (1938: 260) concludes that:

> The Western Shoshoni, probably Southern Paiute, and perhaps some Northern Paiute
> fall outside the scope of the previous generalizations, which were too inclusive. They
> lacked bands and any form of land ownership. The only stable social and political unit
> was the family. Larger groupings for social and economics purposes were temporary
> and shifting.

Other groups (e.g. Owens Valley Paiute, Northern Shoshone, Utes) were basically
organized into composite bands.

In the intervening years between 1938 and 1955, Steward gradually developed
his theoretical orientation and gained practical experience as expert witness for the
federal government's Indian Claims Commission cases in the far west (see
Pinkoski and Asch, this volume). With *Theory of Culture Change* (1955a),
Steward formalized the theory of multilinear evolution with cultural ecology to

form a coherent approach to cultural evolution. His theory of cultural evolution uses three different kinds of hunter-gatherer sociocultural phenomena: families, patrilineal bands and composite bands (Steward 1955a: 101–21, 122–42, 143–50). All three levels of sociocultural integration resulted from the 'cultural ecological process' between culture and environment. Steward reiterated that only the Western Shoshone (and Eskimo populations) were classed at the basic or lowest level of his cultural evolutionary scheme. Steward deemed the pedestrian Shoshone (Diggers) in Nevada and Utah, as 'typologically unique' and repre- senting a 'nonrecurrent line of development in a scheme of multilinear evolution' (1955a: 120).

## Steward's Contributions and Influences on Great Basin Ethnography

Steward's contributions to ecology and evolution had the greatest impact in the late 1950s through the 1970s. During this time the notion of 'band' and 'band-related' literature reached its zenith in America. Service (1962: 52–3) modified Steward's theory by focusing on residence instead of ancestry or descent. Service hypothe- sized that the patrilocal band, which takes precedent over Steward's patrilineal classification, was the primary organization in human history. Specific histories accounted for the presence of other types of band organization (i.e., family and composite). Owens (1965) clarified Service's 'patrilocal' organization by pro- posing a 'patrifocus' organization. Service (1962: 64–5, 94–9) classed the Western Shoshone (Numic) as 'anomalous', due to their family-oriented organization. In 1966, *Man the Hunter* essays clarified and expanded on the notion of the 'band' (Lee and DeVore 1968c). A year later, Steward (1969), in a rejoinder to Service and Owens, questioned the use of patrilocal or patrifocus band type by throwing the whole concept of 'band' into doubt.

Steward's cultural ecological approach was a catalyst for both archaeologists and ethnographers in the Great Basin. Great Basin anthropology was dominated by prehistoric archaeological research aims and goals from a growing community of archaeologists. The few ethnographers working in the region either continued to work on applied and acculturation studies, or re-examined facets of Numic culture using localized ethnographic data (e.g. d'Azevedo, Davis, Fowler and Suttles 1966; Swanson 1970: 172–264). Steward's (1970: 201–31) 'Foundation of Basin-Plateau Shoshonean Society' re-evaluated and reassessed Great Basin hunter-gatherers in light of the recent advances in the Great Basin anthropology.[3] Steward reconsidered the basic unit of analysis, from the nuclear family to the family cluster, reminiscent of what others called camp groups, local bands, primary subsistence bands, etc. (Steward 1970: 114; Harris 1940: 44–72). In so doing, his conventional functional model was reconsidered through advances of process, model and system analysis on the one hand, and on the other, a renewed interest in social phenomenon (e.g. kinship and marriage) and their interactions, interrelations, and structural properties in forming the group (Lévi-Strauss 1989[1962]: 31–51).

## Cognitive Approaches in the Great Basin Region

While Steward was formulating his behavioural approach in the mid 1950s, Goodenough (1956a,b, 1957, 1967) introduced an 'ideational' or 'cognitive' approach based on linguistic and language studies (cf. Keesing 1994). The 'new ethnography' (e.g. 'ethnolinguistic', 'ethnoscience', 'ethnosemantic', etc.), as it was called, gave a unique focus to American ethnography and ethnology. Centring on knowledge and cognitive processes, Goodenough (1957: 167) defined the concept of 'culture' as '. . . not a material phenomenon; it does not consist of things, people, behaviour, or emotions' but rather '. . . an organization of these things. It is the forms of things that people have in mind, the models for perceiving, relating, and otherwise interpreting them.' Cognitive models, based on linguistic properties (i.e. phoneme, morpheme, syntax and semantic) were used to form a 'Native' or 'emic' point of view. This 'emic' perspective was contrasted to a 'etic' or 'scientific' behavioural perspective by Harris (1968: 568–604) and later, by Keesing (1974) under the term 'adaptationists' for the latter 'etic' perspectives and 'ideationalists' for 'emic' perspectives. In America and the Great Basin region, both types of approaches reached a high point by the 1970s.

This 'new ethnography' was followed by a number of scholars (e.g. Bye 1972; Fowler 1971, 1972; Fowler and Leland 1967; Goss 1972; Hage and Miller 1976; Smith 1972; Zigmond 1972) in the Great Basin. Out of these, Fowler and Leland (1967) led the way with ethnobotanical studies for the Northern Paiute (Western Numic) of the western Great Basin region. They found that a limited number of categories were employed to classify 125 plants into an implicit taxonomic order depending on use. Their description and analysis of the Northern Paiute categories and their elicitation and interviewing techniques provided a powerful means by which to gain access into the semantic structure and organization of Northern Paiute thought. Other practitioners provided similar analysis regarding ethnobotany or pharmacopoeia (Bye 1972; Smith 1972), ethnobiology (Zigmond 1972), and ethno-ornithology (Hage and Miller 1976). In addition to these ethno-studies was Goss's (1972) preliminary analysis of Ute cosmology. Based on Lévi-Strauss's structural paradigm, Goss (1972: 123–8) examined different lexicose-mantic domains (e.g. orientation, cosmology, shamanism, eco-systematics) for binary oppositions in Ute culture that operate on many levels but with a similar structure.

## Numic Studies

One year after Steward's (1970) *Foundations of Basin-Plateau Shoshonean Society*, Fowler and Fowler (1971) edited John Wesley Powell's writings on the Numic-speaking hunter-gatherers of the Great Basin. While linguists such as Lamb (1958, 1964) and Miller (1964, 1966, 1970) opted for the classification of Numic people on purely linguistic grounds, Fowler and Fowler were the first to recognize the importance of this classification as a phenomenon in its own right. As a distinct subject matter, the Numic classification system recognized a common linguistic infrastructure for Basin peoples. Synonymous with the traditional linguistic classification of the Mono-Pavisto, Shoshoni-Comanche, Southern Paiute-Ute language families, the new classification (Western, Central and Southern Numic languages) served to enlist common goals of research and contributed directly to the idea of a Numic research area (Myers 1997, 1999).

Ethnographic research in the Great Basin region continued to be intermittent; funded by federal, corporate and academic monies and founded on assumptions and premises developed since the mid 1970s. Practitioners (Franklin and Bunte 1983; Clemmer 1973, 1974, 1978; Eggan 1980; Fowler 1977, 1982a, 1982b; Inter-tribal Council of Nevada 1976a, 1976b, 1976c; Knack 1978, 1980; Knack and Stewart 1984; Rusco 1982a, 1982b; Shimkin 1980; Stewart 1977, 1978, 1979, 1980, 1982, 1984; Vander 1978, 1983; and Zigmond 1977, 1980, 1981) conducted superior work during this time. Most of these works were in the context of applied, acculturation, or ethno-historic research, highlighted by specific problems or issues with local populations in the Basin area. The highly productive period of time for Great Basin anthropology between the mid 1960s and the 1980s culminates in d'Azevedo's (1986a) *Handbook of American Indians: Great Basin* volume.

## Recent approaches

While the majority of practitioners still follow traditional behavioural models (e.g. functionalism, neo-functionalism, materialism), there has been a resurgent and revival of ethnographically based anthropological concerns and issues in the Great Basin region. As the community of Great Basin ethnographers grew and diverged, other cognitive approaches (e.g. structuralism and symbolism) as well as 'post-modern' or 'post-traditional' approaches began to emerge (Marcus and Fischer 1986: 5). Except for Goss's (1972) structural analysis of Ute cosmology, ideational approaches (e.g. symbolism and critical theory) appear to have been late in coming to the Great Basin region. At the forefront, practitioners presented ethnographic studies that analysed original or previous data to conduct 'emic' studies (Loether 1990; 1992; cf., Fowler and Leland 1967). Even stronger is was a combination of structuralism with symbolism (e.g. Clemmer 1996; Franklin 1990; Franklin and Bunte 1992; Gelo 1994; Myers 1997, 2001) or a more radical Marxist approach (Whitley 1990, 1992). Still others have employed a contextual approach to normative problems or issues (Stoffle, Halmo and Austin 1997; Stoffle, Loendorf, Austin, Malmo and Bulletts 2000; Myers 1987). All suggest, however, that cultures are more than a group of 'behaviours' or 'behavioural types', and focus on characteristics of cognition, mind, or thought and knowledge. By this latter focus, religious (e.g. ritual, myth, shamanism, cosmology, worldview) and social (e.g. residential, kinship, political, economic) aspects of Numic culture are intensively analysed and interpreted.

With an emphasis on context and interpretation, a number of the latter approaches encompass a radical conversion from linguistic models, in the 1950s and 1960s, to literary criticism and rhetorical studies of the 1970s and 1980s (Marcus and Fischer 1986: x).[4] Along with this change, these approaches offered a more 'humane' concept for ethnography and ethnographic endeavours. This, in turn, allows for the development of a critical and reflective look at social and cultural trends within the 'human' science.[5] These trends suggest a discursive approach to the study of ethnography and of culture, itself (e.g. Geertz 1973; 1983). Text and textual forms, cultural representations, discourse, literary theory, rhetoric, etc. all suggest a new dimension within which anthropology can be examined. Blurring the line between science and art, these trends embrace a more humanitarian view of the discipline and treat, for the most part, ethnography as literature (Clifford 1986: 3) and anthropologist as author (Geertz 1988).

Like all things innovative and new, these trends have been late in coming to the Great Basin (Blackhawk 1999; Crum 1999). Blackhawk notes that:

> Steward's texts produced fixed, categorical understanding of the Great Basin Indian and reduced vibrant, resilient, and infinity complex peoples to static, materially and ecological determined generalizations. Such generalizations fundamentally obscured the innumerable ways in which these Indian peoples express and represent themselves. The meanings, beliefs, and values they give to themselves, their lands, and their histories never enter into Steward's works. Their philosophy, cosmology, and hermeneutics are thus denied both contemporaneity and past as well as future existence. Interpreting how Steward accomplishes this does not warrant the same attention as what it is he silences. Although they are the subject of literally hundreds of sentences, the Great Basin Indians do not speak in Steward's text. (1999: 218)

Blackhawk's words still hold currency for interpretation, past and present. Factors such as resiliency, vibrancy, and infinite complexity are as present in the modern populations as they were in the past.

## Conclusion

Steward's contributions to hunters and gatherers research had a profound influence and impact on American anthropologists and the discipline itself. By the early 1960s, scholars from North America quickly adopted, modified or elabourated on cultural ecology and/or multilinear evolution. Steward's impact transcended sub-disciplines (American archaeology, ethnography and ethnology) and has had a significant influence on a number of anthropological topics and subject matters. These range from kinship (Fox 1967), social organization (Service 1962), ecology (Vayda and Rappaport 1968; Rappaport 1968), medical (Alland 1970), cultural theory (Kaplan and Manners 1972), to hunter-gatherer studies in general (Bicchieri 1972; Damas 1969; Lee and Devore 1968c, 1976; Leacock and Lee 1982; Schrire 1984; Ingold, Riches and Woodbur 1988; Wilmsen 1989a; Burch and Ellanna 1994).

Due to Steward's exalted position and the significance of his achievements among Great Basin anthropologists, the cultural ecological paradigm has reached a zenith here, compared to other culture areas or regions. Steward placed primary emphasis on subsistence and settlement patterns and those manifest economies they supported. In the 1970s and 1980s, this had largely been replaced by a focus on systems analysis, process and model. However, subsistence and settlement practices and activities were still in the forefront. By the time the Great Basin *Handbook* (d'Azevedo 1986a) was published, anthropological research in the Great Basin had refined, articulated or reformulated Steward's orientation.

In the Great Basin, ethnographic studies evolved with the discipline of anthropology. Purely 'emic' studies represented a transformation of thought and knowledge when compared to function and behaviour. With its strong linguistic foundation, the 'new' ethnography stressed meaning, semantics and taxonomies in an attempt to get into the minds of the natives. By the late 1970s, emic studies were on the decline, but are continued to the present by some (e.g., Loether 1990). As a competing paradigm, the 'new ethnography' complimented and supported 'cultural ecology' to a high degree. At the same time, other researchers endeavoured to produce a number of 'culture histories' or 'ethnohistories' (e.g. applied and acculturation studies) documenting the various facets of Numic culture.

From the late 1980s to the present, a resurgence of ethnography has bought a number of ideational approaches to develop in the Great Basin. These new approaches of structuralism, symbolism, critical theory, etc. began to use key concepts (i.e. identify and reflection, text and context, symbols and meaning, discourse and interpretation) to explain and discuss Numic cultures and lifeways. Other scholars have done, in part, a historical revision of the development of anthropology in the Great Basin.

Scholars have noted that Steward's records on Numic lifeways stressed only a few aspects of Numic cultures. Religion, ritual and much of the social order were dismissed or completely abandoned in Steward's work. As such, a number of topics, issues and subject matters have gone largely unexplored due to Steward's bias that was passed to succeeding generations of anthropologists. The strength of this bias is persuasive.

Steward's use of Great Basin hunter-gatherers in his theoretical paradigm has led to a slowing of the acceptance of new approaches in the Great Basin. But it is clear that Steward's work enabled and empowered subsequent researchers in areas he was blind to or avoided. Recent scholars who have taken the Great Basin and hunter-gatherer studies to new heights owe Steward a debt of gratitude.

## Dedication and Acknowledgements

This essay is dedicated to Marco G. Bicchieri, one of the original contributors to the *Man the Hunter* symposium. His approach to the study of hunters and gatherers gave a clear view of the paramount role of hunters and gatherers in the discipline's development. As a mentor, scholar and a beloved friend, his inspiration and guidance are only enhanced by his creativity, generosity and love of life.

The essay would not have possible without the assistance of Drs Gary Hennen, Deborah J. Gangloff and Alan Barnard. Their suggestions and comments were much appreciated. Nevertheless, I take full responsibility for its content.

## Notes

1. From total indifference, as in acculturation studies or applied research, to highly significant and pre-eminent as in cultural evolutionary models, hunter-gatherer studies vary both in context and purpose.
2. This categorization relied on implicit assumptions and explicit conceptions. Steward (1955a: 31), after Kroeber (1917), utilized a 'super-organic' concept of culture in the treatment of Great Basin hunters and gatherers. Defined by 'traits and institutions', culture, as Steward saw it, was amenable to quantitative manipulation and statistical inference that possessed a unique and powerful distinction separating human beings or 'man' from all other known animal species. As a consequence, a number of assumptions and assertions were implicit. Steward assumed that due to the harsh and unpredictable environment, the Numic people lacked 'leisure time'.
3. In 1970, Steward (1970: 114) substituted family cluster for the nuclear or biological family on evidence from the 'Man the Hunter' conference of 1966.
4. These postmodern or post-traditional schools were an outgrowth of the interpretative anthropology of the 1970s and 1980s.
5. Marcus and Fischer (1986: 7) designated 'human science' as 'broader than and

inclusive of the conventional social science' and 'extending to law, art, archi-
tecture, philosophy, literature, and even the natural sciences'.

# –15–

## Anthropology and Indigenous Rights in Canada and the United States: Implications in Steward's Theoretical Project

### *Marc Pinkoski and Michael Asch*

In the last three decades the manner in which anthropology constructs and under-takes its basic project has come under scrutiny. This reassessment has revealed, for example with respect to our role in support of colonialism, a less than heroic side to our discipline (Lewis 1973). One domain that has not been addressed suffi-ciently, however, is the relationship between anthropological theory and colonial law. It is an area that the authors and others are examining in a common research project undertaken through a Social Sciences and Humanities Research Council of Canada grant. In this paper we turn to a lacuna in the literature in this regard. It is the connection between Julian Steward's theoretical project and the manner in which the governments of Canada and the United States seek to have Indigenous rights defined through litigation.

We address this question for two reasons. First, it provides a window into the larger issues that we are addressing in our project. Second, it opens up an avenue through which we may gain insight into the context within which a seminal figure in the discipline developed his theoretical project. While we will refer briefly to the role of anthropologists as experts, our primary goal in this paper is to examine the relationship between anthropological theory and colonial legal ideology as it appears in the work of Julian Steward.

Given space and time constraints, we will limit our presentation as follows. We begin with a discussion of the position of the US Department of Justice in the Great Basin Indian Claims cases in which Steward was called as an expert. Our examples include the case of the Northern Paiute, a Great Basin Shoshone Tribe, whose existence is marked by their categorization as one of the lowest forms of civilization; and by the importance of their geographic location. The Great Basin cases are an important point of analysis because most of the 325,000,000 acres of land the US government was able to acquire without cost or treaty agreement was located in this area (Rigsby 1997). We will show that the strategy of the government was to seek to deny title to the Indian plaintiffs on the grounds that they were not organized societies, and thus, could not own land. We will then address Steward's theory of cultural ecology and particularly his development of the family level of sociocultural integration. We will show that Steward's depiction of Shoshone society, based on these ideas, corresponded precisely with the picture of Indigenous society favoured by the Department of Justice; that they were developed in the context of his employment as an expert witness in these cases; and that his results appear by implication to be connected closely to his strongly held views on Indian policy. Before closing, we will briefly discuss the impact his approach has had in recent Canadian jurisprudence. In our conclusions, we will address the question as to whether the presumed objectivity of Steward's theoretical project as a means to further our understanding of Indigenous societies, particularly those we describe as hunter-gatherers, and to provide an unbiased framework with which to evaluate the factual basis for establishing Aboriginal rights in Canadian law needs to be reconsidered.

## The US Department of Justice View on Property Rights in the Great Basin Cases

Following the Dawes Allotment Act of 1887, the United States Congress struggled to solve the multitude of claims by Indian Nations for breaches of their treaties. For the first three decades of the century, the Senate and Congress debated the necessity of forming a judicial body that could hear these claims specifically, inexpensively and expeditiously. The political jostling, lasting through sixteen years of open debate in Congress, finally led to enactment, in 1946, of the Indian Claims Commission (ICC), which would hear these cases (Rosenthal 1985).

Beginning with the appointment of Superintendent of Indian Affairs, John Collier, in 1933, and the Indian Reorganization Act (IRA) of 1934, there is an impression of a genuine progressive movement in the relationship between the US government and Indian nations (Rigsby 1997). This impression is derived from the attempt to rectify the political relationship between both parties through a common institutional process that was based on a belief that a mutually beneficial system could be implemented to resolve outstanding political issues. Although, through the enactment of the IRA and the ICC, some progress was made in the resolution of outstanding land claims, this progress was tenuous, and opposition to these claims was supported on financial, social-scientific and legal grounds (Beals 1985; Rosenthal 1990). The twenty-year period, from the appointment of Collier to the ICC's first decade (1934 to 1955), is crucial for understanding contemporary anthropological theory of Indigenous Peoples – for the argument surrounding the premises of the political relationship was greatly divided, and anthropologists were integral to both sides of the debate.

The ICC's mandate was to 'hear and determine . . . claims against the United States on behalf of any Indian tribe, band, or Nation of American Indians'. In specifying that claims could be advanced by Indian tribes, bands and Nations, it seems clear (although one cannot be certain without explicit review) that Congress intended to exhaust the full range of political societies that comprise the category 'North American Indians'. Nonetheless, for the careful and perhaps unsympathetic reader, the specifications allow for another possibility; namely that there could be a class of 'North American Indians' who did not fit any of the three categories listed in the ICC mandate, and therefore unable to bring claims, regardless of the merits, on other grounds. A most likely candidate for such a type of society would be one that, using evolutionary logic, would be too primitive to even meet the criteria of a 'band'. It would be a society that, in effect, could be considered unorganized (cf. Lurie 1957). Thus, although unintended, the ambiguity of the mandate allowed for the argument that there were Indian peoples who did not live in an organized society. In fact, the Department of Justice advanced such a line of argumentation, and forced the Indian group making the claim to demonstrate that their society fit into one of the specified categories and hence had a socio-political organization.

In asserting that there were Indian peoples who did not live in organized societies, the Department of Justice was following a line of reasoning well developed in colonial law. This perspective is clearly expressed in the doctrine of *terra nullius* as that was applied with respect to the legitimization of assertions of sovereignty in colonial territories by Britain during the days of empire and, currently, in Australian and Canadian law. At heart, this asserts that when peoples living in newly acquired territories are too 'primitive' to live in societies that require recognition by 'civilized' peoples, then the territory is considered 'unoccupied' and sovereignty may be acquired merely by settlement. This proposition is expressed clearly in the following passage from *in Re Southern Rhodesia* a judgement of the Lord Lords of the Privy Council in 1919, which serves as the precedent for the justification of the acquisition of sovereignty in Canadian law (Asch 1984); the Law Lords said:

> The estimation of the rights of aboriginal tribes is always inherently difficult. Some tribes are so low in the scale of social organization that their usages and conceptions of rights and duties are not to be reconciled with the institutions or legal ideas of civilized society . . . Such a gulf cannot be bridged. It would be idle to impute to such people some shadow of the rights known to our law and then to transmute it into the substance of transferable rights of property as we know them.

Recognition by the ICC that an Indian claimant group had attained a certain level in the hierarchy of socio-political status transcended anthropological considerations regarding its place in social evolutionary theory to become a matter of core legal and political significance for the very continued existence of that group. Given the preoccupation with evolutionary framings on the part of many anthropologists and their presumed expertise with respect to the cultures and societies of American Indians, Ronaasen, Clemmer and Rudden (1999: 171) quite appropriately conclude that the 'very nature of ICC itself placed anthropologists in a position to legitimize the denial of indigenous rights to collectively held land and to other collective rights guaranteed by treaty with the U.S. government'.

## The Department of Justice View of Northern Paiute's Claim to Property Rights

In the late 1940s, the Northern Paiute Indians, of the Great Basin, filed a petition with the ICC for damages related to their loss without proper compensation of Indian (or Aboriginal) title to lands in Nevada, Oregon and Utah (Stewart 1959). In its defence the Department of Justice responded that 'the government (of the United States) was not liable for any claims because the petitioners [the Northern Paiute] did not hold original Indian title' (Stewart 1959: 51). Specifically, the Department of Justice argued that the Northern Paiute were not an 'organized society'. That is, to quote their words:

1) The purported petitioner, the so-called Northern Paiute Nation, was not an aboriginal tribe or entity united in a community under one leadership or government and was therefore inherently incapable of acquiring and/or holding 'original Indian Title.'

2) All of the aborigines who (either allegedly or in fact) inhabited land in the claimed area were never an aboriginal tribe or entity united in a community under one leadership or government and were therefore inherently incapable of acquiring and/or holding 'original Indian Title' (Defendant's Requested Findings of Fact, Northern Paiute Nation 1975: 1).

As a consequence, the Department of Justice argued that the Northern Paiute did not constitute a socio-political entity that could, legally, bring forward a claim under the technical mandate of the ICC. To justify their assertion in law, the Department of Justice needed an expert report that would indicate that their legal argument was grounded on fact. That is, the expert report needed to state that the Northern Paiute were too primitive to belong to any of the three categories, 'band, tribe or Nation', specified as potential claimants in the ICC, and that they could not hold property. To write this report, they turned to Julian Steward.

## The Family Level of Sociocultural Integration and the Northern Paiute Case

In order to understand the basis of this decision and Steward's contribution, it is useful to recall three central concepts in Steward's work. The first is 'multilinear evolution'. Steward writes that 'multilinear evolution' is 'essentially a methodology based on the assumption that significant regularities in cultural change occur, and it is concerned with the determination of cultural laws' (1955a: 18–19). He argues that its method allows for 'concreteness and specificity' in the comparison and understanding of culture change. Its concern is the generation of taxonomic features, conceptions of historic change and cultural causality (1955a: 11). This piece is the foundation for the notion that societies exist on a true evolutionary continuum that can be discerned through scientific means.

The framework to discern how multilinear evolution plays out is developed in 'Concept and Method of Cultural Ecology' (Steward 1955a). Here, Steward asserts that the determinable and relevant characteristics of cultures are those which are most closely linked with the physical environment, and the subsistence technologies used to exploit it. These elements make up the 'culture core', a concept that forms the basis of comparison between cultures and provides the motor for evolutionary development. Schematically, the techno-environment becomes the base upon which the culture core rests. That is, in Steward's thesis, it is the marriage of a particular form of subsistence technology with a specific set of culturally defined environmental possibilities that constitutes the culture core. The social organization and superstructure arise as a consequence of how the core is shaped, and are seen as epiphenomena. In this manner, the techno-environment is the base that allows for the cultural expression and the advent of new technologies; thus, ecological adaptations are the driving force for cultural change – and, in the manner that Steward conceives of, human evolution (1955a: 11).

What Steward suggests he has accomplished with this paradigm is the identification of empirically identifiable characteristics of the culture core that explain the relationship between environment and culture (Steward 1955a: 163). Cultural development or change is a function of the technological and ecological adaptations to a given environment.

The third key concept is contained in 'Levels of Sociocultural Integration.' Here, Steward combines the approach of multilinear evolution with the methodology of cultural ecology to establish a schema for evaluating the 'level' of a specific society. He introduces the notion of the levels of social forms, and categorizes them in a framework of simple to complex societies, which, as Myers points out, range from family to 'band' to 'tribe' to 'nation'. Although he asserts that the evolutionary trajectory of each society is not unilinear, in this piece he actually hypothesizes that the 'family represents a level that is lower in a structural sense, and in some cases it appears to have been historically antecedent to higher forms' (1955a: 53–4). A determination of the sociocultural levels of groups, he argues, demonstrates the 'growth continuum' of increasingly complex and newly emergent forms. He specifically patterns this schema after the biological understanding of evolution (Steward 1955a: 51; Murphy 1981). The bottom level of the scale of sociocultural integration is known as the 'family-level', where the 'family was the reproductive, economic, educational, political, and religious unit' (Steward 1955a: 54). Each level is marked by increasing complexity, as evidenced by inventories of cultural traits, increasing heterogeneity and formal political structures. Given the context within which we are writing, the 'family level' is the most germane to the discussion. In Steward's view, this level of sociocultural integration arises when a society is organized so that each family exists in virtual isolation from all others, where there are few forms of collective activity and a lack of development in task specialization. Among other characteristics the keys for our discussion include the absence of a permanent, ongoing leadership so that each family remains independent and self-sufficient; and, 'the absence of property claims of local groups to limitable areas of natural resources upon which work had not been expended . . .' (1955a: 108). Another crucial factor in determining whether a society is at the family level, at least under 'pristine' conditions, is the paucity of their trait or element lists. Another is that 'the food quest was of overwhelming importance, but, owing to the differences in environment and exploitive techniques, it entailed very unlike activities and associations between families' (1955a: 120). According to Steward, the family level of sociocultural integration was rather rare in the world in the pre-contact period. He suggests that 'this level' is represented 'in South America by the Nambicuara, Guató, Mura and perhaps other groups,' and in North America by only two such groups: 'the Eskimo' and the 'Shoshonean peoples' (1955a: 119). Further, he says, '[p]erhaps there have been people similar to the Shoshoneans in other parts of the world; for the present, however, the Shoshoneans must be regarded as typologically unique' (1955a: 120).

Steward's report proved very favourable to the position advanced by the Department of Justice for it agreed completely with the core propositions that the Shoshone had not achieved a level of society that had institutions that could hold title to land. The key concept that lay behind Steward's strong assertion on these points was his designation that the Shoshone were properly classified as belonging to the 'family level of sociocultural integration.' That is, as outlined above, the Shoshone belonged to a class of society that, while rare in pre-contact, formed a distinct level below that of the band. One of the determinations of this characteristic was the absence of institutions respecting property in land. Steward's report provides the following rationale for this designation:

I classify the Shoshoneans as an exemplification of the family level of sociocultural integration because in the few forms of collective activity the same group of families did not co-operate with one another or accept the same leader on successive occasions. By another definition, however, it might be entirely permissible to view this ever-changing membership and leadership as a special form of suprafamily integration. While the Shoshoneans represent a family level of sociocultural integration in a relative sense, their suprafamilial patterns of integration involved no permanent social groups of fixed membership despite several kinds of interfamilial co-operation (1955a: 109).

## Discussion

As we see it, at least three implications arise from the finding of a close correspondence between Steward's 'family level of sociocultural integration' and the requirements of a colonial legal ideology consistent with the doctrine of *terra nullius*. The first is the fact of the connection itself. We think it fair to state that anthropology can only benefit from reflections on the larger contexts within which our project is situated. When one takes seriously the proposition that no theoretical stance, at least in the social sciences, is value neutral (Hymes 1972), then it is incumbent upon researchers to be cognisant of values foregrounded in every stance, especially when, as is commonly the case, these are unintended and/or unconscious.[1] This caution becomes even more urgent when the stances that we use have consequences in the real lives of others, such as the Shoshone in this case or the Sto:lo, as we will discuss below. The implication here is that the close tie between the delineation of the family level of sociocultural integration and the depiction of indigenous society favourable to colonial legal ideology invites anthropologists to take particular care when using Steward's paradigm in colonial or politically charged contexts, to avoid inadvertently biasing ethnographic descriptions of Indigenous peoples in that direction; such as by presuming that because a society is at the so-called 'family' level it is not worth examining whether or not they have socio-political institutions or institutions related to holding property.[2]

The second implication concerns the scholarly reputation of Steward's project. Steward is a seminal figure in our discipline, notwithstanding that he developed his theoretical project over a half a century ago.[3] As Myers (this volume) reiterates, the reputation of Steward's project rests on the presumption that it is scientific and objective, rather than ideological and interpretative. It is a reputation underscored by Marvin Harris, another prominent theorist in our field, who argues strongly in favour of naming Steward as the founder of a scientific anthropology (Harris 1968) and by the fact, as Myers points out, that Steward's orientation remains central in the study of hunting-gathering societies across the subfields to the present day (see also Ichikawa, this volume). It is therefore worthwhile to ask whether there are grounds to call into question the objectivity of Steward's project. Here, we wish to proceed with caution as we have only preliminary information. Nonetheless, our findings thus far, along with those of others, raise a concern that Steward's theoretical project may have been biased to favour the position of the Department of Justice in particular and the orientation of colonial legal ideology in general with respect to the depiction of Indigenous societies. Our reasons follow.

Much of Steward's theoretical work was written during his stint as an expert witness for the Department of Justice. This concern arises not specifically because he was an expert witness or that much of his theoretical discussions originated in expert reports. When expert testimony is done with integrity and without prejudice, anthropologists and other professionals play a crucial role when they offer their expertise to parties in disputes. However, concerns arise because Steward acted as an expert for one side in a number of litigations over many years, including a seven-year period while in the employ of the Department of Justice. As such, the possibility exists that Steward's theoretical project may have been influenced, if not determined, by his close association with a particular perspective in litigation.

Secondly, Steward held the view, even prior to his expert reports, that Indian institutions in general were either extinct or at the very least broken-down and that, as a matter of social policy, the only recourse was to advocate the assimilation of Indians into mainstream society (Murphy 1981: 183). It was a position that he held from the outset of his career. For Steward, the Shoshone represented a singular case and he advocated applying a policy of assimilation in their regard even in his first report to the BIA on their socio-political organization. He stated his view on policy with sufficient clarity in reports for the BIA in the period from 1936 to 1946 that he ran afoul of the Director, John Collier. Collier was engaged in the implementation of a policy under the IRA (Rosenthal 1990) that would ensure Indian self-government, the continuation of traditional societies, and the preservation of Indian cultural and socio-political structures that differed from those of the mainstream.

As Rusco (1999) points out, Steward's advocacy of assimilation for the Shoshone raised concerns that his perspective coloured the objectivity of his first report. In fact, when Alida Bowler, then Superintendent of the BIA in Carson City, Nevada, reviewed the report, she recommended that its publication be rejected on the basis of its methodological weaknesses and its biased reportage, specifically a perceived hostility towards the Indians (Rusco 1999: 103–5). Collier, himself, later reviewed the report and produced a lengthy and scathing assessment. He agreed with Bowler's recommendation, and rejected the report outright on its merits. His decision was based, in part, on his qualms with the methods that Steward used, though it is clear that it was based equally on what he perceived to be Steward's biased reporting. Writing to Bowler, he said:

I am tempted to excerpt other and lengthier dicta from Dr. Steward's report, but the one which I have quoted indicate most of the reason why the report does not prepossess me as social philosophy or as factual reporting . . . In determining Indian Service policies, and in attempting to evaluate human beings and to chart the future of human spirits, there are needed some endowments of enthusiasm, confidence in the human nature one is dealing with, and social philosophy. . . . the shedding of light upon our complicated Indian problem needs something more [than what Steward's report offers]. This is another case showing that achievements in a special science, anthropology or any other, provides no assurance of competency to deal with social problems (Collier (1936), cited in Rusco 1999: 106).

It is therefore quite clear that Steward's preconceived views on Indian policy shaped his reportage on the Shoshone to a sufficient extent that readers of that material felt there was both an apprehension of bias and a concern with advocating a direction for social policy in what were intended as 'objective' and factual reports. In this regard, providing expert testimony that opposed the Shoshone claims and which emphasized the breakdown of their institutions would fit well with Steward's own policy agenda. Given this background, it is conceivable that Steward's depiction of Shoshone society, both in his expert reports and later academic writings, resulted from his strong perspective that advocated their assimilation at the expense of impartial assessment.

Thirdly, there is information to indicate that his designation of the 'family level of sociocultural integration' may have been the result, at least in part, of his firm views respecting the inappropriateness of attributing ownership of property to Indian peoples. It may be true, as Myers suggests, that in the 1930s Steward considered that societies at the band level, at least those with a patrilineal form of descent, could have had institutions respecting ownership and inheritance of land in the pre-contact period. However, at least by the 1950s, Steward expressed a very strong position in support of the view that ownership of property, properly speaking, only existed when the form of land holding explicitly fit the characteristics of land ownership as defined in American law. It is a perspective made abundantly clear in the following statement, which represents Steward's counter to Kroeber's view on property as reported from an early ethnohistory conference:

Property in the modern United States has several characteristics . . . Property rights are validated by a transferable title, which is registered with and protected by a higher authority, or state, which has an appropriate system of property laws. Certainly, no one would argue that the aboriginal Indians attached any of these features to their concept of property, despite such common and bare assertions in ethnographic monographs as that the 'band owned the land up to certain clearly defined boundaries' (1955b: 293).

This is a view that echoes the *terra nullius* perspective and is one that dovetails precisely with the requirements of the Department of Justice's legal argument.

However, it was necessary, following Myers (this volume) to square this proposition with Steward's view, held earlier, that band societies could hold title to their lands. To this end, he argued that, while it is true that patrilineal bands in pre-contact times could have institutions that held land, under the influence of colonial penetration, as for example through the fur trade, these bands reverted to an earlier evolutionary stage; such a stage would be the family level of sociocultural integration (1955a: 120; 1955b).

Hence, whether under 'pristine' pre-contact conditions or under the influence of the colonial project, Steward's steadfast position was that contemporary Indian societies were largely at a level of sociocultural integration in which they were not sufficiently evolved, either in socio-political organization or with respect to institutions of land ownership, to fall within the terms of reference as the Department of Justice defined them (Lurie 1957; Stewart 1985; Ronaasen, Clemmer and Rudder 1999).

Given the context within which Steward was working and given his strongly held views on policy matters and on land tenure, it is reasonable to become concerned about the objectivity and dispassion with which he developed his theoretical project.

## Steward and Canadian Law

The third implication concerns the adoption of Steward's theoretical frame as the means through which the Canadian courts assess the factual basis of evaluating the scope and content of an Aboriginal right in litigation. The need to undertake such an evaluation arises because the 1982 Constitution Act includes a provision that 'the aboriginal and treaty rights of the aboriginal peoples of Canada are recognized and affirmed.' And, in recent years, it has fallen largely to the courts to interpret what this phrase means through litigation on specific Aboriginal rights claims. It is a process that parallels, in significant respects, the one that took place in the United States during the ICC proceedings.

In developing jurisprudence on these questions, the Canadian courts have negotiated between two propositions. On the one hand, as has been argued elsewhere (Asch 2002), the courts by implication rest the legitimacy of Canada's assertion of sovereignty and jurisdiction over its territory without the consent of Indigenous peoples on the doctrine of *terra nullius*.[4] On the other hand, since 1973, the courts have acknowledged the principle that Indigenous peoples lived in societies prior to the arrival of settlers and that Aboriginal rights, in principle, flow from that fact (*Calder*).

The courts have reconciled these propositions through the adoption of a test that arose out of a 1979 judgement concerning the Aboriginal rights of the Inuit of

Baker Lake in what was then the Northwest Territories. This test makes, as its first requirement states, that the Indigenous party must demonstrate that they lived in an 'organized society' in the pre-settlement period. It is a test to which every Indigenous litigant must submit.

In seeking to establish this fact, the courts are not intending to differentiate between 'societies' and 'ad hoc' collections of individuals. Rather, as the jurisprudence clearly shows, the test is intended to ensure that the indigenous party lived in an organized society in contrast with something 'more primitive' and that the 'level of organization' established as fact is sufficient to sustain the Aboriginal right they are asserting in law. In this regard, the Canadian courts also parallel the approach taken at the ICC. And, as was the case in the ICC proceedings, this has meant that anthropological theory and expert testimony has become an important component in the factual assessment of legal rights to be determined through litigation.

In developing their legal arguments in the two post-1982 precedent setting cases we have examined thus far, the Crown has explicitly adopted the same line of reasoning as did the Department of Justice in the ICC cases. That is, they have argued that the Indigenous party lived in societies that were unorganized or, at the very best, insufficiently organized to establish a factual basis upon which to establish the right in law. In both cases, their assertions were supported by expert testimony that relied on a Stewardian framework. In the first, *Delgamuuk'w*, the expert, a cultural geographer who was trained by anthropologists and calls herself an anthropologist, argued that the Gitksan and Westsuwe'ten were living at a societal level below a threshold to establish that they could own land. While the anthropologists acting on behalf of the claimants strongly disagreed, the trial judge adopted the perspective of the cultural geographer and concluded that these peoples lived at what can only be termed a 'family level of sociocultural integration' and thus had no right to hold title to lands. It was a decision that was overturned at the Supreme Court largely on the ground that the judge took inadequate notice of the oral testimony that could establish a factual basis for the assertion. The Court also established the terms within which a claim to Aboriginal title could be assessed and sent the case back for retrial. In establishing those terms, the Court accepted as a general principle that there could be societies that, perhaps because they were 'nomadic' could not establish an attachment to land sufficient to sustain a title claim. In reading their judgement on this point, the possibility that they have the difference between what is known as 'band' and 'tribal' levels of integration comes easily to mind.

In the second, *van der Peet*, the issue concerned whether the Sto:lo First Nation of what is now British Columbia, had an Aboriginal right, in law, to fish salmon commercially. Again, the Crown argued that the Sto:lo were not a society sufficiently organized to ground this commercial right in practices that originated prior to settlement. The Crown relied in this instance on an archaeologist who argued that the Sto:lo did not have a factual basis for such an assertion because they were at the 'band' rather than the 'tribal' level of sociocultural integration. The expert for the Sto:lo, an anthropologist, argued to the contrary that they were at a 'tribal' level. Thus, the Stewardian framework was adopted by both parties. It was a correspondence of moment to the Supreme Court for their reasons for judgement make the influence of Stewardian ideas apparent. Specifically they reasoned:

> . . . that the Sto:lo were at a band level of social organization rather than at a tribal level. As noted by the various experts, one of the central distinctions between a band society and a tribal society relates to specialization and division of labour. In a tribal society there tends to be specialization of labour – for example, specialization in the gathering and trade of fish – whereas in a band society division of labour tends to occur only on the basis of gender or age. The absence of specialization in the exploitation of the fishery is suggestive, in the same way that the absence of regularized trade or a market is suggestive, that the exchange of fish was not a central part of Sto:lo culture. I would note here as well Scarlett Prov. Ct. J.'s finding that the Sto:lo did not have the means for preserving fish for extended periods of time, something which is also suggestive that the exchange or trade of fish was not central to the Sto:lo way of life. [para. 90]

> On the basis of the evidence from members of the appellant's band, and anthropological experts, he found that, historically, the Sto:lo people clearly fished for food and ceremonial purposes, but that any trade in salmon that occurred was incidental and occasional only. He found, at p. 160, that there was no trade of salmon 'in any regularized or market sense' but only 'opportunistic exchanges taking place on a casual basis'. He found that the Sto:lo could not preserve or store fish for extended periods of time and that the Sto:lo were a band rather than a tribal culture; he held both of these facts to be significant in suggesting that the Sto:lo did not engage in a market system of exchange. On the basis of these findings regarding the nature of the Sto:lo trade in salmon, Scarlett Prov. Ct. J. held that the Sto:lo's aboriginal right to fish for food and ceremonial purposes does not include the right to sell such fish. He therefore found the accused guilty . . . [para. 7]

This judgement underscores the continuing importance of Steward's anthropology for the public arena. In Canada, it is clear, the courts, from *Baker Lake* to *van der Peet* have accepted a framework for the determination of Aboriginal rights that favours an interpretation of fact foregrounded in Steward's paradigm. This raises the question: Is Steward's theoretical project, and particularly his hierarchic differentiation between levels of sociocultural integration, a fair and unbiased paradigm in which to assess ethnographic and political facts? Clearly, many experts and the courts believe that it is. In our view, it is not. Based on our assessment of these cases and others under consideration as well as the information on the ICC, we believe that Steward's orientation constructs an image of Indigenous society that favours an interpretation of fact more compatible with the view of the Crown than the First Nation. Whether this is due to his advocacy of a policy of assimilation, his strongly held views on the appropriateness of attributing property-like concepts to Indigenous peoples, and/or other personal factors and/or to a general bias in evolutionary approaches identified by Trigger (1998) as an ideological mechanism in defence of privilege, is beyond the scope of this contribution. But, even should these assertions prove too definitive for others to accept based on the information we have brought forward, we believe what we have presented provides a context for reconsidering the faith that the Court and some anthropological experts seem to have that, whatever its other shortcomings, Steward's paradigm provides an objective and scientific way to assess the facts upon which Aboriginal rights are determined in Canadian jurisprudence.

## Conclusions

There can be no dispute that Julian Steward's theoretical project remains seminal in the field, and has become an important source of inspiration for many generations of anthropologists engaged in the theorization and understanding of Indigenous societies. His ideas have had influence, as in the Canadian judicial system, beyond the confines of the discipline with which he is associated. There was a time when the objectivity and scientific nature of his work was virtually unquestioned. However, in recent years work such as that of Ronaasen (1993) with respect to hunting-gathering societies, Bettinger (1983) on Steward's work in the Owens Valley, Clemmer (1969) on his assumptions concerning assimilation and Rusco (1999) as discussed elsewhere in this paper, have challenged this assessment. In this paper, we have extended this assessment by examining the relationship between Steward's theoretical project and the premises of colonial legal ideology. We have found that there is information to indicate that, whether consciously or not, Steward's project displays a bias that depicts Indigenous peoples as lacking qualities of socio-political organization and institutions of land holding that necessitate recognition of their rights by the legal systems of Canada and the United States. It is a systemic bias that, we believe, has implications for the Canadian courts, for experts who appear in those courts and, more generally, for those members of the anthropological community who seek a better understanding of relationship between anthropological projects and the larger contexts within which we work.

## Acknowledgements

The authors acknowledge the assistance of the Social Sciences and Humanities Research Council of Canada (SSHRCC), whose funding has supported this research in the form of a Standard Research Grant (Asch) and a Doctoral Fellowship (Pinkoski).

## Notes

1. This is not to argue in favour of a completely interpretivist approach. Rather, it is to suggest that every theoretical stance only provides a partial understanding, but that, ultimately, it is our view that there is an objective reality to which we are attending.
2. We are not limiting this to approaches that are consonant with colonial legal ideology. We believe it equally incumbent on researchers to consider implications of models that may have biases in favour of Indigenous peoples.
3. Cf. Hatch 1973; Kerns 2003.
4. We are distinguishing here between areas where treaties were negotiated and where they were not. In areas where they were negotiated, the written document states that the Indians ceded and surrendered their underlying title and rights. It is an assertion that is under dispute.
5. This does not mean that the Sto:lo were required to have practiced a 'commercial' fishery prior to contact, but rather that they had institutions that could have developed into a commercial fishery at a later date.

## Cases Cited

*Calder v. Attorney-General of British Columbia (1973) 34 D.L.R. (3d.)*
*Delgamuuk'w v. British Columbia (1997) 3 S.C.R.*
*Hamlet of Baker Lake v. The Minister of Indian Affairs and Northern Development (1979) 1 F.C. 487.*
*In Re: Southern Rhodesia (1919) AC 210 (PC)*
*R. v. van der Peet (1996) 2 S.C.R.*

# 16

# Hunting for Histories: Rethinking Historicity in the Western Kalahari

## *James Suzman*

This paper examines the emergence of a form of historical consciousness among the Omaheke Ju/'hoansi of the western Kalahari desert, in eastern Namibia. In doing so I hijack some of their models of history and historicity to reassess, and, hopefully rejuvenate debate on the once popular distinction in social anthropology between historical and ahistorical societies – albeit with a number of important caveats. I will argue that we need to distinguish more carefully between historical consciousness (as manifest in a societies' tendency to historicize the past and their capacity to imagine a potentially different future) and the past as exposed through historical inquiry. On the basis of this I will argue that, if there is now a wide consensus within anthropology that (a) the dominant conventions of historical representation are no longer sacrosanct, that (b) history itself constitutes a genre for the 'representation of pastness', and that (c) world history can therefore be rewritten as a 'non-domesticated multiple history' (Hastrup 1992: 3), then it is not unreasonable to suggest that some societies may be ahistorical in some important ways.

## Historicizing Kalahari Hunter-Gatherers

The understanding that twentieth-century hunter-gatherers represented our 'contemporary ancestors' and therefore that they embodied some essence of the human condition unadulterated by the 'complications and accretions brought about by agriculture, urbanisation, advanced technology, class and national conflict' (Lee 1984: 169) contributed greatly to the appeal of hunter-gatherer studies during the 1960s and 1970s. However, with the juggernaut of modernity steaming inexorably forward, researchers seeking 'authentic' exemplars of hunting-and-gathering life found themselves having to travel ever further afield. The 1960s and 1970s was the final hour of 'lost world' anthropology as researchers scudded through arctic tundra; hacked paths through equatorial forests; and trekked into the sandy depths of Africa's deserts in search of isolated communities still embedded in the rhythms of hunter-gatherer life. Because of the ground-breaking work of the Harvard Kalahari Research Group during this period the Ju/'hoansi (!Kung) of Dobe emerged as the sine qua non of anthropology's foragers.

That Kalahari San populations like the Ju/'hoansi and G/wikhoe continued to hunt and gather well into the second half of the twentieth century was assumed to be a function of their spatial isolation (Marshall 1976: 13; Lee 1979a: 33; 1976: 18; etc.). Their spatial isolation was also taken as an index of their temporal isolation and members of the Harvard Kalahari Research Group framed their work among the Ju/'hoansi during the 1960s and 1970s as a race against time. Such was the urgency of the project in the light of Lee and DeVore's fears that 'acculturation' was rapidly transforming this 'cold' society into a 'hot' one that between 1963 and 1971 the Harvard Group dispatched no less than ten researchers to Dobe to document a way of life practised by what appeared to be a rapidly diminishing reservoir of living subjects.

The prehistoricity of the hunting-and-gathering San was axiomatic for the Harvard researchers' work. Richard Lee, for example, proclaimed that his research served to 'place this ahistorical society in history' (Lee 1979a: 6). While Lee carefully qualified his assertions concerning Ju/'hoan antiquity, this did not dispose of the underlying premise that he understood them to be a contemporary analogue of Upper Palaeolithic life. The endurance of hunting-and-gathering as a life strategy in the Kalahari was however not solely attributed to the apparent spatial isolation of these people. Lee's nutritional studies of Ju/'hoansi in the late 1960s, taken alongside similar studies among the Fish Creek Aboriginals of Hemple Bay and Tanzania's Hadzabe suggested that hunter gatherers were not Hobbes's miserable wretches, but rather were the 'original affluent society' (Sahlins 1972; Bird-David 1992b).

By the late 1980s, however, the thesis of original affluence was unpopular. Some disputed its evidentiary basis. Others struck at the evolutionary underpinnings to the thesis and queried whether hunters and gatherers like the Kalahari San were as isolated as initially supposed (Wilmsen 1989a). Further interrogation of this latter point suggested that hunter-gatherer specialists' preoccupation with antiquity had paradoxically encouraged complacency about history. Indeed, a growing corpus of archaeological and historical research suggested that (Australia notwithstanding) even the remotest hunter-gatherers had been in sustained contact with peoples engaged in other economic strategies for a considerable period of time. As Carmel Schrire was quick to note, anthropological writing on hunter-gatherers somewhat paradoxically highlighted the present as an analogue for the past 'while neatly ignoring the effect of past interactions on present populations' (Schrire 1982: 11). The implications of this research were tremendous and struck at the very foundations of hunter-gatherer studies. How was anthropology to account for the perseverance of hunting-and-gathering in evolutionary terms if hunters and gatherers had been in sustained contact with people engaged in other forms of economic activity?

Edwin Wilmsen was the first anthropologist to grapple with the implications of sustained historical contact between hunter-gatherers and others in the Kalahari. He eschewed social evolutionary models in favour of a world systems political economy approach. He argued that archaeological and ethnohistorical evidence suggested that the Bushmen, far from being a primitive isolate were an ethnic category forged out of the dramatic political and economic processes that shook the southern African subcontinent over the preceding millennium. For Wilmsen the San were the 'have-nots' of a dystopian southern Africa, and their reliance on hunting and gathering was a sophisticated adaptation to sustained poverty. He intended his analysis to bridge what Faubion (1993) refers to as the 'Great Divide' between peoples 'indifferent to history and peoples devoted to history' and in so doing finally to exorcize ahistoricity from academic representations of San. Inspired by the likes of Eric Wolf (1982: 385), for whom no society is outside of the 'global processes set in motion by European expansion', Wilmsen's Bushmen are not history makers. Rather they are peripheral players in the unfolding of a grander global historical narrative.

Wilmsen's gate-crashing of the hunter-gatherer party precipitated one of the most ferocious debates in late twentieth-century social anthropology. Khoisanists and (to a lesser extent) other hunter-gatherer specialists involved in what subsequently came to be referred as the Kalahari Debate found themselves coalescing into two camps: the revisionists and the traditionalists headed by Edwin Wilmsen and Richard Lee respectively. Where traditionalists defended the isolationist paradigm, revisionists championed political economy and the radical shake-up of hunter-gatherer studies that acceptance of their new data entailed. They accused the traditionalists of having granted the Bushman antiquity while denying them history. The traditionalists countered by accusing the revisionists of overstatement, obscurationism, strawmanism and dishonesty.

Like the Kalahari Wilmsen describes, the Bushman voice struggles to be heard above the din of grander narratives in his analysis of the Kalahari political economy (Wilmsen 1989a). Wilmsen's treatise is not unique in this respect. The overwhelming majority of publications on San history in the past decade owe more to ferreting in the archives than sweating in the Kalahari sunshine. While much has been written about how colonial administrators, conservation officials, magistrates, farmers, show-ground entertainers, anthropologists and others dealt with San and the degree to which San have remained in service to their fantasies we have learnt little of the past from a San perspective. Only a few ethnographers have sought to capture and grant space to the 'native voice' (see, e.g. Shostak 1981;

2000; Biesele 1993; Guenther 1989) or engage San in conversations about 'history'.

The widespread reliance on archival rather than oral sources to map out a history of San in Namibia and Botswana is not simply a function of the fact that San studies has increasingly become the stomping ground of historians keen to avoid sunburn. It is also because San themselves placed little or no emphasis on narrating the past.

## The Northern Omaheke

Namibia's Omaheke Region lies on the western edge of Kalahari. It stretches northwards from the town of Gobabis, through two hundred kilometres of commercial ranch land into the vast Hereroland East communal area, the one-time native reserve of the primarily pastoralist Herero and Mbanderu peoples. This area is also home to the Omaheke Ju/'hoansi, often spuriously referred to in the anthropological literature as the ≠Au//eisi (Suzman 2000). To the north of the Omaheke lies Nyae-Nyae, home to the Ju/'hoansi that were the darlings of 1960s and 1970s anthropological research. Unlike the Ju/'hoansi of Nyae-Nyae, who managed to escape the worst excesses of Namibia's colonial regime until the onset of bush war during the 1970s, the Ju/'hoansi in the Omaheke found themselves at the sharp end of the colonial encounter from the beginning of the twentieth century.

Although a century ago, the Omaheke was the almost exclusive domain of the Ju/'hoansi, they now constitute a small, highly dependent, marginalized and landless minority forced to eke out a living as farm-labourers, beggars and serfs. Their marginalization was effected through the rapid colonial penetration of the Omaheke during the first half of the twentieth century and its subsequent designation as a white commercial farming area and native reserve for the Herero.

Subject to the dominant representations and coercive authority of others Ju/'hoansi in the Omaheke now define themselves as a regional underclass. By 1990, when Namibia finally achieved its independence from South Africa, Ju/'hoansi comprized a minority population in the Omaheke. With hunting and gathering no longer options, most Ju/'hoansi relied on labour exchange in order to secure a place to stay, food to eat and water to drink.

## Hunting for Histories

During my first couple of years in the Omaheke I was keen to add a Ju/'hoan voice to the rapidly growing literature on San history – a task that I discovered was far from straightforward. Given the dramatic changes visited upon Ju/'hoansi in the Omaheke over the preceding eighty years I assumed somewhat naively that some sort of collective history would be presented to me, or at the very least that that there would be some consensus about the impact of the past on the present. My search for a dominant historical narrative failed. Although some informants willingly engaged me in conversation about the recent past, none would stray too far from the immediacies of their own experience. If I happened to ask someone a question about a matter they were not directly involved in, the question would almost inevitably be deferred to someone else. Indeed, the only relatively detailed 'historical' narratives that I was told either involved the narrator or one of her of his immediate kin.[1] Tied to this, as much as elderly Ju/'hoansi were often willing to talk about the past, the same could not be said of younger Ju/'hoansi. Usually, they would greet my inquiries with a glazed expression and suggest that our shared time might be more fruitfully spent playing a game of one-two-three, having a smoke or taking my truck for a spin in the bush in the hope that we might 'find' some meat.

In the end the process of compiling a history of the Omaheke involved synthesizing a fragmentary set of individual recollections, broad generalizations about the past and life histories with other voices, materials and traces from the colonial record. Notwithstanding these difficulties, there soon emerged several clear points of continuity in the ways that Ju/'hoansi spoke about the past and these in turn provided a framework for analysing how Ju/'hoansi related the past to the present and the future. The clearest point of unity in otherwise idiosyncratic renditions of the past was the distinction posited between *old times* and *new times*. Old times it was explained to me was the time before the whites and the Hereros came and when the 'first people' hunted and gathered. New times on the other hand referred to the period after the whites and the Hereros came and 'when the Ju/'hoansi became poor'. The transition from old times and new times was not viewed as a rupture in the course of unilinear time so much as a qualitative distinction between kinds of time. For Ju/'hoansi it was an epochal transition in which their world and their place in it was irreversibly transformed.

Although Ju/'hoansi invoked the distinction between old times and new times in numerous different contexts it was done so most frequently and forcefully when referring to specific individuals or groups of people as either old-time people or new-time people. Most Omaheke Ju/'hoansi described themselves as *jusa o //'eike* – new-time people (literally, 'today's people'). While there was consensus that a significant proportion Ju/'hoansi living north of the Omaheke in the Nyae-Nyae were still old-time people only a few elderly Ju/'hoansi in the Omaheke embraced the label. Old-time people drew their identity and outlook from their days as hunter-gatherers. They kept the physical ephemera of the past – like their bows and arrows – stashed secretively under their mattresses; spoke longingly of hunting and the ways of the animals the once shared their world; they were skilled narrators of contemporary folklore and they knew of the healing force of *n/um*. Although the majority of elderly Ju/'hoansi I knew in the Omaheke were 'old-time' people, having grown up largely independently of white farmers and Herero and having learnt the 'old manners', not all were.

That not all old people were old-time people reflected the fact that Ju/'hoansi in different areas experienced the transition from old times to new at different times. Where some Ju/'hoansi were roped into labour on the white farms in the Omaheke during the early years of white settlement, others maintained their autonomy as hunters and gatherers well into the 1960s and beyond. Still others straddled these two spaces, hunting and gathering during good seasons and engaging in farm labour during bad until white farmers made it brutally clear that they would not tolerate such a laissez-faire attitude to labour. Having noted this, the allocation of old-time and new-time identities was fairly clear-cut. Ju/'hoansi describe the transition from old times to new as a generational process: hunting-and-gathering Ju/'hoansi cajoled, coerced and conscripted into farm labour were still old-time people who maintained an appropriately old-time perspective. New-time people were those that had been born into farm life. As such there is no single moment that bridged old times with new so much as a series of qualitatively similar moments, that occurred in different places at different times.

## Old Times

New-time people were characteristically ambivalent about old times. While they agreed that Ju/'hoansi were 'free' during old times, many considered their contemporary poverty to be a direct consequence of the shortcomings of their ancestors. This was for two related reasons. Firstly, they claimed that their ancestors were with G//aua (now glossed as 'Satan') during old times and reasoned that their current woes were a form of cosmological retribution for their naïve allegiance to what they now thought of as an evil agency. Secondly and more pragmatically, new-time people castigated old-time people for their ignorance and weakness; where Herero and Tswana knew of cattle and Boers knew of borehole pumps, motor vehicles and guns, they explained, the Ju/'hoansi knew only of 'their world'. Both explanations were understood to be mutually reaffirming. Old time people were with G//aua because they were ignorant and likewise, they were ignorant because they were in thrall to G//aua. To this extent Ju/'hoansi echoed dominant colonial narratives that positioned them as the authors of their own misfortunes. As one young Ju/'hoan man explained:

> They were *dom* those old-time people. Look the whites were clever, they came with lots of things, guns, cars, diesel and wind pumps all of that sort of things . . . And also the Hereros and Namas, some of them had these things also, and they knew goats and cattle, but the Ju/'hoansi – they had nothing. They knew fuck all! They were weak people! People struggle in this place because the Hereros say, 'you people are *dom*, you are not people, you cannot make anything!'

New-time people's descriptions of old times were also vague and often speculative. Save for the small group of new-time people seeking to actively promote a Ju/'hoan political identity, few others expressed any interest in old-time things at all. With all Ju/'hoansi painfully conscious of the predominantly negative stereotypes of them held by their various neighbours, many young Ju/'hoansi viewed old-time things as symbolic of a weak and submissive past. Over the past decade in particular a trend among some younger Ju/'hoansi has been to become 'Nama' to avoid the stigma of being a 'Bushman'.

Old-time people on the other hand were less bothered by this negative imagery. Their descriptions of old times were not coloured by contemporary anxieties about social identity so much as tinged with nostalgia and disaffection with the hardships of the present. Nostalgia notwithstanding, old-time people did not consider old times to be a Golden Age. Indeed, they happily conceded some of the benefits of new time life like penknives, tinned meat, sugar, Toyotas and Grandpa's Headache Powders.

Old-time peoples' descriptions of old times were more elabourate than those offered by new-time people. Because old-time people considered themselves corporeal echoes of a conceptually distant yet chronologically recent past they also claimed a privileged position from which to narrate the relationship between new times and old times. This stemmed from the double perspective they claimed because they were *of* that time yet *in* this time. This alienation from both times granted them a degree of reflexivity absent in new-time people's narrations of the past, present or future. This double perspective also allowed old-time people to deploy both old-time and new-time narrative forms to describe their world: the former in the highly specialized idiom of folklore and the latter in the form of 'histories'. Their descriptions of old times however operated at a level of generalization that, while not denying the pastness of this period, did not historicize it. They were qualitative narratives that described *how things were* rather than *what happened*. Old times were portrayed as a homogenous time-space in which temporality was embedded in the practicalities of life and expressed through the periodicity of the diurnal-nocturnal round, the flow of the seasons and the certainty that death came to all that were born. Additionally, old times were populated by an anonymous cast: I was told no tales of great hunters, leaders or shamans. I was told no tales of desperate droughts, dismal dry seasons or great floods. Instead I was told that sometimes there were terrible droughts and great hunger and that sometimes there were great rains when the pans and the *omurambas* (fossilized river valleys) filled with water. I was told that among the Ju/'hoansi there were always good hunters and bad hunters, jealous lovers and powerful shamans and that this 'was always how things were during old times'. In effect, to borrow Lévi-Strauss's terminology, old-time people conveyed old times by reference to structures rather than events. Individual characters with agentive capacity only enter the Ju/'hoan narrative landscape at the onset of new times. The 'oldest' historical story that I was told in which clearly individuated characters appeared is the story of the murder of the white magistrate Van Rynveld during the conflict between the Bushman *Kaptein* Tsemkxau (Zameko) and the redoubtable widow Mrs Bullick in the northern Omaheke in 1923 (see Suzman 2000).

Old-time people described the transition from old times to new times as a process in which Ju/'hoansi were either seduced or coerced out of their *n!oresi* and subjected to the cruel domination of the 'animals of the town' as Ju/'hoansi then referred to whites. This process was often described as one of separation from the environment and ways of being in it. Echoing narrative forms used by foraging Ju/'hoansi, old-time people's descriptions of old times would often include a carefully and forcefully enunciated list of the meat animals that Ju/'hoansi once shared their world with. The absence of most of these species in the contemporary Omaheke meant these narratives gained increasing poignancy.

> They [old-time people] were not like these Bushmen here at Skoonheid. When they married, they married with meat; elands kudus, blue wildebeest, hartebeest, duikers. They would give meat to their wives and their wives would give some to their fathers and mothers and afterwards give even more meat away.

The ahistoricity of old times was expressed through the stress on continuous engagement and the asserted absence of any external agency capable of upsetting the essential sameness of things over time. Thus, while Ju/'hoansi do not deny the presence of others in the Kalahari during old times, they do not concede them the agentive capacity to have induced discontinuity. It was explained to me that:

> Ju/'hoansi were the strongest people in the old times. The strongest! They had bows and arrows with that poison worm. Everyone was scared of that poison, Hereros, everyone. They knew that if they fought with Ju/'hoansi then they might die from that poison. No man they were strong! . . . That is why the South Africans went to take them into the army.[2]

In spite of the endurance of the various structures of San marginalization through and beyond the colonial era, the expectation of change is paradigmatic of new times. New times are perceived of as a period of constant transition motivated by multiple agencies. Change in itself is seen to be inconstant and unpredictable. Different things change at different times, different rates and on different scales. Moreover changes in one area of life are understood to lead to changes in others. While there is consensus that change is contingent on the activities of various agencies, the precise roles of different agencies vary from one narrator's perspective to the next. For some, the status of the Ju/'hoansi was attributable to the actions of the Boers 'who used our hands to make them rich'. Some attributed their status to the Hereros 'who give fuck all for the Bushmen' whereas others blamed themselves. Equally, the hierarchical and causal affinities existing between various agencies were unclear in particular vis-à-vis the sacred and profane.

My faltering inquiries into the past were also impeded by vocabulary. While Ju/'hoansi in the Omaheke employed a more elabourate set of tense qualifiers than Ju/'hoansi in Nyae-Nyae (Van der Westhuizen 1972), these were not well suited to locating events chronologically. Usually only two imprecise qualifiers were used to denote the past: long ago (*goaq* or *g≠'ha*) and very long ago (*n//aaxa*). Even when attempting to locate events in new times, narrators rarely used the Western calendar. For the most part, they relied on broad chronological contextualizations such as 'in the time of the Boers', 'in the time of the pass [identity books]', 'before independence', or 'in the time of the ox wagons', etc. In addition to this, whereas new-time people were often relatively precise about chronology, old-time people were gloriously imprecise even when talking about new times, a fact that made the compilation of life histories something of a headache. While Ju/'hoansi in the Omaheke knew the Afrikaans word for history (*geskiedenis*) none was able to translate the term into Ju/'hoan. When pushed, most Ju/'hoansi agreed that the most appropriate translation was probably *n≠oahnsi* although it wasn't entirely satisfactory since it referred to any of factual stories or news shared around the evening fire.

## Tradition, Revision and the Problem of History

If a history of 'history' queries the possibility of a 'concrete history' and disposes of it as an ongoing theoretical problem (Young 1990: 23), it also highlights the different ways that the past is deployed in a range of contexts. Similarly, the more anthropologists have attended to local models of past, the more apparent it has become that historicity is mediated by perceptions of chronology, temporality and causality and likewise by social status and practical activity. As Hastrup (19942: 3) notes, history does not easily offer itself up to theorization in anthropology because anthropology 'questions the dominant conventions of historical representation'.

Despite the myriad theoretical problems to afflict historical anthropology many anthropologists and historians alike remain wedded to the possibility of a concrete history and theoretical sabre rattling notwithstanding, the Kalahari Debate is ultimately about 'concrete history'. The key protagonists of the debate all claim to render accurate histories of the Kalahari grounded in the diverse discursive and material ephemera of the past.

### People without History
A trend in post-colonial African scholarship has been to view all societies as historical. Two theoretical approaches have been dominant in this process. The first

seeks to locate all peoples in terms of global historical processes whereas the second seeks to explore the indigenous historicity of all peoples. Proponents of this second approach while noting the merits of the first are critical of it for failing to demonstrate the 'internal capacity for transformation' of all societies (Commaroff and Commaroff 1992: 24). While I am sympathetic to this critique, I doubt its universal applicability. It seems to me that presuming the historicity of peoples is as blinkered an approach as presuming their ahsitoricity. Indeed, it strikes me that if models of pre-capitalist orders have almost universally tended to focus on elucidating the mechanics of social reproduction rather than the internal dynamics of transformation, then we should not be so hasty to rush headlong into exposing the perhaps concealed historicity of all and sundry. While it is important that we recognize that different ways of narrating the past are histories, it is something completely different to assume that, just because all peoples have pasts, they are all historically conscious.

The distinction Ju/'hoansi make between old times and new times suggests that we should consider the possibility that hunting-and-gathering Ju/'hoansi were ahistorical in some important ways. Lévi-Strauss's now famous distinction between hot and cold societies provides a useful starting point for inquiry. Although Lévi-Strauss has never repudiated the efficacy of his hot/cold dichotomy, more critics have sought to bury it than praise it. Lévi-Strauss views historicity as a key distinction between 'primitive' and other societies. He is however dissatisfied with the clumsy Lévy-Bruhlian distinction between 'peoples without history and others' (Lévi-Strauss 1989 [1962]: 233). For Lévi-Strauss primitive societies annul history by means of an intellectual form of *bricolage* or 'mythical thought' (1989: 19) that predisposes them to salvage the 'debris of past events' and build structures from them. He contrasts this with hot societies who 'resolutely' internalize 'the historical process, making it the moving power of their development' (Lévi-Strauss 1989: 234). As such, Lévi-Strauss does not deny primitive societies their pasts so much as highlight their adroitness in nullifying the influence of the 'order of temporal succession' (1989: 234). For Lévi-Strauss, the primitive predilection for the 'science of the concrete' disposes of the possibility of their appreciation of concrete history.

An obvious problem with Lévi-Strauss's hot/cold dichotomy is that it renders immaterial the divergent ways that people in different societies engage with the past or whether they place any emphasis on narrating the past at all. However, many of those societies that fall into Lévi-Strauss's 'cold' category clearly place special emphasis on representing the past and moreover summon it as a cipher for social action. Complex genealogies, lists of ancestors and the invocation of tradition in ritual practice all indicate a form of temporal consciousness that extends well beyond the here and now. Also, somewhat at odds with his thermometric conceit, the hot/cold dichotomy allows little room for flexibility and copes poorly with transformation. What of societies that are positively scorching, one might ask, or those that are merely tepid?

A different line of approach is to ask what is it that spurs us develop a sense of ourselves as beings in history? Historical consciousness we are led to understand is contingent on the subject's awareness of change over time. Thus Diane Owen-Hughes (1995) argues that 'without change there is no temporal reality' and moreover that 'the most drastic recognitions of change . . . evoke the most powerful historical narratives' (see also Tonkin 1992; Kubler 1962). In other words one's ability to locate oneself *in* time is contingent on one's perception of change *over* time. But what of societies that assert a lack of change over time? The anthropological literature is replete with examples of apparently 'cold' societies that invoke 'tradition' as a means to resist forces of change or innovation and tradition is eminently historical insofar as it explicitly appeals to the then and there to substantiate the here and now – there is no tradition without history. Whenever tradition is invoked it is done so, at least in part, to banish the spectre of change. In other words, societies that narrate their present in terms of continuity with the past implicitly acknowledge the potential for change. This suggests the productivity of viewing historical consciousness as dependent not only on whether members of a society define their present against a past but also on whether they imagine a potentially different future.

## Rethinking Historicity

Anthropologists and others have often remarked on the 'live for the day attitude' of hunter-gatherers expressed through their apparent lack of concern for the future or the past and evidenced, among other things, by the absence of complex genealogies and oral histories. To be sure this simplistic characterization of hunter-gatherers owes something to the colonial processes that led to the emergence and elabouration of popular mythologies concerning many so-called 'primitives'. Having acknowledged this, however, there is more to the characterization of hunter-gatherers and some others as ahistorical than the ranting of colonizers projecting their evolutionary fantasies onto much-maligned natives. At one stage there was consensus in anthropology that hunter-gatherers paid little heed to either the past or future, a view expressed most forthrightly by the likes of Woodburn (1968), Turnbull (1961), Silberbauer (1981) and later Meillassoux (1981). During the 1970s many anthropologists considered 'immediate return' hunter-gatherer societies to be archetypal ahistorical societies.

Subsequently critics have questioned the veracity of this model of hunter-gatherer temporality. Feit (1994) for example asserts that hunter-gatherers engage in future related activities like moving camps in anticipation of seasonal changes, burning land or even preparing hunting equipment. However, it does not follow that, just because hunter-gatherers engage in future-oriented action, the temporal thinking behind it is qualitatively similar to that of pastoralists, bankers or anthropologists. I am beguiled by the ethnographic data that suggests that the practical engagement of hunter-gatherers (in particular those hunter-gatherers classified by Woodburn (1980) as 'immediate return' hunter-gatherers') encouraged a very different attitude to the past and the future.

Whether tainted by the 'poverty of a misappropriated theory' (Wilmsen 1989a) or not, traditionalist scholarship, suggests fairly unequivocally that the practical and cognitive engagement that hunting-and-gathering peoples like the Ju/'hoansi had with their 'lived in worlds' did not predispose them towards developing a sense of themselves as beings in history. Like Ju/'hoan oral histories traditionalist scholarship suggests that during old times Ju/'hoansi understood their world, and their relationship with it, to be enduring. Changes were predictable as they were underwritten by the systemic continuity of their surroundings: seasons followed one another as surely as night followed day, land that is burnt, as Ju/'hoansi point out, will always rejuvenate – it will be different, but the same. Traditionalist scholarship suggests that, during old times, the systemic continuity of the Ju/'hoan surroundings and their continuous engagement with it, to paraphrase Lévi-Strauss, effaced events of their particularity (1989: 236) and the past and the future were knotted seamlessly together into a perpetual present. In other words, future-oriented action undertaken by hunter-gatherers was mediated by the broad systemic predictability of their surroundings and their confidence in its abundance and generosity. Silberbauer's (1981) writing on the cosmology of G/wi hunter-gatherers in the central Kalahari shows how the broad predictability of the old-time world was underwritten by its systemic continuity. He notes that despite a clear sense of causality, G/wi 'prognostications are based on annual cycles and do not extend beyond one such cycle'. This sense of periodicity he argues is further illustrated by the fact that even the divine creator's desires to transform the world (by changing the weather for example) are ultimately 'bound by his own ordinance' (1981: 100) and that the integrity of the system is 'inviolate' (1981: 52). This ensures the world presents itself as predictable and explicable within certain constraints. Silberbauer (1981: 110) also includes an extraordinary anecdote concerning the extent to which even remarkable events in the 'past' with no enduring impact on the present were simply erased from the collective consciousness. He describes seeing the 'spectacular' Ikeya-Seki comet with the G/wi in 1965, noting that it caused the G/wi some concern. While perhaps none of the Xade band were alive fifty years previously, none had any memory of the even more dramatic Halley's comet that would have been visible in the Kalahari through much of 1910.

If we assume as Ingold (2000a: 187) does that 'the forms that people build arise within the current of their involved activity, in the specific relational context of their practical engagement with their surroundings' then it stands to reason that, if our surroundings change dramatically, the way in which we engage with them must surely follow suit. Given that histories are 'built forms' then historicity – the spur to build histories – must be related to our surroundings and how we engage with them (see Martin 1993: 62). Ju/'hoansi present the transition from old times to new times as a transformation from a world in which the illusion of endurance was a reality to a world in which the expectation and unpredictability of change was unquestioned. Certainly contemporary Ju/'hoan historical consciousness is a function both of change in the recent past, and their shared belief in the potential for change in the future. Thus among Ju/'hoansi 'tradition' as an abstracted conceptual category is very much the progeny of 'new-time' (see also Silberbauer 1981: 112).

By defining historicity as historical consciousness in the broadest possible sense we need no longer seek it in 'inarticulate practices' or the 'implicit language of symbolic activity' (Comaroff and Comaroff 1992: 157). Instead we are liberated to forage in the more certain and arguably more productive realm of explicit representation. Equally importantly we are not bound to conceptualize an ahistorical society as being somehow extra-temporal in the way that Lévy-Bruhl and Lévi-Strauss did. Instead we can examine how the experience of continuity and discontinuity might encourage different attitudes to and understandings of the relationship between the past, the present and the future.

I suspect that further research into concepts like individuality, economy, egalitarianism and social organization might shed further light on how hunter-gatherers engage and engaged with the past, present and future. Likewise, I expect that a better understanding of hunter-gatherer historicity and temporality will contribute to our understandings of other aspects of hunter-gatherer life. The potential of this is well illustrated by Calvin Martin in his treatise aimed at 'shattering history's hammerlock on our imaginations'. For Martin historicity is not only an artefact of the Neolithic but also the 'most important contrivance of that paradigm' (Martin 1993: 59). He argues that the ahistoricity of hunter-gatherers is revealed among other things, the porous relationships they maintained with their environments as evidenced by their belief in other-than-human-persons and the therianthropic capacities of shamans. The Neolithic was the harbinger of the historical, he contends, because farming necessitated the disarticulation of man from his 'surround' and his relocation into an altogether different matrix – the 'river of time'. He sees the emergence of historical consciousness in the appearance of omnipotent and distant deities and the evident desire of humankind to bend their environs to their will. Notwithstanding his outspokenly primitivist bent and arguably superficial treatment of some ethnographic material, Martin's argument tantalizes us with the possible insights a re-evaluation of historicity might offer.

## Conclusion

For much of the latter part of the twentieth century it was perceived that to deny a people history was to query their humanity or the authenticity of their political struggles – points that were of particular concern in southern Africa where apartheid overshadowed regional politics well into the 1990s. The concept of ahistoricity was largely discarded by scholars seeking to clear their closets of the racist baggage that reminded them of the Academy's complicity in the colonial enterprise. But apartheid's demise has now opened the way for inquiry into matters that may once have been viewed as potentially compromising to the aims of 'the struggle'. Nevertheless, research into southern Africa's marginalized San populations remains overshadowed by ethical and moral concerns (see Suzman 2001a).

These problems are not unique to southern Africa. Few societies that hunted and gathered at the turn of the twentieth century do so today. While some retain control over land and maintain aspects to their traditional livelihoods, for most life and livelihood are now shaped by the interplay between local, national and supranational political and economic constraints (Schweitzer, Biesele and Hitchcock 2000). This raises a range of new practical problems concerning one-time hunting-and-gathering populations without necessarily disposing of earlier theoretical problems. In this paper I have explored an earlier problem (historicity) with one eye focused squarely on a contemporary one (indigenous rights). I have argued that the distinction between old times and new times taken in tandem with traditionalist scholarship suggests that we should not dismiss the possibility that certain peoples were ahistorical in some important respects. In broad strokes I have suggested that sustained engagement with a systemically enduring world disposed of their inclination to locate the present in terms of a different past or potentially different future. Like those anthropologists that Johannes Fabian (1983) chides, Ju/'hoansi deny the coevality of old times by not conceding others the capacity to have disrupted the continuity of their engagement with their world.

I have also suggested that it is useful to distinguish the past from consciousness of it or, in other words, concrete history from historicity. While this distinction owes much to theorizing of Lévy-Bruhl and Lévi-Strauss, it makes no presuppositions about the endurance of social structures or the constitution of primitive mentalities. On the contrary, it neither queries the value of concrete historical inquiry nor disputes the relevance or importance of an historical anthropology. As such, the intention behind resuscitating this dichotomy is its potentially beneficial contribution to contemporary historiography and historical anthropology.

It is difficult to ignore the irony of using the transition from old times to new times as a vehicle to advocate the qualified resurrection of the historical/ahistorical-society dichotomy since it questions the utility of such a category for the description of contemporary populations. At the cusp of the third millennium there are few societies that have not experienced kinds of changes that force them to imagine the possibility of a radically different future. For many, to paraphrase Faubion (1993: 36) history has become the primary matter of any ultimate analysis, the primary substance of social identity and the primary source of all entitlements. In the case of the Ju/'hoansi, while historical narratives may well be disjointed, contested and idiosyncratic, there is no doubt that they are historically conscious. Ahistoricality, in other words, is an old-time thing, ill-suited to describing contemporary predicaments. This does not, however, diminish its importance as far as our understandings of the past are concerned. If we accept that some societies, like the Ju/'hoansi were ahistorical in the sense that I have proposed, we are freed to reopen inquiry into a range of questions, that to my mind have been neglected for too long by social anthropology. While I have not got into the problem here, I expect it may well also have some important repercussions concerning the way we interpret and animate historical material that pertains to societies that do not historicize their experience. As far as Bushmen peoples are concerned it does suggest that the extent of their historical contact with Bantu was of a much smaller scale than the revisionists suggest.

## Acknowledgements

This paper draws substantially on continuous fieldwork conducted in the Omaheke initially through 1994 and 1995 and thereafter in the Caprivi, Central Kalahari, Etosha region and Nyae-Nyae over the period 1997 through to 2002. I am grateful to the ESRC, the James Swan Fund, the Smuts Memorial Fund, Open Channels and the European Commission for supporting this research at various times.

## Notes

1. This also appears to be the case among San other than the Ju/'hoansi. Even the Omaheke Ju/'hoansi's south-eastern neighbours, the Nharo who had to contend with the presence of Bantu and white settlers in the Kalahari earlier than many other San populations, historical narratives collected by Matthias Guenther almost all suggest a personal connection between the narrator and the tale. In my experience, the Hai//om San that traditionally inhabited areas in and adjacent to Namibia's Etosha National Park stand out among contemporary San populations because they articulate historical narratives that clearly transcend individual experience.
2. The narrator was referring to the fact that from 1976 onwards, many Ju/'hoansi in the Dobe-Nyae-Nyae region and also in the Omaheke were enlisted into the South African Defence Force to fight in the war in southern Angola (see Gordon 1992: 1; Marshall and Ritchie 1984).

# 17

# (Re-)current Doubts on Hunter-Gatherer Studies as Contemporary History

## Thomas Widlok

This chapter is the revised version of a paper entitled 'On recent attempts to rede-fine anthropology as contemporary history', presented at CHAGS 9. It is the result of debates that I have witnessed over the last few years in the aftermath of the so-called Kalahari Debate and into which I have been recently drawn myself (see Woodburn et al. 2001). It is not meant to be a continuation of these debates but a reflection upon them based on the conviction that there is something more funda-mental at stake for anthropology than simply the Kalahari Debate spilling from one generation into the next. In this contribution I want to highlight patterns in the history of ideas and I therefore have only limited space to refer to the 'San' or 'Bushman' ethnography that forms the background of my argument. A more detailed ethnographic discussion is laid out in Widlok (1999) where I also include full acknowledgements to the field research I have conducted in Namibia.

## Current Issues

Should hunter-gatherer studies be transformed into a contemporary history of people with a hunter-gatherer background or, to put it more cautiously, a contem-porary history of people who (or whose ancestors) used to be classified as hunter-gatherers? An initial reaction to this suggestion is to insist, as probably most anthropologists would, that anthropology as a discipline has something to con-tribute that is not usually contained in history, namely ethnography and compar-ison. However, an even stronger case than that can be made because disciplinary boundaries are only one part of the story. They are an important part in so far, as for instance, in Namibia there is still no department of anthropology at the univer-sity and it is unlikely that there will be one in the near future (see Gordon 2000; Widlok 2001). In such a context, talk about replacing anthropology with history can have very direct influences on higher education and research policies in Namibia and elsewhere. But theoretically, at least, the work that is done under the roof of these disciplines is only vaguely defined. It can encompass a wide spectrum of activities. There is no reason why historians should not be doing ethnography or comparison, and in southern Africa they occasionally do both, just as anthropologists turn to history. Moreover, as anthropology increasingly comes to lean towards practice theory it is likely that 'history' becomes redefined as 'the process of cultural construction through practice' (Pauketat 2001: 87) resolving the old boundary between generalization and history as well as that between archaeology, anthropology and history. 'A theory of practice' Pauketat writes 'makes perfect history' (2001: 87).

The argument I want to make here is therefore not one against history, nor one concerning the politics and history of disciplines (see Widlok 1992), but more broadly an argument about recurring problems in the development of knowledge. In other words, in the phrase 'contemporary history' it is not so much the history bit that worries me but an exclusive focus on the contemporary. This demands further comment because it is fairly easy to see why many anthropologists – who may have objections against a redefinition of their work as history – are rather reluctant to object to 'contemporariness'. First, none of us wants to be blamed for treating the subjects of our research as non-contemporaries, as being stone-age people, survivals of the past, primitive, etc. (see Fabian 1983). Second, we all hope to produce state of the art research that is relevant to our contemporaries. Third, none of the representatives of the groups involved wants to be treated as being non-contemporary and increasingly they have the power to insist on this vis-à-vis research being conducted. Therefore, in a very real and immediate sense, and not merely in an abstract philosophical sense, the political representatives, say, of Namibia's 'San' are as much contemporaneous as the director of a research institute or as members of a university faculty. Researchers have to argue with all these parties; they need to try and convince them that they have interesting and relevant research questions and that these questions can be solved with the methods of the discipline.

Thus, the people involved are all contemporaries and I have not really heard anyone involved in research recently claiming anything to the contrary. In fact, to be mutually engaging with one another is part of the definition of what it means to be contemporary. This does not preclude the spread of a rhetoric of contemporariness. Revisionists have occasionally equated their victims with nineteenth-century racialist evolutionists (see Woodburn et al. 2001). In response, proponents of the 'classic' approach in hunter-gatherer studies emphasize the particular attention they give to contemporary problems and their close relationship with indigenous and support organizations (see Lee and Daly 1999). Since talk about more or less contemporariness in this context is not more than a rhetorical device, I suggest that we focus on the notion of 'currency' instead. Thereby I want to highlight the fact that all parties are contemporary but that none of them is eternal or able to define once and for all what the research or teaching agenda should be. As contemporaries they have to negotiate which concerns are currently on the agenda and which are not. There are issues that receive high currency and those with lower currency – and there are recurrent problems. It would be a rather restricted and restrictive frame if we were to consider only issues related to current history, i.e. to present-day events that constitute the status quo or, more precisely, that are currently thought to constitute the status quo. As a consequence of such a restriction we would be in danger of losing sight of recurrent problems. How do we know what 'recurrent problems' are? It is by relating contemporary events with processes that reach into the past and into the future, by making good use of analogies, comparisons and generalizations.

## Analogies

The use of analogies has a long history in hunter-gatherer studies, but it seems to have fallen somewhat into disrepute. The critique of propositions made with the help of analogies has readily been expanded to a dismissal of analogy as a method and as an analytical tool. My main point is that we need to separate the two. In other words, analogy is a generic and indispensable tool of analysis. Because analogy is such a general-purpose tool it is also used in arguments that invite criticisms. In fact it is part of its productiveness as a tool that we can argue with it. The alternative would consist of implicit and vague analogies that are far less open to scrutiny.

Archaeologists have confronted the question of analogy much more forcefully than social and cultural anthropologists who sometimes think of analogy as 'an archaeological problem'. Moreover, there is a certain degree of asynchrony between the two disciplines (or subdisciplines as some would see it). In an early phase ethnographers were keen to make analogies with the archaeological past. The emergence and subsequent disappearance of the phrase 'stone-age man' (or 'stone-age economics' or stone-age this and that) in the ethnographic discourse on hunter-gatherers is indicative here. Towards the middle of the twentieth century anthropologists made inflationary use of these labels (see Spencer and Gillen 1927; Sahlins 1972) and reluctance to accept these analogies initially came from the archaeologists. They came to envisage their work to be as a self-contained enterprise relying on the recovered materials only, not needing any non-material and therefore dubious anthropological analogies. Today the situation in some ways is almost reversed. It is the archaeologists who are rediscovering the importance of ethnographic analogies to make sense of their data (see Eggert 1998). They readily make use of ethnography and of anthropological models based on ethnography.

Hunter-gatherer ethnographers report that they find their work nowadays cited primarily by archaeologists so that Lee and Daly consider archaeologists to be 'the largest 'consumer' (and producers) of research on hunting and gathering peoples' (1999: 11). Social and cultural anthropologists, by contrast, now (or currently) largely reject the use of analogies. A number of reasons are given for this rejection. Sometimes it is claimed that this in compliance with the demands of the indigenous people that feature in ethnographies who do not want to be portrait as stone-age people. However, in many cases indigenous people explicitly emphasize their connection to a prehistoric past, often where researchers find it difficult to demonstrate that there is such a direct link. In any case, there is an element of inversion here insofar as some European archaeologists have in the past rejected analogies from non-European ethnography because they thought it to be condescending to their European forefathers, whereas it is now the non-Europeans who may find such an analogy condescending from their point of view. Leaving these shifting concerns aside for a moment, some recurrent problems emerge. There is what may be called the temporal fallacy, which assumes that similar results (in terms of material production, settlement layouts, etc) at different points in time allow us to infer the reasons that have motivated the action that has led to these results. Even where there is continuity, stability and homology in the results there may have been shifts in the course of processes that have led to these results. However, there is also an element of a spatial fallacy involved, namely that of assuming that settings observed in the same region, even though in periods far apart, have as it were a natural link and can be explained in terms of one another. This strong genealogical model of the continuity of traditions in certain places also needs to be questioned. It represents the opposite pole to the danger of exoticizing, namely that of a form of 'incorporatism' that subsumes settings in spatial proximity to represent a single case.

To make the matter more concrete, let me refer to the Namibian ethnography and to shift the focus slightly to the more general question of comparison. After all, analogy is a specific form of comparison and the two issues are clearly connected.

## Comparisons

Comparison can be a powerful tool. In the absence of 'experiments' and other such techniques in the social sciences, comparison may indeed be the most powerful tool available to us. I believe that anthropology has to play a particular role in delivering the insights from comparison to fellow researchers and to the public at large. However, the success of any comparative project depends on what is compared and for what purpose, and on being aware and clear about this (see Widlok 2001). Comparisons take place at different levels of analysis. At a micro level I have, for instance, made use of the fact that the people at and around my main field site in northern Namibia switch between a variety of externally defined living spaces, namely 'communal, commercial, or State land controlled by other people' (1999: 37). Comparing personal and social strategies of people at and around Mangetti who switch between these contexts gives an insight into a more general dilemma of accommodating oneself to such a variety of living spaces (1999: 37). In the context of the suggestion that anthropology should be contemporary history, it has been suggested that working exclusively with farm labourers, for instance, would be the right choice for an anthropologist in Namibia today because wage labourers seem to be the most numerous and would best represent 'the Bushmen' of today (see Sullivan 2001). I think this is as self-defeating as the earlier suggestion to study 'the last remnants of true hunter-gatherers' tucked away somewhere in the Kalahari. Both strategies deprive us of the potential of comparison. It is only the comparison between different settings that allows us to see patterns as social relations are transformed in changing contexts. Moreover, a focus on the farm-worker majority would also deprive the people we write about from recognizing the potential for diversity in their own way of doing things. In fact many 'Bushmen' today are as much *former* farm workers as they are former full-time hunters and gatherers having lost both their land and their jobs.

Research with farm labourers may nevertheless be a good starting point for exploring this diversity. When starting work with Ju/'hoansi today it may in fact make more sense to study life on the farms, as Renée Sylvain (1999) and James Suzman (2000) have recently done. The next step in the research process could then be a comparison with life outside the farms which is so well documented for southern African hunter-gatherers. When working with Hai//om, I was faced with the situation that there were no good studies on their contemporary life either on farms or away from farms. There was some work on Hai//om people in the Etosha region, some on Hai//om living on the farms but virtually nothing on Hai//om living in the sparsely populated communal area given to the Owambo. Therefore working with the people 'sitting on the red line' who moved into and out of 'Owamboland', the communal land of agropastoralists to the north, and the 'white farms' in the south necessarily involved a comparative dimension.

At a higher level of abstraction, anthropological work, even in the classic format of an ethnographic monograph, commonly deals with fundamental social problems that necessarily have a comparative dimension. In my case study of the Hai//om of Mangetti this applies to the 'tension between independence, or the ability to choose among extensive options, and autonomy, or the enjoyment of autonomous modes of social organization' (1999: vii). These problems concern people in Europe as much as in Namibia or elsewhere. A monographic case study can contribute to such fundamental issues by comparing all results of the case study in question with what has been reported about the dynamics of social institutions across the world in other contexts. The units of comparison are therefore processes rather than 'cultures' or 'societies'. The flexibility and seemingly disorganized dynamic of 'San' ways of doing things bears a resemblance to many other social and cultural phenomena in today's world in that they force us to take a different approach which no longer assumes that 'society' and 'culture' are ultimate causes which determine human actions and ideas.

In the presentation of anthropological knowledge in ethnographic writing careful indexing is one simple technique of positively working towards a comparison of processes. Referring to indexing in this context may sound like a formality, but it is not. Doing an index for a book is a tiresome task, and one that publishers like to do away with or to pass on to authors, but for one thing it is a systematic way of including reflexive thought and comparative concepts at the same time. When compiling an index, and when using it, we can trace the concepts that are used in a monograph (or any other case material), their distribution across the account that is given, the way they overlap, complement one another or form logical oppositions (or do not). And we can relate the monograph in question to other ethnographic works. For this reason the fact that in recent times indexes are either left to a machine or are left out completely does indicate a more fundamental shift away from good comparative analysis. And it should be pointed out that using ideas or concepts across contexts or cases does not automatically 'reify' them. By contrast, we need to acknowledge that the categories of hunter-gatherer studies can be useful across cases because they are sufficiently abstract. They are not things in themselves but they can be related to empirical phenomena. The concepts developed in 'hunter-gatherer studies' are not 'out there' in the Kalahari inseparably tied to the cases from which they may have originally arisen, but they can be applied to make sense of a changing world of ongoing processes.

## Generalizations

Comparisons and analogies can be used in very different ways and for very diverse purposes so that it is useful to discuss them with regard to specific contexts (see below). However, whatever the specific context, both comparison and analogy necessarily involve a generalizing tendency. Analogies and any other comparisons shed light on the supra-individual, structural level (Eggert 1998: 116). Correspondingly, the usefulness of analogies and comparisons is most pronounced in questions that emerge from a long-term perspective of recurrent problems. Again, many anthropologists today tend to take a critical view towards generalization (see Ingold 1996), either because they fear the superimposition of natural science methodology or because the more sophisticated research of recent decades has increasingly pointed at intracultural diversity which seems to go against generalizations within 'a case' and consequently also across cases. Whether one thinks that anthropology should strive towards more generalization or not, I want to argue that once comparison and analogy are recognized as necessary research tools, anthropology in a sense cannot help generalizing because these tools inherently require a certain degree of generalization (see Widlok, in press).

Moreover, the alternative to systematic analogy and comparison is uncontrolled and vague analogy and comparison. Another example from the recent debates on southern African 'San' may illustrate this point. In one of the contributions that has sparked off from revisionism, it has been claimed that the economic flexibility of 'Bushmen' or 'San' could well be explained by an ecologist who would predict this kind of 'instability' for any population living under unpredictably varying dryland conditions (Sullivan 2001: 185). Without discussing the question of environmental determinism of cultural forms here, the point that I want to highlight is that in this argument too, comparison is being applied as a tool, namely comparative knowledge of other people living in dryland areas. And there is little doubt that such comparative knowledge can indeed be instructive. But again we need to consider carefully what is being compared and for what purpose. A general tendency towards ecological 'instability', even within the same geographical region, will not help to explain, for instance, why the well-known Herero songs are highly formalized while 'San' storytelling is so flexible, why the recorded Himba settlement layouts are highly formalized while 'San' settlement layouts are not, why most Owambo herds constantly grow while 'San' herds do not, why Nama leadership positions are strong while 'San' leadership positions are weak in the current setting. To assume that ecological conditions can be used to explain cultural features of this sort is taking the comparison of dryland populations beyond its useful limits. The comparison can still be made, but only to show that unpredictable dryland conditions *cannot* be used to predict how flexible a social and cultural organization will be.

Similarly, the vague notion of southern African 'San' as an 'underclass' is an analogy of this sort. There is no space to provide a detailed discussion of this issue here. It should suffice to say that the main vagueness about the notion of underclass is whether it is considered to be a social stratum *outside* the class formation or whether it is simply a synonym for the lowest classes. It seems that in Europe the notion was originally used in the former sense while with regard to the 'San' it is usually used in the latter sense. The difference matters because a *Lumpenproletariat* in the original sense can be expected to develop cultural forms that are of considerable autonomy and which are not watered-down versions of, or predictable responses to, those of the dominant classes (see Stewart 2002). It has been suggested that the way in which 'San' make use of the by-products from other economic enterprises does not require any cultural analysis because it is a feature of impoverished people the world over. A simple encounter with 'desperately poor Bangladeshis' on Dhaka's rubbish tip would therefore tell us how to understand what Hai//om or other 'San' are doing (Sullivan 2001: 183). Clearly, this is making a strong claim of analogy between the Bangladeshi poor and the Hai//om of northern Namibia. While I cannot discuss the Bangladeshi case with any authority, I do not think that Hai//om would be so worried about land rights if they thought that the Etosha National Park or their huge mangetti groves were nothing but a rubbish tip (on the contrary some seem to realize that these are potential gold-mines). Also, one need not be romantic about the rich wild food of the northern Namibian bush, the individual autonomy in a Hai//om social network, the joy of storytelling and making music, or the enthusiasm of trance dancers, to realize that this comparison is condescending to the Hai//om of Mangetti and not improving our understanding of the situation. But leaving these points aside, the method-ological point has to be made that the usefulness of making analogies across space, continents in this case, and contexts requires as much explicit justification as making analogies across time. Generalized analogies between contemporary people in very different settings are not in themselves theoretically better justified than analogies between people in different time periods.

There is a final twist to the argument in so far as an exclusive focus on the con-temporary needs to be criticized not only on the basis of long-term perspectives into the past, but also on the basis of a perspective that encompasses the future as well as the present and the past. In fact, concern about the future, beyond the ques-tion of future research opportunities, continues to be somewhat of a blind spot in hunter-gatherer studies. Hunter-gatherer research of all kinds and directions (including revisionism) has been preoccupied with origins and causes. We have not begun to seriously tap the potential of the teleological dimension in our field. Logically there is no reason to give privilege to explanations that refer to situations of the past as causes for what is happening today and to refer to what was before as the explanation of what came afterwards. As philosophers of science point out, explanations that refer to events occurring later have as much dignity and logical legitimacy as explanations that refer to events occurring earlier. And of course there is no reason why an explanation should not contain both temporal perspec-tives. A good example is the explanation of hunter-gatherer mobility. An appro-priate explanation of the size and shape of settlements needs to consider not only the resource-depletion or the conflicts of the recent past (or the present) which may cause a camp to move but also the expectations of various people in the group, the expected length of residence, the purpose for which the settlement is being estab-lished as well as the expected destination to which the camp moves on (see Barnard and Widlok 1996). These are clearly teleological elements which have to do not only with intentions and motives but more generally with inducements relating to the future which allow people to decide in one way (to keep on staying) or another (to move camp). Any explanation of practices is predicated not only on the structurating 'habitus' from the past but also on this teleological element. For something to be called social action proper, it must include the possibility that people could have acted differently. Behaviour may be caused by past events but *social practice* cannot be determined in such a way because by definition it relates to the option of acting in more than one way. More generally, a teleological perspective always presses us to ask what the purpose and the value of a certain action is or has been for the practitioners, what future states are aspired for. One can ask this question in the framework of history or of anthropology. But in any case they lead us beyond 'contemporary' history.

## Conclusion

Debates in hunter-gatherer studies can be fuelled by a number of short-term agendas. As James Woodburn has recently remarked 'the enthusiasm of one generation of anthropologists are typically rejected or much modified by the succeeding generation' (Widlok 2002: 19). This applies not only to shifts within the field of hunter-gatherer studies, or any other specialized field for that matter, but also with regard to the recognition of hunter-gatherer studies as a useful and legitimate field of study. The suggestion to redefine hunter-gatherer studies as contemporary history and the rejection of the applicability of the term 'hunter-gatherer' itself have been instrumental for such short-term agendas. The revisionist debate of recent years has been called 'a tale of patricide' although the main proponents are part of the same generation (Hudelson 1995: 29). As I have argued elsewhere there is too much shared common ground and too little innovation in this debate to consider it a proper paradigm shift (see Widlok, in press). The challenge, it seems, is to transform the antagonistic, often personalized style of debate as in the Kalahari Debate (Barnard 1992b) positively into what has been called confrontational theory (see Reyna 2001). A confrontational stance in this sense is not to be confused with the antagonism of two sides in an episode like the Kalahari Debate but it is confrontational through productively 'confronting generalization with observation, and observation with generalization' (Reyna 2001: 11). In this process of confrontation recurrent issues do emerge, they involve questions of analogy, comparison and generalization as I have highlighted in this short contribution.

I have suggested that it is wrong to consider these issues to be restricted to archaeology only. The transfer from archaeology back into social and cultural anthropology may indeed be very instructive. Archaeologists know that not all aspects of life are equally well captured by archaeological data. This is quite clear in the case of the analysis of settlement patterns for instance. For those aspects that leave few material traces, ethnographic analogies are therefore most welcome. What is frequently overlooked, however, is that the same holds true for ethnography. Not all aspects of life are equally well captured through our standard ethnographic methods, in particular our tendency to privilege interview material. For instance, the claim has been made that what has been described in 'San' ethnography 'can be almost entirely interpreted as due to systematic and progressive exclusion from land and from access to formal decision-making and economic structures' (Sullivan 2001: 182). However, it has not been demonstrated that the diversity of social practices described, including storytelling, accessing resources, creating name and kin relations, settlement patterns and religious activities can be explained solely with reference to exclusion. The evidence is usually restricted to discourses and the construction of identity, meaning that 'Bushmen' tend to accept the labels that they are given as a consequence of being subject to stereotyping (see Gordon 1992). As has been show with regard to central African hunter-gatherers, learning the dominant language and using its terms may – from the hunter-gatherer perspective – be considered to be part of a more fundamental hunting strategy of mimicking the prey (Köhler and Lewis 2002: 297). In the words of an elder Mbendjele 'Pygmy' dealing with a village of farmers is like hunting elephant: 'You must smear its fresh excrement on yourself' (Köhler and Lewis 2002: 296). Ethnographers continue to get a host of information from dominant discourses about hunter-gatherers but the effects of long term practices, economic transfers or marriage patterns are not as easily grasped by ethnography (see Widlok and Tadesse, forthcoming). As ethnographers we are often inundated with stereotypes and attitudes given by informants, but to see forms and patterns that persist over time is not all that easy. As I have tried to indicate, a productive study of the contemporary world always needs to be based on the explanatory potential of analogies and of other forms of comparison.

# References

Adams, J. (1789), *Curious Thoughts on the History of Man; Chiefly Abridged or Selected from the Celebrated Works of Lord Kaimes, Lord Monboddo, Dr. Dunbar, and the Immortal Montesquieu*, London: G. Kearsley.

Albright, W. (1965), 'Primitivism in Ancient Western Asia (Mesopotamia and Israel)', in A. Lovejoy and G. Boas (eds), *Primitivism and Related Ideas in Antiquity*, New York: Octagon Books.

Alekseenko, E.A. (1967), *Kety. Istoriko-etnograficheskie ocherki*, Leningrad: Nauka.

Alexander, R. (1987), *The Biology of Moral Systems*. New York: de Gruyter.

Alland, A. (1970), *Adaptation in Cultural Evolution: An Approach to Medical Anthropology*, New York: Columbia University Press.

Allchin, B. (1985), 'Ethnoarchaeology in South Asia', in J. Schotsmans and M. Taddei (eds), *South Asian Archaeology 1983*, Naples: Instituto Universitario Orientale.

—— (ed.) (1994), *Living Traditions: Studies in the Ethnoarchaeology of South Asia*, New Delhi: Oxford and IBH.

Anderson, D.D., and Orekhova, N.A. (2002), 'The Suslov's Legacy: The Story of one Family's Struggle with Shamanism', *Sibirica*, 2: 88–112.

Andresen, J., Byrd, B., Elson, M., McGuire, R., Mendoza, R., Staski, E. and White, J. (1981), 'The Deer Hunters: Star Carr Reconsidered', *World Archaeology*, 13: 31–46.

Ansari, S. (2000), 'Clay Storage Bins in India: An Ethnoarchaeological Study', *Man and Environment*, 25: 51–78.

Arnold, J. (1996), 'The Archaeology of Complex Hunter-Gatherers', *Journal of Archaeological Method and Theory*, 3: 77–126.

Arom Simha (1987), *Anthologie de la Musique des Pygmées Aka (Cenrafrique)*, 2CD, Paris: OCORA, C559012–13.

—— (1991), *African Polyphony and Polyrhythm*, Cambridge: Cambridge University Press.

—— Bahuchet, S., Epelboin, A., Furniss, S., Guillaume, H. and Thomas, J. (1998*)*, *Les Pygmées – Peuple & Musique*, CD-ROM, Montparnass: Multimedia-CNRS-ORSTOM.

Artemova, O.Yu. (1997), 'Maksimov i ego issledovaniya', in O. Artemova and A. Pershits (eds), Maksimov A.N. *Izbrannye trudy*. Moscow: Vostochnaya Literatura RAN.

Asch, M. (1984), *Home and Native Land: Aboriginal Rights and the Canadian Constitution*. Toronto: Methuen.

—— (2002), 'From Terra Nullius to Affirmation: Reconciling Aboriginal Rights with the Canadian Constitution', *Canadian Journal of Law and Society* 17(2): 23–39.

Ashton, M. (1985), *Interpreting the Landscape: Landscape Archaeology in Local Studies*, London: Batsford.

Augstein, H.F. (1999), *James Cowles Prichard's Anthropology: Remaking the Science of Man in Early Nineteenth Century Britain*, Clio Medica 52, Amsterdam: Rodopi.

Badam, G.L and Sathe, V. (1995), 'Palaeontological Research in India: Retrospect and Prospect', in S. Wadia, R. Korisettar and V. S. Kale (eds), *Quaternary Environments and Geoarchaeology of India,* Bangalore: Geological Society of India.

Bahuchet, S. (1985), *Les Pygmées et la Forêt Centrafricaine*, Paris: SELAF.

—— Mckey, D., and de Garine, I. (1991), 'Wild Yam Revisited', *Human Ecology*, 19: 213–43.

Bailey, R. C. (1986), *The Socioecology of Efe Pygmy Men in the Ituri Forest, Zaire,* Ph.D. Dissertation, Cambridge, MA: Harvard University.

—— (1989), 'Research on the Efe and Lese Populations of the Ituri Forest', *American Journal of Physical Anthropology*, 78: 459–71.

—— Head, G., Jenike, M., Owen, B., Rechtman, R. and Zechenter, E. (1989), 'Hunting and Gathering in Tropical Forest: Is It Possible?' *American Anthropologist*, 91: 59–82.

Baldus, H. (1951), 'Max Schmidt 1874–1950', *Zeitschrift für Ethnologie*, 76: 301–5.

Barnard, A. (1983), 'Contemporary Hunter-Gatherers: Current Theoretical Issues in Ecology and Social Organization,' *Annual Review of Anthropology*, 12: 193214.

—— (1987), 'Hunting and Gathering Societies: Fourth International Conference', *Current Anthropology* 16: 121–42.

—— (1989), 'The Lost World of Laurens van der Post?', *Current Anthropology* 30: 104–14.

—— (1992a), 'Through Radcliffe-Brown's Spectacles: Reflections on the History of Anthropology, *History of the Human Sciences* 5: 1–20.

—— (1992b), *The Kalahari Debate: A Bibliographic Essay*. Edinburgh: University of Edinburgh. Centre of African Studies.

—— (1992c), *Hunters and Herders of Southern Africa: A Comparative Ethnography of the Khoisan Peoples*, Cambridge/New York: Cambridge University Press.

—— (1994) 'Tarzan and the Lost Races: Parallels between Anthropology and Early Science Fiction', in E.P. Archetti (ed.), *Exploring the Written: Anthropology and the Multiplicity of Writing*. Oslo: Scandinavian University Press.

—— (1995), '*Orang Outang* and the Definition of *Man*: The Legacy of Lord Monboddo', in H.F. Vermeulen and A. Alvarez Roldan (eds), *Fieldwork and Footnotes: Studies in the History of European Anthropology*. London: Routledge.

—— (1998), 'Hunter-Gatherers and Bureaucrats: Reconciling Opposing Worldviews', in S. Saugestad (ed.), *Indigenous Peoples in Modern Nation-States: Proceedings from an International Workshop, University of Tromsø, October 13–16, 1997*. Tromsø: Faculty of Social Science, University of Tromsø (Occasional Papers Series A No. 90).

—— (1999), 'Images of Hunters and Gatherers in European Social Thought', in R.

Lee and R. Daly (eds), *The Cambridge Encyclopedia of Hunters and Gatherers*. Cambridge: Cambridge University Press.

—— (2000), *The Hunter-Gatherer Mode of Thought*. Buenos Aires: Annales de La Academia Nacional de Ciencias de Buenos Aires.

—— (2001), 'La cuestión de los cazadores-recolectores en la ciencia hoy', *Avá: Revista de Antropología*, 3: 17–28.

—— (2002a), 'Observations on the Historical Development of Ecological Anthropology and Hunter-Gatherer Studies', Paper Presented at the National Museum of Ethnology, Osaka, 8 April 2002.

—— (2002b), 'The Foraging Mode of Thought', in H. Stewart, A. Barnard and K.Omura (eds), *Self- and Other-Images of Hunter-Gatherers* (*Senri Ethnological Studies* 60), Osaka: National Museum of Ethnology.

—— and Widlok, T. (1996), 'Nharo and Hai//om Settlement Patterns in Comparative Perspective,' in S.Kent (ed.), *Cultural Diversity among Twentieth-Century Foragers: An African Perspective*, Cambridge: Cambridge University Press.

—— and Woodburn, J. (1988), 'Property, Power and Ideology in Hunting and Gathering Societies: An Introduction', in T. Ingold, D. Riches and J. Woodburn (eds), *Hunters and Gatherers 2: Property, Power and Ideology*, Oxford: Berg.

Bartram, L., Kroll, E., and Bunn, H. (1991), 'Variability in Camp Structure and Bone Food Refuse Patterning at Kua San Hunter-Gatherer Camps', in E. Kroll and T. Price (eds), *The Interpretation of Archaeological Spatial Patterning*, New York: Plenum.

Baumhoff, M.A. (1958), 'History of Great Basin Ethnography', *University of California Archaeology Survey Report No. 42*: 1–6.

Bayham, F. (1979), 'Factors Influencing the Archaic Pattern of Animal Exploitation', *The Kiva* 44: 219–33.

Bayly, S. (1999), *Caste, society and politics in India from the eighteenth century to the modern age* (New Cambridge History of India IV, 3), Cambridge: Cambridge University Press.

Beals, R. (1985), 'The Anthropologist as Expert Witness: Illustrations from the California Indian Land Claims Case', in I. Sutton (ed.), *Irredeemable America: The Indians' Estate and Land Claims*, Albuquerque: University of New Mexico Press.

Beattie, J. (1817[1793]), *Elements of Moral Science* (third edition), Vol. 2. Edinburgh: T. Cadell.

Bender, B. (1978), 'Gatherer-Hunter to Farmer: A Social Perspective', *World Archaeology*, 10: 204–22.

—— and B. Morris (1988), 'Twenty Years of History, Evolution and Social Change in Gatherer-Hunter Studies', in T. Ingold, D. Riches and J. Woodburn (eds), *Hunters and Gatherers 1: History, Evolution and Social Change*, Oxford: Berg.

Berry, C. J. (1997), *Social Theory of the Scottish Enlightenment*. Edinburgh: Edinburgh University Press.

Bettinger, R.L. (1983), 'Aboriginal Sociopolitical Organization in Owens Valley: Beyond the Family Band', in E. Tooker (ed.), *The Development of Political Organization in Native North America*, Washington: American Ethnological Society.

—— (1991), *Hunter-Gatherers: Archaeological and Evolutionary Theory*. New York: Plenum Press.

Bicchieri, M.G. (1972), *Hunters and Gatherers Today,* New York: Holt, Rinehart, and Winston, Inc.

Bieder, R. (1986), *Science encounters the Indian, 1820–1880. The early years of American ethnology*, Norman: University of Oaklahoma Press.

Biesele, M. (1993), *Women Like Meat.* Witwatersrand University Press: Johannesburg.

Binford, L. (1967), 'Smudge Pits and Hide Smoking: The Use of Analogy in Archaeological Reasoning', *American Antiquity* 32: 1–12.

—— (1968), 'Methodological Considerations of the Archeological Use of Ethnographic Data', in R.B. Lee and I. Devore (eds), *Man the Hunter*, New York: Aldine de Gruyter.

—— (1977), *For Theory Building in Archaeology*, Orlando: Academic Press.

—— (1978), *Nunamiut Ethnoarchaeology*. London: Academic Press.

—— (1980), 'Willow Smoke and Dogs' Tails: Hunter-Gatherer Settlement Systems and Archaeological Site Formation Processes', *American Antiquity*, 45: 4–20.

—— (1982), 'The Archaeology of Place', *Journal of Anthropological Archaeology*, 1: 5–31.

—— (1983), 'Long-term Land Use Patterns: Some Implications for Archaeology', in L.R. Binford (ed.), *Working at Archaeology*, New York: Academic Press.

—— (2001), *Constructing Frames of Reference,* Berkeley: University of California Press.

Bird-David, N. (1990), 'The Giving Environment: Another Perspective on the Economic System of Hunter-Gatherers', *Current Anthropology*, 31: 189–96.

—— (1992a), 'Beyond "The Hunting and Gathering Mode of Subsistence": Culture-Sensitive Observations on the Nayaka and Other Modern Hunter-Gatherers', *Man* (n.s.), 27: 19–44.

—— (1992b), 'Beyond The 'Original Affluent Society: A Culturalist Reformulation', *Current Anthropology*, 33: 25–35.

—— (1994), 'Sociality and Immediacy: Or, Past and Present Conversations on Bands', *Man* (n.s.), 29: 583–603.

—— (1999), 'Introduction: South Asia', in R. Lee and R. Daly (eds), *The Cambridge Encyclopedia of Hunters and Gatherers*, Cambridge: Cambridge University Press.

Black, A. (1989), *Man and Nature in the Philosophical Thought of Wang Fu-chih*, Seattle: University of Washington Press.

Blackhawk, N. (1999), 'Julian Steward and the Politics of Representation', in R.O., L.D. Myers, and E. Rudden (eds), *Julian Steward and the Great Basin,* Salt Lake City: University of Utah Press.

Bodde, D. (1981), 'Harmony and Conflict in Chinese Philosophy', in C. Le Blanc and D. Borei (eds), *Essays on Chinese Civilization*, Princeton, NJ: Princeton University Press.

Boivin, N. and Fuller, D. Q. (2002), 'Looking for Post-Processual Theory in South Asian archaeology', in S. Settar and R. Korisettar (eds), *Indian Archaeology in Retrospect. Archaeology and Historiography. History, Theory and Method*, Volume IV. Indian Council for Historical Research, New Delhi: Manohar Publishers.

Bonsall, C. and Smith, C. (1990), 'Bone and Antler Technology in the British Late Upper Palaeolithic and Mesolithic: The Impact of Accelerator Dating', in P. Vermeersch and P. Van Peer (eds), *Contributions to the Mesolithic in Europe*, Leuven: Leuven University Press.

Borrero, L.A. (1994), 'The Extermination of the Selk'nam', in E.S. Burch, Jr. and L.J. Ellanna (eds), *Key Issues in Hunter-Gatherer Research*, Oxford: Berg.

Bowler, P. (1992), 'From Savage to Primitive: Victorian Evolutionism and the Interpretation of Marginalized Peoples', *Antiquity*, 66: 721–9.

Bray, W. and Trump, D. (1970), *A Dictionary of Archaeology*, London: Allen Lane.

Brody, H. (2001), *The Other Side of Eden: Hunter-Gatherers, Farmers, and the Shaping of the World*, London: Faber & Faber.

Bromley, Yu.V. (1983), *Ocherki teorii etnosa*, Moscow: Nauka.

Bundo, D. (2001), 'Social Relationship Embodied in the Singing and Dancing Performances among the Baka', *African Study Monographs*, Supplementary Issue, 26: 85–102.

Burch, E. (1994), 'The Future of Hunter-Gatherer Research', in E. Burch and L. Ellanna (eds), *Key Issues in Hunter-Gatherer Research*. Exploration in Anthropology Series, Oxford: Berg.

—— Ellanna, L. (eds) (1994), *Key Issues in Hunter-Gatherer Research*. Exploration in Anthropology Series, Oxford: Berg.

Bye, R.A. (1972), 'Ethnobotany of the Southern Paiute Indians in the 1870's', in D.D. Fowler (ed.), *Great Basin Cultural Ecology,* Reno: Desert Research Institute.

Carter, R. (1997), 'Age Estimation of the Roe Deer (Capreolus capreolus) Mandibles from the Mesolithic Site of Star Carr, Yorkshire, based on Radiographs of Mandibular Tooth Development', *Journal of the Zoological Society of London,* 241: 495–502.

—— (1998), 'Reassessment of Seasonality at the Early Mesolithic Site of Star Carr, Yorkshire based on Radiographs of Mandibular Tooth Development in Red Deer (*Cervus elaphus*)', *Journal of Archaeological Science,* 25: 851–6.

Catt, J. (1987), 'The Quaternary of East Yorkshire and Adjacent Areas', in S. Ellis (ed.), *East Yorkshire Field Guide*, Cambridge: Quaternary Research Association.

Caulfield, S. (1978), 'Star Carr: An Alternative View', *Irish Archaeological Research Forum*, 5: 15–22.

Chakrabarti, D.K. (1994), 'Some Ethnographic Dimensions of the Archaeology of the Chhotanagpur Plateau and Adjoining areas in West Bengal in Eastern India', in B. Allchin (ed.), *Living Traditions: Studies in the Ethnoarchaeology of South Asia*, New Delhi: Oxford-IBH.

Champion, T., Gamble, C., Shennan, S. and Whittle, A. (1984), *Prehistoric Europe*, London: Academic Press.

Chanock, M. (2000), 'Culture' and Human Rights: Orientalising, Occidentalising and Authenticity' , in M. Mamdani (ed.), *Beyond Rights Talk and Culture Talk: Comparative Essays on the Politics of Rights and Culture*, Cape Town: David Philip Publishers.

Clark, J.D. and Sharma, G.R. (1983), 'A Discussion of Preliminary Results and Assessment of Future Research Potential', in G.R. Sharma and J.D. Clark (eds),

*Palaeoenvironment and Prehistory in the Middle Son Valley (Madhya Pradesh, North Central India),* Allahabad: Avinash Publications.

Clark, J.G.D. (1936), *The Mesolithic Settlement of Northern Europe,* London: Cambridge University Press.

—— (1952a), *Prehistoric Europe: The Economic Basis,* London: Methuen.

—— (1952b), 'The Mesolithic Hunters of Star Carr', *Transactions of the Lancashire and Cheshire Antiquarian Society,* 63: 183–90.

—— (1953), 'The Economic Approach to Prehistory: Albert Reckitt Archaeological Lecture, 1953', *Proceedings of the British Academy,* 39: 215–38.

—— (1954), *Excavations at Star Carr: an Early Mesolithic Site at Seamer, near Scarborough, Yorkshire,* Cambridge: Cambridge University Press.

—— (1967), *The Stone Age Hunters,* London: Thames and Hudson.

—— (1972a), 'The Archaeology of Stone Age Settlement: Oliver Davies Lecture for 1972', *Ulster Journal of Archaeology,* 35: 3–16.

—— (1972b), *Star Carr: A Case Study in Bioarchaeology,* Reading, Mass.: Addison-Wesley.

—— (1973), 'Bioarchaeology: Some Extracts on the Theme', *Current Anthropology,* 14: 464–70.

—— (1974), 'Prehistoric Europe: The Economic Basis', in G. Willey (ed.), *Archaeological Researches in Retrospect,* Cambridge, Mass.: Winthrop Publishers Inc.

—— (1975), *World Prehistory: A New Outline,* Cambridge: Cambridge University Press.

Clarke, D.L. (1973), 'Archaeology: The Loss of Innocence', *Antiquity* 47: 6–18.

—— (1976), 'Mesolithic Europe: The Economic Basis', in G. Sievking, I. Longworth and K. Wilson (eds), *Problems in Economic and Social Archaeology,* London: Duckworth.

Clemmer, R. (1969), 'The Fed-Up Hopi: Resistance of The American Indian and the Silence of the Good Anthropologists', *Journal of the Steward Anthropological Society,* 1 (1): 18–40.

—— (1973), 'Channels of Political Expression Among the Western Shoshone-Goshute of Nevada, in R.M. Houghton (ed.), *Native American Politics: Power Relationships in the Western Great Basin Today,* Reno: University of Nevada Bureau of Governmental Research.

—— (1974), 'Land Use Patterns and Aboriginal Rights: Northern and Eastern Nevada, 1858–1971', *The Indian Historian,* 7: 24–49.

—— (1978), 'Pine Nuts, Cattle, and the Ely Chain: Rip-off Resource Replacement vs. Homeostatic Equilibrium', in D.R. Tuoby (ed.), *Selected Papers from the 14th Great Basin Anthropological Conference* (Ballena Press Publications in Archaeology, Ethnology, and History 11), Ramona, CA: Ballena Press.

—— (1996), 'Ideology and Identity: Western Shoshoni "Cannibal Myth" as Ethnonational Narrative', *Journal of Anthropological Research,* 52: 207–23.

—— and Myers, L.D. (1999), 'Introduction', in R.O. Clemmer, L.D. Myers, and E. Rudden (eds), *Julian Steward and the Great Basin,* Salt Lake City: University of Utah Press.

Clifford, J. (1986), 'Introduction', in J. Clifford and G.E. Marcus (eds), *Writing*

*Culture: The Poetic and Politic of Ethnography*, Berkeley: University of California Press.

—— (1988), *The Predicament of Culture: Twentieth Century Ethnography, Literature, and Art*, Cambridge: Harvard University Press.

—— and G.E. Marcus (eds), (1986), *Writing Culture: The Poetic and Politics of Ethnography*, Berkeley: University of California Press.

Cloutman, E. (1988), 'Palaeoenvironments in the Vale of Pickering. Part 1: Stratigraphy and Palaeogeography of Seamer Carr, Star Carr and Flixton Carr', *Proceedings of the Prehistoric Society*, 54: 1–20.

—— and Smith, A. (1988), 'Palaeoenvironments in the Vale of Pickering. Part 3: Environmental history at Star Carr', *Proceedings of the Prehistoric Society*, 54: 37–58.

Clutton-Brock, J. and Noe-Nygaard, N. (1990), 'New Osteological and C-isotope Evidence on Mesolithic Dogs: Companions to Hunters and Fishers at Star Carr, Seamer Carr and Kongemos', *Journal of Archaeological Science*, 17: 643–53.

Coles, J. (1999), 'Appendix: John Grahame Douglas Clark 1907–1995 (the British Academy memoir)', in J. Coles, R. Bewley and P. Mellars (eds), *World Prehistory: Studies in memory of Grahame Clark*, London: Oxford University Press (Proceedings of the British Academy 1990).

—— and Coles, B. (1989), *People of the Wetlands: Bog's Bodies and Lake-Dwellers*, London: Thames and Hudson.

—— and Orme, B. (1983), 'Homo sapiens or Castor fiber?', *Antiquity*, 57: 95–102.

Comaroff J. and Comaroff, J. (1992*), Ethnography and the Historical Imagination*, Boulder, CO: Westview Press.

Coon, C. S. (1948), *A Reader in General Anthropology*. New York: Henry Holt and Company.

Cooper, Z. M. (1986), 'The Kuruk Fishermen of Bastar District, Central India', *Eastern Anthropologist*, 39: 1–20.

—— (1990), 'Archaeological Evidence for Resource Exploitation in the Andaman Islands', *Man and Environment*, 15: 73–81.

—— (1992), 'The Relevance of the Forager/Collector Model to Island Communities in the Bay of Bengal', *Man and Environment*, 17: 111–22.

—— (1994), 'Abandoned Onge Encampments and their Relevance in Understanding the Archaeological Record in the Andaman islands', in B. Allchin (ed.), *Living Traditions: Studies in the Ethnoarchaeology of South Asia*, New Delhi: Oxford-IBH.

—— (1997), *Prehistory of the Chitrakot Falls, Central India*, Pune: Ravish Publishers.

Cope, J. (1998), *The Modern Antiquarian: A Pre-millennial Odyssey through Megalithic Britain*, London: Thorsons.

Cosgrove, D. (1993), 'Landscapes and myths, gods and humans', in B. Bender (ed.), *Landscape: Politics and perspectives*, Oxford: Berg.

Crum, S. J. (1999), 'Julian Steward's Vision of the Great Basin', in R.O. Clemmer, L.D. Myers, and E. Rudden (eds), *Julian Steward and the Great Basin*, Salt Lake City: University of Utah Press.

Cummins, G., Innes, J.B. and Simmons, I. (forthcoming), 'The environmental setting', in P. Lane and R.T. Schadla-Hall (eds), *Hunter-Gatherers in the Landscape: The Archaeology of the Early Mesolithic in the Vale of Pickering, North Yorkshire*, Cambridge: Macdonald Institute for Archaeological Research.

Cunow, H. (1926), *Allgemeine Wirtschaftsgeschichte. Erster Band: Die Wirtschaft der Natur- und Halbkulturvölker*, Berlin: J.H.W. Dietz Nachfolger.

Curran, K.B. and R. K. Tshombe (2001), 'Integrating Local Communities into the Management of Protected Areas', in Weber, W., L.J.T. White, A. Vedder and L. Naughton-Treves (eds), *African Rain Forest Ecology and Conservation*, New Haven: Yale University Press.

Dalrymple, Sir John. (1758 [1757]), *Essay Towards a General History of Feudal Property in Great Britain* (second edition). London: A. Millar.

Damas, D. (1969), *Contributions to Anthropology: Band Societies*, Ottawa: National Museum of Canada (Bulletin No. 228).

Dark, P. (2003), 'Dogs, a Crane (Not Duck) and Diet at Star Carr: A Response to Schulting and Richards', *Journal of Archaeological Science*, 30: 1353–6.

Darvill, T. (1987), *Prehistoric Britain*, London: Batsford.

Darwin, C. (1871), *The Descent of Man, and Sexual Selection in Relation to Sex*. London: Murray.

Dash, G. (1998), *Hindus and Tribals: Quest for a Co-Existence (Social Dynamics in Medieval Orissa)*, New Delhi: Decent Books.

Day, P. (1996), 'Dogs, Deer and Diet at Star Carr: A Reconsideration of C-isotope Evidence from Early Mesolithic Dog Remains from the Vale of Pickering, Yorkshire, England', *Journal of Archaeological Science,* 23: 783–7.

—— and Mellars, P. (1994), '"Absolute" Dating of Mesolithic Human Activity at Star Carr, Yorkshire: New Palaeoecological Studies and Identification of the 9600 BP radiocarbon "plateau" ', *Proceedings of the Prehistoric Society,* 60: 417–22.

d'Azevedo, W.L. (ed.) (1986a), *Handbook of North American Indians 11: Great Basin*. Washington, D.C.: Smithsonian Institution.

—— (1986b), 'Introduction', In W.L. d'Azevedo (ed.), *Handbook of North American Indians 11: Great Basin*, Washington, D.C.: Smithsonian Institution.

—— Davis, W.A., Fowler, D.D. and Suttles, W. (eds), (1966), *Current Status of Anthropological Research in the Great Basin: 1964*. Reno: Desert Research Institute.

Degerbøl, M. (1961), 'On the Find of a Preboreal Dog (*Canis familiaris*) Star Carr, Yorkshire, with Remarks on other Mesolithic Dogs', *Proceedings of the Prehistoric Society*, 27: 35–65.

Deshpande-Mukherjee, A. (2000), 'An Ethnographic Account of Contemporary Shellfish Gathering on the Konkan Coast, Maharashtra', *Man and Environment*, 25: 70–92.

Dincauze, D.F. (2000), *Environmental Archaeology*, Cambridge: Cambridge University Press.

Doig, D. (1792), *Two Letters on the Savage State Addressed to the Late Lord Kaims*. London: G.G.J. and J. Robinson.

Dolgikh, B.O. (1960), *Rodovoy i plemennoy sostav narodov Sibiri v XVII veke*. Moscow: Izdatel'stvo Akademii Nauk SSSR.

Donovan, A. (1996), *Antoine Lavoisier: Science, Administration, and Revolution*. Cambridge: Cambridge University Press.

Dounias, E. (2001), 'The Management of Wild Yam Tubers by the Baka Pygmies in Southern Cameroon', *African Study Monographs, Supplementary Issue*, 26: 135–56.

Duchet, M. (1971) *Antropologie et histoire au siècle des lumières: Buffon, Voltaire, Rousseau, Helvétius, Diderot*, Paris: Maspero.

Dumont, J. (1989), *A Microwear Analysis of Selected Artefact Types from the Mesolithic Sites of Star Carr and Mount Sandel*, Oxford: British Archaeological Reports.

Dumont, L. (1977), *From Mandeville to Marx: The Genesis and Triumph of Economic Ideology*, Chicago: University of Chicago Press.

Dumont, P.-E. (1965), 'Primitivism in Indian Literature', in A. Lovejoy and G. Boas (eds), *Primitivism and Related Ideas in Antiquity*, New York: Octagon Books.

Dunbar, J. (1781 [1780]), *Essays on the History of Mankind in Rude and Cultivated Ages* (second edition). London: W. Strahan and T. Cadell. Edinburgh: J. Balfour.

Eggan, F. (1980), 'Shoshone Kinship Structures and Their Significance for Anthropological Theory', *Journal of the Steward Anthropological Society* 11: 165–93.

—— and d'Azevedo, W.L. (1966), 'Introduction', in W.L. d'Azevedo et al. (eds), *The Current Status of Anthropological Research in the Great Basin: 1964*, Reno: Desert Research Institute.

Eggert, M. (1998), 'Archäologie und Analogie: Bemerkungen zu einer Wissenschaft vom Fremden', *Mitteilungen der Anthropologischen Gesellschaft in Wien* 128: 107–24.

Elgee, F. (1930), *Early Man in NE Yorkshire*, Gloucester: North Bellows.

Eliade, M. (1991 [1949]), *The Myth of the Eternal Return, or, Cosmos and History,* Princeton, N.J.: Princeton University Press.

Engels, F. (1972[1834]), *The Origin of the Family, Private Property and the State, in Light of the Researches of Lewis M. Morgan*, London: Lawrence &Wishart.

Fabian, J. (1983), *Time and the Other. How Anthropology Makes Its Object.* New York: Columbia University Press.

Faculty and Students (1989), 'Archaeology of a Vacant Land in Poona: An Experimental Study', *Bulletin of the Deccan College Post-graduate and Research Institute,* 47–48: 249–76.

Fagan, B. (1995), *Ancient North America: The Archaeology of a Continent,* London: Thames and Hudson.

—— (1997), *In the Beginning,* New York: Longman.

—— (1999), 'Grahame Clark and American archaeology', in J. Coles, R. Bewley and P. Mellars (eds), *World Prehistory: Studies in Memory of Grahame Clark*, London: Oxford University Press (Proceedings of the British Academy 1990).

—— (2001), *Grahame Clark: An Intellectual Life of an Archaeologist.* Boulder: Westview Press.

Faubion D.J. (1993), 'History in Anthropology', *Annual Review of Anthropology*, 22: 35–54.

Feit, H. (1994), 'The Enduring Pursuit: Land, Time, and Social Relationships in

Anthropological Models of Hunter Gathers and Subarctic Hunters' Images', in E.H. Burch, Jr and L.J. Ellanna (eds), *Key Issues in Hunter-Gather Research*, Ocford: Borg.

Ferguson, Arthur B. (1993), *Utter Antiquity: Perceptions of Prehistory in Renaissance England*, Durham, NC: Yale University Press.

Ferguson, Adam (1966 [1767]), *An Essay on the History of Civil Society*. Edinburgh: Edinburgh University Press.

Fischer, H. (1990), *Völkerkunde im Nationalsozialismus. Aspekte der Anpassung, Affinität und Behauptung einer wissenschaftlichen Disziplin*, Berlin: Dietrich Reimer.

Foley, R. (1992), 'Evolutionary Ecology of Fossil Hominids', in E.A. Smith and B. Winterhalder (eds), *Evolutionary Ecology and Human Behavior*, New York: Aldine de Gruyter.

Foote, R.B. (1866), 'On the Occurrence of Stone Implements in Lateritic Formations in Various Parts of the Madras and North Arcot districts', *Madras Journal of Literature and Science*, 3rd series Part II: 1–35.

—— (1868), 'On the Distribution of Stone Implements in Southern India', *Quarterly Journal of the Geological Survey*, 24: 484–95.

—— (1881), 'Sketch of the Work of the Geological Survey of India', *Madras Journal of Literature and Science* 1881: 279–328.

Forde, C. D. (1934), *Habitat, Economy and Society*. New York: Harcourt Brace and Company.

Fowler, C.S. (1971), 'Some Notes on Comparative Numic Ethnobotany', in C.M. Aikens (ed.), *Great Basin Anthropological Conference, 1970: Selected Papers*, Eugene: University of Oregon Anthropology Papers 1.

—— (1972), 'Some Ecological Clues to Proto-Numic Homelands', in D.D. Fowler (ed.), *Great Basin Cultural Ecology*, Reno: Desert Research Institute.

—— (1977), 'Ethnography and Great Basin Prehistory', i D.D. Fowler (ed.), *Models and Great Basin Prehistory: A Symposium,* Reno: Desert Research Institute.

—— (1982a), 'Settlement Patterns and Subsistence Systems in the Great Basin: The Ethnographic Record', in D.B. Madsen and J.F. O'Connell (eds), *Man and Environment in the Great Basin*. Washington, DC: Society for American Archaeology (Papers No. 2).

—— (1982b), 'Food-Named Groups Among the Northern Paiute in North America's Great Basin: An Ecological Interpretation', in N. Williams and E. Hunn (eds), *Resource Managers: North American and Australia hunter-gatherers, Washington, DC:* American Association for the Advancement of Science (Selected Symposium 67).

—— and Leland, J. (1967), 'Some Northern Paiute Native Categories', *Ethnology* 6: 381–404.

—— Duport, M., Rusco, M.K., and Esteves. P. (1999), 'In the Field in Death Valley: Julian Steward's Panamint Shoshone Fieldwork', in R.O. Clemmer, L.D. Myers, and E. Rudden (eds), *Julian Steward and the Great Basin,* Salt Lake City: University of Utah Press.

Fowler, D.D. (1980), 'History of Great Basin Anthropological Research', *Journal of California and Great Basin Anthropology*, 2: 8–36.

—— (1986), 'History of Research', in W.L. d'Azevedo (ed.), *Handbook of North American Indians 11: Great Basin,* Washington, D.C.: Smithsonian Institution.

—— and Fowler, C.S. (1971), *Anthropology of the Numa: John Wesley Powell's Manuscripts on the Numic Peoples of Western North America 1868–1880*, (Smithsonian Contributions to Anthropology, No. 14). Washington: Smithsonian Institution.

Fox, R. (1967), *Kinship and Marriage: An Anthropological Perspective,* Baltimore: Penguin Books.

Fox, R.G. (1969), 'Professional Primitives: Hunters and Gatherers of Nuclear South East Asia', *Man in India*, 49: 139–40, 154–60.

Franklin, R. J. (1990), 'Encounters at the Boundary of Wilderness and Civilization: Southern Paiute "True Stories" of Animal-Human Relations', Paper presented at the Southwest Anthropology Association Annual Meeting, Long Beach, CA.

Franklin, R. J. and Bunte, P.A. (1983), *The Paiute.* New York: Chelsea House Publishers.

—— (1992), 'Animals and Humans, Sex and Death: Towards a Symbolic Analysis of Four Southern Numic Rituals', Paper presented at the 23rd Great Basin Anthropological Conference, October 8–10, Boise, Idaho.

Fraser, F. and King, J. (1954), 'Faunal Remains', in J.D.G. Clark (ed.), *Excavations at Star Carr*, Cambridge: Cambridge University Press.

Freeman, L. (1968), 'A Theoretical Framework for Interpreting Archeological Materials', in R.B. Lee & I. Devore (eds), *Man the Hunter*, New York: Aldine de Gruyter.

Freud, S. (1960 [1913]), *Totem and Taboo* (translated by J. Strachey), London: Routledge & Kegan Paul.

Fuller, D.Q. and Boivin, N. (2002), 'Beyond Description and Diffusion: A History of Processual Theory in the Archaeology of South Asia', in S. Settar and R. Korisettar (eds), *Indian Archaeology in Retrospect. Arcahaeology and Historiography. History, Theory and Method*, Volume I, Indian Council for Historical Research, New Delhi: Manohar Publishers.

Fung Yu-Lan (1953), *A history of Chinese Philosophy Volume 2*, translation by D. Bodde, Princeton: Princeton University Press.

Gardner, P.M. (1982), 'Ascribed Austerity: A Tribal Path to Purity', *Man* 17: 462–469.

Garland, E. (1999), 'Developing Bushmen: Building Civil(ized) Society in the Kalahari and Beyond', in J. Comaroff and J. Comaroff (eds), *Civil Society and the Political Imagination in Africa.* Chicago University Press: Chicago.

Geertz, C. (1963), *Agricultural Involution,* Berkeley: University of California Press.

—— (1973), *The Interpretation of Culture,* New York: Basic Books.

—— (1983), *Local Knowledge: Further Essays in Interpretive Anthropology,* New York: Basic Books.

—— (1988), *Works and Lives: The Anthropologist as Author,* Stanford, CA: Stanford University Press.

Gelo, D. J. (1986), *Comanche Belief and Ritual*, Ph.D. dissertation, Rutgers University, New Brunswick, NJ.

—— (1994), 'Recalling the Past in Creating the Present: Topographic References in Comanche Narrative', *Western Folklore*, 53: 295–312.

Gernet, J. (1982), *A History of Chinese Civilization*, Cambridge: Cambridge University Press.

Gingrich, A. (forthcoming), 'Ruptures, Schools, and Non-Traditions: Re-Assessing the History of Socio-Cultural Anthropology in German', in F. Barth, A. Gingrich, R. Parkin, and S. Silverman (eds), *Four Traditions in Anthropology: The Halle Lectures*, Chicago: The University of Chicago Press.

Glacken, C. (1967), *Traces on the Rhodian shore: Nature and Culture in Western Thought from Classical Times to the End of the Eighteenth Century*, Berkeley: University of California Press.

Glasgow, K. (1994), *Burarra-Gunnartpa Dictionary*. Darwin: Summer Institute of Linguistics.

Goodenough, W. H. (1956a), 'Componential Analysis and the Study of Meaning', *Language*, 32: 195–216.

—— (1956b), 'Residence Rules', *Southwestern Journal of Anthropology* 12: 22–37.

—— (1957), 'Cultural Anthropology and Linguistics', in P.L. Garvin (ed.), *Monograph Series on Languages and Linguistics*, No. 9, Washington, D.C.: Georgetown University.

—— (1967), Componential Analysis, *Science*, 156: 1203–9.

Gordon, R. (1992), *The Bushman Myth: The Making of a Namibian Underclass*. Boulder, CO: Westview Press.

—— (2000), 'The Stat(u)s of Namibian Anthropology: A Review', *Cimbebasia*, 16: 1–23.

Goss, J. A. (1972), 'Basin-Plateau Shoshonian Ecological Model', in D.D. Fowler (ed.), *Great Basin Cultural Ecology,* Reno: Desert Research Institute.

—— (1977), 'Linguistic Tools for the Great Basin Prehistorian, in D.D. Fowler (ed.), *Models and Great Basin Prehistory: A Symposium,* Reno: Desert Research Institute.

—— (1990), 'Ute Myth as Cultural Charter', Paper presented at the 22nd Great Basin Anthropological Conference, October, Reno, NV.

—— (1999), 'The Yamparika – Shoshones, Comanches, or Utes – or Does It Matter', in R.O. Clemmer, L.D. Myers, and E. Rudden (eds), *Julian Steward and the Great Basin*, Salt Lake City: University of Utah Press.

Gould, R. (1978), 'Beyond Analogy in Ethnoarchaeology', in R. Gould (ed.), *Explorations in Ethnoarchaeology*, Albuquerque: University of New Mexico Press.

—— (1980), *Living Archaeology*, Cambridge: Cambridge University Press.

—— (1981), 'Comparative Ecology of Food-Sharing in Australia and Northwest California', in R. Harding and G. Teleki (eds), *Omnivorous Primates: Gathering and Hunting in Human Evolution*, New York: Columbia University Press.

Gracheva, G.N. (1984), *Traditsionnoe mirovozzrenie okhotnikov Taymyra*. Leningrad: Nauka.

—— (1993), 'Etnograf po prizvaniyu. K 90–letiyu Andreya Aleksandrovicha Popova', *Kunstkamera. Etnograficheskie tetradi*, 2–3: 406–24.

Grinker, R.R. (1994), *Houses in the Rain Forest*, Berkeley: University of California Press.

Grosse, E. (1890), *Herbert Spencer's Lehre von dem Unerkennbaren*, Leipzig: Verlag von Veit & Comp.

—— (1896), *Die Formen der Familie und die Formen der Wirthschaft*, Freiburg i. B.: Akademische Verlagsbuchhandlung von J. C. B. Mohr.

—— (1898), *The Beginnings of Art*, New York: D. Appleton.

Guenther, M. (1989), *Bushman Folktales; Oral traditions of the Nharo of Botswana and the /Xam of the Cape*. Franz Steiner Verlag Wiesbaden GMBH: Stuttgart.

—— (1999), *Tricksters and Trancers: Bushman Religion and Society*. Bloomington: Indiana University Press.

Guha, S. (1994), 'Recognising 'Harappan': A Critical Review of the Position of Hunter-Gatherers within Harappan Society', *South Asian Studies,* 10: 91–7.

—— (1996), 'Forest Polities and Agrarian Empires: The Khandesh Bhils, c. 1700–1850', *The Indian Economic and Social History Review*, 33: 133–53.

Gumilev, L.N. (1989), Etnogenez i biosfera zemli. 2$^{nd}$ edn. Leningrad: Izdatel'stvo LGU.

Gurrmanamana. F., Hiatt, L. and McKenzie, K. (2002), *People of the Rivermouth: The Joborr Texts of Frank Gurrmanamana*. Canberra: National Museum of Australia and Aboriginal Studies Press.

Gusinde, M. (1931–39), *Die Feuerland Indianer*, 3 vols. Mödling bei Wien: Verlag der Internationalen Zeitschrift Anthropos.

Hage, P. and Miller, W.R. (1976), ' "Eagle=Bird": A Note on the Structure and Evolution of Shoshoni Ethnoornithological Nomenclature', *American Ethnologist*, 3: 481–8.

Hahn, E. (1891), 'Waren die Menschen der Urzeit zwischen der Jägerstufe und der Stufe des Ackerbaues Nomaden?', *Das Ausland*, 64: 481–7.

—— (1914), *Von der Hacke zum Pflug*, Leipzig: Quelle & Meyer.

Halbfass, W. (1988), *India and Europe: an essay in understanding*, Albany: SUNY Press.

Hamilton, W. (1964), 'The Evolution of Social Behavior', *Journal of Theoretical Biology*, 12: 12–45.

Hann, C. (1994), *When History Accelerates: Essays on Rapid Social Change, Complexity and Creativity*, Athlone Press: London.

Harako, R. (1976), 'The Mbuti as Hunters', *Kyoto University African Studies*, 10: 37–99.

—— (1980), 'The Mbuti Children and Their Play', *Meiji University Bulletin*, 137: 1–44 (in Japanese).

—— (1984), 'The Religious World of the Mbuti Pygmies', in J. Itani and T. Yoneyama (eds), *Studies in African Cultures*, Kyoto: Academia Shuppankai (in Japanese).

Harris, J. (1940), 'The White Knife Shoshoni of Nevada', in R. Linton (ed.), *Acculturation in Seven American Indians Tribes,* New York: Appleton-Century.

Harris, M. (1968), The Rise of Anthropological Theory: A History of Theories of Culture, New York: Thomas Y. Crowell.

Hastrup, K. (1992), *Other Histories*, Routledge: London.

Hatch, E. (1973), *Theories of Man and Culture*. New York: Columbia University Press.

Headland, T. (1997), 'Revisionism in Ecological Anthropology', *Current Anthropology* 38: 605–30.

240 · *References*

Hegmon, M. (2003), 'Setting Theoretical Egos Aside: Issues and Theory in North American Archaeology', *American Antiquity*, 68: 213–43.

Henderson, J. and Dobson, V. (1994), *Eastern and Central Arrernte to English Dictionary*. Alice Springs: IAD Press.

Hester, T., Heizer, R. and Graham, J. (1975), *Field Methods in Archaeology* (sixth edition), Palo Alto: Mayfield Publishing Co.

Hewlett, B. (1991), *Intimate Fathers*, Ann Arbor: University of Michigan Press.

Hiatt, L. (1996), *Arguments about Aborigines: Australia and the Evolution of Social Anthropology*. Cambridge: Cambridge University Press.

Hirasawa, A. (2002), 'Infant Care among the Sendentarized Baka Pygmies in Cameroon', Paper presented at the Ninth International Conference on Hunting and Gathering Societies, Edinburgh, September 2002.

Hittman, M. (1996), *Corbett Mack*, Lincoln: University of Nebraska Press.

Hobbes, T. (1973 [1651]), *Leviathan*, London: J.M. Dent & Sons.

Hodgen, M.T. (1964), *Early Anthropology in the Sixteenth and Seventeenth Centuries*, Philadelphia: University of Pennsyvania Press.

Hooja, R. (1988), *The Ahar Culture,* Oxford: BAR International Series 412.

—— (1994), 'Contacts, Conflicts and Coexistence: Bhils and Non-Bhils in Southeastern Rajasthan', in B. Allchin (ed.), *Living Traditions: Studies in the Ethnoarchaeology of South Asia*, New Delhi: Oxford-IBH.

Hudelson, J. (1995), 'One Hundred Years Among the San: A Social History of San Research,' in A. Sanders (ed.), *Speaking for the Bushmen*, Gaborone: Botswana Society.

Hume, D. (1987 [1748]), 'Of National Characters', in *Essays Moral, Political and Literary* (revised edition, edited by Eugene F. Miller). Indianapolis: Liberty Press.

Huxley, T. (1888), 'The Struggle for Existence', *The Nineteenth Century*, 23: 161–80.

—— (1894), *Evolution and Ethics*. London: Macmillan.

Hymes, D. (1972), 'The Use of Anthropology: Critical, Political, Personal', in D. Hymes (ed.), *Reinventing Anthropology*, New York: Pantheon.

Ibn Khaldûn (1967 [c. 1380–1400]), *The Muqaddimah: An Introduction to History*, traslated by F. Rosenthal (three volumes), v. 1, London: Routledge & Kegan Paul.

Ichikawa, M. (1978), 'The Residential Groups of the Mbuti Pygmies', *Senri Ethnological Studies,* 1: 131–88.

—— (1987), 'Food Restrictions of the Mbuti Pygmies, Eastern Zaire', *African Study Monographs,* Supplementary Issue, 6: 97–121.

—— (1991), 'Impact of Commoditisation on the Mbuti of Zaire', *Senri Ethnological Studies*, 30: 135–62.

—— (1996), 'The Co-existence of Man and Nature in the Central African Rain Forest', in R. Ellen and K. Fukui (eds), *Redefining Nature*, Oxford: Berg.

—— (2001), 'The Forest World as a Circulation System', *African Study Monographs, Supplementary Issue*, 26: 157–68.

—— (2002), 'Tropical Forest Destruction in a Local Context: An Example from Cameroon', *Asian and African Area Studies*, 2: 292–305.

Ikeya, K. (1993), 'Goat Raising among the San in the Central Kalahari', *African Study Monographs,* 14: 39–52.

—— (1994), 'Hunting with Dogs among the San in the Central Kalahari', *African Study Monographs*, 15: 119–34.

—— (1996a), 'Road Construction and Handicraft Production in the Xade Area, Botswana', *African Study Monographs, Supplementary Issue*, 22: 67–84.

—— (1996b), 'Dry Farming among the San in the Central Kalahari', *African Study Monographs, Supplementary Issue*, 22: 85–100.

—— (2001), 'Some Changes among the San under the Influence of Relocation Plan in Botswana', in D. G. Anderson and K. Ikeya (eds), *Parks, Property and Power: Managing Hunting Practice and Identity within State Policy Regimes* (Senri Ethnological Studies, 59), Osaka: National Museum of Ethnology.

Imamura, K. (1996), 'Gathering Activity among the Central Kalahari San', *African Study Monographs, Supplementary Issue*, 22: 47–65.

—— (2001), 'Water in the Desert: Rituals and Vital Power among the Central Kalahari Hunter-Gatherers', *African Study Monographs, Supplementary Issue*, 27: 125–63.

Ingold, T. (1986), *The Appropriation of Nature: Essays on Human Ecology and Social Relations*, Manchester: Manchester University Press.

—— (1990), Comment on 'Foragers, genuine or spurious? Situating the Kalahari San in history' (J.S. Solway and R.B. Lee), *Current Anthropology*: 130–31.

—— (1996), 'Huntering and Gathering as Ways of Perceiving the Envcironment', in R. Ellen and K. Fukui (eds), *Redefining Nature: Ecology, Culture and Domestication*, Oxford: Berg.

—— (1999), 'On the social relations of the hunter-gatherer band', in R. Lee and R. Daly (eds), *The Cambridge Encyclopedia of Hunters and Gatherers*. Cambridge: Cambridge University Press.

—— (2000a), *The Perception of the Environment: Essays in Livelihood, Dwelling and Skill*. Routledge: London.

—— (2000b), 'The Poverty of Selectionism', *Anthropology Today*, 16: 1–2.

—— Riches, D. and Woodburn, J. (1988), *Hunters and Gatherers*, vol.1 & 2, Washington, D.C.: Berg.

Inter-Tribal Council of Nevada (1976a), *Nuwuvi: A Southern Paiute History*, Reno: Inter-Tribal Council of Nevada.

—— (1976b), *Numa: A Northern Paiute History*, Reno: Inter-Tribal Council of Nevada.

—— (1976c), *Newe: A Western Shoshone History*, Reno: Inter-Tribal Council of Nevada.

Isaac, G. (1968), 'Traces of Pleistocene Hunters: An East African Example', in R.B. Lee & I. Devore (eds), *Man the Hunter*, New York: Aldine de Gruyter.

Itani, J. (1988), 'The Origins of Human Equality', in M. R. A. Chance (ed.), *Social Fabrics of the Mind*, London: Lawrence Erlbaum Associates.

Ivanova, Yu.V. (1999), 'Petr Fedorovich Preobrazhenskiy: zhiznennyy put' i nauchnoe nasledie', in D.Tumarkin (ed.), *Repressirovannye Etnografy,*. Moscow: Vostochnaya Literatura RAN.

Jacobi, R. (1978), 'Northern England in the Eight Millenium BC: An Essay', in P. Mellars (ed.), *The Early Post-Glacial Settlement of Northern Europe*, London: Duckworth.

Jacobsen, J. (1985), 'Acheulian Surface Sites in Central India', in V.N. Misra and P. Bellwood (eds), *Recent Advances in Indo-Pacific Prehistory*, New Delhi: Oxford-IBH.

Janko, J. (1997), 'Two Concepts of the World in Greek and Roman Thought: Cyclicity and Degeneration', in M. Teich, R. Porter and B. Gustaffson (eds), *Nature and Society in Historical Context*, Cambridge: Cambridge University Press.

Jayraj, J.S. (1983), *Early Hunter-Gatherer Adaptations in the Tirupati Valley, South India,* Ph.D. Dissertation, Deccan College, Pune, India.

Jessop, R. (1967), *Age by Age: Landmarks of British Archaeology*, London: Michael Joseph.

Joiris, D.V. and S. Bahuchet (1994), 'Afrique Equatoriale', in S. Bahuchet and P. De Maret (eds), *Situation des Populations Indigenes des Forêts Denses Humides*, Brussels and Paris: ULB-LACITO.

Kabo, V.R. (1981) Obshchina i rod u nivkhov, in *Puti razvitiya Avstralii i Okeanii: Istoriaya, economica, etnografiya.* Moscow: Nauka.

Kahn, J.S. (1990), 'Towards a History of the Critique of Economism: The Nineteenth-Century German Origins of the Ethnographer's Dilemma', *Man* (n.s.) 25: 230–49.

Kajale, M.D., Murty, M.L.K., Sharma, B.L., Dayal, R., and Vijendra Rao, R. (1991), 'Archaeological Wood Remains from the Prehistoric Cave Site at Betamcherla (Muchchatla Chintamanu Gavi), District Kurnool, Andhra Pradesh', *Man and Environment,* 16: 115–19.

Kamei, N. (2002), *Anthropological Study of Children's Daily Activities and Socialization among the Baka Hunter-Gatherers.* Doctoral Thesis, Kyoto University.

Kames, H. Home, Lord (1758), *Historical Law Tracts*, Edinburgh: A. Kincaid and J. Bell.

—— (1788 [1774]), *Sketches of the History of Man* (second edition), Vol. I, Edinburgh: A. Strahan.

—— (1789 [1774]), *Sketches of the History of Man* (third edition), Vol. I, Dublin: James Williams.

Kaping, T. (1998), *The Southern Nagas: An Ethnoarchaeological Study*, Ph.D. Dissertation, Deccan College, Pune, India.

Kaplan, D. and Manners, R.A. (1972), *Culture Theory*. Englewood Cliffs, NJ: Prentice-Hall Inc.

Kaplan, H. and Hill, K. (1992), 'The Evolutionary Ecology of Food Acquisition', in E.A. Smith and B. Winterhalder (eds), *Evolutionary Ecology and Human Behavior*, New York: Aldine de Gruyter.

Keen, I. (1988), 'Twenty-five Years of Aboriginal Kinship Studies', in R.M. Berndt and R. Tonkinson (eds), *Social Anthropology and Australian Aboriginal Studies. A Contemporary Overview,* Canberra: Aboriginal Studies Press.

Keene, A. (1981), 'Optimal Foraging in a Nonmarginal Environment: A Model of Prehistoric Subsistence Strategies in Michigan', in B. Winterhalder and E.A. Smith (eds), *Hunter-Gatherer Foraging Strategies: Ethnographic and Archeological Analyses*, Chicago: University of Chicago Press.

Keesing, R.M. (1974), 'Theories of Culture', *Annual Review of Anthropology,* 3: 75–97.

—— (1987), 'Anthropology as Interpretive Quest', *Current Anthropology,* 28: 161–76.

—— (1994), 'Theories of Culture Revisited', in R. Borofsky (ed.), *Assessing Cultural Anthropology,* New York: McGraw-Hill, Inc.

Kelly, R. L. (1995), *The Foraging Spectrum: Diversity in Hunter-Gatherer Lifeways,* Washington: Smithsonian Institution Press.

Kennedy, K. A. R. (2000), *God-Apes and Fossil Men: Palaeoanthropology of South Asia,* Ann Arbor: University of Michigan Press.

Kenoyer, J.M., Clark, J.D., Pal, J.N., and Sharma, G.R. (1983), 'An Upper Palaeolithic Shrine in India?', *Antiquity,* LVII: 88–94.

Kenrick, J. (2001), 'Present Predicament of Hunter-Gatherers and Former Hunter-Gatherers of the Central African Rainforests', in A. Barnard and J. Kenrick (eds), *Africa's Indigenous Peoples:'First Peoples' or 'Marginalised Minorities?',* Edinburgh: Centre of African Studies.

—— (2002), 'Anthropology and Anthropocentrism: Images of Hunter-Gatherers, Westerners and the Environment', in H. Stewart, A. Barnard and K.Omura (eds), *Self- and Other-Images of Hunter-Gatherers (Senri Ethnological Studies* 60), Osaka: National Museum of Ethnology.

Kent, S. (1993), 'Sharing in an Egalitarian Kalahari Community', *Man* (n.s.), 28: 479–514.

—— (ed.) (1996), *Cultural Diversity among Twentieth-Century Foragers: An African Perspective,* Cambridge: Cambridge University Press.

Kerns, V. (2003), *Scenes from the High Desert,* Urbana: University of Illinois Press.

Khanna, G. S. (1988), *Reassessing the Mesolithic of India (With Special Reference to the Site of Bagor, Rajasthan),* Ph.D. Dissertation, University of California at Berkeley.

Khare, R. (1990), 'Indian Sociology and the Cultural Other', *Contributions to Indian Sociology* (n.s.), 24: 177–99.

—— (2001), *The Singing Bow. Song Poems of the Bhil,* India: Harper Collins.

Kimura, D. (2001), 'Difference in Conversation Style between the Baka and Bantu', *African Study Monographs,* Supplementary Issue, 26: 103–21.

Kirk, R. (1974*), Hunters of the Whale: An Adventure in NW Coast Archaeology* (with R. Daugherty), New York: William Morrow.

Kitamura, K. (1990), 'Interactional Synchrony: A Fundamental Condition for Communication', in M. Moerman and M. Nomura (eds), *Culture Embodied* (Senri Ethnological Studies 27), Osaka: National Museum of Ethnology.

Kitanishi, K. (1995), 'Seasonal Changes in the Subsistence Activities and Food Intake of the Aka Hunter-gatherers in Northeastern Congo', *African Study Monographs,* 16: 73–118.

—— (1998), 'Food Sharing among the Aka Hunter-Gatherers in Northeastern Congo', *African Study Monographs,* Supplementary Issue, 25: 3–28.

Klein, R., Alwarden, K. and Wolf, C. (1983), 'The Calculation and Interpretation of Ungulate Age Profiles from Dental Crown Heights', in G. Bailey (ed.), *Hunter-Gatherer Economy in Prehistory,* Cambridge: Cambridge University Press.

Knack, M.C. (1978), 'Beyond a Difference: An Inquiry into Southern Paiute Indian Experience with Public Schools', *Anthropology and Education Quarterly*, 9: 216–34.

—— (1980), *Life Is With People: Household Organization of the Contemporary Southern Paiute Indians* (Ballena Press Anthropological Papers 19) Socorra, NM: Ballena Press.

—— and Stewart, O.C. (1984), *As Long as the River Shall Rise: An Economic Ethnohistory of the Pyramid Lake Indian Reservation*, Berkeley: University of California Press.

Knight, C., Power, C., and Watts, I. (1995), 'The Human Symbolic Revolution: A Darwinian Account', *Cambridge Archaeological Journal*, 5: 75–114.

Köcke, J. (1979), 'Some Early German Contributions to Economic Anthropology', *Research in Economic Anthropology*, 2: 119–67.

Köhler, A., and Lewis, J. (2002), 'Putting Hunter-Gatherer and Farmer Relations in Perspective: A Commentary from Central Africa,' in S. Kent (ed.), *Ethnicity, Hunter-Gatherers, and the 'Other'. Association and Assimilation in Africa*, Washington, DC: Smithsonian Institution.

Koppers, W. (1915–16), 'Die ethnologische Wirtschaftsforschung. Eine kritisch-historische Studie', *Anthropos*, 10/11: 611–51, 971–1079.

Krader, L. (1972), *The Ethnological Notebooks of Karl Marx*, transcribed and edited, with an Introduction by Lawrence Krader, Assen: Van Gorcum and Company.

Krause, F. (1924), *Das Wirtschaftsleben der Völker*, Breslau: Ferdinand Hirt.

Kreynovich E.A. (1973), *Nivkhgu: Zagadochnye obitateli Sakhalina i Amura*. Moscow: Nauka.

Kroeber, A.L. (1917),'The Superorganic', *American Anthropologist,* 19: 163–213.

—— (1925), *Handbook of the Indians of California*, Washington, DC: Bureau of American Ethnology (Bulletin 78).

Kropotkin, P. (1890), 'Mutual Aid among Animals', *The Nineteenth Century,* 28: 699–719.

Krupnik, I. (1998), 'Jesup Genealogy: Intellectual Partnership and Russian-American Cooperation in Arctic/North Pacific Anthropology', *Arctic Anthropology,* 35: 199–226.

Kubler, G. (1962), *The Shape of Time: Remarks on the History of Things,* New Haven: Yale University Press.

Kuper, A. (2003), 'The Return of the Native', *Current Anthropology*, 44: 389–402.

LACITO (1981–), *Encyclopédie des Pygmées Aka*, Paris and Louvain: SELAF-Peeters.

Laden, G. (1992), *Ethnoarchaeology and Land Use Ecology of the Efe of the Ituri Rain Forest*. Ph.D. Dissertation, Harvard University, Cambridge, MA.

Laing, L. and Laing, J. (1980), *The Origins of Britain*, London: Routledge and Keegan Paul.

Lamb, S.M. (1958), 'Linguistic Prehistory in the Great Basin', *International Journal of American Linguistics*, 24: 95–100.

—— (1964), 'The Classification of Uto-Aztecan Languages: A Historical Survey', *University of California Publication in Linguistics*, 34: 106–25.

Lane, P. and Schadla-Hall, R.T. (eds) (forthcoming), *Hunter-Gatherers in the*

*Landscape: The Archaeology of the Early Mesolithic in the Vale of Pickering, North Yorkshire*, Cambridge: Macdonald Institute for Archaeological Research.

Lar'kin, V.G. (1958), *Udegeytsy (istoriko-etnograficheskiy ocherk s serediny XIX v. do nashikh dney)*. Vladivostok: Nauka.

Layton, R. (1989), 'Introduction: who needs the past?', in R. Layton (ed.), *Who Needs the Past? Indigenous Values and Archaeology*, London: Unwin Hyman.

—— (2001), 'Hunter-Gatherers, their Neighbours and the Nation State', in C. Panter-Brick, R. Layton and P. Rowley-Conwy (eds), *Hunter-Gatherers: an Interdisciplinary Perspective*, Cambridge: Cambridge University Press.

Leacock, E. and Lee, R. (eds) (1982), *Politics and History in Band Societies.* Cambridge University Press: Cambridge.

Lee, R. B. (1976), 'Introduction', in R.B. Lee and I. DeVore (eds), *Kalahari: Hunter-Gatherers: Studies of the !Kung San and their Neighbors*, Cambridge, MA: Harvard University press.

—— (1979a), *The !Kung San: Men, Women, and Work in a Foraging Society*, Cambridge: Cambridge University Press.

—— (1979b), 'Hunter-Gatherers in Process: The Kalahari Research project, 1963–1976', in G.M. Foster, T. Scudder, E Colson, and R.V. Kemper (eds), *Long-Term Field Research in Social Anthropology*, New York: Academic Press.

—— (1984), *The Dobe !Kung*, New York: Holt, Rinehart and Winston.

—— (1992), 'Art, science, or politics? The Crisis in hunter-Gatherer Studies', *American Anthropologist*, 94: 21–54.

—— (1993), 'Problems in Kalahari Historical Ethnography and the Tolerance of Error', *History in Africa*, 20: 185–235.

—— and Daly, R. (1999), 'Introduction: Foragers and Others', in R. Lee and R. Daly (eds), *The Cambridge Encyclopedia of Hunters and Gatherers*, Cambridge: Cambridge University Press.

—— and DeVore, I. (1968a), 'Preface', in R.B. Lee and I. DeVore (eds), *Man the Hunter*, Chicago: Aldine Publishing Company.

—— and DeVore, I. (1968b), 'Problems in the Study of Hunters and Gatherers', in R.B. Lee and I DeVore (eds), *Man the Hunter*, Chicago: Aldine Publishing Company.

—— and DeVore, I. (eds) (1968c), *Man the Hunter*, Chicago: Aldine Publishing Company.

—— and DeVore, I. (eds) (1976), *Kalahari Hunters-Gatherers: Studies of the !Kung San and Their Neighbors,* Cambridge: Harvard University Press.

—— and Guenther, M. (1991), 'Oxen or Onions: The Search for Trade (and Truth) in the Kalahari', *Current Anthropology 32*: 592–601.

Legge, A. and Rowley-Conwy, P. (1988), *Star Carr Revisited. A Re-Analysis of the Large Mammals*, London: Centre for Extramural Studies, University of London.

Lévi-Strauss, C. (1989 [1962]), *The Savage Mind*, London: Weidenfeld & Nicholson.

Levin, M. (1958), 'Etnicheskaya antropologiya i problemy etnogeneza narodov Dal'nego Vostoka', in G. Debets (ed.), *Trudy Instituta Etnografii. Trudy Severo-Vostochnoy Ekspeditsii*: XXVI. Moscow: Izdatel'stvo Akademii Nauk SSSR.

—— and Cheboksarov, N. (1955), 'Khozyaystvenno-kul'turnye tipy i istoriko-etnograficheskie oblasti', *Sovetskaya etnografiya*, 4: 3–17.

—— and Potapov, L. (eds) (1961), *Istoriko-etnograficheskiy atlas narodov Sibiri*. Moscow-Leningrad: Izdatel'stvo Akademii Nauk SSSR.

Lewis, D. (1973), 'Anthropology and Colonialism', *Current Anthropology*, 14: 581–602

Lewis, J. (2001), 'Forest People or Village People: Whose Voice Will Be Heard?, in A. Barnard and J. Kenrick (eds), *Africa's Indigenous Peoples: 'First Peoples' or 'Marginalised Minorities'?*, Edinburgh: Edinburgh University.

Lewis, R. (1982), 'Phytolith Studies', in G. Frison and D. Stanford (eds), *The Agate Basin Site: A Record of the Paleoindian Occupation of the Northwestern High Plains*, Orlando: Academic Press.

Lips, J. (1928), 'Die Anfänge des Rechts an Grund und Boden bei den Naturvölkern und der Begriff der Erntevölker', in W. Koppers (ed.), *Festschrift P.W. Schmidt*, Vienna.

Lister, A. (1981), *Evolutionary Studies on Pleistocene Deer*, Ph.D. Thesis, University of Cambridge.

Liu, J. (2002), 'Wang Fu-chih', http://www.geneseo.edu/~liu/WangFuChih.htm

Locke, J. 1988 [1690]. *Two Treatises of Government*. Cambridge: Cambridge University Press.

Loether, C. (1990), 'Western Mono Mythology: A Numic Oral Tradition in California', Paper presented at the Twenty-second Great Basin Anthropological Conference, October 8–10, Boise, Idaho.

—— (1992), 'The California Mourning Anniversary in the Great Basin', Paper presented at the Twenty-third Great Basin Anthropological Conference, October 8–10, Boise, Idaho.

Longworth, I., Ashton, N., and Rigby, V. (1986), 'Prehistoric Britain', in I. Longworth and J. Cherry (eds), *Archaeology in Britain Since 1945*, London: British Museum Publications.

Lovejoy, A. and Boas, G. (1965), *Primitivism and Related Ideas in Antiquity*, New York: Octagon Books.

Lowie, R.H. (1909), 'The Northern Shoshoni', *Anthropological Papers, American Museum of Natural History* 2: 165–306.

Luganskii, Yu., et al. (1979) *Vladimir Klavdievich Arsen'ev. Biografiya v fotografiyakh, vospominaniyakh druzey, svidetel'stvakh epokhi*. G.Aleksyuk (ed.), Vladivostok: Ussuri.

Lukas, H. (1998), 'Paul Schebesta und H. A. Bernatzig, die österreichischen Pioniere in der ethnologischen Erforschung der Malaiischen Halbinsel', in *21. Österreichischer Historikertag in Wien 1996, Tagungsbericht*, Vienna.

Lurie, N. O. (1957), 'The Indian Claims Commission Act,' The *Annals of the American Academy of Political and Social Science*, 311: 56–70.

Lyapunova, R.G. (1975), *Ocherki po etnografii aleutov*. Moscow: Nauka.

Maksimov, A.N (1898), K voprosu o metodakh izucheniya istorii sem'i, *Etnograficheskoe obozrenie* 4: 1–35.

—— (1908), Ogranicheniya otnosheniy mezhdu odnim iz suprugov i rodstvennikami drugogo, *Etnograficheskoe obozrenie* 1908 (1–2): 1–77.

—— (1909), Brachnye klassy avstraliytsev, *Etnograficheskoe obozrenie* 1901 (2–3): 1–32.

—— (1912), Systemy rodstva avstraliytsev, *Etnograficheskoe obozrenie* 1912 (1–2): 35–100.

Malik, S.C. (1968), *Indian Civilization. The Formative Period. A Study of Archaeology as Anthropology,* Simla: Indian Institute of Advanced Study.

Malouf, C. (1966), 'Ethnohistory in the Great Basin', in W.L. d'Azevedo et al (eds), *The Current Status of Anthropological Research in the Great Basin: 1964,* Reno: Desert Research Institute.

Marcus, G. and Fischer, M.M.J. (1986), *Anthropology as Cultural Critique.* Chicago: University of Chicago Press.

Marks, S. (1972), 'Khoisan resistance to the Dutch in the Seventeenth and Eighteenth Centuries', *Journal of African History*, 13: 55–80.

Marshall, L. (1976), *The !Kung of Nyae Nyae*, Cambridge, MA: Harvard University Press.

—— (1999), *Nyae Nyae !Kung Beliefs and Rites*, Cambridge, MA: Peabody Museum Monographs, No. 8.

—— and Ritchie, C. (1984), *Where Are the Ju/was: of Nyae Nyae? Changes in a Bushman Society, 1958–1981*, Cape Town: Centre for African Studies, University of Cape Town.

Martin, C. (1993), *In the Spirit of the Earth: Rethinking History and Time*, Baltimore: John Hopkins University Press.

Maruyama, J. (2002), 'Resettlement, Livelihood and Social Relationships among the /Gui and //Gana in Central Kalahari', Paper presented at Ninth International Conference on Hunting and Gathering Societies, Edinburgh, September 2002.

Mauss, M. (in collaboration with H. Beuchat) (1979 [1904–5]), *Seasonal Variations of the Eskimo: A Study in Social Morphology*, London: Routledge & Kegan Paul.

Meek, R. L. (1976), *Social Science and the Ignoble Savage.* Cambridge: Cambridge University Press.

—— (1977), 'Smith, Turgot and the "Four Stage Theory" ', in *Smith, Marx and After: Ten Essays in the Development of Economic Thought.* London: Chapman & Hall.

Meillassoux, C. (1981), *Maidens, Meal and Money: Capitalism and the Domestic Community*, Cambridge University Press: Cambridge.

Mellars, P. (1998), "Postscript: Major Issues in the Interpretation of Star Carr', in P. Mellars and P. Dark (eds), *Star Carr in Context*, Cambridge: Macdonald Institute for Archaeological Research.

—— and Dark, P. (eds) (1998), *Star Carr in Context*, Cambridge: Macdonald Institute for Archaeological Research.

—— Schadla-Hall, T. and Lane, P. (1998), 'Excavations in Trench A: 1985 and 1989', in P. Mellars and P. Dark (eds), *Star Carr in Context*, Cambridge: Macdonald Institute for Archaeological Research.

Menovshchikov, G.A. (1959), *Eskimosy*, Magadan: Magadanskoe knizhnoe izdatel'stvo.

Mercader, J., Runge, F., Vrydaghs, L., Doutrelepont, H., Ewango, C. E. N., and Juan-Tresseras, J. (2000), 'Phytoliths from Archaeological Sites in the Tropical Forest of Ituri, Democratic Republic of Congo', *Quaternary Research*, 54: 102–12.

Millar, J. (1806 [1771]), *The Origin of the Distinction of Ranks* (fourth edition). Edinburgh: William Blackwood.

Miller, W.R. (1964), 'The Shoshonean Languages of Uto-Aztecan', *University of California Publications in Linguistics*, 34: 145–8.

—— (1966), 'Anthropological Linquistics in the Great Basin', in W.L. d'Azevedo et al (eds), *The Current Status of Anthropological Research in the Great Basin: 1964*, Reno: Reno Desert Research Institute.

—— (1970), 'Western Shoshoni Dialects', in E.H. Swanson (ed.), *Language and Cultures of Western North American*, Caldwell, ID: Caxton Printers.

Ministry of Tribal Affairs (2002), http://tribal.nic.in/

Mishra, B.B. and Clark, J.D. (1983), 'Contemporary Abandoned Shelters and Temporary Camps: Some Implications for Ethno-archaeological Interpretation', in G.R. Sharma and J.D. Clark (eds), *Palaeoenvironment and Prehistory in the Middle Son Valley (Madhya Pradesh, North Central India)*, Allahabad: Avinash Publications.

Misra, V.N. (1989a), 'Hasmukh Dhirajlal Sankalia (1908–1989): Scholar and Man', *Man and Environment*, 14: 1–20.

—— (1989b), 'Stone Age India: an Ecological Perspective', *Man and Environment*, 14: 17–64.

—— (1990), 'The Van Vagris-"Lost" Hunters of the Thar Desert, Rajasthan', *Man and Environment*, 15: 89–108.

—— and Nagar, M. (1993), 'The Pardhis: A Hunting-Gathering Community of Central and Western India', *Man and Environment*, 18: 115–40.

Mogilyanskiy, M. (1916), 'Predmet i zadachi etnografii', *Zhivaya Starina*, 1: 3–17.

Mohanty, P. (1989), *Mesolithic Settlement System of Keonjhar district, Orissa*, Ph.D. Dissertation. Deccan College, Pune.

—— and Mishra, J. (2002), 'Fifty years of Ethnoarchaeological research in India: A Review', in S. Settar and R. Korisettar (eds), *Indian Archaeology in Retrospect. Archaeology and Interactive Disciplines*, Vol. III. New Delhi: Manohar Publishers.

Monboddo, J. Burnet, Lord. (1774 [1773]), *Of the Origin and Progress of Language*, Vol. I (second edition), Edinburgh: J. Balfour. London: T. Cadell.

Montesquieu, Charles de Secondat, baron de (1989 [1748]), *The Spirit of the Laws*, Cambridge: Cambridge University Press.

Moore, J. (1950), 'Mesolithic Sites in the Neighbourhood of Flixton, North-East Yorkshire', *Proceedings of the Prehistoric Society*, 16: 101–8.

—— (1951), *Lake Flixton: A Late-Glacial Structure*, Scarborough: Scarborough & District Archaeological Society Publication No. 1.

—— (1954), 'Excavations at Flixton, Site 2', in J. Clark (ed.), *Excavations at Star Carr: an Early Mesolithic Site at Seamer, near Scarborough, Yorkshire*, Cambridge: Cambridge University Press.

Morris, B. (1982), *Forest Traders. A Socio-Economic Study of the Hill Pandaram*, New Jersey: Athlone Press.

Motte, E. (1980), *Les Plantes chez les Monzombo de la Lobaye (Cenrafrique)*, Paris: SELAF.

Munn, N. (1992), 'The Cultural Anthropology of Time: A Critical Essay', *Annual Review of Anthropology*, 21: 93–123.

Murphy, R.F. (1970), 'Basin Ethnography and Ecological Theory', in E.H. Swanson (ed.), *Language and Cultures of Western North American*, Caldwell: Idaho Caxton Printers.

——— (1977), 'Introduction', in *Evolution and Ecology*. Urbana: University of Illinois Press.

——— (1981), 'Julian Steward', in S. Silverman (ed.), *Totems and Teachers*, New York: Columbia University Press.

Murty, M.L.K. (1978–1979), 'Symbiosis and Traditional Behaviour in the Subsistence Economies of the Kunchapuri Yerkulas of South India: A Predictive model', *Purattatva*, 10: 50–61.

——— (1981), 'Hunter-Gatherer Ecosystems and Archaeological Patterns of Subsistence Behaviour on the Southeast Coast of India: an Ethnographic Model', *World Archaeology*, 13: 47–58.

——— (1985a), 'Ethnoarchaeology of the Kurnool Cave areas, South India', *World Archaeology*, 17: 192–205.

——— (1985b), 'The Use of Plant Foods by some Hunter-Gatherer Communities in Andhra Pradesh', in V.N. Misra and P. Bellwood (eds), *Recent Advances in Indo-Pacific Prehistory*, New Delhi: Oxford-IBH.

——— (1994), 'Forest Peoples and Historical Traditions in the Eastern Ghats, South India', in B. Allchin (ed.), *Living Traditions: Studies in the Ethnoarchaeology of South Asia*, New Delhi: Oxford-IBH.

Myers, F. (1979), 'Emotions and the Self: A Theory of Personhood and Political Order among Pintupi Aborigines', *Ethos*, 7: 343–70.

——— (1986), *Pintupi Country, Pintupi Self: Sentiment, Place, and Politics Among Western Desert Aborigines*. Washington: Smithsonian Institution.

——— (1988), 'The Logic and Meaning of Anger among Pintupi Aborigines', *Man*, 23: 589–610.

Myers, L.D. (1987), *Levels of Context: A Symbolic Analysis of Numic Origin Myths*, Ph.D Dissertation, Rutgers University, New Brunswick, NJ.

——— (1988), 'Hunters and Gatherers as Anthropological Exemplars: An Illustration from the American Great Basin', Paper presented at the Fifth International Conference on Hunting and Gathering Societies, Darwin, Australia, September 1988.

——— (1997), 'Animal Symbolism Among the Numa: Symbolic Analysis of Numic Origin Myths', *Journal of California and Great Basin Anthropology*, 19: 32–43.

——— (1999), 'A Frame for Culture: Observations on the Culture-Element Distribution of the Snake River Shoshone', in R.O. Clemmer, L.D. Myers, and E. Rudden (eds), *Julian Steward and the Great Basin*, Salt Lake City: University of Utah Press.

——— (2001), 'Myth as Ritual: Thoughts from a Symbolic Analysis of Numic Origin Myths', *Journal of California and Great Basin Anthropology* 24: 39–50.

Nagar, M. (1967), *The Ahar Culture: An Archaeological and Ethnographic study*, Ph.D. Dissertation, Deccan College, Pune, India.

——— (1969), 'Clues to Aharian Prehistory in Contemporary Mewar Village Life', *The Eastern Anthropologist*, 22: 55–73.

——— (1977), 'Living Prehistory Around Bhimbetka', in V.N. Misra, Y. Mathpal and

M. Nagar (eds), *Bhimbetka: Prehistoric Man and His Art in Central India*, Pune: Poona Exhibition Souvenir.

—— (1978), 'Role of Ethnographic Evidence in the Reconstruction of Archaeological data', *The Eastern Anthropologist,* 28: 13–22.

—— (1982), 'Fishing among the Tribal Communities of Bastar and its Implications for Archaeology', *Bulletin of the Deccan College Postgraduate and Research Institute,* 42: 116–25.

—— (1983), 'Ethnoarchaeology of the Bhimbetka Region', *Man and Environment,* 7: 61–69.

—— (1985), 'The Use of Wild Plant Foods by Aboriginal Communities in Central India', in V.N. Misra and P. Bellwood (eds), *Recent Advances in Indo-Pacific Prehistory,* New Delhi: Oxford-IBH.

—— and Misra, V.N. (1989), 'Hunter-Gatherers in an Agrarian Setting: The Nineteenth Century Situation in the Ganga Plains', *Man and Environment,* 13: 65–78.

—— and Misra, V.N. (1990), 'The Kanjars-A Hunting-Gathering Community of the Ganga Valley, Uttar Pradesh', *Man and Environment,* 15: 71–88.

—— and Misra, V.N. (1993), 'The Pardhis: A Hunting-Gathering Community of Central and Western India', *Man and Environment'* 18: 115–44.

—— and Misra, V.N. (1994), 'Survival of the Hunting-Gathering Tradition in the Ganga Plains and Central India', in B. Allchin (ed.), *Living Traditions: Studies in the Ethnoarchaeology of South Asia*, New Delhi: Oxford-IBH.

Nanda, S.C. (1983), *Stone Age Cultures of Indravati Basin, Koraput district, Orissa,* Ph.D. Dissertation, Deccan College, Pune, India.

Needham, J. (1965), *Time and Eastern Man* (Royal Anthropological Institute Occasional Paper 21), London: RAI.

Noe-Nygaard, N. (1975), 'Two Shoulder Blades with Healed Lessions from Star Carr', *Proceedings of the Prehistoric Society*, 41: 10–16.

—— (1977), 'Butchering and Marrow Fracturing as a Taphonomic Factor in Archaeological Deposits', *Palaeobiology*, 3: 218–37.

—— (1988), 'Taphonomy in Archaeology with Special Emphasis on Man as a Biasing Factor', *Journal of Danish Archaeology*, 6: 7–52.

Nonaka, K. (1996), 'Ethnoentomology of the Central Kalahari San', *African Study Monographs,* Supplementary Issue, 22: 29–46.

Northern Paiute Nation (1975), *Indian Claims Commission, Docket 87.* New York: Clearwater Publishing Company.

O'Connell, J. and Hawkes, K. (1981), 'Alywara Plant Use and Optimal Foraging Theory', in B. Winterhalder and E.A. Smith (eds), *Hunter-Gatherer Foraging Strategies: Ethnographic and Archeological Analyses*, Chicago: University of Chicago Press.

—— (1984), 'Food Choice and Foraging Sites Among the Alywara', *Journal of Anthropological Research*, 40: 504–35.

—— Hawkes, K., and Jones, B. (1991), 'Distribution of Refuse-Producing Activities at Hadza Residential Base Camps: Implications for Analyses of Archaeological Site Structure', in E. Kroll and T. Price (eds), *The Interpretation of Archaeological Spatial Patterning*, New York: Plenum.

Olivier, E. and S. Furniss (1999), 'Pygmy and Bushman Music: A New Comparative Study', in K. Biesbrouck, S. Elders and G. Rossel (eds), *Central African Hunter-Gatherers in a Multidisciplinary Perspective: Challenging Elusiveness*, Leiden: Universiteit Leiden.

Omvedt, G. (1980), 'Adivasis, Culture and Modes of Production in India', *Bulletin of Concerned Asian Scholars*, 12: 15–22.

Osaki, M. (1984), 'The Social Influence of Change in Hunting Technique among the Central Kalahari San', *African Study Monographs*, 5: 49–62.

—— (1990), 'The Influence of Sedentism on Sharing among the Central Kalahari Hunter-Gatherers', *African Study Monographs,* Supplementary Issue, 12: 59–87.

—— (1998), 'Reconstructing the Recent History of the /Gui and //Gana Bushmen', Paper presented at the Eigth International Conference on Hunting and Gathering Societies, Osaka, October 1998.

Osnitskaya, I.A. (1993), 'Shest'desyat let v Kunstkamere: k 90–letiyu D.A. Ol'derogge' *Kunstkamera. Etnograficheskie tetradi*, 2–3: 356–73.

Owen-Hughes, D. (1995), 'Introduction', in D. Owen-Hughes and T. Trautman (eds), *Time: Histories and Ethologies*, Ann Arbor: University of Michigan Press.

Owens, R.C. (1965),'The Patrilocal Band: A Linguistically and Cultural Hybrid Social Unit, *American Anthropologist*, 67: 673–90.

Paddayya, K. (1979), 'Palaeoethnography vis-à-vis the Stone Age Cultures of India: Some Methodological Considerations', *Bulletin of the Deccan College Postgraduate and Research Institute,* 38: 63–90.

—— (1981), 'Water Supply as a Key Determinant in the Acheulian Occupation of the Hunsgi valley, Peninsular India', *Bulletin of the Deccan College Post-graduate and Research Institute,* 40: 39–51.

—— (1982), *The Acheulian Culture of the Hunsgi Valley (Peninsular India): A Settlement System Perspective,* Pune: Deccan College.

—— (1987), 'The Place of Site Formation Processes in Prehistoric Research in India', in D.T. Nash and M.D. Petraglia (eds), *Natural Formation Processes and the Archaeological Record,* Oxford: BAR International Series 352.

—— (1990), *The New Archaeology and Aftermath: A View from Outside the Anglo-American world,* Pune: Ravish Publishers.

—— (1995), 'Theoretical Perspectives in Indian Archaeology', in P.J. Ucko (ed.), *Theory in Archaeology: A World Perspective*, London: Routledge.

Pagden, A. (1982), *The Fall of Natural Man: The American Indian and the Origins of Comparative Ethnology*, Cambridge: Cambridge University Press.

Pandey, D. (1989), 'An 11th Century Literary Reference to Prehistoric Times in India', in R.Layton (ed.), *Who Needs the Past? Indigenous Values and Archaeology*, London: Unwin Hyman.

Pant, P.C. and Jayaswal, V. (1991), *Paisra: The Stone Age Settlement of Bihar,* Delhi: Agam Kala Prakashan.

Panter-Brick, C., Layton, R. and Rowley-Conwy, P. (eds) (2001), *Hunter-Gatherers: An Interdisciplinary Perspective*, Cambridge: Cambridge University Press.

Pappu, S. (1991–92), 'Robert Bruce Foote and the Study of Site Formation Processes of the Archaeological record', *Bulletin of the Deccan College Post-graduate and Research Institute,* 51–52: 647–54.

—— (2001), *A Re-examination of the Palaeolithic Archaeological Record of Northern Tamil Nadu, South India,* Oxford: BAR-International Series 1003.

Patterson, T. (2001), *A Social History of Anthropology in the United States,* Oxford: Berg.

Pauketat, T. (2001), 'Practice and History in Archaeology: An Emerging Paradigm', *Anthropological Theory,* 1: 73–98.

Pearsall, D. (1985), *Paleoethnobotany: A Handbook of Procedures,* Orlando: Academic Press.

Petraglia, M.D. (1995), 'Pursuing Site Formation Research in India', in S. Wadia, R. Korisettar and V. S. Kale (eds), *Quaternary Environments and Geoarchaeology of India,* Bangalore: Geological Society of India.

Piperno, D. (1988), *Phytolith Analysis: An Archaeological and Geological Perspective,* Orlando: Academic Press.

Pitts, M. (1979), 'Hides and Antlers: A New Look at the Hunter-Gatherer Site at Star Carr, North Yorkshire, England', *World Archaeology,* 11: 32–42.

Pluciennik, M. (2001), 'Archaeology, Anthropology and Subsistence', *Journal of the Royal Anthropological Institute* (n.s.), 7: 741–58.

—— (2002), 'The Invention of Hunter-Gatherers in Seventeenth-Century Europe', *Archaeological Dialogues,* 9: 98–151.

Popov, A.A. (1958), 'Perezhitki drevnikh doreligioznykh vozzreniy Dolganov na prirodu', *Sovetskaya etnografiya,* 2: 77–99.

—— (1966), *The Nganassan: The Material Culture of the Tavgi Samoyeds.* Bloomington: Indiana University Press.

—— (1984), *Nganasany. Sotsial'noe ustroystvo i verovaniya.* Leningrad: Nauka.

Possehl, G. and Kennedy, K.A.R. (1979), 'Hunter-Gatherer/Agriculturalist Exchange in Prehistory: An Indian Example', *Current Anthropology,* 20: 592–3.

Prasad, R. (1989), 'Beginning of Agriculture: A Synchronism Between Puranic and Archaeological Evidence', in R.Layton (ed.), *Who Needs the Past? Indigenous Values and Archaeology,* London: Unwin Hyman.

Preobrazhenskiy, P.F. (1929), 'Pervobytnyy monoteizm u ognezemel'tsev', *Uchenye zapiski instituta istorii,* 1: 201–53.

Price, T. (1982), 'Willow Tales and Dog Smoke', *Quarterly Review of Anthropology,* 3: 4–7.

—— and Brown, J. (eds) (1985), *Prehistoric Hunter-Gatherers. The Emergence of Cultural Complexity,* Orlando: Academic Press.

Pufendorf, S. von. 1991 [1673]. *On the Duty of Man and Citizen according to Natural Law* (translated by M. Silverthorne and edited by J. Tully). Cambridge: Cambridge University Press.

Radcliffe-Brown, A.R. (1952), *Structure and Function in Primitive Society.* London: Cohen and West.

Radley, J. and Mellars, P. (1964), 'A Mesolithic Structure at Deepcar, Yorkshire, England and the Affinities of its Associated Flint Industries', *Proceedings of the Prehistoric Society,* 30: 1–24.

Raju D.R. (1988), *Stone Age Hunter-Gatherers: An Ethno-Archaeology of Cuddapah Region, South-East India,* Pune: Ravish Publishers.

Raman K.V. (1959), *The Early History of the Madras Region,* Madras: National Art Press.

Rao, N. (1994), 'Subsistence and Settlement Patterns in Central India: An Ethnoarchaeological Analysis', in B. Allchin (ed.), *Living Traditions: Studies in the Ethnoarchaeology of South Asia,* New Delhi: Oxford-IBH.

Rappaport, R.A. (1968), *Pigs For The Ancestors: Ritual in the Ecology of a New Guinea People,* New Haven: Yale University Press.

Ratzel, F. (1896 [1894]), *The History of Mankind,* Volume 1, London: Macmillan.

Reid, A. (1994), 'Early Southeast Asian Categorizations of Europeans', in S. Schwarts (eds), *Implicit Understandings: Observing, Reporting and Reflecting on the Encounters between European and other Peoples in the Early Modern Era,* Cambridge: Cambridge University Press.

Reshetov, A.M. (1972), 'Vvedenie', in A. Reshetov (ed.), *Okhotniki, sobirateli, rybolovy. Problemy sotsial'no-ekonomicheskikh otnosheniy v dozemledel'cheskom obshchestve.* Leningrad: Nauka.

Reyna, S. (2001), 'Theory Counts: (Discounting) Discourse to the Contrary by Adopting a Confrontational Stance, *Anthropological Theory,* 1: 9–29.

Rigsby, B. (1997), 'Anthropologists, Indian Title, and the Indian Claims Commission: The California and Great Basin Cases', in D.E. Smith and J. Finlayson (eds), *Fighting Over Country: Anthropological Perspectives,* Canberra: Centre for Aboriginal Economic Policy Research, The Australia National University, Research Monograph No. 12.

Rival, L. (1999), 'Introduction: South America', in R.B. Lee and R. Daly (eds), *The Cambridge Encyclopedia of Hunters and Gatherers,* Cambridge: Cambridge University Press.

Roberts, N. (1989), *The Holocene,* Oxford: Blackwell.

Robertson, W. (1809 [1777]), *The History of America,* Volume 2, Alston, Cumberland: T. Walton & Co.

Ronaasen, S. (1993). *Cultural Ecology and Functionalism: Social Theory Framed by a Colonial Political Context.* Master's Thesis, University of Alberta, Edmonton.

——Clemmer, R.O., and M.E. Rudden (1999), 'Rethinking Cultural Ecology, Multilinear Evolution, and Expert Witnesses: Julian Steward and the Indian Claims Commission Proceedings', in R.O. Clemmer, L.D. Myers, and E. Rudden (eds), *Julian Steward and the Great Basin,* Salt Lake City: University of Utah Press.

Roon, T.P. and Sirina, A.A. (2003), 'E.A. Kreynovich: zhizn' i sud'ba', in D.Tumarkin (ed.), *Repressirovannye etnografy.* 2. Moscow: Vostochnaya Literatura RAN.

Rosaldo, R. (1982), 'Utter Savages of Scientific Value', in E. Leacock and R. Lee (eds), *Politics and History in Band Societies,* Cambridge: Cambridge University Press.

Roscoe, P. (2002), 'The Hunters and Gatherers of New Guinea', *Current Anthropology,* 43: 153–62.

Rosenthal, F. (1967), 'The Muqaddimah', in Ibn Khaldûn. *The Muqaddimah: an introduction to history,* translated by. F. Rosenthal, v. 1, lxviii-lxxxvii, London: Routledge & Kegan Paul.

Rosenthal, H. (1985), 'Indian Claims and the American Conscience: A Brief History of the Indian Claims Commission', in I. Sutton (ed.), *Irredeemable America: The Indians' Estate and Land Claims*, Albuquerque: University of New Mexico Press.
—— (1990), *Their Day in Court: A History of the Indian Claims Commission*. New York: Garland.
Rousseau, J.J. (1973 [1755]), 'A Discourse on the Origin of Inequality', in *The Social Contract and Discourses*. London: J.M. Dent & Sons.
Rovner, I. (1971), 'Potential of Opal Phytoliths for Use in Paleoecological Reconstruction', *Quaternary Research*, 1: 345–59.
—— (1983), 'Plant Opal Phytolith Analysis: Major Advances in Archaeobotanical Research', in M. Schiffer (ed.), *Advances in Archaeological Method and Theory*, Vol. 6, New York: Academic Press.
—— (1988), 'Macro- and Micro-Ecological Reconstruction Using Plant Opal Phytolith Data from Archaeological Sediments', *Geoarchaeology* 3: 155–63.
Rowley-Conwy, P. (1983), 'Sedentary Hunters: The Ertebølle Example', in G. Bailey (ed.), *Hunter-Gatherer Economies in Prehistory*, Cambridge: Cambridge University Press.
—— (1986), 'From Cave Painters to Crop Planters: Aspects of the West Temperate Mesolithic' in M. Zvelebil (ed.), *Hunters in Transition*, Cambridge: Cambridge University Press.
—— (1995), 'Mesolithic Settlement Patterns: New Zooarchaeological Evidence from the Vale of Pickering, Yorkshire', in P. Loutter and G. Phillips (eds), *University of Durham and University of Newcastle Archaeological Reports 1994*, Durham: University of Durham.
—— (2001), 'Time, Change and the Archaeology of Hunter-Gatherers: How Original is the 'Original Affluent Society'?, in C. Panter-Brick, R. Layton and P. Rowley-Conwy (eds), *Hunter-Gatherers: an Interdisciplinary Perspective*, Cambridge: Cambridge University Press.
Rudebeck, E. (2000), *Tilling Nature, Harvesting Culture: Exploring Images of the Human Being in the Transition to Agriculture* (Acta Archaeologica Lundensia, 8th Series, 32), Stockholm: Almqvist & Wiksell International.
Rusco, E.R. (1982a), 'The MX Missile and the Western Shoshone Land Claims', *Nevada Public Affairs Review*, 2: 45–54.
—— (1982b), 'Organization of the Te-Moak Bands of Western Shoshone, *Nevada Historical Society Quarterly*, 25: 175–6.
—— (1999), 'Julian Steward, the Western Shoshones, and the Bureau of Indian Affairs: A Failure to Communicate.' In R.O. Clemmer, L.D. Myers and E. Rudden (eds), *Julian Steward and the Great Basin*, Salt Lake City: University of Utah Press.
Sahlins, M. (1972), *Stone Age Economics*, Chicago: Aldine.
Sato, H. (1992), 'Notes on the Distribution and Settlement Pattern of Hunter-Gatherers in Northwestern Congo', *African Study Monographs*, 13: 203–16.
—— (2001), 'The Potential of Edible Wild Yams and Yam-like Plants as a Staple Food Resource in the African Tropical Rain Forest', *African Study Monographs*, Supplementary Issue, 26: 123–34.
Saugestad, S. (2001), *The Inconvenient Indigenous: Remote Area Development in*

*Botswana, Donor Assistance, and the First People of the Kalahari*, Uppsala: Nordiska Afrikainstitutet.

Savyasaachi, (2001), 'Forest Dwellers and Tribals in India', in S. Visvanathan (ed.), *Structure and Transformation: Theory and Society in India*, New Delhi: Oxford University Press.

Sawada, M. (1990), 'Two Patterns of Chorus among the Efe, Forest Hunter-Gatherers in Northeastern Zaire', *African Study Monographs*, 10: 159–95.

Schadla-Hall, R. (1987), 'Recent Investigations of the Early Mesolithic Landscape and Settlement in the Vale of Pickering, North Yorkshire', in P. Rowley-Conwy, M. Zvelebil and H. Blankholm (eds), *Mesolithic Northwest Europe: Recent trends*, Sheffield: Department of Archaeology & Prehistory, University of Sheffield.

—— (1989), 'The Vale of Pickering in the Early Mesolithic in context', in C. Bonsall (ed.), *The Mesolithic in Europe*, Edinburgh: John Donald Publishers.

Schebesta, P. (1938–50), *Die Bambuti Pygmaen vom Ituri* (3 vols), Bruxelles: Librairie Falk fils.

—— (1952–57), *Die Negrito Asiens*, 2 vols. Mödling bei Wien: St.-Gabriel-Verlag.

Schiffer, M.B. (1976), *Behavioral Archaeology*, London: Academic Press.

—— (1987), *Formation Processes of the Archaeological Record*, Albuquerque: University of New Mexico Press.

Schmidt, M. (1920–21), *Grundriss der ethnologischen Volkswirtschaftslehre*, 2 vols. Stuttgart: F. Enke.

—— (1924), *Völkerkunde*, Berlin: Ullstein.

Schmidt, W. (1973 [1939]), *The Culture Historical Method of Ethnology: The Scientific Approach to the Racial Question*, Westport, CT: Greenwood Press.

Schott, R. (1956), *Anfänge der Privat- und Planwirtschaft. Wirtschaftsordnung und Nahrungsverteilung bei Wildbeutervölker*, Braunschweig: Albert Limbach Verlag.

Schrire, C. (1982), 'Wild Surmises on Savage Thoughts' In C. Schrire (ed.), *Past and Present in Hunter-Gatherer Studies*. Orlando, Florida: Academic Press.

—— (1984), *Past and Present in Hunter-Gatherer Studies*, New York: Academic Press.

Schulting, R.J. and Richards, M.P. (2002), 'Dogs, Ducks, Deer and Diet: New Stable Isotope Evidence on Early Mesolithic Dogs from the Vale of Pickering, North-East England', *Journal of Archaeological Science*, 29: 327–33.

Schweinfurth, G. (1873), *The Heart of Africa*, London: Sampson Low, Marson Low, and Searle.

Schweitzer, P. (2000a), 'Silence and Other Misunderstandings: Russian Anthropology, Western Hunter-Gatherers Debates, and Siberian Peoples', in P.P. Schweitzer, M.Biesele, and R.K. Hitchcock (eds), *Hunters and Gatherers in the Modern World: Conflict, Resistance and Self-Determination*, New York: Berghahn.

—— (2000b), 'The Social Anthropology of the Russian Far North', in M.Nuttall and T.V.Callaghan (eds), *The Arctic: Environment, People, Policy*, Amsterdam: Harwood Academic Publishers.

—— Biesele, M. and Hitchcock, R. (2000), *Hunters and Gatherers in the Modern World: Conflict, Resistance and Self-Determination*, New York: Berghahn.

Selvakumar, V. (1996), *Investigations into the Prehistoric and Protohistoric Cultures of the Upper Gundar basin, Madurai district, Tamil Nadu,* Ph.D. Dissertation, Deccan College, Pune, India

Service, E.R. (1962), *Primitive Social Organization: An Evolutionary Perspective,* New York: Random House.

—— (1971) *Primitive Social Organization: An Evolutionary Perspective* (second edition), New York: Random House.

—— (1978 [1958]), *Profiles in Ethnology* (third edition). New York: Harper and Row.

Shakhnovich, M. (1958), 'O 'psikho-analiticheskom metode' izucheniya pervobytnoy religii (po povodu stat'i A.A.Popova)', *Sovetskaya etnografiya,* 5: 71–76.

Sharma, G.R., Mishra, V.D., Mandal, D., Misra, B.B. and Pal, J.N. (1980), *Beginnings of Agriculture (Epi-Palaeolithic to Neolithic): Excavations at Chopani-Mando, Mahadaha and Mahagara,* Allahabad: Avinash Publications.

Shawcross, W. (1972), 'Energy and Ecology: Thermodynamic Models in Archaeology', in D. Clarke (ed.), *Models in Archaeology,* London: Methuen.

Sheehan, M. (2002), 'Dietary Responses to Mid-Holocene Climatic Change', *North American Archaeologist,* 22: 117–43.

Sheppard, T. (1923), 'The Maglemose Harpoons', *The Naturalist,* May 1923: 169–78.

Sherratt, A. (1980), *The Cambridge Encyclopedia of Archaeology,* Cambridge: Cambridge University Press.

Shimkin, D.B. (1964), 'Julian H. Steward: A Contributor to Fact and Theory in Cultural Anthropology', in R.A. Manners (ed.), *Process and Pattern in Culture,* Chicago: Aldine Publishing Company.

—— (1980), 'Comanche-Shoshone Words of Acculturation, 1786–1848', *Journal of the Steward Anthropological Society,* 11: 195–248.

—— (1990), 'Eastern Shoshone Myths: A Cognitive System?', Paper presented at the 22nd Great Basin Anthropological Conference, Reno, NV, October 1990.

Shirokogorov, S. M. (1922), *Etnos. Issledovanie osnovnykh printsipov izmeneniya etnicheskikh i etnograficheskikh yavleniy,* Vladivostok.

Shostak, M. (1981), *Nisa: The Life and Words of a !Kung Woman,* Cambridge, MA: Harvard University Press.

—— (2000), *Return to Nisa,* Cambridge, MA: Harvard University Press.

Silberbauer, G. (1981), *Hunter and Habit in the Central Kalahari Desert,* Cambridge: Cambridge University Press.

Simchenko, Yu.B. (1976), *Kul'tura okhotnikov na oleney Severnoy Evrazii. Etnograficheskaya rekonstruktsiya.* Moscow: Nauka.

Simmons, I. (1969), 'Evidence for Vegetation Changes Associated with Mesolithic Man in Britain', in P. Ucko and G. Dimbleby (eds), *The Domestication and Exploitation of Plants and Animals,* London: Duckworth.

Singer, P. (1981), *The Expanding Circle: Ethics and Sociobiology.* New York: Farrar Strauss.

Singh, C., (1988), 'Conformity and Conflict: Tribes and the 'Agrarian System' of Mughal India', *The Indian Economic and Social History Review,* 23: 319–40.

Singh, K. (1994), *The Scheduled Tribes* (People of India National Series volume 3), Calcutta: Anthropological Survey of India/Oxford University Press.

Sinopoli, C. (1991), 'Seeking the Past through the Present: Recent Ethnoarchaeological Research in South Asia', *Asian Perspectives,* 30: 177–92.

Sirina, A. A. (1993), 'Vydayushchiysya etnograf i fol'klorist G. S. Vinogradov (1887–1945)', *Etnograficheskoe obozrenie,* 1: 115–28.

—— (1999), 'Zabytye stranitsy sibirskoy etnografii: B.E. Petri', in D.D.Tumarkin (ed.), *Repressirovannye Etnografy,* Moscow: Vostochnaya Literatura RAN.

Slattery, B. (1979), *The Land Rights of Indigenous Canadian Peoples, as Affected by The Crown's Acquisition of their Territory.* D. Phil. Thesis, Oxford University.

Slezkine, Yu. (1994), *Arctic Mirrors: Russia and the Small Peoples of the North.* Ithaca, NY: Cornell University Press.

Slocum, S. (1975), 'Woman the Gatherer', in R.P. Reiter (ed.), *Toward an Anthropology of Women,* New York: Monthly Review Press.

Smith, A. (1776), *An Inquiry into the Nature and Causes of the Wealth of Nations* (two volumes). London: W. Strahan and T. Cadell.

—— (1896 [Lectures delivered 1762–63]), *Lectures on Justice, Police, Revenue and Arms, Delivered in the University of Glasgow* (edited by E. Cannan), Oxford: The Clarendon Press.

—— (1978 [Lectures delivered 1762–63]), *Lectures on Jurisprudence,* edited by R.L. Meek, D.D. Raphael and P.G. Stein, Oxford: The Clarendon Press.

Smith, C. (1989), 'British Antler Mattocks', in C. Bonsall (ed.), *The Mesolithic in Europe,* Edinburgh: John Donald Publishers.

—— (1992), *Late Stone Age Hunters of the British Isles,* London: Routledge.

Smith, E.A. (1991), *Inujjuamiut Foraging Strategies: Evolutionary Ecology of an Arctic Hunting Economy,* New York: Aldine de Gruyter.

—— and B. Winterhalder (1992), *Evolutionary Ecology and Human Behavior,* New York: Aldine de Gruyter.

Smith, J.A. (1972), 'Native Pharmacopoeia of the Eastern Great Basin: A Report on Work in Progress', in D.D. Fowler (ed.), *Great Basin Cultural Ecology: A Symposium,* Reno: Desert Research Institute.

Smith, W.D. (1991), *Politics and the Sciences of Culture in Germany, 1840–1920,* New York: Oxford University Press.

Smolyak, A.V. (1966), *Ul'chi. Khozyaystvo, kul'tura i byt v proshlom i nastoy-ashchem.* Moscow: Nauka.

—— (1991), *Shaman: lichnost', funktsii, mirovozzrenie (narody Nizhnego Amura).* Moscow: Nauka.

Solovey, T.D. (1998), *Ot 'burzhuaznoy' etnologii k 'sovetskoy' etnografii.* Moscow: Izdatel'stvo Koordinatsionno-metodicheskogo tsentra IEA RAN.

—— (2001), 'Korennoy perelom' v otechestvennoy etnografii (diskussiya o predmete etnograficheskoy nauki: konets 1920-kh – nachalo 1930-kh godov), *Etnograficheskoe obozrenie,* 3: 101–20.

Solway, J. and Lee, R. (1990), 'Foragers, Genuine or Spurious: Situating the Kalahari San in History', *Current Anthropology* 31: 109–46.

Sorrell, A. (1951), 'Yorkshire Men of Ten Thousand Years Ago: A Reconstruction of Life on the Middle Stone Age Lakeside Site of Star Carr, Near Scarborough, Showing Typical Artefacts and Activities', *Illustrated London News,* February 3, 1951: 172–3.

Spadafora, D. (1990), *The Idea of Progress in Eighteenth-Century Britain*. New Haven: Yale University Press.

Spencer, B., and Gillen, F. (1927), *The Arunta: A study of a Stone Age People*. London: Macmillan.

Sterns, F. (1918), 'The Peopling of the American Plains by the Indians', *Scientific American Supplement*, 85: 234–5.

Steward, J.H. (1933), 'Ethnography of the Owens Valley Paiute', *University of California Publications in American Archaeology and Ethnology* 33: 233–350.

—— (1936), 'The Economic and Social Basis of Primitive Bands', in R.H. Lowie (ed.), *Essays in Anthropology Presented to A.L. Kroeber,* Berkeley: University of California Press.

—— (1938), *Basin-Plateau Aboriginal Sociopolitical Groups* (Bureau of American Ethnology Bulletin 120), Washington, DC: Smithsonian Institution.

—— (1941), 'Culture Element Distribution, XIII: Nevada Shoshoni', *University of California Anthropological Records*, 4(2): 209–360.

—— (1943), 'Culture Element Distribution, XXIII: Northern and Gosiute Shoshoni', *University of California Anthropological Records*, 8(3): 263–392.

—— (1955a), *Theory of Culture Change: The Methodology of Multilinear Evolution,* Urbana: University of Illinois Press.

—— (1955b), 'Theory and Application in a Social Science', *Ethnohistory*, 2: 291–302.

—— (1965), 'Some problems raised by Roger C. Owen's "The Patrilocal Band" ', *American Anthropologist*, 67: 732– 3.

—— (1968), 'Causal Factors and Processes in the Evolution of Pre-farming Societies', in R.B. Lee and I. DeVore (eds), *Man the Hunter,* Chicago: Aldine Publishing Company.

—— (1969), 'Observations on Band', in D. Damas (ed.), *Contributions to Anthropology: Band Societies*, Ottawa: National Museum of Canada (Bulletin No. 228).

—— (1970), 'The Foundations of Basin-Plateau Shoshonean Society', in E.H. Swanson, (ed.), *Language and Culture of Western North American*, Caldwell, ID: Caxton Printers.

Stewart, M. (2002), 'Deprivation, the Roma and 'the Underclass',' in C. Hann (ed.), *Postsocialism. Ideals, Ideologies and Practices in Eurasia*, London: Routledge.

Stewart, O.C. (1959), 'Anthropology and the Indian Claims,' *Delphian Quarterly*, 42: 8–13.

—— (1977), 'Contemporary Document on Wovoka (Jack Wilson) Prophet of the Ghost Dance in 1890', *Ethnohistory*, 24: 219–22.

—— (1978), 'The Western Shoshone of Nevada and the U.S. Government, 1863–1900', in D.R. Tuoby (ed.), *Selected Papers from the 14th Great Basin Anthropological Conference*, (Ballena Press Publications in Archaeology, Ethnology, and History, No. 4) Socorra, NM: Ballena Press.

—— (1979), 'An Expert Witness Answers Rosen', *American Anthropologist*, 81: 108–11.

—— (1980), 'Temoke Band of Shoshone and the Oasis Concept', *Nevada Historical Society Quarterly*, 23: 246–61.

—— (1982), 'The History of Peyotism in Nevada' *Nevada Historical Society Quarterly*, 25: 197–209.

—— (1984), 'Friend to the Ute: Omer C. Stewart Crusades for Indian Religious Freedom', *University of Utah Anthropological Papers*, 108: 269–75.

—— (1985), 'The Shoshone Claims Cases', in I. Sutton (ed.), *Irredeemable America: The Indians' Estate and Land Claims*, Albuquerque: University of New Mexico Press.

Stocking, G. (1982), 'The Persistence of Polygenist Thought in Post-Darwinian Anthropology', in *Race, Culture, and Evolution*, Chicago: University of Chicago Press.

Stoffle, R.W. and Evans, M. J. (1990), 'Holistic Conservation and Cultural Triage: American Indian Perspectives on Cultural Resources', *Human Organization*, 49: 91–9.

——, Halmo, D.B. and Austin, D.E. (1997), 'Cultural Landscapes and Traditional Cultural Properties: A Southern Painte View of the Grand Canyon and Colorado River', *American Indian Quarterly* 21: 229–49.

—— Loendorf, L., Austin, D. E., Halmo, D. B. and Bulletts, A. (2000), 'Ghost Dancing the Grand Canyon: Southern Paiute Rock Art, Ceremony, and Cultural Landscapes', *Current Anthropology*, 41: 11–38.

Stuart, G. (1797 [1791]), *A View of Society in Europe in its Progress from Rudeness to Refinement: Or, Inquiries Concerning the History of Law, Government, and Manners*, new edition, Basil: J.J. Tourneisen.

Sugawara, K. (1984), 'Spatial Proximity and Bodily Contact among the Central Kalahari San', *African Study Monographs,* Supplementary Issue, 3: 1–43.

—— (1988), 'Social Relations and Interactions between Residential Groups among the Central Kalahari San: Hunter-Gatherer Camp as a Micro-Territory', *African Study Monographs,* 8: 173–211.

—— (1990), 'Interactional Aspects of the Body in Co-presence: Observations on the Central Kalahari San', in M. Moerman and M. Nomura (eds), *Culture Embodied* (Senri Ethnological Studies 27), Osaka: National Museum of Ethnology.

—— (1991), 'The Economics of Social Life among the Central Kalahari San (G/wikhwe and G//anakwe) in the Sedentary Community at !Koi!kom', in N. Peterson and T. Matsuyama (eds), *Cash, Commoditisation and Changing Forgers* (Senri Ethnological Studies, 30), Osaka: National Museum of Ethnology.

—— (1993), *Shintai no Jinruigaku* (Anthropology of the Body), Tokyo: Kawadeshobo-shinsha.

—— (1996), 'Some Methodological Issues for the Analysis of Everyday Conversation among the /Gui', *African Study Monographs,* Supplementary Issue, 22: 145–61.

—— (1998a), 'The "Egalitarian" Attitude in Everyday Conversations among the /Gui', In A. Bank (ed.), *The Proceedings of the Khoisan Identities & Cultural Heritage Conference,* Cape Town: The Institute for Historical Research, University of Cape Town /Infosource.

—— (1998b), *Kataru Shintai no Minzokushi* (Ethnography of Speaking Body), Kyoto: Kyoto University Academic Press.

—— (1998c), *Kaiwa no Jinruigaku* (Anthropology of Conversation), Kyoto: Kyoto University Academic Press.

—— (1998d), 'Ecology and Communication in Egalitarian Societies: Japanese Studies of the Cultural Anthropology of Southern Africa', *Japanese Review of Cultural Anthropology,* 1: 97–129.

—— (2001), 'Cognitive Space Concerning Habitual Thought and Practice toward Animals among the Central Kalahari San (/Gui and //Gana): Deictic/Indirect Cognition and Prospective/Retrospective Intention', *African Study Monographs*, Supplementary Issue, 27: 61–98.

—— (2002a), 'Speech Acts, Moves, and Meta-communication in Negotiation: Three cases of everyday conversation observed in the /Gui society', Paper presented at Ninth International Conference on Hunting and Gathering Societies, Edinburgh, September 2002.

—— (2002b), 'Optimistic Realism or Opportunistic Subordination?: The Interaction of the G/wi and G//ana with Outsiders', in S. Kent (ed.), *Ethnicity, Hunter-Gatherers, and the 'Other': Association or Assimilation in Africa*, Washington: Smithonian Institution Press.

—— (in press), 'Possession, Equality and Gender Relations in /Gui Discourse', in T. Widlok and W. Tadesse (eds), *Property and Equality Vol. 1: Ritualization, Sharing, Egalitarianism*, Oxford: Berghahn.

Sullivan, S. (2001), 'Difference, Identity, and Access to Official Discourses. Hai//om, 'Bushmen,' and a Recent Namibian Ethnography', *Anthropos*, 96: 179–92.

Sumner, W.G. and Keller, A.G. (1927), *The Science of Society*, Vol. I, New Haven : Yale University Press.

Suzman J. 2000 *'Things from the Bush': A Contemporary History of the Omaheke Bushmen*, Basel : PSP Publishing.

—— (2001a), *An Assessment of the Status of Namibia's San Population*, Windhoek: Legal Assistance Centre/EU.

—— (2001b), *An Introduction to the Regional Assessment of the Status of the San in southern Africa*, Windhoek: Legal Assistance Centre/EU.

—— (2001c), 'Human Rights and Indigenous Wrongs: National Policy International Resolutions and the Status of the San in Southern Africa', in J. Kenrick and A. Barnard (eds), *Africa's Indigenous Minorities: First Peoples or Marginalized Minorities*, Edinburgh: CAS (University of Edinburgh).

—— (2002), 'Difference, Domination and "Under-development" – Notes on the Marginalisation of Namibia's San Population', in B. Winterhalder (ed.), *Namibia–Society–Sociology*, Windhoek: Gamsberg Macmillan.

Swanson, E.H. (ed.) (1970), *Languages and Cultures of Western North American: Essays in Honor of Sven S. Liljeblad*, Pocatello: The Idaho State University Press.

Sylvain, R. (1999), *'We Work to Have Life': Ju/hoan Women, Work and Survival in the Omaheke Region*, Ph.D. Dissertation, University of Toronto.

Takeuchi, K. (1994), 'Food Avoidance among the Aka Hunter-Gatherers of Northeastern Congo', *Africa Kenkyu*, 44: 1–28.

—— (1995), 'Ritual Aspects and Pleasure in Hunting Activities: Cooperation and Distribution in the Net Hunting Activities of Aka Hunter-Gatherers in Northeastern Congo', *Africa Kenkyu*, 46: 57–76.

Tanaka, J. (1969), 'The Ecology and Social Structure of Central Kalahari Bushmen: A Preliminary Report', *Kyoto University African Studies*, 3: 1–26.

—— (1971), *Busshuman: Seitai Jinruigaku teki Kenkyu* (The Bushmen: A Study in Ecological Anthropology), Tokyo: Shisaku-sha.

—— (1976), 'Subsistence Ecology of Central Kalahari San', in R. B. Lee and I. DeVore (eds), *Kalahari Hunter-Gatherers: Studies of the !Kung San and Their Neighbors,* Cambridge, MA: Harvard University Press.

—— (1978), 'A Study of the Comparative Ecology of African Gatherer-Hunters with Special Reference to San (Bushman-speaking People) and Pygmies', *Senri Ethnological Studies* 1 (Africa 1): 189–212.

—— (1980), *The San, Hunter-Gatherers of the Kalahari: A Study in Ecological Anthropology,* Tokyo: University of Tokyo Press.

—— (1987), 'The Recent Changes in the Life and Society of the Central Kalahari San', *African Study Monographs*, 7: 37–51.

—— (1989), 'Social Integration of the San Society from the Viewpoint of Sexual Relationships', *African Study Monographs,* 9: 55–64.

—— (1991), 'Egalitarianism and the Cash Economy among the Central Kalahari San', in N. Peterson and T. Matsuyama (eds), *Cash, Commoditisation and Changing Foragers* (Senri Ethnological Studies, 30), Osaka: National Museum of Ethnology.

—— (1994), *Saigo no Shuryo-Saishu-Min* (The Last Hunter-Gatherers), Tokyo: Dobutsu-sha.

—— (1996), 'The World of Animals Viewed by the San Hunter-Gatherers in Kalahari', *African Study Monographs*, Supplementary Issue, 22: 11–28.

—— and Sugawara, K. (1996), 'Introduction', *African Study Monographs*, Supplementary Issue, 22: 3–9.

Tanno, T. (1976), 'The Mbuti Net-Hunters in the Ituri Forest, Eastern Zaire: Their Hunting Activities and Band Composition', *Kyoto University African Studies*, 10: 101–35.

—— (1981), 'Plant Utilization of the Mbuti Pygmies: With Special Reference to Their Material Culture and Use of Wild Vegetable Food', *African Study Monographs*, 1: 1–53.

Tavares, A. (1997), *Paleopathology: its Implications in the Archaeological record,* Ph.D. Disseration: Deccan College, Pune, India.

Taylor, W. (1948), *A Study of Archeology*, Washington, DC: Memoir of the American Anthropological Association, No. 69.

Teng, S. Y. (1968), 'Wang Fu-chih's Views on History and Historical Writing', *Journal of Asian Studies*, 28: 111–23.

Terashima, H. (1983), 'Mota and Other Hunting of the Mbuti Archers', *African Study Monographs*, 3: 71–85.

—— (1986), 'Economic Exchange and Symbiotic Relationship between the Mbuti (Efe) Pygmies and Neighbouring Farmers', *Sprache und Geschichte in Afrika*, 7: 391–408.

Testart, A. (1982), 'The Significance of Food Storage among Hunter-Gatherers: Residence Patterns, Population Densities and Social Inequalities', *Current Anthropology*, 23: 523–37.

Thomas, D. (1986), 'Contemporary Hunter-Gatherer Archaeology in America', in D. Meltzer, D. Fowler, and J. Sabloff (eds), *American Archaeology: Past and Future*, Washington, DC: Smithsonian Institution Press.

Tishkov, V.A. (ed.) (1994), *Narody Rossii. Entsiklopediya*. Moscow: Nauchnoe izdatel'stvo 'Bol'shaya Rossiyskaya Entsiklopediya'.

Toby, R. (1994), 'The "Indianness" of Iberia and Changing Japanese Iconographies of the Other', in S. Schwartz (ed.), *Implicit Understandings*, Cambridge: Cambridge University Press.

Todorov, T. (1984), *The Conquest of America: The Question of the Other*, New York: Harper & Row.

Tokarev, S.A. (1929), 'O systemakh rodstva avstraliytsev' *Etnografiya*, No. 1.

—— (1949), 'K postanovke problem etnogeneza', *Sovetskaya etnografiya*, 3: 12–36.

—— (1966), *Istoriya russkoy etnografii (Dooktyabr'skiy period)*. Moscow: Nauka.

Tolstov, S.P. (1931), 'Problemy dorodovogo obshchestva', *Sovetskaya etnografiya*, 3–4: 30.

Tonkin, E. (1992), *Narrating Our Pasts: The Social Construction of History*, Cambridge: Cambridge University Press.

Tribe, K., (1978), *Land, Labour and Economic Discourse*, London: Routledge & Kegan Paul.

Trigger, B. (1989), *A History of Archaeological Thought*, Cambridge: Cambridge University Press.

—— (1998), *Sociocultural Evolution*, Oxford: Blackwell.

Trivers, R. (1971), 'The Evolution of Reciprocal Altruism', *Quarterly Review of Biology*, 46: 35–57.

Tsuru, D. (1998), 'Diversity of Ritual Spirit Performances among the Baka Pygmies in Southwestern Cameroon', *African Study Monographs*, Supplementary Issue, 25: 47–84.

—— (2001), *A Study of Behavioural Anthropology of Ritual Performances of the Baka Pygmies*, Doctoral Thesis, Kyoto University.

Turgot, A.R.J. (1973 [1808]), 'On Universal History', in *Turgot on Progress, Sociology and Economics* (translated and edited by Ronald L. Meek). Cambridge: Cambridge University Press.

Turnbull, C. (1961), *The Forest People*, New York: Simon and Schuster.

—— (1965), *Wayward Servants: The Two Worlds of the African Pygmies*, New York: Natural History Press.

Vainshtein, S. and Kryukov, M. (1988), 'Sovetskaya etnograficheskaya shkola', in M.Kryukov and I. Zel'nov (eds), *Svod etnograficheskikh ponyatiy i terminov*. Moscow: Nauka.

Vaktin, N.B. and Sirina, A.A. (2003), ' "Komu prinadlezhit Sibirskaya Etnogriafiya?" Razmyshleniya posle mezdunarodnogo seminara po metodike, metodologii I etike etnograficheskikh issledovanii na severe Sibiri'. *Etnograficheskoe obozrenie* 2002, no. 3, 141–8.

Vajda, L. (1968), *Untersuchungen zur Geschichte der Hirtenkulturen*, Wiesbaden: Otto Harrassowitz.

Van der Sluys, C. (2000), 'Gifts from the Immortal Ancestors: Cosmology and Ideology of Jahai Sharing', in P.P. Schweitzer, M.Biesele, and R.K. Hitchcock (eds), *Hunters and Gatherers in the Modern World: Conflict, Resistance and Self-Determination.* New York: Berghahn.

Van der Westhuizen, P. (1972), *Tydsaanduiding in die Gobabis !Xu,* MA Thesis, University of Cape Town.

Vander, J. (1978), A View of Wind River Shoshone Music Through Four Ceremonies, M.A. Thesis, University of Michigan, Ann Arbor.

—— (1983), '17 Ghost Dance Songs of Emily Hill, a Wind River Shoshone', Unpublished manuscript in Vander's possession

—— (1995), 'The Shoshone Ghost Dance and Numic Myth: Common Heritage, Common Themes', *Journal of California and Great Basin Anthropology,* 17: 174–90.

Vansina, J. (1985), *Oral Tradition as History,* London: James Currey.

Vasilevich, G.M. (1969), *Evenki. Istoriko-etnograficheskie ocherki (XVIII-nachalo XX v.).* Leningrad: Nauka.

Vayda, A.P. and Rappaport, R. (1968), 'Ecology, Cultural and Non-Cultural', in J.A. Clifton (ed.), *Introduction to Cultural Anthropology,* New York: Houghton Mifflin Publishing Company.

Vdovin, I.S. (ed.), (1976), *Priroda i chelovek v religioznykh predstavleniyakh narodov Sibiri i Severa (vtoraya polovina XIX-nachalo XX v.),* Leningrad: Nauka.

—- (ed.) (1981), *Problemy istorii obshchestvennogo soznaniya aborigenov Sibiri (po materialam vtoroy poloviny XIX-nachala XX v.),* Leningrad: Nauka.

Veniaminov, I. (1984), *Notes on the Islands of the Unalashka District* (edited by R. Pierce), Kingston, Ontario: Limenstone Press; Fairbanks: Elmer E.Rasmuson Library Translation Program, University of Alaska.

—— (1993[1823–36]), *Journals of the Priest Ioann Veniaminov in Alaska, 1823 to 1836* (introduction and commentary by S.A. Mousalimas, translation by J. Kisslinger), Fairbanks: University of Alaska Press.

Vita-Finzi, C. and Higgs, E. (1970), 'Prehistoric Economy in the Mount Carmel Area: Site Catchment Analysis', *Proceedings of the Prehistoric Society,* 36: 1–37.

Waal, F. de (1996), *Good Natured: The Origins of Right and Wrong in Humans and Animals,* Cambridge: Harvard University.

Walimbe, S.R. and Tavares, A. (1992), 'Bio-cultural Study of Man in India', *Man and Environment,* 12: 81–91.

Walker, D. and Godwin, H. (1954), 'Lake Stratigraphy, Pollen Analysis and Vegetational History', in J. Clark (ed.), *Excavations at Star Carr: An Early Mesolithic Site at Seamer, near Scarborough, Yorkshire,* Cambridge: Cambridge University Press.

Walker, R. (1994), 'Social Movements/World Politics', *Millennium Journal of International Studies,* 23: 669–700

Warder, A. (1961), 'The Pali Canon and its Commentaries as an Historical Record', in C. Philips (ed.), *Historians of India, Pakistan and Ceylon,* London: Oxford University Press.

Watanabe, H. (1968), 'Subsistence and Ecology of Northern Food Gatherers with Special Reference to the Ainu', in R. B. Lee and I. DeVore (eds), *Man the Hunter,* Chicago: Aldine.

Weber, M. (1948),*The Theory of Social and Economic Organization,* New York: Free Press.

Westermarck, E. (1891), *The History of Human Marriage*. London: Macmillan.

—— (1906), *The Origin and Development of the Moral Ideas*. London: Macmillan.

Wheeler, A. (1978), 'Why Were There No Fish Remains at Star Carr?', *Journal of Archaeological Science*, 5: 85–9.

Whitley, D.S. (1990), 'Etiology and Ideology in the Great Basin', Paper presented at the 22nd Great Basin Anthropological Conference, October, Reno, NV.

—— (1992), 'The Vision Quest in the Great Basin', Paper presented at the 23rd Great Basin Anthropological Conference, October, Boise, ID.

Widlok, T. (1992), 'The Independent Anthropologist in Independent Namibia', *Newsletter of the Namibia Scientific Society*, 33: 38–42.

—— (1999), *Living on Mangetti. 'Bushman' Autonomy and Namibian Independence*. Oxford: Oxford University Press.

—— (2001), 'Living on Ethnography and Comparison. What Difference Do Hai//om 'Bushmen' Make to Anthropology (and Vice Versa)?', *Anthropos*, 96: 359–78.

—— (2002), 'The Long Walk IV - Hunter-Gatherers and Anthropology: an Interview with James Woodburn', *Nomadic Peoples*, 6: 7–22.

—— (in press), 'Theoretical Shifts in the Anthropology of Desert Hunter-Gatherers,' in P. Veth and M. Smith (ed.), *Desert Peoples: archaeological perspectives*, Oxford: Blackwell.

—— and Tadesse, W. (ed.) (forthcoming), *Property and Equality*. Oxford: Berghahn.

Wilkie, D. S. and Carpenter, J.F. (1999), 'Bushmeat Hunting in the Congo Basin: An Assessment of Impacts and Options for Mitigation', *Biodiversity and Conservation*, 8: 927–55.

Williams, G. (1966), *Adaptation and Natural Selection: A Critique of some Current Evolutionary Thought*, Princeton: Princeton University Press.

—— (1989), 'A Sociobiological Expansion of 'Evolution and Ethics', in J. Paradis and G. Williams (ed.), *Evolution and Ethics*, New Jersey: Princeton University.

Wilmsen, E. N. (1983), 'The Ecology of Illusion: Anthropological Foraging in the Kalahari', *Reviews in Anthropology*, 10: 9–20.

—— (1989a), *Land Filled with Flies: A Political Economy of the Kalahari*. Chicago: University of Chicago Press.

—— (1989b), *We Are Here: Politics of Aboriginal Land Tenure*, Berkeley: University of California Press.

—— (1996), 'First People? Images and Imaginations in South African Iconography', *Critical Arts*, 9: 1–27.

—— and Denbow, J. R. (1990), 'Paradigmatic History of San-speaking Peoples and Current Attempts at Revision', *Current Anthropology*, 31: 489–524.

Winterhalder, B. (1981), 'Optimal Foraging Strategies and Hunter-Gatherer Research in Anthropology: Theory and Models', in B. Winterhalder and E.A. Smith (eds), *Hunter-Gatherer Foraging Strategies: Ethnographic and Archeological Analyses*, Chicago: University of Chicago Press.

—— (1986), 'Diet Choice, Risk, and Food Sharing in a Stochastic Environment', *Journal of Anthropological Archaeology*, 5: 369–92.

—— (1988), 'The Population Ecology of Hunter-Gatherers and Their Prey', *Journal of Anthropology Archaeological*, 7: 289–328.

—— (1990), 'Open Field, Common Pot: Harvest Variability and Risk Avoidance in

Agricultural Societies', in E. Cashdan (ed.), *Risk and Uncertainty in Tribal and Peasant Economies*, Boulder: Westview Press

—— and Smith, E. A. (1981), *Hunter-Gatherer Foraging Strategies: Ethnographic and Archeological Analyses*, Chicago: University of Chicago Press.

—— (1992), 'Evolutionary Ecology and the Social Sciences', in E.A. Smith and B. Winterhalder (eds), *Evolutionary Ecology and Human Behavior*, New York: Aldine De Gruyter.

—— (2000), 'Analyzing Adaptive Strategies: Human Behavioral Ecology at Twenty-Five', *Evolutionary Anthropology*, 9: 51–72.

Wissler, C. (1914), 'The Influence of the Horse in the Development of Plains Culture', *American Anthropologist*, 16: 1–25.

Wolf, E. (1982), *Europe and the People without History*, Berkeley: University of California Press.

Wood, P. (1995), 'Introduction', in S. S. Smith, *An Essay on the Causes of Complexion and Figure in the Human Species*, and D. Doig, *Two Letters on the Savage State, Addressed to the Late Lord Kaims*. Bristol: Thoemmes Press.

Woodburn, J. (1968), 'An Introduction to Hadza Ecology', in R.B. Lee and I. de Vore (eds), *Man The Hunter*. Chicago: Aldine.

—— (1980), 'Hunters and Gatherers Today and Reconstruction of the Past', in E. Gellner (ed.), *Soviet and Western Anthropology*, London: Duckworth.

—— (1982), 'Egalitarian Societies', *Man* (n.s.), 17: 431–51.

—— (1988), 'African Hunter-Gatherer Social Organization: Is It Best Understood as a Product of Encapsulation?', in T. Ingold, D. Riches and J. Woodburn (eds), *Hunters and Gatherers 2: Property, Power and Ideology*, Oxford: Berg.

—— (1997), 'Indigenous Discrimination: The Ideological Basis for Local Discrimination Against Hunter-Gatherer Minorities in sub-Saharan Africa', *Ethnic and Racial Studies*, 20: 345–61.

—— (2001), 'The Political Status of Hunter-Gatherers in Present-Day and Future Africa, in A. Barnard and J. Kenrick (eds), *Africa's Indigenous Peoples: 'First Peoples' or 'Marginalized Minorities'?* Edinburgh: Centre of African Studies, University of Edinburgh.

—— Widlok, T., Wilmsen, E. and Ingold, T. (2001), 'Comment: Primitive Mentality', *Journal of the Royal Anthropological Institute*, 7: 767–9.

Wylie, A. M. (1985), 'The Reaction Against Analogy', in M.B. Schiffer (ed.), *Advances in Archaeological Method and Theory*, Volume 8, New York: Academic Press.

Yamashita, S. (1998), 'Introduction: A Viewing Anthropology from Japan', *Japanese Review of Cultural Anthropology*, 1: 3–6.

Yellen, J. (1976), 'Settlement Pattern of the !Kung Bushman: An Archaeological Perspective', in R. Lee and I. DeVore (eds), *Kalahari Hunter Gatherers*, Cambridge: Harvard University Press.

—— (1977a), *Archaeological Approaches to the Present: Models for Reconstructing the Past,* New York: Academic Press.

—— (1977b), 'Long Term Hunter-Gatherer Adaptation to Desert Environments: A Biogeographical Perspective', *World Archaeology*, 8: 262–74.

—— (1982), 'Spatial Patterning in a Hunting and Gathering Society', *National Geographic Research Reports* 14: 711–18.

—— (1986), 'Optimization and Risk in Human Foraging Strategies', *Journal of Human Evolution*, 15: 733–50.

Yengoyan, A.A. (1998), 'No Exit: Aboriginal Australians and the Historicizing of Interpretation and Theory', *American Anthropologist*, 100: 181–4.

Yesner, D. (1981), 'Archeological Applications of Optimal Foraging Theory: Harvest Strategies of Aleut Hunter-Gatherers', in B. Winterhalder and E.A. Smith (eds), *Hunter-Gatherer Foraging Strategies: Ethnographic and Archeological Analyses*, Chicago: University of Chicago Press.

Young, R. (2000), *White Mythologies: Writing History and the West*, London: Routledge.

Zigmond, M.L. (1972), 'Some Mythological and Supernatural Aspects of Kawaiisu Ethnography and Ethnobiology', in D.D. Fowler (ed.), *Great Basin Cultural Ecology*, Reno: Reno Desert Research Institute.

—— (1977), 'The Supernatural World of the Kawaiisu', in T.C. Blackburn (ed.), *Flowers of the Wind: Papers on Ritual, Myth, and Symbolism in California and the Southwest*, Socorro, NM: Ballena Press.

—— (1980*), Kawaiisu Mythology: An Oral Tradition of South-Central California*, Ballena Press Anthropological Papers No. 18, Socorro, NM: Ballena Press.

—— (1981), *Kawaiisu Ethnobotany*, Salt Lake City: University of Utah Press.

Zimmerman, A. (2001), *Anthropology and Antihumanism in Imperial Germany*, Chicago: University of Chicago Press.

Zolotarev, A.M. (1931), 'Proiskhozhdenie ekzogamii, *Izvestiya Gosydarstvennoy akademii istorii material'noy kul'tury*, 10 (2–4): 1–67.

Zvelebil, K. (1988), *The Irulas of the Blue Mountains*, Ithaica, NY: Maxwell School of Citizenship and Public Affairs, Syracuse University.

Zvelebil, M. (2002), 'The Invention of Hunter-Gatherers in Seventeenth Century Europe? A Comment on Mark Pluciennik', *Archaeological Dialogues*, 9: 123–9.

—— and Fewster, K. (2001), 'Ethnoarchaeology and Hunter-Gatherers: Pictures at an Exhibition', in K. Fewster and M. Zvelebil (eds), *Ethnoarchaeology and Hunter-Gatherers: Pictures at an Exhibition (BAR International Series 955)*, Oxford: Archaeopress.

# Notes on Contributors

**Olga Artemova** is a Senior Researcher at the Institute of Ethnology and Anthropology in Moscow and Deputy Director of the Centre of Social Anthropology in the Russian State University for Humanities. She has done fieldwork in Chukotka and Kalmykia. Her publications include papers on anthropological theory and hunter-gatherers and a book on personality in Australian Aboriginal society.

**Michael Asch** is Professor Emeritus at the University of Alberta and Visiting Professor in Anthropology at the University of Victoria. He has worked with various First Nations, especially the Dene. Among his books are *Home and Native Land: Aboriginal Rights and the Constitution* and *Aboriginal and Treaty Rights in Canada*.

**Alan Barnard** is Professor of the Anthropology of Southern Africa at the University of Edinburgh. He has done fieldwork with the Nharo (Naro) of Botswana and other hunter-gatherer and former hunter-gatherer groups, and research on the history of anthropological ideas. His books include *Hunters and Herders of Southern Africa* and *History and Theory in Anthropology*.

**L.R. Hiatt** was, until his retirement in 1991, Reader in Anthropology at the University of Sydney. He was also President of the Australian Institute of Aboriginal Studies from 1974 to 1982. His most recent book is *Arguments about Aborigines: Australia and the Evolution of Social Anthropology*.

**Mitsuo Ichikawa** is Professor in Ecological Anthropology at the Graduate School of Asian and African Area Studies, Kyoto University. He has carried out field research in the Democratic Republic of Congo, Kenya, Zambia and Cameroon and is author of *Forest Hunters: The Life of the Mbuti Pygmies*.

**Paul Lane** is Director of the British Institute in Eastern Africa, Nairobi. He has done research in both European and African prehistory, as well as historical archaeology and ethnoarchaeology in Botswana, and has published widely in archaeology journals and volumes.

**Daniel Myers** is Director of Epochs Past, a private archaeological and ethnographic consulting firm in Maryland. He has conducted ethnographic studies with Numic populations of the North American Great Basin and with peoples of the Pacific Northwest He is the author of *Numic Mythologies* and co-author of *Julian Steward and the Great Basin*.

**Shanti Pappu** is the founder and Director of the Sharma Centre for Heritage Education, in Pune/Chennai, India. She has carried out field research in prehistoric archaeology and ethnoarchaeology in South India and is the author of *A Re-examination of the Palaeolithic Archaeological Record of Northern Tamil Nadu, South India*.

**Marc Pinkoski** is a Doctoral Fellow in the Department of Anthropology at the University of Victoria, British Columbia. He is currently doing research on the politics of cultural ecological theory, focusing on its implication in bolstering the doctrine of *terra nullius* in current Aboriginal rights claims in Canada.

**Mark Pluciennik** is Director of Distance Learning and Lecturer in Archaeology at the University of Leicester. His current fieldwork involves multi-period survey and excavation in Sicily, and his publications include articles on the analysis of archaeological narratives, European cultural politics and the transition to agriculture in the Mediterranean.

**Tim Schadla-Hall** is Reader in Public Archaeology in the Institute of Archaeology, University College London. His interests include post-glacial settlement in north-western Europe, landscape archaeology, and post-medieval country houses. He has edited and written widely on these topics, as well as on public involvement in archaeology.

**Peter Schweitzer** is Professor of Anthropology at the University of Alaska, Fairbanks and also teaches at the University of Vienna. He has worked in Siberian hunter-gatherer and reindeer-herding communities and has written widely on these peoples. He is editor of *Dividends in Kinship* and co-editor of *Hunter-Gatherers in the Modern World*.

**Michael Sheehan** is Director of the Program for Applied Archaeological Research at the Illinois State Museum. He has conducted fieldwork in many parts of the United States, and in Hungary, and his research focuses on the archaeology of hunter-gatherer responses to climatic change. He has published extensively in paleoecology, archaeometry, and geoarchaeology.

**Anna Sirina** is a Senior Researcher at the Institute of Ethnology and Anthropology, Moscow. She has carried out field research in central, south and north-eastern Siberia and the Russian Far East, and is author of *Katangskie Evenki v XX veke (The Katanga Evenki in the Twentieth Century)*, as well as publications in applied and juridical anthropology, cultural geography and history of Siberian ethnology.

**Kazuyoshi Sugawara** is Professor of Cultural Anthropology in the Faculty of Integrated Human Studies, Kyoto University. He has carried out extensive research with the G/wi and G//ana of Botswana, especially on communication, cognition, and social relationships. He has published several books on the G/wi and G//ana in Japanese, as well as a number of articles in English.

**James Suzman** is Smuts Fellow in African Studies, University of Cambridge. He formerly directed the European Union Regional Assessment of the Status of the San in Southern Africa and has done extensive fieldwork in Namibia and Botswana. He is the author of *'Things from the Bush': A Contemporary History of the Omaheke Bushmen*.

**Thomas Widlok** is Lecturer in Anthropology at the University of Heidelberg. He has carried out field research in northern and central Namibia and in north-western Australia and is author of *Living on Mangetti: 'Bushman' Autonomy and Namibian Independence*, as well as works on property relations and in cognitive and linguistic anthropology.

**Aram Yengoyan** is Professor of Anthropology at the University of California at Davis. He has done fieldwork in Australia and the Philippines. His research interests include cultural theory, language and culture, and the history of anthropology, and he has published widely in these areas as well as in the ethnography of Aboriginal Australia. His latest book is *Modes of Comparison: Theory and Practice*.

# Index